REDEEMING EVE

ELAINE V. BEILIN

Redeeming Eve

WOMEN WRITERS
OF THE ENGLISH
RENAISSANCE

PRINCETON
UNIVERSITY
PRESS

Copyright © 1987 by Princeton University Press

Published by Princeton University Press, 41 William Street,
Princeton, New Jersey 08540
In the United Kingdom: Princeton University Press, Guildford, Surrey

All Rights Reserved

Library of Congress Cataloging in Publication Data will be found on the last
printed page of this book

ISBN 0-691-06715-5

This book has been composed in Linotron Granjon

Clothbound editions of Princeton University Press books
are printed on acid-free paper, and binding materials are
chosen for strength and durability. Paperbacks, although satisfactory
for personal collections, are not usually suitable for library rebinding

Printed in the United States of America by Princeton University Press,
Princeton, New Jersey

Designed by Laury A. Egan

FOR BOB

FOR HANNAH AND RACHEL

CONTENTS

CONTENTS

ACKNOWLEDGMENTS

*T*HIS BOOK germinated during a long bus ride with Patricia Spacks, for whose insight and encouragement I will always be grateful. Mount Holyoke College gave me a Faculty Grant to support the initial research in England. From the beginning, I have been fortunate to have had the support of Carolyn Collette as a scholar, colleague, and friend. At crucial stages, Lynn and Linck Johnson offered criticism, editing, and moral support; Lynn has shared her wisdom and friendship in generous measure. John Lemly nobly read the entire manuscript, suggested many improvements, and cheered me on. Betsy Seifter read early chapters and contributed her scholarly and editorial expertise. My debt to Bill Carroll is manifold: for reading the manuscript, for offering sound advice and practical help, for being an ideal colleague.

To those who taught me about the Renaissance and provided models of scholarship and teaching to which I have always aspired, I am grateful: Anne Lancashire, G. E. Bentley, and in particular, Thomas P. Roche. I owe a considerable debt to scholars whose work has shown the way: D. W. Robertson, Jr., Barbara Lewalski, John King.

I have been educated and inspired by the scholarship on women that has flowered in the last fifteen years. The work of predecessors and companions in women's studies is acknowledged in every chapter.

I am grateful for a National Endowment for the Humanities Fellowship for College Teachers in Residence at Boston University in 1977–1978, which gave me the time to begin writing. To the members of the N.E.H. Seminar, I owe an enlightening year of poetry and writing. Helen Vendler taught me much about both; her advice helped shape the material that became Chapter Six, as did that of Paul Gaston, Molly Oates, Cheryl Walker, and Martha Collins.

ACKNOWLEDGMENTS

The Alliance of Independent Scholars in Cambridge, Massachusetts, has given me intellectual support and extraordinary colleagues since 1981. Particular thanks are due to Nancy Zumwalt who assisted with Latin and Greek and read part of the manuscript. I have profited greatly from discussions at research colloquia, and from the Renaissance scholarship of Claudia Limbert, Elizabeth Coons, and Sherrin Marshall Wyntjes.

Elizabeth Hageman and John King read the manuscript for the Press and I am indebted to them for their close attention and excellent suggestions for improving substance and style. I am, however, entirely responsible for any remaining errors or omissions. I thank Robert E. Brown of Princeton University Press for being a cordial and patient guide.

For assistance in research, I am grateful to the librarians and staff of the Bodleian Library, the British Library, Houghton and Widener Libraries of Harvard University, Firestone Library of Princeton University, Mugar Memorial Library of Boston University, Williston Library of Mount Holyoke College, and the Boston Public Library. For her painstaking assistance in researching patronage by women, I am grateful to Janice Broder. Diane Kilday typed the manuscript and cheerfully amended it as often as requested.

My extended family has given me truly extended support over ten years of research and writing, and they have my gratitude for their tolerance and interest. My parents offered continual encouragement. All of them, especially my two daughters, Hannah and Rachel, are pleased that the book is finished. The help and advice of my husband, Bob Brown, has been essential at every stage; I thank him for keeping the book and me on course.

Chapter Two incorporates and expands "Anne Askew's Self-Portrait in the *Examinations*," in *Silent But for the Word*, ed. Margaret P. Hannay (Kent, Ohio: Kent State University Press, 1985). Chapter Six includes material from "Elizabeth Cary and *The Tragedie of Mariam*," in *Papers on Language and Literature* 16 (1980). Part of Chapter Eight first appeared in

ACKNOWLEDGMENTS

" 'The Onely Perfect Vertue': Constancy in Mary Wroth's *Pamphilia to Amphilanthus*" in *Spenser Studies* II (1981). I am grateful for permission to republish parts of these articles.

Unless otherwise noted, translations are mine and textual references are to the earliest printed edition. Contractions have been expanded and i/j and u/v have been modernized. Verso and recto designations have not been printed superscript. When "v" (verso) appears next to lower-case roman numerals, it has been separated from them by a half space to avoid ambiguity.

INTRODUCTION

$\mathbb{R}$ ESPONDING directly to the ceaseless defamation of women's intellect and creativity, the late medieval writer, Christine de Pisan, wrote the *Cité des Dames*. In 1521 an English translation, *The Cyte of Ladyes*, appeared, and although it does not seem to have been widely known, the work vividly and poignantly expresses some of the feelings and ideas that English women writers later voice.

In her first chapter, Christine's unhappy persona, Christine, details the psychological effects of believing that one is evil merely because one is female. She comments on her overwhelming sense that "in all treatyses of phylosophres, poetes and all rethorycyens which sholde be longe to reherce all theyr names speaketh as it were by one mouthe and accordeth all in semble conclusyon determynynge that the condycyons of women ben fully enclyned to all vyces."[1] Although she examines her own nature and that of women of all degrees whom she knows, she cannot justify such opinions; yet Christine concludes that it is probably her own intelligence that is lacking: "myne understandynge for his symplenesse and ygnoraunce ne coude not knowe my grete defautes ... and soo I reported me more to the Jugement of other then to that I felte or knowe myselfe" (Bbii-Bbii v). Being led to contemplate woman as the source of evil, Christine feels in herself "a grete dyspleasaunce and sorowe of courage in dyspraysynge myselfe and all womenkynde." Momentarily, she comforts herself by remembering that God made woman and that all God makes is good; but so many men have said the contrary that Christine's doubts return: "Alas good lorde why haddest thou not made me to be borne in to this worlde in the masculyne kynde ..." (Bbii v-Bbiii). These forays into self-doubt and self-deprecation are not unfamiliar to us today. In various ways, such feelings arise in the group of educated women who are the subject of this book.

Christine's metaphor for women's sense of insecurity under men's constant attacks is that women are "as a felde without a hedge." Even women's defenders, who also imply their frailty, might evoke such an image. But her countering image is the city of ladies itself, a walled city that women themselves must build under the direction of Reason, Righteousness, and Justice to provide "some manere of place to come to or a cloystre of defence agaynst all those that wolde assayle them" (Bbvi v). Christine responds to destruction with creation, building a city as a tribute to women's virtue. Her definition of virtue may well disturb her twentieth-century sisters, but it was an important model both in early fifteenth-century France and throughout the sixteenth century in England. Having chosen the Virgin Mary as queen of the city, Christine concludes her work by dignifying humility, benignity, patience, piety, and chastity. For her, there seems to be no contradiction between detailing for several hundred pages the intelligence, creativity, courage, and accomplishments of women throughout history and concluding in the final pages that they must be obedient to men, humble, patient, and chaste. She can praise the active life, strongly advocate women's education, and defend women against all the conventional charges of frailty, inconstancy, and lechery; yet, her final exhortation might to us depict a silent, passive creature. If we suspect that the narrator meant the weight of the previous evidence ironically to undermine the ending, we must turn again to the final pages.[2]

The very last words of the book are crucial. Christine invites her "ryght redoubted ladyes to drawe to the vertues and flee vyces to encreace and multeplye our Cyte," and for herself, she wishes to live in God's service and to be granted with them "the Joye which endures evermore." At the center of Christine's thought is salvation, and we must recognize the close links in a Renaissance mind between the qualities of humility, patience, obedience, and chastity—and salvation. These are, after all, the spiritual virtues of Christ and the

Virgin Mary, and therefore the ideals of a Christian life. The argument against narrative irony is that in Christine's book, the women she praises, whether they are actually saints or proto-Christians like Sarah, Susanna, Lucretia, or Penelope, are always chaste, and always faithful and obedient to authority, be it husband, church, or God. Indeed, their source of strength and ability to act grow out of their radical adherence to the precepts of Christianity which always demand self-sacrifice and obedience. When she says "yt is tyme that theyre Juste cause be put out of the handes of Pharao," Christine means to associate the coming of the new law with women, who will establish a commonwealth built on their— and Christianity's—essential virtues.[3]

The building of a city to glorify feminine virtue is a metaphor profoundly appropriate to the architects of a women's literary tradition in English. Their writing reveals constant awareness of the masculine view of women and continually seeks to counter it by the "virtue" of what they write. In praising chastity, piety, humility, constancy, and obedience, they aligned themselves with traditional definitions of women designed to maintain their secondary, domestic status. But if their writings always seem conservative, acknowledging women's traditional place, certain texts go beyond reclaiming woman's nature to suggesting a redefinition of the importance and domain of the feminine virtues. Thus, chastity and humility are not merely the attributes of a weak woman, but more precisely, those of a good Christian. They are not the virtues commonly attached to public life and to the heroic, but from the pens of Christine de Pisan's descendants come poetry and prose glorifying their transcendence. Placing women at the very heart of Christianity, they, like Christine, envision woman's proper place, which if lower than men's in the hierarchies of the world, is often higher in the beauties of the spirit.

These women writers of sixteenth- and seventeenth-century England have been continually noticed from their own time to the present, but until recently, observers have uneasily described their accomplishments as anomalous or surprising.

This book will show that these women were not so much wonders as signs: that they were a significant and comprehensible part of English culture.

In the sixteenth century, commentators consistently praised a few English women for their learning and virtue, thus initiating the habits of isolating them as exceptional women and insisting that women's intellectual attainments consort with their feminine goodness. Over succeeding centuries, women like the daughters of Thomas More or the daughters of Antony Cooke became legendary examples of the learned and virtuous woman; even in the present century, they have retained the aura of "Tudor paragons."[4] While such titles are not entirely undeserved, the "paragons" become much more interesting when examined in a cultural context which clarifies the conflicts inherent in their being both women and writers.

Not until the 1930s, when Ruth Hughey and Charlotte Kohler documented the works of the many hidden behind the legends of the few were these writers treated systematically and seriously. Hughey studied printed matter, manuscripts, letters, and diaries, and concluded that religious devotion could both liberate women as writers and hobble their intellectual confidence. Kohler began the task of serious literary criticism. But their work, left largely unpublished in their Ph.D. dissertations, did not have the impact on scholarship and teaching that it deserved.[5] Fifty years after their pioneering studies, this book carries on their work by analyzing women writers of the English Renaissance as a group, and arguing that they form an early modern tradition of women's writing.

Many recent studies have analyzed the portrayal of women in Renaissance literature. Feminist critics have generated lively debate, particularly on Shakespeare, and in the process have evoked a healthy discussion of the relationship between literature and life as well as between the writer's environment and the writer's art. Scholars have offered new information about Renaissance attitudes toward women and new insights into the canon, so that present-day readers can more readily understand the Renaissance as a complex period, very different from the modern, in which, nevertheless, questions of gender and the position of women in society were continually discussed. In one of the most interesting of recent works, *Still Harping on Daughters: Women and Drama in the Age of Shakespeare*, Lisa Jardine provides Renaissance contexts for studying Elizabethan and Jacobean drama and can thus offer many valuable insights into Shakespeare's female heroes. Jardine also raises the interesting problem of how contemporary feminism can best help us to understand the Renaissance.[6] Certainly, some Renaissance women writers speak eloquently for women, and they appeal immediately to a desire to find our historical roots; nevertheless, this study will show that to ask whether sixteenth-century women writers were feminists is to ask an anachronistic question. These writers, in keeping with their era, devoted themselves to regenerating the image of women in the familiar terms of their own culture, not to imagining or advocating a different society in which all women might change their ordained feminine nature for equality with men or public power.[7]

Current interest in Renaissance women has also increased the volume of essays on individual women writers. Within the last two decades, scholars have provided new critical editions, making more writers available for research and teaching. The Countess of Pembroke and her niece, Mary Wroth, have attracted most attention, although work has also appeared on the defenders of women, and on less well-known figures like the religious writer, Katherine Parr, the poet, Isabella Whitney, and the dramatist, Elizabeth Cary.[8]

But if scholarship has revealed much about cultural attitudes toward women in the Renaissance and about the works of some women writers, too little has been done to put together these two aspects: to ask how social and literary attitudes toward women influenced women writers in Renaissance England. This book is the result of such an inquiry. Evidence from some thirty writers indicates that the concept of woman had a pervasive and crucial influence on women writers in three principal ways: by motivating them to write;

by circumscribing what they wrote and how they wrote it; and in some seemingly paradoxical cases, by encouraging them to subvert cultural expectations of women's writing.

What then was the Renaissance concept of woman? It is, of course, a composite, often contradictory, portrait, but its very ambiguities made it a perennial topic of interest among many different kinds of Renaissance writers. Woman was, in fact, the subject of a longstanding controversy, the "woman question," which over the course of a hundred years continued the medieval debate about the inherent virtue or vice of women and added material drawn from Neoplatonism, Christian humanism, and Protestant theology. Recently, Linda Woodbridge has persuasively demonstrated that the formal controversy over women was a separate genre with its own rules, forms, and techniques; that it developed as an elaborate literary game appropriate to the persona of attacker or defender of women (and did not necessarily reflect the author's own views); and that it had a wide influence on many other kinds of literature.[9] Woodbridge's book, like Jardine's, offers proof that there was a high level of interest in the nature of woman in a wide variety of sixteenth- and early seventeenth-century literature. The formal controversy was only the most visible result. Because the most eminent writers—Agrippa, Juan Vives, Thomas Elyot—as well as the most scurrilous pamphleteers discussed woman's nature, often addressing their works to women, it was a topic that could hardly escape the attention of a woman of letters.

But even if she did ignore the literary controversy, she would still learn its content, because as Ruth Kelso so thoroughly documented thirty years ago, doctrine on women was being delivered from the pulpit, in prayer books, in educational treatises, and household manuals. The nature of woman, her duties, and her limitations were topics constantly in the air.[10] Here, a brief summary of what a woman would most probably have read and heard about her sex will be useful.

Invariably returning to the first woman, the attackers, whether writing a jest-book or preaching a sermon, would point out that Eve listened to Satan and thus initiated all of humankind's future woe. Since then, women had followed their guilty foremother by being disobedient, talkative, lascivious shrews. Implied in this attack is that women should be the opposite—obedient, silent, and chaste—and indeed, these are precisely the virtues that women's defenders claim. Also acknowledging Eve's fault, they nevertheless propose that the second Eve, the Virgin Mary, is the source of all redemption. Their image of the virtuous woman is a domesticated version of the Virgin: remaining at home to keep the household goods, a good woman was pious, humble, constant, and patient, as well as obedient, chaste, and silent.[11]

I do not know precisely what effect these doctrines had on the everyday lives of women in the sixteenth century. In a real home, many accommodations and compromises might have been sought between parents and daughters, husband and wife, whatever social doctrines might prescribe. One extant sixteenth-century diary does suggest that at least for this writer, the injunctions to privacy, domesticity, obedience, piety, and humility were serious tenets of her daily life. Grace Sherrington Mildmay, married as a girl to the Elizabethan courtier, Anthony Mildmay, writes that she refused to go to court with great ladies she knew, instead remaining at home, because "God had placed me in the world in this house; and if I found no comfort here, I would never seek it out of this house; and this was my certaine resolution." Her "good delights" consisted in reading "in divinitie every day, as my leasure would give me leave, and the Grace of God permitt and drawe me"; studying her "Herball" and ministering to the sick; doing needlework and drawing. "And, though I was but meanly furnished to be excellent in any of those exercises, yet they did me good, inasmuch as I found myselfe that God wrought with me in all."[12] Perhaps Grace Mildmay writes as a countrywoman wishing to avoid the temptations of court; perhaps she expresses a pious withdrawal from the world; but her diary also seems to reveal how thoroughly a woman might internalize and acknowledge the doctrine of domestic feminine virtue.

If women might successfully adapt in the private sphere to their cultural limitations, these doctrines posed dilemmas for women who wrote and published their work. No author composes his or her works independently of other literature or of the cultural environment. That her society ordained a woman to legal, theological, and familial subjugation almost certainly had an inhibiting effect on women writers. The Renaissance Englishwoman who set out to write faced particular difficulties: early in the period, at least, she knew of few women who had been writers before her, leaving her still to discover an appropriate persona, subject, and form; she knew that almost everything in her culture either described women as intellectually and morally inferior or created models of impossible perfection. Thus, the woman writer confronted major obstacles from the moment when she began to write to the moment when she apologized to her readers for having written. Even the woman who did not write for immediate publication was aware of social and literary attitudes toward women as she tried to create her own literary persona, the very voice in which to express her ideas.

Almost every aspect of Renaissance society distinguished between the characteristics, the abilities, the essential nature of men and women. In particular, while everything encouraged educated men to be public servants, the continued insistence that the virtuous woman was private, domestic, and silent was an acknowledged difficulty for many writers who wished to address an audience. Perhaps many women writers specifically invoked a female audience partly out of legitimate sympathy, but partly to camouflage their public voice, to pretend that addressing other women was not really talking to the world. More important, the social injunctions also produced a recognizable and sometimes articulated feminine decorum, the adherence to subjects, images, and language that conformed to the type of the virtuous woman. Yet, in their very restrictions, women would discover their voice and their art.

For it is indeed the persona of the virtuous woman that dominates each of these women as she writes. At a time when writing could be considered an inappropriate activity for women, the woman writer early on created a little island for herself in the literary stream by writing pious works. The Reformation, with its emphasis on individual salvation and the reading of Scripture, was in fact the single most important influence on women writers, who added to the huge volume of works bearing witness to the Reformed faith. More significant, women also adopted the persona of the preacher or teacher of the faithful. From Katherine Parr's *Prayers* to Anne Bacon's translation of Bishop Jewel's *Apology of the Church of England*, to Rachel Speght's *Mortalities Memorandum*, women writers made themselves responsible for the well-being of their readers' souls.

Piety was the lifeblood of Renaissance women writers, as it was of many men. Anne Askew, the Protestant martyr, in recording her examination for heresy, wrote a witty, dramatic, and gripping spiritual autobiography. Jane Grey composed an impassioned, highly crafted letter to convince an apostate to return to the Reformed faith. Anne Dowriche wrote a blood-and-thunder account of the struggles of the French Huguenots, a fascinating study in the language and imagery of religious propaganda. Mary Sidney translated the Psalms into an extraordinary variety of Elizabethan lyrics. Out of their piety came their vocation as writers, and if some women wrote only functional religious works in mediocre verse or plodding prose, others, like Isabella Whitney, seem to develop as poets before the reader's eyes as they struggled toward the fullest expression of their feelings and ideas.

But if pious writers could assume legitimacy from their obvious learning and virtue, over the course of this study, it will become clear from the words of women themselves as well as from the praises of men, that the phrase "learned and virtuous" was both praise and limitation. To men and perhaps to some women, a woman's desire for knowledge was a frightening prospect, recalling images of Eve's hand reaching for the apple. But by claiming that learning would increase a woman's virtue (her chastity, obedience, humility), the humanists and their successors reassured society that a woman's

INTRODUCTION

knowledge was under control and directed only to enhancing her womanliness. In their writing, many women took pains to endorse this attitude, to emphasize that they themselves were virtuous—specifically chaste, modest, and obedient—and that women, far from inheriting Eve's penchant for rebellion, were determined to redeem her through virtuous words and deeds. Such conservatism almost guaranteed that most women would not participate in the literary experimentation or secularization carried on by men of the period; yet, they would embrace the image of the learned and virtuous women and make it their own by creating a distinctively feminine persona and eventually feminine genres. Ultimately, their learning would provide the means to glorify feminine virtue on their own terms by the creation of female heroes.

To understand how a particular writer played her part in creating this tradition of women's writing involves uniting the general social and literary context with the particular details of her life and work. While my approach to the treatises, poems, translations, and plays is fundamentally literary, I have also sought to clarify choices of persona, genre, language, and imagery by referring to the broader cultural environment. From the theorists, men who wrote treatises about women's education, I indicate specifically what English readers would expect from the learned woman. Biographical material about individual writers has often been a problem, because it varies from adequate in the case of Elizabeth Cary, whose daughter wrote a life of her mother, to scattered references in most cases, to almost nonexistent for women like Elizabeth Colville or Anne Dowriche. We may rely on a certain amount of internal evidence to reveal details of the writer's life, but many of these women remain shadowy figures known to us only through a single printed edition, a diary, or letters.

The first work studied here is Margaret More Roper's translation of Erasmus's treatise on the Paternoster, published in 1524; the last is an advice book, *The Mothers Counsell*, entered in the Stationer's Register in 1623. In those hundred years appeared more translations, varied feminine personae, and experiments with genre, style, and voice as women steadily strove to establish a legitimate place for their own literary experience. If this constitutes a literary Renaissance for women, it does not conform to that of masculine culture, nor does it extend much beyond the death of James I. At the quarter-century mark, whether the interest in women's education had faltered, or whether women had exhausted this particular vein of writing, they briefly turned away from building their city to other pursuits.[13]

To reflect the gradual establishment of a women's tradition, I have divided the book into three parts, each designated by one of Christine de Pisan's architectural metaphors. The first part, "The sturdy foundations," comprising Chapters One through Four, establishes the cultural setting and examines the growing tradition of women's pious writing in prose, poetry, and translation. Margaret More Roper, who epitomizes the humanist ideal of the learned and virtuous woman is followed by Anne Askew whose learned and virtuous persona ironically subverts the restrictions on women's roles. Chapter Three considers how the Reformation provided women with the opportunity and the language for literary preaching and fostered both a feminine persona, the true Christian woman, and a feminine imagery. Chapter Four studies the relationship of women's piety to their development as poets.

In part Two, "Mighty towers and strong bastions," I focus on four major figures, Mary Sidney, Elizabeth Cary, Aemilia Lanyer, and Mary Wroth. Each of these writers expanded the possibilities for writers of her sex by experimenting with persona, modifying and adapting existing genres, and technically mastering the task of writing good poetry while conveying doctrine. Each breathed new life into the concept of the virtuous woman, the redeemed Eve: Mary Sidney by her own assumption of the role of divine poet; Elizabeth Cary by creating a conflicted hero who suffers for her virtue and yet triumphs over tyranny; Aemilia Lanyer by envisioning a world which reflects women's Christian virtue, manifested both in Biblical personages and in great English women of her own day; Mary Wroth by creating a fictional character, a lover, a queen, and a poet whose heroic constancy dominates her world.

In Part Three, "Lofty walls all around," the final chapter, "Redeeming Eve," presents both the women who wrote defenses of women and those who composed mother's advice books. In harmonious discord, these two groups clearly represent both the distance women writers had journeyed over the course of one hundred years and the limitations that still beset their work. While each group diversifies the voice and style of women's writing, to varying degrees, their subject matter ultimately reinforces traditional definitions of feminine virtue.

PART I

"The sturdy foundations"

ONE

LEARNING AND VIRTUE: MARGARET MORE ROPER

*I*N THEIR PROLIFIC writings about women, sixteenth-century men gave only minor consideration to the question of women's education. Even in those few books devoted exclusively to women's upbringing, authors lingered but briefly on intellectual development before hurrying on to detailed advice about feminine conduct. Such general neglect gives particular prominence to the writings of the humanists, Juan Luis Vives, Thomas More, Richard Hyrde, and Thomas Elyot, who appear to advocate something akin to a liberal education for women. Indeed, the obvious assumption might be that only because certain humanists gave certain women access to books and encouraged their studies did the number of women writers increase so dramatically in the sixteenth century. But if women did indeed gain an education, they also confronted restrictions upon their knowledge. As this chapter will show, Tudor educational theorists were at best ambivalent and at worst prohibitive when considering how women might use their education.[1]

What was the relationship between women's education and the establishment of a women's literary tradition? Part of the answer lies within the books that considered whether and how women should be educated. While these writings were not necessarily closely followed prescriptions, they nonetheless recorded the contemporary attitudes, beliefs, rationalizations, prejudices, and expectations which confronted, and may even have formed, women writers. Whether advocating or proscribing women's education, these writers expressed a devastatingly consistent cultural doctrine on women's function in society, establishing in the process an image of the ideal learned and virtuous woman.

The main problem for women writers evolved from the nature of the virtue that their learning was intended to foster. While male virtue might be expressed by an active life in the world or public service or eloquence, women were taught that feminine virtue meant a private, domestic existence, lived in "obedience, silence, and chastity." Indeed, writers on female education seem obsessed with these three traditional feminine virtues at the very moment when they are considering the untraditional topic of improving women's minds. Discussing change in so important an area seems to have summoned fears that women would step beyond the private sphere, and so these educators compensated by insisting on women's "natural" domestic attributes. As their own writings consistently show, women received this message and often felt compelled to reveal how their learning had indeed increased their virtue.

It is important to realize about these treatises that those who argue for and against women's education proceed from the same assumptions about woman's nature. The belief in woman's inherent intellectual weakness justified both advocating that her mind be improved and insisting that she was incapable of learning. The conviction that woman's sphere was domestic warranted both the prohibition of women's education and the establishment of a curriculum appropriate to her place in society. In considering the works of Juan Vives (as translated by Richard Hyrde), Thomas Elyot, Richard Mulcaster, and Giovanni Michele Bruto (as translated by "W.P."), we will find that while all but Bruto advocate the intellectual improvement of daughters, all four writers assume women are lesser creatures belonging to the private domain. Their advice would pose particular problems for an incipient writer and prohibitions like theirs may well have influenced the kind of writing women did.

An influential voice on women's education was that of Juan Luis Vives, tutor in the service of Catherine of Aragon, Henry VIII's highly educated queen. Vives's *Instruction of a Christen*

uintilian and St. Jerome praised eloquence in the
Cornelia and Hortentia, Vives does not wholly
it, but because of its public aspect, it is not a goal
ucation and may interfere with her female virtue.
never dies during the period, and even a century
1631, Richard Brathwaite can advise gentlewomen
nly "of such arguments as may best improve your
ge in household affaires, and other private employ-
o discourse of State-matters, will not become your
; nor to dispute of high poynts of Divinity, will it
l with women of your quality. These Shee-Clarkes
mes broach strange opinions, which, as they under-
em not themselves, so they labour to intangle others
ll understanding to themselves."[6] The old patristic
on that with chastity went obedience and silence finds
uing place in Renaissance doctrine for women.
r in the sixteenth century, some writers did approve
nen writing poetry, but the tendency is to trivialize
fforts. In his *Arte of English Poesie* (1589), George Put-
h designates the chapter, "A division of figures, and
hey serve in exornation of language," "for the learning
ies and young Gentlewomen, or idle Courtiers, desirous
ome skilful in their owne mother tongue, and for their
e recreation to make now and then ditties of pleasure,
ing for our parte none other science so fit for them and
lace as that which teacheth *beau semblant*, the chiefe
ssion as well of Courting as of poesie: since to such
her of mindes nothing is more combersome then tedious
ines and schollarly methodes of discipline, we have in
owne conceit devised a new and strange modell of this
fitter to please the Court then the schoole."[7] Even al-
ng for Puttenham's inculcation of gentility in courtiers,
e or female, he assumes that a woman, like an idle courtier,
ld not be capable of scholarly discipline. If, surmounting
hese barriers, a woman should still seriously wish to write
try, she is confronted by hostility and by poetic traditions
conventions that had been adapted to masculine expe-
nce.

woman (1523), translated into English in 1529 by Richard
Hyrde, a tutor in Sir Thomas More's household, had over
forty editions and translations in the sixteenth century, including eight reprintings of the English version between 1540
and 1592.[2] According to Hyrde's preface, More fully approved
of Vives's program and had himself considered translating
the *Instruction*. He did in fact oversee Hyrde's work, making
corrections and endorsing the final copy.

The humanists did indeed see themselves as women's ben-
efactors, countering the streams of vilification from misogynist
writers. Hyrde, in his preface to the *Instruction*, says he often
wonders at the "unreasonable oversyght of men whiche never
ceace to compleyne of womens conditions. And yet having
the education and order of them in theyr owne handes not
only do litell diligence to teache them and bryng them up
better but also purposely withdrawe them from lernyng by
whiche they myght have occasyons to waxe better by their
selfe."[3] Like every other sixteenth-century educator, Vives
focuses women's education on the development of her virtue,
primarily defined as chastity, and with it, the attendant qualities of domesticity, privacy, and piety. All of his analysis of
woman's nature and his recommendations for her upbringing
conform to his fundamental insistence on her chastity. For
Vives, chastity certainly means physical purity, as the admonitions to girls, wives, and widows to avoid male company
and to dress modestly confirm; occasionally he seems to refer
to a larger sense of spiritual purity.

In Chapter Six, "Of virginite," significantly juxtaposed to
the chapter, "What bokes be to be redde and what not," Vives
remarks that even the pagans valued virginity, and cites the
example of Pallas who, born of Jupiter's brain, signified that
"virginitie and wysedome were joyned together. And they
dedicated the nombre of seven both to chastite and wysdome.
. . ." This coupling is not new, as for centuries church fathers
and ecclesiastical scholars had waged a vigorous battle against
women for the cause of a celibate clergy. They too insisted
that chastity and wisdom were joined together, that chastity
allowed the triumph of the mind over the flesh, and that sex

and marriage destroyed the ability to serve God. Women were of course the main temptation, and everyone from Eve on was a potential danger to the holy living of mankind.[4] But where chastity for men was by no means central, for women it was prescribed as the preeminent goal for all, whether celibate, maiden, wife, or widow. "For as a man nedeth many thynges as wysedome, eloquence, knowledge of thynges with remembrance, some crafte to live by, Justice, Liberalitie, lusty stomake, and other thynges mo ... in a woman the honestie is in stede of all" (Giv). And again, "chastyte is the principall vertue of a woman and counterpeyseth with all the reste: ... shamfastnes and sobrenes be the inseperable companyons of chastite" (Liv v). For Vives, chastity is the fountainhead of all virtues necessary for a woman, as "demureness/measure/ frugalite/scarsite/diligence in house/cure of devotion/mekenes ..." (Mii). As the end point of an education, however, chastity so defined transforms a potential widening of spirit and growth of mind into something which allies piety, good manners, and efficient housekeeping. The vigilant censorship that Vives enjoins on a girl's teachers provides her with the examples of chaste women from history and literature and the injunctions to be found in "the Gospelles and the actes and the epistoles of thapostles and ye olde Testament saint Hieronyme/saint Cyprian/Augustine/Ambrose/Hilary/Gregory/ Plato/Cicero/Senec/ and such other...." These she must study only under the tutelage of "some wyse and sad Men" to avoid her depending on her own judgment and misconstruing her texts. Instead of the free exploration of his world that would lead a man to develop judgment and the virtues suitable for public life and action, a woman would receive pieces of information about the world, filtered through her preceptor whose goal was to make her a chaste wife, mother, and if it so happened, widow. The only role another woman might take was as governess to modify the girl's behavior, to act as a virtuous role model, or as a duenna to keep her cloistered.

Vives himself provides specific lists for women's reading, and in so doing, helps us to understand more about women's writing.[5] While some of his injunctions resemble the cautions

teachers leveled at mal
women because of the
woman should "lerne t
out of bokes whiche she
redde ..." (Liv-Liv v), V
to women, notably roma
mance, Vives feared cont
..." and naming such wo
he decries books "idell m
upon filthe and vitiousnes
Sir Philip Sidney's remark
have known men that ever
which, God knoweth, want
found their hearts moved to
and especially courage.") Viv
merely to tempt women's ch
craftes. ..." To offer example
ently to risk inclining a woma
ment is so weak. As for poet
gerous Ovid himself warned
witty and well lerned poetes
wryte of love [as] Calimachus
Tibullus, Propertius and Gall
should beware of all these book
snakes. And if there be any wo
in these bokes that she wyl nat le
she shuld nat only be kept from
good bokes with an yll wyl and
frendes shuld provyde that she m
ynge" (F v-Fii). Prohibiting imagi
been the single most damaging ste
as the education of a potential wr
those who do not read it, will not wr
is almost as prohibitive, discouraging
guage, rhetoric, and particularly elo
Vives remarks, "As for eloquence I
woman nedeth it nat: but she nedeth
Nor it is no shame for a woman t

Because
exemplar
condemn
of her e
This vie
later, in
to talk
knowle
ments.
auditory
sort we
many t
stand t
of equa
injunct
a conti
Late
of wo
their e
tenhan
how t
of Lad
to bec
priva
think
the
profe
man
doct
our
arte
low
mal
wou
all
po
an
rie

Because of his service to Catherine of Aragon and through his translator, Richard Hyrde, Vives may have influenced the education of specific women like the Princess Mary and the daughters of Thomas More. Probably more theoretical was the work of Sir Thomas Elyot, the scholar, diplomat, and author, also an admirer of Queen Catherine and a friend of Thomas More. Elyot supported the education of women, while seemingly unable to relinquish a belief in their secondary position and limited sphere. What emerges even more clearly in Elyot's *Defence of Good Women* (1540) are the inherent contradictions in the programs for women's education that might create particular anxieties for the beneficiaries. *The Defence of Good Women* is a dialogue between Candidus and Caninius, who argue for and against women's education, and concludes with the arrival and evidence of Zenobia, the legendary queen of Palmyra. As the antagonist, Caninius has to concede at the end of the dialogue, "I see well inoghe, that women beinge well and vertuously brought up, do not only with men participate in reason, but some also in fidelitie and constauncie be equall unto them."[8] The presence of Zenobia, now a Roman captive, provides dramatic evidence of woman's ability to learn moral philosophy and to become a ruler with all the appropriate virtues of that position. Candidus introduces Zenobia, pardoned by Rome for "her nobilitye vertue and courage" as "well lerned in greke ... and doth competently understand latine, but excellently the Egyptian language." She teaches her children and "wryteth as they say of Alexandria and the orient eloquent stories" (51-52). Zenobia herself evinces becoming reluctance to be away from home, for fear of her reputation, and then testifies to the importance of studying moral philosophy before she married "late" at age twenty, "for I knewe the better what longed to my duety" (55). And what Zenobia learned between sixteen and twenty was "that without prudence and constancy, women mought be broughte lyghtely into errour and foly, and made therefore unmete for that companye, wherunto they were ordeyned: I meane, to be assistence and comfort to man through theyr fidelitie ..." (56). Adapting the virtues to woman's special case, Zenobia explains that "Justyce teacheth us womenne, to honour our husbands nexte after god: which honour resteth in due obedience ...," that Fortitude keeps women in a "vertuouse constancy" and that "in a woman, no vertue is equall to Temperaunce, wherby in her wordes and dedes she alway useth a just moderation, knowynge when tyme is to speke, and whan to kepe silence, whan to be occupyed and whan to be merye. And if she measure it to the wyll of her husbande, she doth the more wysely ..." (57). As a wife, Zenobia never said or did anything which did not please her husband; when a widow, she was able to assume command of her country's government so capably that the country thrived:

> And to the intente that the name of a woman, shulde not amonge the people be had in contempt, I used so my procedynges, that none of them mought be sayd, to be done womanly. Wherfore I sate alway abrode amonge my counsaylours, and sayde myne opinion, so that it seemed to them all, that it stode with good reason. ... More over, I caused good lawes to be publyshed ... I made justice chiefe ruler of myne affection ... to the whiche wysedome and polycy I atteyned by the study of noble philosophy. Also thereby I acquired such magnanimitie, that nowe I kepe in as strayt subjection al affections, and passions, as the Romaynes doo nowe me and my chyldren. (61-64)

Zenobia conducted matters of state, spoke publicly, gave laws, meted justice, and acquired magnanimity, that supreme virtue jealously guarded as the goal of a gentleman's education. But none of these activities "mought be sayd to be done womanly"; that is, as a ruler, Zenobia did not act like the rest of weak and inconstant womankind but like a reasonable man. In public, she was manly; in private, she surpassed the virtue of all other women. Earlier in the dialogue, Candidus, the supposed defender, had suggested as much when he admitted that "in al kyndes of thinges, are commonly founde more warse than better" and "althoghe a greatte numbre of women

perchance were viciouse, yet oughte not a man reproche therfore the hole kynde of women, sense of them undoubtedly
many be vertuouse." It was a commonplace in writings about
women to separate the few good, the striking examples, from
the rest, so that educated, virtuous women would see themselves as isolated and hybrid figures: bearing the inherent
inferiority of their sex, relegated to ancillary roles, and yet
capable through education of attaining unwomanly reason. It
is no accident that Elyot shows his virtuous and learned lady
as a captive queen, now removed from the public sphere, but
naturally quite content to be out of the limelight.[9] To Elyot,
there seems to be no problem inherent in educating a woman
while assuming that she will continue content to be private
and domestic. The writers against women's education may
have more nearly analyzed the reality when they claimed, as
Bruto would, that once a woman began to learn, men would
no longer be able to choose her reading lists or prevent her
from preferring the pen to the needle.

Throughout the sixteenth century, theories about women's
abilities and sphere changed very little, but at least by 1581,
the prominent educator Richard Mulcaster can support education for girls because it is "the manner and custome of
my countrey."[10] However, with the customary refusal of discussions on women's education to challenge preconceptions,
Mulcaster clarifies that this cannot mean education in public
grammar school, nor university, but "with distinction in degrees, with difference of their calling, with respect to their
endes ..." (168). English girls may be taught to read, write,
sing, play, and learn Latin and Greek very successfully, for
they are as capable as, even superior to the Roman and Greek
paragons, to German and French ladies, and even to Italian
ladies "who dare write themselves, and deserve fame for so
doing. Whose excellencie is so geason [uncommon, amazing],
as they be rather wonders to gaze at, then presidentes to
follow" (168). Again, the conventional view is that a woman
must dare to step out of her sphere to write and that she
becomes a comet flashing once across the sky, not a steady
beacon of light to guide other women. Mulcaster reiterates

this point several times, remarking later that there may be "rare excellencies in some women," but "there is neither president to be fetcht nor precept to be framed ... these singularities be above the comon ... those pictures passe beyond all hope" (177).

Echoing Hyrde's preface to Vives, Mulcaster finds it to be men's duty to educate girls "to have our childrens mothers well furnished in minde, well strengthened in bodie." Since women are by nature weaker, "is there any better meane to strengthen their minde, then that knowledge of God, of religion, of civil, of domesticall dueties ...?" In what he obviously considers an apt comparison, Mulcaster cites the analogy of Augustus Caesar's horse who had a weak dam, concluding that much benefit will derive from exercising girls' bodies as well as their minds (169).

Mulcaster does believe that women's own "naturall towardnesse" deserves the nurturance of education to bring them to their own particular excellence. "And yet thereby in no point to let [i.e., hinder] their most laudable dueties in marriage and matche, but rather to bewtifie them, with most singular ornamentes ..." (170). Citing Plato and Aristotle for support, Mulcaster claims that each advocates that the distinctive qualities of women be brought to their naturally endowed potential and performance. He also points to the "excellent effectes" of those women who have been educated, calling on Plutarch and "all good and generally authorised histories," which show "that not onely private and particular wymen, being very well trained, but also great princesses and gallant troupes of the same sex have shewed fourth in them selves mervelous effectes of vertue and valure" (172-73). As long as she is admired from afar, the supreme example and exception is of course Queen Elizabeth herself, and with her stand "many singuler ladies and gentlwymen so skilfull in all cunning, of the most laudable, and loveworthy qualities of learning, as they may well be alleaged for a president to prayse, not for a patern to prove like by ..." (174).

Unlike boys, whose education is "without restraint for either matter or maner, bycause our employment is so generall in all thinges" (174), girls must be kept within limits. Pointing out that sometimes girls' minds seem to ripen earlier than boys', "yet it is not so. Their naturall weaknesse which cannot holde long, delivers very soone. . . . Besides, their braines be not so much charged, neither with weight nor with multitude of matters, as boyes heades be, and therefore like empty caske they make the greater noise" (176).

On this kind of false reasoning, Mulcaster builds his curriculum, where he recommends reading, so as to make available religious works and "comfortable and wise discourses, penned either in forme of historie, or for direction to live by." Writing will be useful particularly to tradeswomen, and playing and singing will please parents and potential spouses, if girls would only keep practicing once they become mothers. He has no domestic advice, "though I thinke it, and knowe it, to be a principall commendation in a woman: to be able to governe and direct her housild, to looke to her house and familie, to provide and keepe necessaries, though the goodman pay, to know the force of her kitchen, for sicknes and health . . ." (178).

In the upper classes, women need education more, "to honour themselves and to discharge the duetie" to their country. He censors geometry, law, physics, and divinity; but philosophy may be allowed, "and those faculties also, which do belong to the furniture of speache, may be verie well allowed them, bycause toungues be most proper, where they do naturally arise" (181). He concludes,

> And is not a young gentlewoman, thinke you, throughly furnished, which can reade plainly and distinctly, write faire and swiftly, sing cleare and sweetely, play wel and finely, understand and speake the learned languages, and those tongues also which the time most embraseth, with some *logicall* helpe to chop, and some *Rhetoricke* to brave. (181-82)

The endorsement here is of an education providing basic literacy, the fundamentals of good companionship, and some measure of polite accomplishment. Mulcaster does not want stupid women, but he does not wish for intellectual ones either. The boy's freedom to range over all knowledge, to follow his spirit as high as it will go is for the girl replaced by confinement. It is no wonder that in many cases, any real learning women of this era did was achieved through self-education.[11]

Unlike Mulcaster, Elyot, and Vives, in his 1598 translation of Giovanni Bruto's 1555 treatise, *The Necessarie, Fit, and Convenient Education of a yong Gentlewoman*, "W.P." does not merely limit intellectual instruction for women, he prohibits it. He clarifies in great detail what a woman would have to fear if she acquired learning, or more precisely, he reveals what men feared in a well-educated woman, and perhaps what lay behind the tentativeness of women's prologues and the apologies of her publishers. Continually repeated, Bruto's message is clear and simple:

> I am not therfore of opinion, in any sort whatsoever, that a young gentlewoman should be instructed in learning and humane Arts, in whome we account honestie and true vertue to be more comely and a better ornament, than the report and light renowme of great science and knowledge by her attained unto.[12]

The nature of this true virtue is explicitly laid out in a discussion of why learning with its two purposes of profit and recreation is not for women. If learning is for profit,

> that cannot be hoped for in a woman, who as by nature shee is given us for a companion in our labors, so she ought to be active and attentive to governe our houses, nor this manner of studie which procureth delight may not bee granted unto her, without great daunger to offend the beautie and glory of her minde. (F8v)

Bruto's compliments barely mask his absolute prohibitions or his fear that women might quit their domestic sphere.

If learning is for recreation, the danger is that women will learn to be "subtil and impudent lovers" or "learnedly to write verses, poetrie, ballads and songs." Their care should be their houses, not verses, and "how much more convenient the needle, the wheele, the distaffe, and the spindle, with the name and reputation of grave and honest matrons is for them, then the book and pen with an uncertaine report: if in them there be more learning than honestie and vertue" (G2). Bruto's image of a woman's mind seems to be of a tiny, fixed space that can only contain so much—if more learning, then less virtue. In a similar vein, he recommends that the young gentlewoman develop humility, because it is the foundation of Christian virtue, and "because it ingendreth in us the knowing of our selves, as much as her weake mind may comprehend, she shall shew her of the wisdom of God, of his goodnes, and his power . . ." (H2). Given her intellectual inferiority, even woman's piety is deficient.

Vives's translator, Richard Hyrde, had actually addressed arguments like Bruto's as early as 1524 in his dedication of Margaret More Roper's translation from Erasmus, *A devout treatise upon the Pater noster*. Reviewing the prohibition against Greek and Latin being taught to women, Hyrde argued that such studies would improve any mind, male or female, and that whereas a woman's mind might wander into evil while only her fingers were busy with sewing, if she learned Greek and Latin, her mind would be fully occupied with good. Indeed, he believed that no learned woman "ever was . . . spotted or infamed as vicious. But on the other side/many by their lernyng taken suche encreace of goodnesse/that many may beare them wytnesse of their vertue."[13]

It is interesting that Hyrde, who twice published his fervent endorsement of the doctrine that women's education increased their feminine virtue, knew Margaret More Roper well, for to her contemporaries, no one was more successful in uniting her erudition and her domestic vocation than Thomas More's eldest daughter. Whether Hyrde was actually her tutor, whether he influenced her or she influenced him, it is clear that Margaret More Roper came to represent for Hyrde, for Vives, and for many others, the ideal learned, virtuous woman.

MARGARET MORE ROPER (1505–1544)

From the sixteenth century to the present, Margaret More Roper has been described as a paragon of learning and virtue.[14] While examination of extant contemporary documents does nothing to contradict her fame, it is time to reconsider the nature of both her erudition and her goodness.

The eldest of three daughters and a son born to Sir Thomas More and his first wife, Jane Colt, Margaret More had the qualities of mind and spirit to be particularly singled out for her father's attention. Indeed, More's letters indicate that he guided Margaret's life to conform both to his principles of education and his beliefs about woman's nature. Simply put, he agreed with Vives that though inferior, women might increase their virtue with learning, and that their virtue should be wholly private and domestic. How thoroughly Margaret Roper assimilated her father's opinions is reflected in her actions, her letters, and her writings, and is verified by all who knew her. Her learning and virtue, so unendingly praised, conformed by definition to the humanist ideal for women, which seems to have become her own self-concept. Since all witnesses wished to view her as Thomas More's ideal daughter, we may never know whether the woman beneath the image was any different.

The myth of perfection surrounding Thomas More has inevitably produced a similarly legendary aura around Margaret Roper. All contemporary information about her comes from her admiring and perhaps self-congratulatory father and from the original More hagiographers, William Roper, Richard Hyrde, Nicholas Harpsfield, and Thomas Stapleton, who all praised the completeness of her womanly virtue and the extent of her learning with the greatest ardor and the utmost conformity. Given that these men idealized everything about More, including his relations with his family, still it is useful to examine their characterization of Margaret Roper, because they find in her the fulfillment of the virtuous and learned woman created by More's educational principles.

The More biographer who knew her best, her husband,

William Roper, surprisingly provides us with the fewest details of her character. In his notes for the biographer Nicholas
Harpsfield, written about 1556, Roper relates only an anecdote
of Margaret's "daughterly affection" as she waited for More
on his final journey from Westminster to the Tower of London. Having rushed forward to embrace her father "openly,
in the sight of all," she,

> not satisfied with the former sight of him, and like one
> that had forgotten herself, being all ravished with the
> entire love of her dear father, having respect neither to
> herself, nor to the press of the people and multitude that
> were there about him, suddenly turned back again, ran
> to him as before, took him about the neck, and divers
> times together most lovingly kissed him, and at last,
> with a full heavy heart, was fain to depart from him.[15]

The description of this episode might recall the weeping
Daughters of Jerusalem following Christ to Calvary, a characterization in keeping with Roper's depiction of More as
saint. One wonders, too, whether Roper is confirming what
all the other documents suggest, that his wife's relationship
with her father overshadowed every other bond.

It is from other sources that we learn of contemporary
views of Margaret Roper's learning and virtue. In his preface
to Margaret Roper's translation of Erasmus, *A devout treatise
upon the Pater noster*, Richard Hyrde names the author as an
example of how learning increases woman's virtue, and tells
us a little more about her marriage. Her

> vertuous conversacion/lyvyng/and sadde demeanoure/
> maye be profe evydent ynough what good lernynge
> dothe/ where it is surely roted: of whom other women
> may take example of prudent/humble/and wyfely be-
> havour/ charitable and very christen vertue/with whiche
> she hath with goddes helpe endevoured herselfe/no lesse
> to garnisshe her soule/than it hath lyked his goodnesse
> with lovely beauty and comelynesse/ to garnysshe and
> sette out her body: And ... with her vertuous/ wor-

shipfull/wyse/and well lerned husbande/she hath by the
occasyon of her lernynge/and his delyte therin/ suche
especiall conforte/pleasure/and pastyme/as were nat well
possyble for one unlerned couple/eyther to take togyder
or to concyve in their myndes/what pleasure is therin.
(A4v-B)

Not only has Roper's education reinforced the traditional
virtues attached to women, but it has improved her wifely
attributes by making her a better companion for her husband,
who clearly approves of her accomplishments. Since he is
introducing one of the earliest published works by a woman,
Hyrde's reiterated insistence on her continuing virtue and
womanliness was probably meant to palliate the public appearance of her work, but it also repeats the generalized,
glowing portrait found everywhere else.

In Nicholas Harpsfield's *Life and Death of Sir Thomas More*
(1557?), based in part on William Roper's recollections, Margaret Roper appears as amazingly learned, but most warmly
commended for her exemplary virtue as daughter, wife, and
mother. Since she was the most like her father, Roper was
of course "to her servants a meek and gentle mistress, to her
brother and sisters a most loving, natural and aimable sister,
to her friends a very sure, steadfast and confortable friend;
yea, which is a rare thing in a woman, accounted of them to
be of such gravity and prudent counsel. ..."[16] If Roper impressed others by her grave, wise talk, "above all other she
was to her father, and to her husband, such a daughter, such
a wife, as I suppose it was hard to match her in all England"
(98). Harpsfield goes on to cite Erasmus who "for her exquisite
learning, wisdom and virtue, made such an account of her,
that he called her the flower of all the learned matrons in
England" (98). And while Harpsfield pays tribute to her
knowledge by noting how she amended an error in St. Cyp-
rian that previous scholars had missed, he is far more concerned to document her miraculous recovery from the sweat-
ing sickness due to the prayers of and divinely inspired cure

recommended by her father. If Thomas More is the phoenix of men, Margaret Roper is the paragon of women.

Thomas Stapleton's *Life and Illustrious Martyrdom of Sir Thomas More* (1588) also glorifies the Mores, but emphasizes Margaret Roper's specific scholarly achievements as a way of praising her father. He describes the More household as an ideal academy of religious instruction, noting how at meals each child took turns reading a passage of Scripture and patristic commentary, intoned in ecclesiastic fashion and ending with "and do thou, O Lord, have mercy on us," as in religious houses.[17] This would be followed by an informal conversation about scriptural passages. The children's tutors taught them Latin and Greek literature, logic, philosophy, mathematics, and the writings of the Church Fathers. Of Roper's particular accomplishments, Stapleton says,

> More than all the rest of his children, she resembled her father, as well in stature, appearance, and voice, as in mind and in general character. She wrote very eloquently prose and verse both in Greek and Latin. Two Latin speeches, written as an exercise, which I have myself seen, are in style elegant and graceful, while in treatment they hardly yield to her father's compositions. Another speech, first written in English, was translated by both the father and the daughter separately into Latin with such great skill that one would not know which to prefer. ... (112)

Both father and daughter wrote a treatise on the *Four Last Things*, and Stapleton claims that More "affirmed most solemnly that the treatise of his daughter was in no way inferior to his own. As St. Augustine had his Adeodatus, whose admirable talents he could never sufficiently admire, so had More his Margaret" (113). While Margaret Roper was viewed as a physical and intellectual reflection of her father, such praise of her erudition may well have been conditioned not only by the biographers' purpose in writing—to canonize More—but by their basic assumptions of what women were capable of achieving. A rational judgment of Roper's intellectual attainments should depend not on who she was but on what she actually wrote. Unfortunately, her contemporaries could not forget she was More's daughter and a woman. Modern appraisal must be partial because very little of her work remains.[18]

In their own correspondence, first during More's service at court and later while he was a prisoner in the Tower, father and daughter provide abundant evidence of their deep bond, but also some clarification of how More perceived Margaret and how she saw herself. While the letters reflect their mutual love and respect, and More continually acknowledges Margaret's brilliance, they also bear witness to the limitations on women, no matter how exceptional. In a letter written in 1521, shortly after Margaret's marriage to William Roper, More, always addressing his daughter as "most dear," gently chides her:

> There was no reason, my darling daughter, why you should have put off writing me for a single day, because in your great self-distrust you feared that your letters would be such that I could not read them without distaste. Even had they not been perfect, yet the honor of your sex would have gained you pardon from anyone, while to a father even a blemish will seem beautiful in the face of a child. But indeed, my dear Margaret, your letters were so elegant and polished and gave so little cause for you to dread the indulgent judgment of a parent, that you might have despised the censorship of an angry Momus.[19]

The letter is loving, but in indicating Margaret's habitual self-deprecation of her own talents, More also makes the crucial point that as a woman she can expect to be judged by less stringent standards. The two points are not unrelated, for a sense of the inferiority of her sex could well have bred insecurity about her abilities. At the moment she is told her letter is "perfect," she is also told that her sex would excuse faults anyway, as would her being More's daughter.

More's subsequent recommendations for Margaret's future

course reflect his belief both that study would improve women's minds and that women were essentially private and domestic beings. He hopes that she will devote the rest of her life "to medical science and sacred literature, so that you may be well furnished for the whole scope of human life (which is to have a sound mind in a sound body) . . ." (*Letters*, 149). These are the arts that will best train her for usefulness within the family circle, as a teacher for her children's spirits and doctor for their bodily ills.[20] And if More's humor surfaces at the end of the letter, as he notes that both Margaret and William Roper are studying astronomy with Nicholas Kratzer, he still has a message about Margaret's place:

> Farewell, my dearest child, and salute for me my beloved son, your husband. I am extremely glad that he is following the same course of study as yourself. I am ever wont to persuade you to yield in everything to your husband; now, on the contrary, I give you full leave to strive to surpass him in the knowledge of the celestial system. (*Letters*, 149)

If Margaret Roper's position sounds difficult, both to excel in learning and virtue, and to give due obedience to her fellow student, she seems to have succeeded to everyone's satisfaction.

Assumptions about women's naturally weak minds seem to be accepted inside and out of the More circle, despite the achievements attributed to Margaret Roper. On another occasion, More delightedly reports to her that John, Bishop of Exeter, reading one of her letters, praised it for "its pure Latinity, its correctness, its erudition, and its expressions of tender affection" (*Letters*, 152) to her father. Until reassured by More, the Bishop could not believe it to be the work of a woman, and his effusive praise increased when More showed him a speech of hers and some poems. Such commendations indicate to Roper that she is exceptional, that she can do what most women cannot; and yet, the limits of her sphere can be no wider.

While showing his concern for the education of Roper's "lofty and exalted character of mind" in an earlier letter to the tutor, Gonnell, More acknowledges the difficulties inherent in educating women. He strongly advocates the addition of "even moderate skill in learning" to a woman's "eminent virtue of mind," and wishes Gonnell to teach all his children "to put virtue in the first place among goods, learning in the second; and in their studies to esteem most whatever may teach them piety towards God, charity to all, and modesty and Christian humility in themselves" (*Letters*, 105). Women are human beings, says More, and "are equally suited for the knowledge of learning by which reason is cultivated," but "if the soil of a woman be naturally bad, and apter to bear fern than grain, by which saying many keep women from study, I think, on the contrary, that a woman's wit is the more diligently to be cultivated, so that nature's defect may be redressed by industry" (*Letters*, 105). With the consciousness that her education must begin by correcting her inherent defects, a woman like Margaret Roper had a kind of double original sin to redeem. Not only was she the daughter of Eve, but her mind was "naturally bad." Roper's close dependence on her father logically follows, since he was offering her a way to redeem those inherent faults, to learn wisdom, and to increase her virtue.

In examining Margaret Roper's authorship, we find that her writings fulfill her father's criteria, and confirm her role as a learned and virtuous woman. As already noted, she composed Latin orations, poems, and in common with her father, a treatise on the *Four Last Things*, all works now apparently lost. Also lost is a translation of Eusebius from Greek to Latin, which she evidently suppressed after hearing that Bishop Christopherson was to publish his own. Thomas Stapleton remarked that "Margaret's learning was of no ordinary or common kind. She had produced works which fully deserved to be published and read by all, although the bashfulness of her sex, or her humility, or the almost incredible novelty of the thing (as More hints) never allowed her to consent to publication" (115). But the one work to be published, her English translation of Erasmus's *Precatio Dominica in Septem Portiones Distributa, A devout treatise upon the Pater noster* (1524), does nothing to detract from her womanly modesty, piety, and humility. Not only is the work suitably pious, but Erasmus was her father's dear friend, a member of the humanist circle, a man who had praised her as the proof that learning deepened virtue. More himself had taught his children the value of translation, first from Latin to English and then back again, as a way to learn prose style in both languages.[21] By translating Erasmus's exposition of the Paternoster, Roper could be identified as a humanist scholar without stepping out of the family circle. A first-rate translation—as Hyrde says of her "erudite and elegant" prose, "such wysedom/suche dyscrete and substancyall judgement in expressynge lyvely the latyn"—would appear as an act of piety, as an extension of her studies, as a tribute to a learned man, as an integral part of her family's interests.[22]

We might also wonder whether Roper's obedience went even further than this. For centuries, women had been faced with the patristic injunction supposedly based on Paul, not to interpret Scripture for themselves. More had advised Gonnell that his daughters should "thoroughly learn" the works of the Fathers, citing how Jerome and Augustine had "not only exhorted excellent matrons and honorable virgins to study, but also, in order to assist them, diligently explained the abstruse meanings of the Scriptures" (*Letters*, 105). A scholar like Roper might find an acceptable outlet for her learning by following the exposition of Erasmus instead of attempting to write her own, by playing Eustochium to his Jerome.

Interestingly, at about this time More sent Margaret a letter commiserating with her because men would doubt her learning and so "rob you of the praise you so richly deserved for your laborious vigils, as they would never believe, when they read what you had written, that you had not often availed yourself of another's help." Still, he turns her lack of recognition into a womanly asset:

> Although you cannot hope for an adequate reward for your labor, yet nevertheless you continue to unite to your

singular love of virtue the pursuit of literature and art. Content with the profit and pleasure of your conscience, in your modesty you do not seek for the praise of the public, nor value it overmuch even if you receive it, but because of the great love you bear us, you regard us— your husband and myself—as a sufficiently large circle of readers for all that you write. (*Letters*, 155)

Instead of public acclaim, Roper works for the approval of the men who love her and whom she loves. Her contentment to remain in the domestic sphere is fueled by ties of affection, but also by her apparent assimilation of current belief about women. Even when he jokes, More brings home his doctrine, for in the same letter, he concludes by referring to Roper's "imminent confinement":

May God and our Blessed Lady grant you happily and safely to increase your family by a little one like to his mother in everything except sex. Yet let it by all means be a girl, if only she will make up for the inferiority of her sex by her zeal to imitate her mother's virtue and learning. Such a girl I should prefer to three boys. (*Letters*, 155)

The most unusual evidence of Roper's obedience and compliance with her father's ideas is the supposedly puzzled authorship of the "letter" from Margaret Roper to Alice Alington, her stepmother's daughter. William Rastell, the editor of More's *English Works*, noted, "whether this aunswere wer writen by syr Thomas More in his daughter Ropers name, or by her selfe, it is not certaynelye knowen."[23] Although Margaret Roper's authorship has always been questioned, the very debate is instructive. Since it is clear that there are two distinct voices in the letter, one appropriate to a young woman and the other to a wise man, the readers and critics who have doubted Roper's authorship seem unable to accept that a woman could mimic a man's language and style.[24] But as we have seen, the close relationship between father and daughter and her devotion to his ideas would make her capable above all others of capturing her father's voice. More important, the letter suggests that at the heart of differences between male and female writers of this period is the decorum of language. Women's language must reflect the traditional feminine virtues and is thus constricted in a way that men's language is not.

As R. W. Chambers remarked, the Alington letter is "about the length of Plato's *Crito*, to which indeed, in many ways, it forms a striking parallel."[25] Chambers' analogy is accurate, because as the subject of *Crito* concerns the imprisoned Socrates' teaching about the integrity of the individual conscience versus the opinion of the multitude, so the Alington letter is a Socratic dialogue in which More instructs his daughter that his determination not to take the Oath of Succession is a matter between him and God, and not to be affected by any other man's—or woman's—threats or entreaties. As Crito's position provides Socrates the opportunity for discourse, so Margaret's role is to state the general opinion that More, like everyone else, should swear in order to live. Recognizing this role, her father characterizes her several times as "maistres Eve," come to "tempte your father again, and for the favour that you beare him labour to make him sweare against his conscience, and so send hym to the devil" (More, 1434). Both More and Roper speak in voices entirely appropriate to their character and to their gender. Whoever wrote the work, he or she was completely capable of ventriloquizing the voice of the other: More appears as the absolute, witty, philosophizing master, and Roper as the humble, loving pupil concerned for his safety. If More was the author, he knew thoroughly his daughter's deference and invented, at times seriously, at times humorously, a language reflecting a virtuous young woman's knowledge and understanding. If Roper was the author, as is more than likely, she created herself with suitable limitations on her woman's knowledge, full of modesty, at once the perfect foil for and the mouthpiece of the ideas of her beloved parent. The letter would be evidence of how thoroughly she had absorbed the thinking, the style of absolute certainty, and the wit of her father, to the point of perfect reproduction.

At one point in the letter, her woman's ignorance of the world becomes the basis for a stylistic jest. Margaret cannot remember the term, "pie powder court," the court at a fair which administers justice on the spot even to the dusty (French, *pied poudré*):

> And with this, he tolde me a tale, I wene I can skant tell it you agayne, because it hangeth upon some tearmes and ceremonies of the law. But as farre as I can call to mind my fathers tale was this, that ther is a court belongyng of course unto everye fayre, to dooe justice in such thynges as happen within the same. Thys court hath a prety fond name, but I cannot happen on it: but it begynneth with a pye, and the remenant goeth much lyke the name of a knyght that I have knowen ... syr William Pounder. But tut let the name of the court go for this once, or call it if ye will a courte of pye syr William Pownder. (More, 1437)

Thus mincingly does Roper appear, unable to report accurately the phrase, because it belongs to the male sphere of law and justice. Even though the tone here is exaggerated and comic, the passage epitomizes the tentativeness and humble self-consciousness of the voice assigned to the daughter, most notably in language like "I wene I can skant tell it you agayne," "as farre as I can call to mind," and "call it if ye will." More's language, by contrast, is assured, controlled, and instructive:

> But Margaret fyrst, as for the lawe of the lande, thoughe everye man beynge borne and inhabityng therein, is bounden to the keepinge in everye case upon some temporall payne, and in many cases uppon payne of Goddes displeasure too, yet is there no manne bounden to sweare that every lawe is well made, nor bounden upon the payne of Goddes dyspleasure, to perfourme anye suche poynte of the lawe, as were in dede unlawefull. (More, 1439)

And all the jokes assigned to him are also at Margaret's expense, as "he smyled upon me and said: 'how now daughter Marget? What howe mother Eve? where is your mind nowe? sit not musing with some serpent in youre brest, upon some new perswasion, to offer father Adam the apple yet once agayne?'" (More, 1441). It is significant that this ventriloquism comes from the Tower period, for at this time Roper's expressions of love for and gratitude to her father are profound and eloquent. This is, to her, the "bitter time of your absense," only alleviated by "reading againe and againe your most fruteful and delectable letter ..." (*Correspondence*, 510). She continually comforts More by telling him that his family's only pleasure now is to recall the "experiens we have had of your lyfe past and godly conversacion, and wholesome counsaile, and verteous example ..." And in one revealing phrase, she describes herself as "your most loving obedient dowghter and handmaide" (*Correspondence*, 510). The Biblical overtones of "handmaide" suggest that Margaret likens herself to such scriptural handmaids as Hannah, Abigail, or Mary, thus assuming the role of More's spiritual companion and helpmeet to a far greater extent than his wife, Alice More, generally portrayed as a good-hearted but simple soul. While he is in prison, through letters and visits, Roper becomes his sole conduit to family and friends, and as the Alington letter suggests, perhaps to a more general audience.

One persistent legend exists about Roper, that after her father's execution, she brought his head from the Tower and, keeping it until her death in 1544, was buried with it in her arms.[26] At the very least, this is a powerful image of the unending influence More had on her life and of her complete devotion. Perhaps it is also a vivid illustration that for this woman, the thoroughly successful union of learning and domestic virtue depended on strong—and in this case, indissoluble—emotional bonds. If Margaret Roper has always been praised as one of the most outstanding sixteenth-century woman of letters and virtue, it is significant that she is equally lauded as the most devoted of daughters.

Being Thomas More's daughter enabled Roper to be a

scholar, yet strictly defined the limits of her endeavors. Obeying his authority as both educator and parent, she learned her philosophy, languages, and astronomy and applied them to an uncompetitive, supportive role within the family. She appeared to be living proof that education made women more dedicated to feminine virtue.

TWO

A CHALLENGE TO
AUTHORITY:
ANNE ASKEW

*A*s much as Margaret Roper seems to define the ideal of
the learned and virtuous woman as a private, modest, silent
being, Anne Askew seems to diverge from it. Converting to
the Reformed church, Askew continually raised her voice in
public to bear witness to her faith, and in so doing, defied
not only her husband, but the whole hierarchy of Church
and State. Her writings movingly document her imprisonment, examinations, and torture, and provide some insight
into a woman who recognized the restrictions on her sex, but
chose to circumvent them because of her beliefs. In 1546, at
the age of twenty-five, this extraordinary woman was burned
at Smithfield as a heretic, so becoming a Protestant martyr
whose legend is still current today.[1]

As in the case of Margaret Roper, many men testified to
the character of Anne Askew. Of course, the Catholic church
and the Reformers differed sharply in their judgments, for
to the former she was a sinner, to the latter, a saint; but both
saw her primarily in the light of their conception of woman.
On the one hand, the Catholic establishment seems to have
assumed that Askew fit their preconceptions of weak and
foolish womanhood and that she could easily be persuaded,
or frightened, into recanting and eventually bowing to the
authority of Church and State. But instead, Askew became
a significant antagonist, a gentlewoman who wanted a divorce,
who defied every Catholic churchman who tried to save her

soul, be he priest or bishop, who argued with her accusers by extensively quoting Scripture and revealing their lack of preparation, who would not recant or inform despite the rack.

On the other hand, the Reformers, although praising this very resistance, also assumed Askew's inherent womanly weakness, and found in it her singular importance for the cause: her courage, constancy, and fortitude, since they could not be a woman's, must have come from God—and so God must have sanctified the New Faith. In her, John Bale, Askew's greatest admirer, claimed the fulfillment of "2 Cor. 12. The strength of God is here made perfyght by weakenesse," so that Askew provided further evidence of the justness of their cause.[2]

With Anne Askew, we are fortunate, as we were not with the self-effacing Margaret Roper, to know something of the woman from her own writings, and they in fact present an interesting series of complications. The *Examinations* themselves are the rarest form of sixteenth-century writing, the self-portrait, and by looking closely at the text, its circumstances, and her biography, we may partly determine why Askew decided to write her first-person narrative—to create herself—and how that creation relates to the concept of woman supported by her society. The most interesting question here is how a woman who deliberately abandoned her private life, who publicly debated with some of the most powerful men in the country, and who therefore became a hero to her coreligionists, would choose to portray herself. Part of Askew's continuing attraction today probably lies in her forthright style, in her direct, dramatic account, and in her avoidance of both extremes of self-aggrandizement and self-effacement. While quite aware of what she was supposed to be, she presented herself independently of current definitions, and in the process, implied an alternate role for the religious woman.

To John Bale, the fiery Protestant propagandist, we owe the first publication of Askew's work, and through his interlinear "Elucydacyon," an insight into the conflict inherent in Askew's being both a woman—supposedly weak, silent, and domestic—and a Reformist martyr—courageous, disputatious, and strong. Interested primarily in the propagandist value of Askew's text, Bale denies the paradox by arguing that Askew's strength came wholly from God and was a sure sign of the truth of the Reformed cause.[3] Continually remarking on her inherent womanly weakness and daintiness, he can safely applaud the unwomanly or unnatural power in her words and deeds by attributing them to divine grace. But to examine Askew's text without Bale's framework is to find Askew's depiction of herself a much less easy assimilation of the "weak vessel of the Lord" with the learned, argumentative, courageous woman who defied the male hierarchy of both Church and State. If we look at the *Examinations* in their two different settings, with and without Bale's commentary, we have an interesting opportunity to compare the way a woman created herself and the way an admiring man adorned her.[4]

Whether Anne Askew was, as Bale believed, the stereotypically weak woman made strong by God, or whether she was a strong woman made stronger by her faith is not the issue here. Although nothing in her earlier life suggested she subscribed to the obedience and silence recommended for her sex, her assertiveness and loquacity do seem to have been motivated by a powerful conversion, and intense Christian belief informs all her writing. Her decision to set down her examinations in such detail (perhaps unique among the Reformist martyrs), to be responsible for her own record, whether inspired by the "good people" of her sect whom she addresses in her opening words, by the "dere frynde in the lorde" whom she wishes to persuade of the symbolic nature of communion, or by the need to clarify her own character and behavior, is in essence a decision to write her autobiography.[5] Though they cover only the period of her imprisonment and questionings, the years 1545 and 1546 were the climactic ones of her life, bringing the confrontation to which all her previous acts had been leading. To write about the crisis of her life suggests Askew possessed a reasonably developed sense of self; however, we need to see this self motivated not by the individualism of modern autobiography, but by the desire to participate in a larger community, the Reformed church. By showing herself to be *not* a weak woman, but a vanquisher of the papist foe, a learned, honest, God-fearing, Scripture-loving comrade in the faith, Askew was seeking to disclose her true identity. Her sense of an audience eager to read her work engenders Askew's careful attention to the nuances of language and a style not of private revelation of self—indeed she carefully omits direct references to her personal life—but of a public celebration of the virtues she values: piety, constancy, learning, and fortitude. What should strike us here is that Askew presents herself in public as fully participant in the "gifts of the Lord" and as a teacher of doctrine and champion of her faith. If a Protestant woman no longer had the possibilities of Catholic mysticism to provide her an acceptable public role within the church hierarchy, she now had another unmediated path to God.[6] By her own learning, she could read Scripture and as a Reformer, trust it to empower her words and deeds. Because Askew professed her faith in the years she did, without cloister, anchorage, or family to protect her, she ran headlong into a political and religious cross fire that gave her a new role, that of martyr. Her autobiography, then, is implicitly the making of a Protestant hero, and possesses the simultaneous self-effacement and self-centeredness that such a role might be expected to entail.

Both the Henrician reaction, represented by Bishops Gardiner, Winchester, and Bonner, Lord Chancellor Wriothsley, and various officials of city and Church, and the Reformers, represented by John Bale, define Askew as "woman." Her inquisitors enunciate all the traditional dogma about a woman's not meddling in Scripture or speaking in church, and the lord chancellor seems particularly vindictive because so weak a vessel proves so immovable in her determination not to recant. But John Bale seizes on this inherent weakness of woman and claims from it his most telling proof that God is with the Reformers: "2 Cor. 12. The strength of God is here made perfyght by weakenesse. Whan she semed most feble, than was she most stronge" (I, Preface, 9v). Bale attributes to Askew herself this interpretation of her role: "And gladlye she rejoyced in that weakenesse, that Christes power myght strongelye dwell in her" (I, Preface, 9v). Bale's lesson for the faithful here is that the sixteenth-century Reformers fulfill Bede's prophecy that a renewal of the faith of the Apostles and prophets will be accompanied by "horryble persecucyon" and martyrdom (I, Preface, 2). He therefore presents Askew, "a gentylwoman verye yonge, dayntye, and tender" (I, Preface, 5), as a latter-day version of the martyrs of the primitive church, particularly comparing her to a second-century martyr, Blandina, whom Eusebius had described as "small and weak and greatly despised, she had put on the great and invincible athlete Christ."[7] As John King has shown, the title page of the 1546 edition clearly reflects this identification, for it pictures Askew, radiant, the Bible in one hand, a palm in the other, triumphing over the Papist Beast.[8]

Bale examines the comparison to Blandina point by point, designing Askew's character and martyrdom to agree with the prototype in every way.

> Blandina was yonge and tender. So was Anne Askewe also. ... Blandina never faynted in torment. No more ded Anne Askewe in sprete, whan she was so terrybly racked of Wrysleye the chaunceller and Ryche, that the strynges of her armes and eyes were peryshed.
> ... Blandina at the stake shewed a vysage unterryfyed. So ded Anne Askewe a countenaunce stowte, myghtye and ernest. ... The stronge sprete of Christ gave stomack to Blandina, both to laugh and daunce. The same myghtye sprete (and not the popes desperate sprete) made Anne Askewe both to rejoyce and synge in the preson. ... Manye were converted by the sufferaunce of Blandina. A farre greatter nombre by the burnynge of Anne Askewe. Though Blandina were yonge, yet was she called the mother of martyrs. Manye men have supposed Anne Askewe, for her Christen constancye, to be no lesse. (I, Preface, 7v-9)

In his account of Askew's ability to face her inquisitors and to withstand "the terrour of all tormentes," Bale attributes to God all the strength given to a naturally feeble woman, and deduces that her courage must be proof that God is with her and that their mutual cause is divinely sanctioned. In his singularly unambiguous polemic, he defines woman's religious role in the words, "Thus choseth the lorde, the folysh of thys worlde to confounde the wyse, and the weake to deface the myghtye..." (I, Preface, 9v).

Askew's text is, however, considerably more complicated, because while she shared Bale's belief in God's strength and her own human weakness, by the very act of writing down her examinations, of self-conceptualizing, Askew created a woman of faith, strength, and purpose. Askew did feel that God worked in her, but not because her female constitution was as inherently dainty as Bale wished to believe.

To compose this counterportrait of Anne Askew, we may consider how the events of her life influenced her authorial persona and style. Her father, Sir William Askew, a Lincolnshire landowner and courtier to Henry VIII, educated his daughters, although he naturally believed that they were still wholly subject to their father where marriage was concerned. Askew found herself married off to Thomas Kyme, son of another large landholder, an uneducated, staunch Catholic, not at all sympathetic to his wife's faith. The priests of Lincoln were apparently responsible for urging Kyme to cast out his heretic wife, and Askew seems then to have seized the initiative by requesting a divorce. According to Bale, whose source also informed him that Askew had two children by Kyme, she justified her action "by thys doctryne of S. Paule I. Cor. 7. If a faythfull woman have an unbelevynge husbande, whych wyll not tarrye with her she may leave hym. For a brother or syster is not in subjeccyon to soch, specyallye where as the marryage afore is unlawfull."[9] Her grounds for divorce, says Bale, were "bycause he so cruellye drove her out of hys howse in despyght of Christes veryte" (II, 15v), but neither at Lincoln nor later in the London courts did she succeed in ending her marriage.[10]

Later, during her first trial in London, she records the antagonism of the priests of Lincoln, but pictures herself as already firm in her beliefs and sure of her ability to conduct a theological dispute. When Bishop Bonner rebuked her for saying that sixty priests of Lincoln were against her, she tells him that despite friends' advice that the priests would "assault" her, she went to Lincoln unafraid to face her foes. With relish, she recounts the meeting:

> And as I was in the mynster, readynge upon the Byble, they resorted unto me by ii and by ii, by v. and by vi, myndynge to have spoken to me, yet went they theyr wayes agayne with out wordes speakynge.
>
> Then my lorde asked, if there were not one that ded speake unto me. I tolde him, yeas, that there was one of them at the last, whych ded speake to me in dede. And my lorde than asked me, what he sayd. And I tolde hym, hys wordes were of so small effecte, that I ded not now remembre them. (I, 33–34)

Askew pictures herself as active and assured as she waits in the minster, ready for dispute, while the priests appear agitated, disorganized, and timid. In her anecdotal climax, she uses Bonner's questions to her own advantage, making him draw out her responses, so centering attention on herself. Her final sentence here is a two-edged slur, for Askew derides the substance of the priest's remarks by apparently forgetting them and puts Bonner in his place by not repeating for him what he knew already. Consistently Askew presents herself in control of her questioners by throwing their questions back, responding with another question, smiling, or reprimanding them for their poor judgment. She never plays the part of a weak woman, but assumes for herself intellect, assurance, and strength.

If such qualities in her persona reflect the real Anne Askew, they may explain her decision to leave Lincolnshire and Thomas Kyme. Her move to London, perhaps motivated by the divorce suit, or perhaps by a desire to join other Reformers, brought Askew completely out of the domestic sphere and directly into the public view. Associating with the Reformers who surrounded Katherine Parr—John Parkhurst, Anne Herbert, the Duchess of Suffolk, Lady Denny, Lady Fitz-william, the Countess of Sussex, John Lascelles—Askew came to the notice of Bishop Gardiner and Lord Chancellor Wriothsley, both of whom saw in her a way to bring down the Reformist queen herself.[11] In March 1545, Askew was brought before the quest for heresy, so becoming the first gentlewoman to be judged by a London jury;[12] whatever she spoke there and recorded afterward established her as a public figure.

In considering Askew's motives for writing down her two examinations, we should remember first how unusual such a step was. Many of the accused Reformers wrote letters, but these were almost entirely to clarify or declare points of doctrine for other Reformers.[13] Few other contemporary auto-biographical documents remain that describe in such detail the questioning and suffering of a heresy trial, or give so vivid a sense of the victim's personality. One hypothesis is that Askew was particularly driven by the need for self-justification. In a society in which all women of her class lived protected by their friends or family, and identified themselves solely within the family circle, Askew was cut off from paternal and marital protection (Sir William Askew died in March 1541; the eldest son, Francis, remained in Lincolnshire and may indeed have betrayed his sister) and belonged only to a religious group whose ability to help her was restricted by its own dangerous position. Although a gentlewoman of "very auncyent and noble stock" (I, Preface, 6v), her unrepentant defiance of the authorities of both Church and State reduced the ability of her friends to aid her, and the power struggle at court between Catholics and Reformers made her more vulnerable to danger. Her record of her experience seeks to establish her firmly as a God-fearing, honest woman who consistently quotes Scripture and attempts to reveal only the truth. Her assertions in the *Examinations* are always positive, filled with a sense of her own rectitude, assured of her own virtue. At one point she is careful to record her wish, "that all men knewe my conversacyon and lyvyng in all poyntes, for I am so sure of my selfe thys houre, that there are non able to prove anye dyshonestie by me" (I, 34v). Writing may have offered Askew a way to create herself as she desired, rather than to be known either as a disobedient wife and heretić by one side, or a distant figurehead by the other. By controlling the persona of Anne Askew and selecting and shaping the events of her imprisonment, Askew fulfills the role she recognized she was to have for the Reformers, but she also becomes an autobiographer who composes the woman, Anne Askew. The work does begin, "To satisfie your expectation, good people" and proceeds to bear witness to the strength of the Reformed faith and the wickedness of its enemies, demanding of the writer that she subjugate herself to a concept: Anne Askew is one of the elect, a vessel filled with God's grace. But the crosscurrents of personality that consistently flow in the narrative do not enhance Askew's role as the weak woman made strong by God. Rather, the combination of her witty rejoinders and the very reticence with which she records her endurance on the rack are a consistently self-conscious, stylized version of herself that portrays a woman who is neither "dainty" nor "tender," but rather, tough in mind and body, learned, and tenacious. While the narrative concentrates mainly on recording conversation, it clearly highlights the occasions on which Askew outfoxes her questioners. Bale finds this to prove God's presence; other readers will find a self-portrait of a woman who lived out an idea of herself as a defender of the faith and teacher, the spiritual equal of any man.

Some of the most striking points in the text occur when Askew clearly asserts herself as a woman confronting the male hierarchy. At these stress points, Askew recounts how her clever responses allowed her to triumph over her questioners. In her first examination, she tells us:

Then the Byshoppes chaunceller rebuked me, and sayd, that I was moche to blame for utterynge the scriptures. For S. Paule (he sayd) forbode women to speak or to

talke of the worde of God. I answered hym, that I knewe
Paules meanynge so well as he, whych is, i Corinthiorum
xiiii, that a woman ought not to speake in the congre-
gacyon by the waye of teachynge. And then I asked hym,
how manye women he had seane, go into the pulpett
and preache. He sayde, he never sawe non. Then I sayd,
he ought to fynde no faute in poore women, except they
had offended the lawe. (I, 10-10v)

Not only does Askew declare she can understand Scripture
as well as the Bishop's chancellor, but she responds by questioning him, exacting an answer, and drawing an appropriate
conclusion to discomfit the questioner. The style here is perfectly suited to Askew's aims, for it is unadorned, understated,
and concise, thus allowing the climactic last sentence to exert
its full force. The choice of "poore" to describe women is an
example of Askew's controlled irony, for she has already
shown herself to be anything but "poore."

Here and elsewhere, Bale is silent on Askew's manner,
applauding only her matter, and zealously associating her
every thought with the earliest members of the Church. Here
he comments extensively on the theme of women learned in
Scripture who speak in public. Aware that the chancellor had
expressed the prevailing view, he justifies Askew's knowledge
by reference to the women at the tomb, to St. Jerome's cor-
respondents, and to early English Christians like Helena,
Ursula, and Hilda. By contrast, he infers that the chancellor's
source is the old *Contra doctrices mulieres* "or else some other
lyke blynde Romysh beggeryes" (I, 11). His strong language
and unflaggingly vociferous style emphasize how restrained,
witty, and subtle Askew is in her verbal defeat of her enemies;
she seems more effective in underscoring their prejudices and
injustices, and more in control. The accepted methods of
rhetorical argument called for citing of past authorities and
exempla, and certainly such means suited Bale's desire to
justify the Reformers. While Askew cites Scripture at every
opportunity, she uses it not as Bale does, but in a directly
pragmatic, situational way: "Paul says women should not

preach in church. No woman has preached in church. Women have not defied Paul." And much of her effectiveness derives from her skilled presentation of the moment's drama, bringing to life through their own words the players and their parts.

Askew continually uses her dramatic abilities and plays upon her lack of formal training—her rhetorical "otherness"—in subsequent contests with her questioners. After the lord mayor sends Askew to the Compter, she records the visit of a priest who attempts to win her confidence and then exact a confession.

> Fortly he asked me, if the host shuld fall, and a beast ded eate it, whether the beast ded receyve God or no? I answered, Seynge ye have taken the paynes to aske thys questyon, I desyre yow also to take so moche payne more, as to assoyle it yourself. For I will not do it, bycause I perceyve ye come to tempt me. And he sayd it was agaynst the ordre of scoles, that he whych asked the questyon, shuld answere it. I tolde hym, I was but a woman, and knewe not the course of scoles. (I, 13v-14)

Again, Askew builds to her needle-jab destruction of the adversary's position. In the middle sentences, she takes the initiative away from the priest, offering two "reasons" why he should answer his own question: he asked it and he asked it with an ulterior motive, to trap Askew into admitting a derogatory view of the host commonly thought to be Reformist. Her ready wit listens for a cue, and once more she ironically plays upon the preconception of woman. "Scoles" belong to the male preserve of formal education—and also to hated Catholic scholasticism—and being "but a woman," Askew is excluded. Here, the "but" is as telling a choice as "poore" was earlier.

It is interesting to contrast Askew's emphasis here with Bale's response. Again, Bale does not remark on Askew's wit, but pounces eagerly on the priest's ignorance of doctrine, scorning his question as a blasphemous rejection of God's spiritual essence. While Askew is of course aware of the doctrinal crux at issue here, in *The first examinacyon* she is less concerned with elucidating her sacramentarian beliefs than with establishing her identity, with asserting her faith in Scripture, needling her inquisitors, and playing upon their preconceptions of woman's weakness and proper place.

For example, during Bishop Bonner's interrogation on the host, she reiterates an emphatic, almost ritualistic, three times, "I believe as the Scripture doth teach me."

> And upon thys argument he tarryed a great whyle, to have dryven me to make him an answere to hys mynde. Howbeit, I wolde not, but concluded thus with hym, that I beleved therin and in all other thynges, as Christ and hys holye apostles ded leave them. Then he asked me, whye I had so fewe wordes. And I answered, God hath geven me the gyfte of knowlege, but not of utter-aunce. And Salomon sayth, that a woman of fewe wordes, is a gyfte of God, Prover. 19. (I, 27-29)

Touching Bonner's sore spot, for Askew's words are few only in the sense that she does not speak the ones he wishes to hear, Askew ironically cites a text often used to support the dogma for woman's obedience and silence. She caps this retort a few sentences later when bidden to say her mind about her citation from Paul, Apostles 17, "God dwelleth not in temples made with hands." Askew tells us, "I answered, that it was agaynst saynt Paules lernynge, that I beynge a woman, shuld interprete the scriptures, specyallye where so many wyse lerned men were" (I, 31v). Underlining her own unsupported appearance before numerous questioners, Askew casts back the text previously used to accuse her, but alters its emphasis to disparage her enemies. Her tone mocks their wisdom and learning, and perhaps even their manhood, since all of them are lined up against one "poore" lone woman.

The linguistic games that Askew plays at these moments convey her as confident and self-possessed in the face of danger, certainly part of the character she wishes to create for her readers. Askew chooses to reveal her strength in *The first examinacyon* by using an ironic, witty style for herself, which she clearly contrasts with the style of her enemies, depicted as superficial, irascible, or insidious, but never righteous and never triumphant. She laughs at Christopher Dare for his ignorance, saying "I wolde not throwe pearles amonge swyne, for acornes were good ynough" (I, 2v). Like a mother reprimanding a child, she cautions the archdeacon who foolishly warned her not to read a book by John Frith:

> Then I asked hym, if he were not ashamed for to judge of the boke before he sawe it within, or yet knew the truthe therof. I sayd also, that soche unadvysed and hastye judgement is a token apparent of a verye slendre wytt. Then I opened the boke and shewed it hym. He sayd, he thought it had bene an other, for he coulde fynde no faulte therin. Then I desyred hym, nomore to be so swyfte in judgement, tyll he throughllye knewe the truthe. And so he departed. (I, 21-21v)

Whatever the "truth" of that exchange, Askew has molded it in her narrative to make herself the active, teaching voice and the archdeacon the abashed respondent; in her reenactment, Askew gains the upper hand, the archdeacon is discomfited and exits.

Askew's full awareness of style is vividly demonstrated by an exchange with Bishop Bonner:

> Then brought he fourth thys unsaverye symylytude, That if a man had a wounde, no wyse surgeon wolde mynystre helpe unto it, before he had seane it uncovered. In lyke case (sayth he) can I geve yow no good counsell, unlesse I knowe wherwith your conscyence is burdened. I answered, that my conscience was clere in all thynges. And for to laye a playstre unto the whole skynne, it might apere moche folye. (I, 23v-24)

Here she objects to the unpleasantness, both moral and figurative, of Bonner's analogy, but resumes the linguistic upper hand by topping his similitude. Normally her prose is devoid of figurative language, but she uses it here to make points: first, that she feels herself innocent and strong before her enemies, and second, that anything Bonner can do, she can do better.

In *The lattre examinacyon*, the record of her second imprisonment, Askew's tone changes to a more uniformly serious, earnest contemplation of her beliefs and her questioners. No doubt she knew that this time she was in far greater danger. She presents her enemies as doggedly evil, and repeats their reiterated questions as often as they are asked, along with her own patient responses. When the Bishop of Winchester wishes to speak to her "famylyarlye," she responds, "So ded Judas whan he unfryndelye betrayed Christ," and demands two or three witnesses to be always present. Bale is clearly delighted by her stand, gloating, "Ded she not (thynke you) hytt the nayle on the head, in thus tauntynge thys Bysshop? yeas" (II, 18v-19). Askew puts the Bishop's next remark, her own death sentence, simply and dramatically, "Then the Byshoppe sayd, I shuld be brente." Not mourning for herself—and as always in control—Askew says that nowhere in the Scriptures can she find that Christ or the Apostles put anyone to death, another clear instance of the Romish contravention of God's word.

Much of *The lattre examinacyon* consists of scriptural quotation and doctrinal statements about communion, once to a friend, once in confession of her belief, once to the Council, and once to the king. Bale accurately notes how even in her danger, "Neyther lasheth thys woman out in her extreme troubles, language of dispayre nor yet blasphemouse wordes agaynst God with the unbelevynge, but uttereth the scriptures in wonderfull habundaunce to hys lawde and prayse..." (II, 27v). Again Bale attributes such constancy in a woman "frayle, tendre, yonge and most delycyouslye brought up" to Christ's spirit in her (II, 27v). Wherever she derived her strength, she convinces the reader of her power by a controlled, dignified, assured style that portrays a woman humble before God, if never before the enemies she considers to be betrayers of God's word.

Askew reveals the tremendous power of a story told without decoration and with restraint when she narrates her experiences in the Tower. Her captivity moved into its explicitly political phase when she was asked for the names of Reformers at court. Hoping to incriminate the Duchesses of Suffolk, Sussex, and Hertford, Lady Denny, Lady Fitzwilliam, and by association, Queen Katherine, Sir Richard Rich and Lord Chancellor Wriothsley questioned and then tortured Askew for a confession. Their proceedings were cruel and vicious, as well as entirely illegal, since the law prohibited the racking of women, and Askew was a gentlewoman besides. Again, their actions probably mark how alone and unprotected she really was. But such considerations pale before the horror of their deeds gathered from Askew's dramatic, sparing account of her profound suffering:

> Then they sayd, there were of the counsell that ded maynteyne me. And I sayd, no. Then they ded put me on the racke, bycause I confessed no ladyes nor gentyllwomen to be of my opynyon, and theron they kepte me a longe tyme. And bycause I laye styll and ded not crye, my lorde Chauncellour and mastre Ryche, toke peynes to racke me [with] their owne handes, tyll I was nygh dead.
>   Then the lyefetenaunt caused me to be loused from the racke. Incontynentlye [immediately] I swounded, and then they recovered me agayne. After that I sate ii longe houres reasonynge with my lorde Chauncellour upon the bare floore, where as he with manye flatterynge wordes, persuaded me to leave my opynyon. But my lord God (I thanke hys everlastynge goodnesse) gave me grace to persever, and wyll do (I hope) to the verye ende. (II, 44v-47).

By understatement, Askew conveys both the silent virtue of her own remarkable fortitude and constancy—"I laye styll and ded not crye"—and by contrast, the vindictiveness of the two men, desperate to break her spirit. Like the devil's temptation, Wriothsley's words are "flatterynge," but if we see Askew as an Eve, she pictures herself filled with God's grace and able to do God's will to the end.[14]

In his concluding remarks, John Bale professes himself convinced that Anne Askew is now an "undoubted cytyzen of heaven" (II, 61) and a "Saynt canonysed in Christes bloude..." (II, 62v). Askew herself had written to her fellow sufferer, John Lascelles, "For I doubt it not, but God wyll perfourme hys worke in me, lyke as he hath begonne" (II, 49v). Bale never swerves from his conviction that Askew's text demonstrates the sanctification of the Reformers' cause. In her more humble, more personal statement, Askew reveals how fundamental her faith was to her life. But her belief that God was working through her did not proceed from any sense of womanly weakness; for her, the source of human weakness before God did not lie in male or female characteristics.

While her prose narrative reveals much about Askew's character, it is her attempt at poetry that provides us with her most focused self-portrait. If she did not season her prose with so much as a simile, in the scripturally based "Ballad which Anne Askewe made and sang when she was in Newgate," she liberally sprinkles figures of speech throughout the 56 lines to convey a vivid poetic personality. Again transcending sexual stereotypes, she chooses the persona of the Christian soldier from Ephesians 6:11ff:

> Lyke as the armed knyght
> Appoynted to the fielde
> With thys world wyll I fyght
> And fayth shall be my shielde.[15]
>
> (ll. 1-4)

So armed, she fears no foe, but continues the battle metaphor, assured that God will hear her knock and will fight "in my steed." In the second half of the ballad, she compresses the experiences of the *Examinations* into lucid images expressing her feeling of strength, her vision of evil, and her gentler Christian compassion. In one metaphor, she conveys her deep assurance of the importance of her cause and her power to see it through:

I am not she that lyst
My anker to lete fall
For everye dryslynge mist
My shippe substancyall.

(ll. 33-36)

Contrasting "dryslynge mist" with "anker" and "shippe substancyall," she conveys the lightness of other matters and the
unshakeable firmness of her present spiritual commitment.

While admitting to an incidental weakness, that she is a
literary novice—"not oft use I to wright/In prose nor yet in
ryme"—Askew professes herself undeterred in her self-im-
posed mission to "shew one sight" that characterizes her enemies:

I sawe a ryall trone,
Where Justice shuld have sytt
But in her stede was one
Of modye cruell wytt.

(ll. 41-44)

Absorpt was rygtwysnesse
As of the ragynge floude
Sathan in hys excesse
Sucte up the gyltelesse bloude.

(ll. 45-48)

Far from being an indictment of Henry VIII, whom, judging
from her letters and comments, she seems to have trusted,
this is an apocalyptic vision of the usurpation of Scriptural
Justice by the Pope, commonly characterized by the Reformers
as a worldly and spiritual tyrant or Antichrist. Resonances of
Jeremiah also echo, recalling God's warning to the King of
Judah to "kepe equite and rightuuousnesse, delyver the op-
pressed from the power of the violent: do not greve nor
oppresse the straunger, the fatherlesse nor the wydowe, and
shed no innocent bloude on this place."[16] Askew's strong
diction here almost belies Bale's praise of her self-restraint,
and indicates both the fervor of her beliefs and the deliberate

control she exercised in the *Examinations* in order to maintain her dignity and credibility.

But the ballad concludes with the same prayer that ended *The lattre examinacyon*, essentially that of the forgiving Christian:

> Yet lorde I the desyre
> For that they do to me
> Lete them not tast the hyre
> Of their inyquyte.
> (ll. 53-56)

As a Christian soldier, Askew must take up the good fight and rely on the promise of mercy. No longer in direct confrontation with the Church hierarchy, she depicts herself in her ballad not as a "poor woman," but as a visionary and a fighter.

For Anne Askew, as for Margaret Roper, contemporary thinking about women reverberated in her life and influenced her writing. No matter how advanced its educational program might have been, the More household and "school" reflected and reinforced the beliefs of traditional doctrine about women, and Roper's attachment to her father seems to have ensured her conformity in all things, whether moral or literary, to his model of learning and virtue. And if no man appears to have ruled Anne Askew, still we find consistent acknowledgment in her text of conventional assumptions about women and an attempt, through irony, to circumvent them.

The differences in their responses to their virtuous womanhood are also reflected in the kind of writers they were. Roper's ventriloquism masks her as a writer, in one case as she translates Erasmus and in the other, Thomas More, so preserving the semblance of feminine modesty and privacy. While she certainly conceived of herself as a virtuous woman, Askew scorned ventriloquism, openly rejecting Bishop Bonner's offer to provide words for her, "to make him an answere to hys mynde." Instead, to create her personae, to generate her language, to authorize her very utterances, Askew drew

on Scripture. In the *Examinations*, both the "wonderfull ha-
bundance" of Biblical quotations and Askew's own scriptural
diction and intonation indicate how thoroughly she conceived
of her authorship as inspired by God's word. The rhythm of
her own sentences often passes imperceptibly into the cadences
of Scripture: "Then he asked me, whye I had so fewe words.
And I answered, God hath geven me the gyfte of knowledge,
but not of utteraunce. And Saloman sayth, that a woman of
fewe wordes, is a gyfte of God." Likewise, in her ballad, she
draws her poetic persona from a central Reformist text, thus
seeming to gain scriptural authority for her vision. To Askew
the Reformer, as Scripture taught her to seek her own salvation, it also authorized her to speak, to bear witness as a
true Christian woman.[17]

Scripturalism is certainly characteristic of many writers of
the time, but it is particularly important for women's literary
history. As Askew moved from reading and knowing the
Bible to quoting it in public to writing it down in the context
of her own story, she was breaking down prohibitions against
women that had stood for centuries. She was also forecasting,
perhaps even influencing, a mode of thinking and writing to
be used by women for the next several decades. The next
chapter will show how pious women found in the Reformed
church what they had rarely had before, a legitimate voice.
Some of these women may have read the widely published
Examinations of Anne Askew, and understanding and remembering her work, they too would attempt to create their
own literary voices.

THREE

BUILDING THE CITY:
WOMEN WRITERS
OF THE REFORMATION

THE APPEARANCE between 1545 and 1605 of fifteen prose religious works and translations by women might not appear significant compared with the hundreds of similar works by men during those sixty years. Yet, when these few women assumed the roles of teacher, preacher, and witness to the faith, they created the vital link between women's traditional spirituality and their developing literary vocation. The very existence of these works indicates the increasing importance for women of recording their religious experiences and beliefs themselves. These Protestant authors, while showing themselves to be "learned and virtuous," were also establishing themselves as writers. While the author or translator of a religious treatise might impersonally focus on the subject matter, arranging given doctrine to convince or teach the reader, women signed their names to their work and took their place as religious polemicists. The subject matter itself conferred authority, even if few of these writers assumed it openly, and some appear to retire almost completely from their work. The voiceprints are there, however, sometimes in a word or phrase, sometimes in an attitude. These are the beginnings, the religious compositions by women who constructed the English city of ladies, who wrote to prove that women would speak for themselves and redeem their good name. In their versions of Protestant doctrine, these writers may have differed from one another in talent, skill, and creativity, but they were alike in their desire to preserve traditional feminine decorum, the suitability of language and matter to the persona of the virtuous woman. Accordingly, the genres and styles they adopted became standard solutions to the difficulties inherent in being a female author.

This chapter and the next—this concerning the prose writers, the next concerning the poets—will examine the authors whose subject, form, and style established the literary presence of religious women in England throughout the century. Short biographies, where available, something of the literary context, and a brief analysis of their work will show how women from both the upper and middle classes created a place for women within the Protestant literary mainstream. From those authorized by the Reformation to add their godly testimony and to teach God's saving grace; to those who translated religious works by men; to those who identified a special feminine piety founded on specific scriptural texts—each of these women found her voice along with her vocation. As Anne Locke Prowse so humbly declared in her 1590 dedication of a translation to the countess of Warwick:

> Everie one in his calling is bound to doo somewhat to the furtherance of the holie building; but because great things by reason of my sex I may not doo, and that which I may, I ought to doo, I have according to my duetie, brought my poore basket of stones to the strengthening of the walls of that Jerusalem, whereof (by grace) wee are all both Citizens and members.[1]

In the Reformed church, the figure of the pious woman, the "learned and virtuous" lady who was chaste, patient, humble, and charitable became an ideal in which women found the perfect voice for public speaking. As Foxe's records indicate, the Reformers' desire to bear witness to their faith had brought forward women of all ranks, and among the educated upper gentry and aristocracy, women with a clear vocation for preaching began to write pious works. The published writings of Reformist luminaries like Katherine Parr, Jane

Grey, and of course, Elizabeth Tudor, as well as religious works by less famous figures like Elizabeth Tyrwhitt, Anne Cooke Bacon, and Anne Locke appeared not to contravene their private virtue, because their Christian virtues in fact coincided with their feminine ones. Each of these women presented a persona who testified that she was a humble and penitent sinner who despised the world, the flesh, and the devil, and who trusted alone in the grace of God. Shining through her work was her faith and her humility, providing her with the strength to endure adversity and to teach the faithful. Of course, given the political status of Katherine Parr, Jane Grey, and above all, Elizabeth, their writings were not simply pious testimonials, but exceedingly useful contributions to the Reformist cause; this alone might guarantee their publication.

Scholars have long recognized how much the press influenced the English Reformation, from printing English Bibles to providing numerous religious commentaries, works of propaganda, and pious literature for the faithful. For a religion that emphasized the individual conscience, the printed word became the means to disseminate widely the personal stories and teachings of those who had found salvation. The most famous example is of course Foxe's *Actes and Monuments* which included numerous narratives and documents concerning women.[2] By the 1540s, women had discovered their audience. In Anne Askew's case, religious controversy and persecution precipitated her work, sharpening her sense of herself as a strong woman with a public voice, and providing her with thousands of readers. Study of other writers like Jane Grey, Anne Cooke Bacon, and Anne Dowriche reveals that with its dual emphasis on individual salvation and reading Scripture, and in the climate of controversy, the Reformation authorized the English woman writer by giving her both a language and a role. Women wrote religious works because literary preaching offered a vocation compatible with their education and society's concept of virtuous womanhood. As pious writers teaching the faithful, they could respond simultaneously to the enemies of their religion and their sex.

The scriptural basis of women's writing in this period manifests itself both in the content and the style of their works. Like Anne Askew and other Reformers, they think Biblically, and their writing modulates, often imperceptibly, between Biblical quotations or references and their own words. Almost without exception, they write in the "Protestant plain style," an unornamented, Biblical English aimed at a universal audience. In some cases, their vivid, colloquial expression suggests that these writers would gladly have joined their brethren in the pulpit.[3]

This chapter begins with Anne Wheathill, who might be called typical, if such a word has meaning for a woman writer in the sixteenth century. Wheathill's concern for the souls of the faithful had been anticipated on a more ambitious scale by the translations of Anne Cooke Bacon; of Anne Locke; and of Bacon's own sister, Elizabeth Russell, each of whom disseminated important Reformist doctrines through the voice of a male author. How important these religious writings were to the development of women's voices becomes apparent in *The Monument of Matrones*, an anthology of women's pious writing that emphasizes women's special spiritual heritage. Here appear the works of Elizabeth Tudor, Katherine Parr, and Jane Grey, as well as the writings of Elizabeth Tyrwhitt, Frances Aburgavennie, and other "vertuous Gentlewomen." In short, this chapter will demonstrate not only the religiosity of these writers, but also their range and their limitations; their successes and their frustrations; their mediocrity and their brilliance.

ANNE WHEATHILL (fl. 1584)

Although unknown today, in many ways Anne Wheathill represents the typical concerns of the sixteenth-century pious woman writer, to spread God's word while reassuring herself and her readers that she is not overstepping the bounds of feminine decorum. She reveals that the apologies of a female author disclose more about the writer than about her work, and she introduces the world of contradictions in which most of these women wrote. Herself a gentlewoman, Wheathill dedicated her work, *A handfull of holesome (though homelie) hearbs, gathered out of the goodlie garden of Gods most holie word* to "all Ladies, Gentlewomen, and others, which love true religion and vertue and be devoutlie disposed . . . ,"[4] and even in this "and others" is the hint of a dilemma. Her implicit wish to address all women, regardless of class, suggests that women have a special interest in pious works; but such universal accessibility might forfeit the interest of learned readers, whether men or women, who might take up her book. As the dedication continues, she appears increasingly concerned that such scholars will find her to be "grose and unwise," so that she makes the dedication part apology, part certification of herself as a woman writer.

The first qualification is of course her chastity: Wheathill asserts that she uses her time wisely "even now in the state of my virginitie or maidenhood." Her task has been to choose scriptural passages, or as she modestly phrases it:

> I dedicate to all good Ladies, Gentlewomen, and others
> . . . a small handfull of grose hearbs; which I have presumed to gather out of Gods most holie word. Not that there is anie unpurenes therein, but that (peradventure) my rudenes may be found to have plucked them up unreverentlie, and without zeale. (A2v)

Her humility, perhaps somewhat mitigated by the "peradventure" and the conditional "may be found," seems to be rooted in her having composed the work alone "without the counsell or helpe of anie" (A2v). Claiming to depend only on "the weakenes of my knowledge and capacitie," Wheathill apologizes for her "grose hearbes" which do not compare with the "fragrant floures of others, gathered with more understanding." Nevertheless, she feels the confidence of one who works with a "willing hart and fervent mind" to advance "Gods glorie" (A3). In sum, Wheathill anticipates criticism of her work by apologizing for her supposed lack of learning and by drawing attention to her chastity, her zeal, and the implied Biblical text that the humblest offerings please God.

Possibly an attempt to exonerate any accomplices, her claim to have worked alone may truly reflect a woman writer's isolation.

In truth, Wheathill's misgivings about her text are unfounded, suggesting that her dedication probably emanated from her self-consciousness as a woman writer. She writes plainly, in the style long established as appropriate for godly instruction. Her work is completely within the tradition of Reformed books for private devotion, deriving prayers from Scripture and emphasizing human depravity, the need for divine grace, and the doctrine of the elect. If Wheathill did not receive the direct "helpe of anie," still her prayers resemble those found in contemporary collections like *A godly Garden out of the which most comfortable herbs may be gathered for the health of the wounded conscience of all penitent sinners* (1574), indicating that she drew from current Reformist doctrine. But where such texts tend to be organized around hours of the day or days of the week, Wheathill's book provides more general prayers, centered on Scripture, and particularly the Psalms. For instance, she includes prayers of lamentation, thanks for God's wisdom and mercy, and professions of faith that God will preserve those who trust Him and bless those who fear Him. She may have been more concerned to adapt her own scriptural learning for the use of the godly than to imitate particular forms.

As in similar devotional texts, Wheathill composes many of the prayers in the first person, offering her readers the voice of the sinner and humble penitent. In these cases, she writes that the sinner "lamenteth his miserable estate," the masculine possessive appearing in recognition of the traditional form of prayers, and indicating the conventional nature of the genre Wheathill has adopted. Indeed, the work reminds us that it is a woman's at only two points: when Wheathill composes "A praier of the creation of mankind," and when she creates a feminine image. Her description of the Fall recalls the emphasis of the defenders of women, for she claims that the fault did not originate with Eve alone, but jointly with both Adam and Eve:

There had they instructions given them, and the lawe
of life for an heritage. Before them was laid both life
and death, good and evill, with a freewill given them
to take which liked them best. But their frailtie was
such, that they, through a small intisement, chose the
evill, and left the good: they left life, and chose death.
(50v-51)

Wheathill avoids both the misogynist attribution of guilt to
Eve and the ingenious acquittals of her defenders. Her reading
of Scripture does not emphasize the seductive temptress nor
the wrongly ambitious mate, nor the naive woman, but simply
by choosing the third-person plural pronoun, she implies the
helpmeet who shares Adam's human frailty and his fate.

This choice, which perhaps issues from a feminine consciousness, echoes briefly later in the text in an image of the
sinner, burdened by guilt and longing for grace: "I cannot
but lament, mourne, and crie for helpe, as dooth a woman,
whose time draweth neere to be delivered of hir child; for
she can take no rest, till she be discharged of hir burthen"
(103-103v). The image may derive from Biblical texts referring
to the pain of women in labor, and a male writer could have
composed a similar passage; but in the context of a woman's
work, the simile stands out momentarily as feminine experience used figuratively to convey doctrine. These passages
deserve brief notice because in other respects Wheathill de-
parts from prayer book convention: she omits prayers designed specifically for women. Ordinarily, such prayers
evolved from the dogma of women's guilt for Eve's sin, and
stressed the punishment of labor pain and the need for obedience.[5] Since Wheathill chooses to attribute no special blame
to Eve, she may have thought that women needed no special
expiation; and her simile of travail expresses simply the intensity of the sinner's desire for God's help.

Anne Wheathill's life is a mystery, but her work seems
designed to help and comfort the godly in their daily trials.
Despite her initial self-deprecation, her goals are clear, to
reach her chosen audience with Scripture and to direct their

prayers. With two minor exceptions in her text, her self-consciousness as a woman is limited to her dedication in which she allays the fears of her assumed critics. More important, Wheathill's work is evidence of how influential Protestant scripturalism was in the development of women's literary voice. Individual close study of the Bible and familiarity with contemporary works derived from Scripture offered women both the knowledge and the language with which to express their piety and to assume the role of preacher.

Anne Cooke Bacon (1528–1610)

Of Anne Cooke Bacon we know a good deal more to supplement the authorial persona of the learned and virtuous lady. In the comments of her contemporaries, in the dedication to her first work, and in her letters appears an intelligent, strong-minded, profoundly pious woman who was, nevertheless, not without ambition. Margaret Roper may have written for her family and Wheathill for the faithful, but Bacon assumed a place at the very center of contemporary religious polemic. To solve the problem of a woman reasoning in public, she provided Bishop John Jewel with a completely unexceptionable English translation of his Latin work, *Apologia Ecclesiae Anglicanae* at a time when he and Archbishop Parker needed one to carry on their defense of the English church. Bacon's considerable contribution to the Reformed cause indicates how much pious women could do despite their restrictions. Had she not been a woman, her brain and her industry might have carried her far in public service and in literature, perhaps in a path similar to that of her son, Francis.

As the second of five daughters among the nine children of Sir Anthony Cooke and Lady Anne Fitzwilliam Cooke, Anne Cooke grew up in a home notable for its espousal of female education. Her father, a country gentleman who probably studied the classics and Scripture alongside his children, is mentioned as a tutor to Edward VI and certainly served at a court known for humanistic learning and piety.[6] Her mother, a merchant's daughter, also had strong moral and intellectual influence on Anne. In her first work, a translation from the Italian of Bernardino Ochino's sermons, she addresses her "right worshypful and worthyly beloved Mother," to whom she attributes all her own goodness.[7] Apparently Lady Cooke had once reproved the vain study of Italian, and so her daughter dedicated to her this Italian work castigating human pride and exalting the glory of God. She committed the translation to her mother's protection "as yeldyng some parte of the fruite of your Motherly admonicions. . . ." Cooke's reference to maternal precepts indicates that both parents supervised their children's upbringing, and the publication of religious works by three of the sisters suggests the communal commitment to learning and piety that existed at Gidea Hall, Essex.

When she was about twenty, Cooke's translation of five of Ochino's sermons was published, followed by an edition of fourteen sermons (1551?), which was prefaced by a publisher's dedication that characterized her in the familiar mold of chastity, virtue, and learning. Whereas Cooke was concerned to live up to her mother's high standards of godly living, her publisher worries about Cooke's feminine modesty. In his address to "the Christen Reader," he describes Cooke and her translations as a "wel occupied Jentelwoman, and verteouse mayden . . . whose shamfastnes would rather have supprest theym, had not I to whose handes they were commytted halfe agaynst her wyll put them fourth" (A2). Not only does he vouch for her virtue, her lack of vanity, and her industry, but he also manages to imply that she stays safely at home: "If oughte be erred in the translacion, remember it is a womans yea, a Gentylwomans, who commenly are wonted to lyve Idelly, a maidens that never gaddid farder than hir fathers house to learne the language" (A2v). Clearly, the publisher was interested less in biography than in reassuring readers that Cooke's learning did not injure her domestic virtue, because at this time, she was actually a member of Edward VI's entourage at court. She was also informed enough to recognize that Ochino, a Protestant exile newly arrived in England and in residence as Cranmer's protégé at Lambeth

Palace, was an important Reformist leader. Translating his sermons expressed her piety, her learning, and her devotion to furthering religious reform, and the work is entirely compatible with the pious translations of her sisters. Mildred translated from the Greek "An Homilie or Sermon of Basile the great" (c. 1548), and Elizabeth translated Ponet's work on the Last Supper, *A Way of Reconciliation of a Good and learned man, touching the Trueth, Nature, and Substance of the Body and Blood of Christ in the Sacrament* (published 1605). And yet Ochino's closeness to Cranmer suggests that even then Cooke aligned herself with the active core of Protestantism in England.[8]

In 1556, Anne Cooke married Nicholas Bacon, assuming the motherhood of his six children by a first marriage and a position near the heart of English politics and religion for the next twenty years. Remaining loyal to Elizabeth during Mary's reign, Bacon was rewarded with the office of Lord Keeper of the Great Seal and head of the Chancery court, and was known for his learning and wisdom in the service of the State. With his brother-in-law, William Cecil, who had married Mildred Cooke in 1546, he served the queen on the Privy Council. But Anne Cooke Bacon wished to make her own contribution to the Elizabethan church, and perhaps taking advantage of her husband's friendship with Matthew Parker, Archbishop of Canterbury, she sent to him her translation of Bishop Jewel's defense of the Church of England, a work commissioned by Cecil to be the English clergy's answer to its foreign detractors and the cornerstone of English doctrine.[9] In it, Jewel argues against the power of the Council of Trent, which England had refused to attend, and so against papal supremacy; he denies schism within the English church itself; and he asserts that the Church of England follows the ancient true church, whereas the Church of Rome emanates from corrupt, non-Scriptural doctrine. Jewel spoke for the entire English clergy and addressed an international audience. The debate following publication of the *Apology* indicated how crucial it was to explaining and clarifying English faith in England and abroad.[10]

Shortly after the Latin *Apologia* appeared, an anonymous translation surfaced, only to prove unacceptable because of errors and inaccuracies. At this point, Archbishop Parker received Anne Cooke Bacon's translation, and in his letter to her, appended to the published work, he claims "that the thinge itselfe hath singularly pleased my judgement, and delighted my mind in reading it."[11] More important, he recognizes the service she has performed for the Church:

> By which your travail (Madame) you have expressed an acceptable dutye to the glorye of God, deserved well of this Churche of Christe, honourablie defended the good fame and estimation of your owne native tongue, shewing it so able to contend with a worke originally written in the most praised speache: and besides the honour ye have done to the kinde of women and to the degree of Ladies, ye have done pleasure to the Author of the Latine boke in deliveringe him by your cleare translation from the perils of ambiguous and doubtful constructions: and in makinge his good worke more publikely beneficialle:

As he praises Bacon's scholarship, he is also aware that the customary language of men to women is flattery, and so he hastens to assure her and the readers that his estimation of her translation is wholly accurate. Not only is she clever enough to recognize flattery, but Parker reminds his readers that the stakes are too high, that Jewel and he "in respecte of our vocations" cannot risk "to have this publike worke not truely and wel translated." The final proof of its excellence was that Jewel himself used this text in his continuing doctrinal disputations with Harding.[12]

If the archbishop's commendations are impressive, they were also a necessary preface to so important a work by a woman. He does not neglect to address Bacon as "learned and virtuous," recognizing that his approbation serves "the commoditie of others, and good incouragement of your selfe." By this he indicates that readers needed the reassurance of a specific formula to accept a woman's work as bona fide, and indeed to encourage Bacon is yet another way of publicly approving her virtue. He praises her modesty three times: for submitting the book to his judgment, for disliking flattery, and for her putative disinclination to have the work published. Each instance represents her possession of a feminine virtue: obedience to men, humility, and privacy. Moreover, in his statement that she has brought honor to "the kinde of women and to the degree of Ladies," Parker underlines, probably with a generous impulse, that she is an exemplary woman first and a writer last. The translation proves she is virtuous, makes of her "so singular a president" [precedent] to "noble youth," and by it "all noble gentlewomen shall (I trust) hereby be allured from vain delights to doinges of more perfect glory." Like the publisher of Ochino's sermons, Parker implies that most women are idle pleasure seekers, and that Bacon is an isolated example of learning and goodness. Indeed, only under these conventional terms would Parker and his readers also admit to the brilliance and public usefulness of Bacon's achievement. It is the paradoxical precondition that confronted learned and creative women throughout the period, that insistence on their private virtue must alway accompany publication of their work. In this case, translation perfectly answered Anne Bacon's desire to participate in the central controversy of her time, because it simultaneously concealed the writer while it accorded her a voice. Jewel's work provided her with a text and an audience, allowing her to bring honor on the English language, as the archbishop claimed, "showing it so able to contend with a worke originally written in the most praised speache." Translation thus appears again as an act of ventriloquism, allowing Bacon to perform the masculine task of public disputation while yet remaining as the ideal, virtuous woman.

Although she lived at least another forty years, Bacon, like most other women writers, was not prolific, publishing only these two works. If she did not, or could not, continue as a writer, she did consider herself as an active participant in religious affairs. For instance, in the 1580s, despite concerted action by Church and State to quell them, she took up the cause of the Poor Preachers, a band of traveling Nonconformists. Her reasons for espousing their cause, stated in a politic letter to William Cecil, now Lord Burghley, appear to emanate from her own spiritual experience:

> I confess as one that hath found mercy, that I have profited more in the inward feeling knowledge of God his holy will, though but in a small measure, by such sincere and sound opening of the scriptures by an ordinary preaching within these seven or eight years, than I did by hearing odd sermons at Paul's wellnigh twenty years together. I mention this unfeignedly the rather to excuse my boldness to your lordship, humbly beseeching your lordship to think upon their suit, and as God shall move your understanding heart, to further it.[13]

The independent spirit reflected here may explain why she had once cast herself as Jewel's translator; the obeisance to Burghley perhaps echoes her strategy in submitting the translation to Matthew Parker for his approval.

Tantalizing details about Anne Bacon's character and her creativity surface in many of her letters to her sons, Anthony and Francis. Perhaps modeling herself after her own mother who took such care for the moral and spiritual education of her children, Bacon devoted a lifelong correspondence to urging her sons to lead the godly life: to pray, to avoid bad company, to shun Catholics, not to drink or indulge the senses. She interested herself in the smallest details of their lives, from the wearing of mufflers to diet, especially in the case of Anthony who had been sickly since childhood; and also in the greatest, particularly in their preferment to state appointments. She was an inexhaustible pleader, manager, and conscience. In one letter to Anthony, styling herself as "your long-grieved mother," she warns him against one Lawson, "that fox," and pushes forward a Mr. Fant as one "able to advise you both very wisely and friendly." Clearly fearing Anthony's apostasy, as his "Christian and natural mother," she begs him to follow "the true religion of Christ." Reminding Anthony that he has no father and that he has little enough "regarded your kind and no simple mother's wholesome advice from time to time," she urges him to change his ways and prays God will protect him. It is a letter well calculated to arouse Anthony's guilt and to assert his mother's spiritual power over him.[14]

Bacon's epistolary attempts to exert complete control over her sons' lives may be another sign of the strong will that resided in her pious soul. Her letters may also reveal a woman trying to live a vicarious public life through her sons, attempting to direct their friendships and their careers where her own could not go. Certainly, as in her translation of Bishop Jewel's *Apology*, she acted out of a strong, assured, practical devotion to her faith.

Other Translators: Anne Locke Prowse and Elizabeth Cooke Hoby Russell

Anne Bacon's work, like Anne Wheathill's, belonged to the religious mainstream, and can certainly be placed in the context of a flourishing translation "movement," for in the sixteenth century, the art of translation was practiced by everyone from Sidney and Chapman to hundreds of anonymous renderers of French, Italian, or Latin treatises. Pride in the English language, interest in great works of the past, the desire to spread works of religious reform are the reasons normally given for this great outpouring of translation, and certainly educated women might share these motives. But men might offer translations to patrons as evidence of their capacity for public service, and this women could not do.[15] What translation did provide for the educated woman was a voice and an identity as a writer, decorously concealed in the work of a known and accepted male author. And from Margaret Beaufort, Henry VIII's grandmother, who translated *The myrrour of golde for the Synfull soule* (published 1522, 1526) to Anne Locke Prowse who translated Calvin's sermons in 1560 and John Taffin's treatise in 1590, women rendered those pious works in which they could assume the voice of a preacher and the persona of Christian virtue. So habitual was this choice that when she presented her translation of a Spanish romance in 1578, Margaret Tyler felt obliged to argue at some length that women could properly translate works other than those of divinity.[16]

While Anne Bacon's work indicates what a determined and well-placed woman might accomplish, other translators appropriate less notable niches for their talents. Yet each wished to leave some mark as an author, and so used her dedication to establish her own literary persona. For example, in her translation of Marguerite de Navarre, to be examined later in this chapter, Elizabeth Tudor demonstrates a youthful humility when she briefly expresses her duty and gratitude to Katherine Parr. With a good deal more thought and maturity, Anne Locke, esteemed friend of John Knox and translator of the *Sermons of John Calvin, upon the songe that Ezechias made after he had bene sicke, and afflicted by the hand of God* (1560), took the opportunity in her dedication to the Duchess of Suffolk to write her own sermon on the theme of spiritual sickness, a metaphor she sustains for eleven pages. She notes near the end that she has translated Calvin's book "so nere as I possibly might, to the very wordes of his text, and that in so plaine Englishe as I could expresse."[17] Plain style very much characterizes her own preaching which outlines the intricate connections between body and soul as found in Scripture and in John Calvin's writing. In her forthright manner, she exploits the medical metaphor to win over her readers:

> And that you maye be assured, that this kinde of medicine is not hurtfull: two moste excellent kinges, Ezechias and David, beside an infinite numbre have tasted the lyke before you, and have founde health therin, such healthe as hathe cured them for ever, and not as common or naturall reasons of Philosophie doe cure a sicke or soore mynde, which with easie and weake not well drawynge or cleansinge plasters, so overheale the wounde that it festreth and breaketh oute afreshe wyth renewed and doublye increased danger. (A3v)

Locke's dedication to saving the sick souls of England seems to have motivated her translation, but it also allows her to identify herself as an active purveyor of God's word, some-where down the line from Calvin, but nevertheless on the same line: "This receipte God the heavenly Physitian hath taught, his most excellent Apothecarie master John Calvine hath compounded, and I your graces most bounden and hum-ble have put into an Englishe box, and do present unto you" (A3). Beyond the dedicatory expressions of humility common to writers of both sexes, Locke does not apologize for her literary efforts. Perhaps a conviction that she was a part of God's Providence overcame any doubts she may have had as a female author.

More typically apologetic is a dedication by Anne Bacon's sister, Elizabeth Cooke Hoby Russell, Dowager Countess of Bedford. In her translation from French of *A Way of Rec-onciliation of a good and learned man, touching the Trueth, Nature, and Substance of the Body and blood of Christ in the Sacrament* (published 1605), Russell claims that at first she "meant not to have set it abroad in Print," but wished only to have for herself a certain guide and justification on the controversial issue of transubstantiation. In a tactic familiar to all dedication writers, she claims to have lent her work to a friend and been "bereft thereof by some." In addition, she fears that after her death a pirated edition might appear "according to the humors of other, and wrong of the dead, who in his life approved my Translation with his owne al-lowance." Nothing remained but to publish and to dedicate the book to her "most vertuous and worthilie beloved daugh-ter," Anne Herbert. Thus in a few lines Russell has touched all points of concern to a woman writer and her readers: she is pious in her concern for the true religion; she is obedient in having her translation approved by the original author; she is essentially private, because the work was not intended for publication, and only respect for the dead compelled her to change its course; and she is a devoted mother, eager to contribute to the spiritual well-being of her child with her "last Legacie, this Booke. A most precious Jewell to the com-fort of your Soule. ..." She is thus accredited and ready to proceed as a peacemaker, to present a work resolving that "cruel and pernitious contention" over communion. She is an example of the pious writer who set herself a particular task to aid the Reformed cause. That such women did find an audience is suggested by the publication in 1582 of *The Monument of Matrones*, an anthology of pious writing by women, collected by Thomas Bentley of Gray's Inn.

The Monument of Matrones

The Monument of Matrones, a volume of a thousand pages, contains "the woorthie works partlie of men partlie of women; compiled for the necessarie use of both sexes out of the sacred Scriptures and other approved authors."[18] Including everything from the prayer of Judith to the last words of Jane Grey, from the song of Deborah to a translation of Marguerite de Navarre's *Miroir de l'Ame pécheresse* by Elizabeth Tudor, its editor, Thomas Bentley more precisely designated the book as "more proper and peculiar for the private use of women than heretofore hath beene set out by anie." While he assumed some men to be in his audience, he clearly anticipated that women would be the primary readers of works by and about other women, thus acknowledging that there was something separate and special about feminine piety. To unify his volume, Bentley relies on the imagery of Matthew 25, the parable of the wise and foolish virgins, for he conceives of the seven books of *The Monument* as seven "Lamps of Virginitie, or distinct treatises," planning the first five to offer prayer and meditation and the last two precepts and examples. The actual writing by contemporary women occupies the "Second Lampe." Recognizing the importance of coupling women's learning with their chastity, Bentley parallels the wise virgins and the authors whom he publishes: the five wise virgins who kept their lamps filled with oil and were prepared to go in to the marriage with the bridegroom, Christ, are types of the women who wrote religious works to prepare themselves and their readers. At first, the analogy may seem to be alarmingly literal, but further consideration suggests that Bentley exploited a connection inherent in the parable, one that a number of women writers had also embraced.

In the Biblical text, and in its traditional exegesis, the sex of the wise virgins is irrelevant to their signification, for they represent the Christian soul prepared for the Day of Judgment. The gloss in the Geneva Bible reads, "By this similitude of the virgins Jesus teacheth every man to watch." Likewise, traditional exegesis of the bridal imagery in the Song of Songs transcends specific gender because the beloved is the soul or the Church and the lover is Christ. Nevertheless, like Bentley, Renaissance women writers themselves singled out these and other passages featuring female figures, believing that such allegories were particularly meaningful for their own spiritual lives. Since allegories of the female soul or of virgins awaiting marriage indeed exploit the archetypal female virtues of chastity, purity, humility, and modesty—virtues heavily imprinted in their own educations—women writers may have found in such scriptural passages a ready-made language and imagery expressing the ideals for which they had been taught to strive. Moreover, the allegorical use of relationships like spouse, sister, daughter, and mother were particularly relevant to women who were used to being exclusively defined by their relations to men. Perhaps the subordination that women were advised to practice as mothers, daughters, sisters, and wives helped them as Christians to begin the necessary obedience and humility of the soul before her God. In any case, as we will see here and in succeeding chapters, it seems that some women writers felt an affinity for female allegory, whether it expressed their spirituality, provided them with an imagery appropriate to women, or called on feminine experience. Bentley recognized the importance for the pious women readers of *The Monument of Matrones* of this telescoping of the literal with the figurative.

This attitude is nowhere more strongly demonstrated than in Bentley's treatment of Queen Elizabeth, who appears in *The Monument* as patron, muse, author, and Biblical symbol. In his opening dedication to the queen, Bentley had cited "obedience of your Maiestie" as one of the reasons for undertaking his work and had referred to his seven books as "these seven Lamps of your perpetuall virginitie" (A3). Elizabeth appears throughout the work as a patron, an archetypal chaste and learned lady, and as "Davids daughter," the champion of the English Reformed church. Joining the queen to her sacred predecessors, Bentley urges women to rejoice with Sara Tobit, Judith, the Virgin Mary, "and with our most gratious Queene ELIZABETH, incessantlie to yeeld all possible praise and hartie thanks for their so often, mightie, and marvellous preservation and deliverance from so manie kinds of dangers, yea deaths and destruction pretended by sathan and his bloudie ministers dailie against them" (B4). And if women fight the good fight, they will also be demonstrating "the pure love of their countrie." These themes are developed fully in the "Third Lampe" in which Elizabeth appears as England's Solomon, queen, and Defender of the Faith.[19]

Bentley was interested both in presenting and justifying the work of contemporary women, and so he did not take lightly his promise to include works "of al ages." Following the historical methodology of Reformers justifying their cause by reference to Scripture, in the "First Lampe of Virginitie" he gathers "the divine PRAIERS, HYMNES, or SONGS, made or sunge by sundrie holie women in the Scripture." Included here, with glosses for the "unlearned Reader," are passages recording the words of women from Hagar to Deborah, from Naomi to Abigail.[20] Given extended attention is a heavily annotated and explicated version of the Song of Solomon as a divine dialogue between Christ the bridegroom and his bride, "the faithful soule, his sanctified, chaste, and holie spouse the Church." Similarly, in the words of Lamentations, a female Church bewails Christ's forsaking her because of her "sinnes, unfaithfulnesse, and rebellion," and Bentley proceeds into the New Testament and Apocrypha to record all the words uttered both by Biblical women and by female allegorical figures, from the woman of Canaan and the foolish virgins to the Virgin and the Apocryphal Esther, Judith, and Sarra of The Book of Tobit. Bentley's apparent purposes were to educate women in their long spiritual history and to place the women of his own time in a framework that authorized their pious utterances: if the Bible recorded the words of women, certainly contemporary books might do no less. Strikingly, Bentley does not distinguish between the reality of a specific historical personage like Deborah and parabolic figures like the foolish virgins, or between these and the allegorical figures of the soul and the Church, because the important concept is that they are all represented by female voices. Women were to understand the song of Deborah as well as the words of the beloved in the Canticles as part of their particular religious heritage. The "first Lampe" explicitly recognizes that feminine piety is nurtured by feminine types and symbols.

Elizabeth I (1533–1603)

This concept is strongly supported by the very first entry in the "Second Lampe of Virginitie," the translation of Marguerite de Navarre's *Miroir de l'Ame pécheresse* executed in 1544 by the eleven-year-old Princess Elizabeth, and soon after published in 1548 by John Bale as *A Godly Medytacyon of the christen sowle concerninge a love towarde God and hys Christe*. Elizabeth, already a student of Latin, Italian, and French, and a pupil of the Cambridge humanist, William Grindal, sent her stepmother, Katherine Parr, a prose translation of Marguerite de Navarre's poem. Written in her own clear, italic hand, Elizabeth's "miroir or glasse of the synnefull Soule," bound in a hand-embroidered cover, was a New Year's gift, perhaps in response to the queen's kindness, or a dutiful exercise, or a recognition of the Reformist beliefs they held in common. In 1533, Marguerite's poem had been briefly declared heretical by the Sorbonne, which disapproved of prayer and scriptural quotation in the vernacular. Very much like Katherine Parr, Marguerite de Navarre did not openly espouse the Reformed church, but welcomed and protected many of its foremost believers.[21] John Bale had perceived the Reformist potential of Elizabeth's translation and printed it to lend the weight of her position to the cause.

In her dedication to Queen Katherine, Elizabeth remarks on "the affectuous wille and fervent zeale, the wich your highnes hath towards all godly lerning," a bond of interest between the two to supplement that of "duetie."[22] As a work of virtuous learning, *Le miroir* is not only appropriate to the beliefs of the young princess, but also suggests that she or her preceptors found it a suitable vehicle to express a young woman's piety. The most notable feature of the work, as Elizabeth herself notes, is its exploration of the traditional allegories of the Christian soul as the "mother, daughter, syster, and wife" of God. To hypothesize that Marguerite de Navarre carefully chose her subject and that Elizabeth or her tutors understood the choice leads to an analysis of the work as more than what Neale called "an excessively dreary French poem in Elizabethan prose," and provides a glimpse into sixteenth-century feminine piety.[23]

Marguerite herself had drawn attention to her sex at the beginning and end of her work. In her concluding lines, she signs her poem, in essence revealing it as the spiritual autobiography of a sinner who hopes that God will "faire de moy sa Marguerite" (l. 1430). And in her opening address to the reader, beginning with her self-effacing "if," Marguerite humbly asks:

> If thou doest rede this whole worke: beholde rather the matter and excuse the speche, consydering it is the worke of a woman wiche hath in her neyther science, or knowledge, but a desyre that eche one might se, what the gifte of god doth when it pleaseth hym to justifie the harte of a man. (5)

> Si vous lisez ceste oeuvre toute entiere,
> Arrestez vous, sans plus, a la matiere,
> En excusant la rhyme et le languaige,
> Voyant que c'est d'une femme l'ouvraige,
> Qui n'a en soy science, ne scavoir,
> Fors un desir, que chascun puisse veoir
> Que fait le don de Dieu le Createur,
> Quand il lui plaist justifier un cueur;
> *(Le Miroir, 99)*

In her dedication, Elizabeth describes her own "symple witte, and small lernyng" (3). Nevertheless, Marguerite reveals a considerable knowledge of Scripture and exegetical tradition, and a comprehension of how to use them in the service of nonsectarian doctrine. Her poetry is fervent, emphatic, and credible as the voice of a sinner despising her sins and continually amazed at the bountiful grace of God. Elizabeth's translation, while consistently flatter in tone and often too literal, occasionally captures some of the original fervor. Its significance lies in what she translates more than how.

Early in her 1,434-line poem, Marguerite initiates her long exposition of scriptural allegories featuring female figures with Christ's rescue of her soul from hell "where against his wille she was willinge to perishe bycause she did not love thee" (12). By contrast, Christ shows infinite love and handles the soul "as a mother, daughter [sic], syster, and wife" (13). Citing every Biblical text that supports these allegorical relationships, Marguerite ranges from Hosea 2, interpreted as the marriage of Christ and the soul ("It pleaseth the to gyve her another name, to call her thy wife, and she to call thee, husbande . . . ," 15), to Proverbs 23, interpreted as the filial relationship ("for [with great swittenes] thou saydest, daugther, lende me thy harte"). From Matthew 12, "Those that shall do the will of my father; they are my brethren and mother," Marguerite launches a disquisition on how she, the sinning Christian, can be mother of Christ: "through love i have begotten the. Therefore withoute any feare will i take upon me the name of a mother, Mother of god" (17-17v). Immediately apostrophizing the Virgin Mary, the "corporall" and through faith, the "spirituall mother" of Christ, Marguerite praises the Virgin's steadfast faith and wonders at God's grace in her, and concludes "than, i (following thy faith with humilitie) am hys spirituall mother." Again, the conventional feminine virtues accord precisely with the Christian virtues, allowing the woman poet to bring together her own spiritual being and scriptural language in dramatic reenactment.

Similarly, the imagery of the Canticles authorizes the relationship of sister and wife:"Thou doest call me, love, and faire spowse, if so it be, suche hast thou made me" (20). While there is little question that Elizabeth would be aware that these terms were allegorical, she was, after all, translating a work composed almost entirely of scriptural references to women. Thus, the literal aspect of the story or parable assumes a new importance for women while they proceed with traditional interpretations. For instance, from 3 Kings 3:16-28 (Vulgate), Marguerite offers an exegesis of the story of the two mothers with one living and one dead child as an allegory of sin: "Nowe have i lost the by mine owne fautte, by cause i toke no hyde to kepe the. My envy, my sensualite (i beyng in my beastely slepe) did steal the frome me, and gave me an other childe havinge no life in hym, wich is called synne" (23v). And when the child (Christ) is restored to her, she praises him because "it hath pleased the, me lesse than nothing to call a mother" (26). The interpretation is theologically sound, but the passage would not have been singled out had it not concerned two mothers.[24]

One of the most striking, impassioned passages in the poem concerns the "old" treatment of wives contrasted with the "new" generosity of Christ to his spouse. Most husbands would not forgive a wife "after that she had offended hym and did returne unto hym." Most husbands would "cause the judges to condemne them to dye," or kill them themselves, sent them away, or "shutte them in a prison" (29v-30). An adulterous wife is "estimed to be poluted, and of no value" (36); yet Christ, the essence of charity, takes her back like a "gratious good, switte and pitiefull husbande ..." (38).[25]

Thus the poem proceeds and concludes as a testament to God's love for the sinner, expressed throughout by the relationships between a male, patriarchal, beneficent God and a sinning, humble, penitent female. Such configurations suggest several conclusions: that the conventional hierarchical distinctions between male and female aptly reflect traditional theological distinctions between God and the sinning mortal; that the recognition of such distinctions influenced the pious woman's conception of herself, and the more literate in the Bible and its exegesis she became, the more she would discover that her inferiority extended even to figurative language and the expression of universal spiritual truth. Gathering from her reading that femaleness could inherently represent the essential sinfulness of humankind, she responded by accepting the burden and with fierce piety reciting her weakness and strongly asserting her inviolable faith in God's grace ad love.

The catalogue of citations in *Le Miroir* reveals, then, a woman writer obsessively detailing the scriptural use of male-female similitudes to express an aspect of her own spiritual struggle. It is important to see that she includes the classic female representations of evil (sin, whore, harlot) and good (the Virgin, humility, faith, purity, love), because the two provide the extreme loci which female symbols signified in Christian theology. And for women, to strive for the ideal virtue of the Virgin meant overcoming the sense of extra sin inherent in femaleness, and because of their additional guilt, feeling extraordinary gratitude for the grace, love, and forgiveness of God. The very existence of the pious woman writer derives not only from her desire to emulate the ideal virtue of the Virgin—or Susanna or Deborah—but from her perceiving how especially sinful her sex was. By speaking or by writing, she could provide tangible signs that she had received grace and that she had joined the elect; she could even hope that through her work her readers would pray and that God would "plante the lively fayth" in them too.

Elizabeth's translation, made "in the tender and maidenlie yeeres of hir youth and virginitie, to the great benefit of God's Church, and comfort of the godlie"(title page, the "Second Lampe of Virginitie") took the prominent first place in Bentley's "Second Lampe," in keeping with his recognition of her important religious and political role for English Protestants. Bentley also includes in the "Second Lampe" three prayers Elizabeth reportedly made in her early days, one when imprisoned in the Tower, one when she feared she might be murdered, and one on the way to her coronation when she compared herself to Daniel being delivered from the lions' den. Each marks a stage in Elizabeth's becoming the figurehead for the English reformers, commemorating her escape from the Church's Romish enemies. In her role as the redeemed princess, she is essential to the Protestant propagandists' belief in their divinely sanctioned cause. As head of the English church, her past history became all the more important as a sign of God's providential care, and so her writings received inordinate attention and praise.

In his edition of Elizabeth's work, Bale likewise devoted much space to praising her learning, virtue, and true Christianity. As he did with Anne Askew, he sets the young princess in a scriptural and a historical context, comparing her to "Christes most blessed mother, whan she sayd with heavenly rejoyce, My sowle magnyfyeth the lorde and my sprete rejoyceth in God my saver," and placing her in an ancient tradition of virtuous English women, from "Cordilla the doughter of kynge Leyer" to her own great-grandmother Margaret. The woodcut on the title page, repeated after Bale's conclusion, depicts Elizabeth kneeling before Christ, Bible in hand. As John King notes, this is "the conventional apostolic pose," and "lends her royal authority to the progress of reform";[26] it also illustrates the close male-female relationships in the *Miroir* between Christ and the true Christian. Despite Bale's fulsome admiration for Elizabeth's achievements as a scholar and writer, someone edited her text, making the translation smoother and more idiomatic. If it was Bale himself, no doubt he believed that if Elizabeth were to aid the cause of reform, she might as well appear as a mature prose stylist.[27]

KATHERINE PARR (1512–1548)

While Elizabeth's juvenile translation retains pride of place in *The Monument*, the work of Katherine Parr was probably in its time a more genuine contribution to Reformist doctrine. Her *Prayers or Meditacyons* went into fifteen editions between 1545 and 1608 and her *Lamentacion of a Sinner* had three editions between 1547 and 1563. Although it was the second of her works, the *Lamentacion* appears first in Bentley's collection, probably because it contained the most explicit Reformist attitudes. A preface by the Reformist politician and statesman, William Cecil, who clarifies for the reader that its purpose is "thine amendment," indicates that the work would have added the status of the dowager queen to the Reformed cause. Bentley's edition asserts that she was a "most vertuous and right gratious Ladie" and that the work is "verie profitable to the amendment of our lives," as always spelling out the necessary qualifications for the publication of a woman's book, even if the author was a queen.

Katherine Parr was a thoroughly pious woman with Reformist tendencies at a very dangerous time, but she had no desire for the martyrdom that overtook Anne Askew.[28] Whether apocryphal or not, Foxe's famous story of how she saved herself from Bishop Gardiner's deadly attack by submitting herself utterly to Henry VIII's will in all things indicates a circumspection corroborated by the timing of the publication of her works. The Reformist *Lamentacion* with its rude words for Papists, while written during Henry's life, was not published until 1547, whereas the universally acceptable *Prayers or Medytacions* "collected out of holy workes"—and demonstrating only the Christian piety of "the most vertuous and graciouse Princesse Katherine"(title page)—appeared in 1545.

In common with Anne Askew, Katherine Parr had a vocation for preaching, and also chose the genre of confession. But unlike the first person in Askew's *Examinations* with its play of irony, Katherine Parr's "I" in the *Lamentacion* "bewailing the ignorance of hir blind life, led in superstition," confesses her sins, repents, glorifies God, and teaches her fellow sinners of the differences between the "carnall Children of Adam" and "the children of light" without naming herself specifically or making any reference to the external events of her life. Rather than draw attention to herself or exploit her womanhood like Askew or Marguerite de Navarre, Parr assumes the voice of the sinner in search of redemption and teaches her fellow sinners. Likewise in the *Prayers or Medytacions*, the voice is that of a Christian supplicant, confessing weakness and, in the *de contemptu mundi* tradition, despising the things of the world and trusting in God alone.[29] Like

Anne Locke, she offers a body of doctrine for the spiritual health of her readers, authorized by her scriptural material and her circumspection. In the queen's case, her position would only enhance the acceptability of her work, perhaps even making it easier for other pious women to write and publish.

Paying obeisance to the rank of his authors, Bentley proceeds from the work of queens to that of ladies and gentlewomen who contributed to Reformist literature. From the saintly figure of Lady Jane Grey to the earnest schoolmistress, Lady Elizabeth Tyrwhitt; from Lady Frances Aburgavennie's deathbed legacy of prayers to the prayers of "Godlie women Martyrs"; from the words of John Bradford's mother to the translation by Mistress Dorcas Martin of a French treatise, to the pious exhortations of anonymous gentlewomen, Bentley presents the work of those women who are "woorthie paternes of all pietie, godlinesse, and religion to their sex," who "in great fervencie of the spirit, and zeale of the truth, even from their tender and maidenlie yeeres," have occupied themselves in studying the "noble and approoved sciences, and in compiling and translating of sundrie most christian and godlie bookes" (B). The key words, "fervencie" and "zeale" indicate their Reformist qualifications, although Bentley is careful to emphasize as well how appropriately feminine these women are. Not only has Bentley himself found their writings beneficial, but his reiterated hope is that his list of learned and pious authors will "incourage, provoke, and allure all godlie women of our time ... to become even more studious imitators, and diligent followers of so godlie and rare examples in their vertuous mothers." In whatever studies are "commendable for women," he hopes "that so being lightened by their good examples both of life and doctrine, they may shine also together with them on earth, as burning lampes of verie virginitie; and in heaven, as bright starres of eternall glorie ..." (B7v-B8).

Bentley here articulates what many women writers knew, that their art was inseparable from a chaste feminine virtue, that they had inherited the mantle of history's "rare examples," and that they were always bound by what was "commendable for women." Whether or not the individual writer composed with these precepts in mind—and the evidence suggests that she did—she knew this was how her audience defined her. Often, her only scope lay in choosing what to translate or what to pray for, a position that could offer either safety or frustration depending on her artistic temperament. And yet, preaching and teaching were important steps in the establishment of a feminine literary presence.

JANE GREY (1537–1554)

Like Elizabeth, Jane Grey lived briefly in Katherine Parr's household, but rather than assuming Parr's circumspect, steady commitment to Reform, Grey's learning and faith propelled her into dangerous, ultimately fatal, political action.[30] Writing became an integral part of Grey's total devotion to the Reformed cause, and the texts she left convey vividly how important it was to her to set down for herself her beliefs, her struggles, and her deep sense of vocation.

Like Margaret More Roper, Jane Grey bears a reputation even today for learning, piety, and virtue, largely based on the famous account by Roger Ascham in *The Scholemaster*. His remembrance of the solitary scholar, reading Plato in Greek while her family is out hunting in the park, finding in her occupation "moch delite" and "trewe pleasure," suggests both Grey's single-mindedness and her reliance on her inner resources. Since Ascham wishes to illustrate the importance of kind schoolmasters, he then relays Grey's explanation of her studiousness, that her parents were "sharpe and severe" and her tutor "gentle"; her parents punish her so severely for anything less than perfect behavior,

> that I thinke my selfe in hell, till tyme cum, that I must go to M. *Elmer* who teacheth me so gentlie, so pleasantlie, with soch faire allurementes to learning, that I thinke all the tyme nothing, whiles I am with him. And when

I am called from him, I fall on weeping, because, what soever I do els, but learning, is ful of grief, trouble, feare, and whole misliking unto me: And thus my booke, hath bene so moch my pleasure, and bringeth dayly to me more pleasure and more, that in respect of it, all other pleasures, in very deede, be but trifles and troubles unto me.[31]

Such devotion to her studies is borne out in the erudition and rhetorical skill of Grey's writings, which reveal an intellectual vigor and a strongly developing sense of herself as a religious teacher and writer. At the age of thirteen, already a scholar of Scripture, Latin, and Greek, she composed a letter, "The Lady Jane to a learned man," a work preserved in manuscript, in Foxe's *Actes and Monuments*, and in a 1615 edition of her works, attesting to its importance for the Reformed cause.

As a composition by a woman, the significance of Grey's "Epistle"—a letter written in 1550 to the apostate, John Harding, "late falne from the truth of gods moste holy word for feare of the world"—lies not only in her assumption of the role of preacher and teacher, but also in her attendant certainty that she was Harding's spiritual equal and could convince him through her written argument to return to the Reformed church.[32] The letter reflects the writer's command of rhetorical techniques, fervent faith in Scripture, and a structured range of moods varying, as appropriate, from righteous anger, to sorrow, to hope. In other words, in the terms of a sixteenth-century Protestant, it is a carefully written and persuasive document that attests both to Grey's piety and her mastery of prose style.

Adopting the tones of a "gospeling" preacher, she claims her own shock and sorrow at his action which she contrasts with his previous state of grace:

I cannot but mervell at thee, and lamente thy case: that thou whiche sometyme wast the lyvely member of Christ: but now the defourmed impe of the divel, some tyme the beutifull temple of God: but now the stinking and filthy kenell of Sathan, sometyme the unspotted

spouse of Christe, but now the unshamefast paramour
of Anti-Christ, somtyme my faythful brother: but now
a straunger and Apostata, Yea some time a stout Christen
souldier, but now a cowardly runaway. (920)

Such striking dichotomies, fueled by Reformist fervor, are
designed to arouse in the apostate immediately and emotionally a horror of his spiritual state. To this, she adds another
highly effective rhetorical technique, a continuing series of
rhetorical questions, each in parallel structure, each building
to a climax, and each designed to make the apostate examine
his soul:

Can neither the punishment of the Israelites (which for
theyr idolatry so oft they receaved) move thee, neither
the terrible threatininges of the auncient prophetes stirre
thee, nor the curses of gods owne mouth feare the to
honour any other God then him? (920)

By referring to the Israelites, the prototypes of the English
Reformers, by reminding Harding of the doctrine of personal
salvation, by summoning the specter of Romish idolatry, Grey
clearly aims her argument at the particular case of the apostate; that is, at a man who had once accepted the basis of her
letter as truth, that the Reformed church is the True Church,
and the Church of Rome a corrupt aberration. This letter
would hardly have much effect on a convinced Catholic, but
to someone who had once doubted Rome's power, yet had
apparently returned to the Catholic faction, Grey's extreme
language would summon all the intense feeling that the Reformers brought to their cause. Likewise, to tell Harding in
measured repetition, "the same Sathan, the same Belsabub,
the same dyvell" that tempted Christ has "prevayled against"
him reminds Harding of an omnipresent tempter who preys
on the naturally depraved human being, that "sincke of
synne," and that "childe of perdicion" (921).

Grey uses strong language, persuasive rhetoric, vivid ap-
peals to the authority of Scripture, and a strong, righteous
voice to scorn the apostate's fall, to exhort him to reconsider,

and to command him to return. But the central proposition of her letter is expressed with devastating simplicity. From Paul she quotes the warning of eternal damnation, "if we that willinglye sinne after we have receaved the knowledge of hys truth, there is no oblation left for synne, but the terrible expectation of judgment and fire . . ." (921). By contrast, and perhaps this provides some insight into Grey's own extraordinary strength and dignity in suffering, she refers to Christ's saying "blessed are you when men revile you and persecute you for my sake: rejoyce, and be glad, for great is your rewarde in heaven" (922).

Having delivered the thunderbolts through such scriptural passages, Grey moderates her tone to conclude her letter with the consolations of faith. Citing the "ensaumples of holy men and women," she exhorts Harding to "returne, returne agayne into Christes warre, and as becommeth a faythfull warriour, put on that armour that S. Paule teacheth to be most necessary for a Christian man. And above all thinges take to you the shilde of fayth" (922). This text, so important to the Reformers as a justification and encouragement for their spiritual struggles and worldly battles, appears again in Grey's "effectual prayer," written shortly before she was executed, and indicates that she too saw herself as a Christian soldier fighting the good fight. For those who have fought and beaten the dark powers, Grey offers the paradisical vision of Christ's welcome, expressed in warm, emotive images of love and redemption. Christ "stretcheth out his armes to receave you, ready to fal upon your necke and kisse you, and laste of all to feaste you with the deinties and delicates of hys own precious bloud . . ."(922). Such a passage, with its emphasis on the personal relationship with the Saviour indicates how thoroughly Grey had committed herself to Reformist doctrine, and perhaps provides an insight into the dignity and strength with which she met her own cruel death.

In *The Monument of Matrones*, Bentley does not publish this letter, but the works more closely associated with Jane Grey's martyrdom, "A certaine effectuall praier" and "An exhortation," both final statements of faith, as well as her purported last words at the scaffold (98-102). Her role in *The Monument* seems to be less as a controversialist and more as a woman of faith.

"A certaine effectuall praier" begins in the voice of a "poore and desolate woman," burdened by afflictions deriving from "the long imprisonment of this vile masse of claie, my sinfull bodie and bloud" (98). The mortal fear that God will not after all visit his grace upon her, strikingly phrased in rhetorical questions, is succeeded by the most profound statement of faith, "assuredlie knowing, that as thou wilt deliver me, when it shall please thee, nothing doubting nor mistrusting thy goodnesse towards me" (99). She concludes the prayer by expressing her "calling" in the same image that inspired Anne Askew, by desiring to become a soldier in the church militant:

> arme me, I beseech thee, with thine armour, that I may stand fast, my loines being girded about with veritie, having on the brestplate of righteousness, and shod with the shoes prepared by the Gospell of peace; above all things taking to me the shield of faith, wherwith I may be able to quench all the firie darts of the wicked; and taking the helmet of salvation, and the sword of the spirit, which is thy most holie word. . . . (100)

From a "poore and desolate woman," Jane Grey transforms herself through prayer to the Christian fighting the good fight, filled with the faith "that it cannot be but well all that thou doest" (100). This brief prayer, written in strong, scriptural language, working to its impressive climax, would clearly bolster the author's position as an inspiration and example to her fellow Reformers. It also indicates Jane Grey's skill and care to compose a doctrinally sound and stirring prayer.

The second work, "An exhortation written by the Ladie Jane, the night before she suffered, in the end of the new Testament in Greeke, which she sent to hir sister the Ladie Katherine," is designed more specifically to be a didactic work, not only for her sister, but for all the faithful. Beginning concretely with the very book that she sends her sister, Grey assures her that "if you, with a good mind reade it, and with an earnest desire folowe it, it shall bring you to an immortall and everlasting life. It will teach you to live, and learne you to die" (100-101). In a firm, assured voice which governs the imperatives of her lesson, Grey exhorts her sister to "live still to die," to "denie the world, defie the divell, despise the flesh, and delight your selfe onlie in the Lord" (101). Bolstering her preaching with favorite scriptural texts, she urges her sister to be ready for death like the good servant, and not to be unready like the foolish virgins. No doubt her readers would remember her own composure at the scaffold, perhaps as she herself intended. With her last words at the time of execution, "Lord into thy hands I commend my spirit," she demonstrated how deed suited word, and assured her place as a martyr in the Protestant cause.

Jane Grey's vocation for preaching is clear. After her death, however, she became the symbol of perfect Christian womanhood, rather than the scholar. Foxe printed her writings as evidence of her true martyrdom, and when her collected works were published in the early seventeenth century, she appeared not only as the "most chast, learned, and Religious Lady," but her editor even went so far as to name her "the Saintlike Lady."[33] From this perspective, he can make her learning and courage exceptional for a woman, urging his readers "to behold in that, which we call the weaker sexe a strength matchlesse and invincible" (A2-A2v). While duly praising her instruction of the faithful, he emphasizes her feminine virtue as exemplary. She is "a Lady in all goodnes so perfect" that to possess part of her shadow would be to gain great virtue. Praise of her virtues far outweighs the acknowledgment of her literary gifts, suggesting that when the editor encourages other women to follow Grey's example, he wishes them to consider her "sober and chast life," her "modest humility," her "zeale," "her most charitable patience," her "blessed and modest boldnes of spirit," her "meeknesse of Spirit, and a Saint-like patience" more prominently than "her sweete ellocution in the schollerlike connexture and marriage of the best words and phrases together" (B3-C3v).

In the "Second Lampe" of *The Monument of Matrones* the brief appearance of Jane Grey precedes 140 pages of prose meditation, translation, and pious verse by Elizabeth Tyrwhitt, Frances Aburgavennie, John Bradford's mother, Dorcas Martin, "godlie women Martyrs," and anonymous "vertuous Gentlewomen." While generally undistinguished as prose stylists or versifiers, these women dedicated themselves to the Reformed faith so deeply as to become preachers and writers for the cause. Like their male counterparts, they wished to aid lay people with daily devotion, providing prayers for all occasions and meditations on key scriptural texts.[34] Taking care of souls was not a new feminine task, but it did demand a new kind of creativity for women as they learned to identify themselves as pious authors.

ELIZABETH TYRWHITT AND
FRANCES MANNERS ABURGAVENNIE

As the governess appointed by the Privy Council to supervise Princess Elizabeth after the removal of the indiscreet Mrs. Ashley, Lady Elizabeth Tyrwhitt would naturally possess sound Reformist credentials. Her section in *The Monument of Matrones*, "Morning and Evening praiers, with diverse Psalmes, Hymns, and Meditations," consists of pious verses written with much attention to doctrine, some to the rhyme, and a little to the rhythm, along with interspersed prose meditations. The author's persona is the sinner, a "miserable wretched woman," and throughout her prayers, she emphasizes the distance between insufficient mortals and a gracious God (113). If her prayers lack the poetic skill to move the reader deeply, still they accomplish their probable intention: to bear witness to Lady Tyrwhitt's faith, to remind the faithful of their debt to God, and to provide a text of daily worship. The Reformers had recognized that verse could convey doctrine in a direct and pleasing way, and Lady Tyrwhitt's dependence on fourteeners suggests that she chose a familiar form for the purpose of conveying a series of pithy and memorable, or memorizable, supplications and lessons.[35]

For instance, her first morning prayer, "The Hymne or praier to the sonne of God," asks for God's blessing for a day beset by the usual worldly trials. In verse notable for clarity rather than skill, Lady Tyrwhitt makes the familiar play on sun/son, associating light and warmth with grace:

Thou art the everlasting daie, which shinst in everie place.
And feedest everie living wight, with plentious gifts of
    grace. (103)

The simplicity of the verse is repeated in a refrain which echoes throughout her work and acts as an anchor of praise, expressing her fundamental concerns with grace and sacrifice:

We laud thee Father for thy grace
    We praise the Sonne which made us free
We thank the holie Spirit for our solace
    Which is one God and persons three. (103)

The third line here reveals how Tyrwhitt's doctrine normally precedes her desire for smooth verse. The rhymes "grace" and "solace" are fortuitously appropriate and seem to be the base around which she composed the lines, but once she has conveyed the necessary idea, she appears to make no attempt to polish the verse.

Similarly in "The Hymne of the passion of Christ," which also uses her basic refrain between its six-line ababcc stanzas, Tyrwhitt narrates events with just enough doctrinal inter-polation to fill out the rhymes:

Beaten was his bodie, defiled was his face,
    And yet God and man, the verie well of grace. (112)

She tends to gather her occasional metaphors from Scripture and insert them into her narrative rather than expanding them to create a new context or signification. Her language serves her doctrine rather than her imagination:

This verie God, Gods onlie begotten child
    Said to his father, why hast thou me forsaken?
Yet receive this sacrifice, and my spirit undefild:

The heavens were darkned, asunder the thrones were
    shaken
Bloud and water then sprang from this blessed lamb,
    Then graves opened, the dead alive foorth came. (112)

If Tyrwhitt's poetic skills are minor, nonetheless, in writing
these verses, she conceived of herself as a religious poet to
the extent that she wished to imprint words of faith vividly
on her reader's mind. Perhaps this attitude becomes even
clearer from the last piece of hers that Bentley prints, "Certaine godlie sentences," a list of 35 maxims by which to live.
Here, conventionally pious wisdom, what to believe and how
to behave, combine to provide advice for the godly which
includes, "Further the just sute of the poore," "Kill anger
with patience," "Make much of modestie," "Speake in season," "Trust not the world," and finally, "Awaie you must,
and turne to dust" (137-38). Such unadorned pithy instruction
suggests plain faith and plain speaking guided Tyrwhitt's
creativity. She is an early example of how the urge to teach
her own religious convictions bridged the private and public
spheres, providing an appropriate channel for feminine piety
and learning to reach the world.

A similar piety inspired the prayers in prose and meter by
Frances Manners Aburgavennie, daughter of the Earl of Rut-
land, wife of Henry, sixth Lord Bergavenny, and mother of
Mary Fane, her only daughter, to whom she dedicates her
work. Her motherly care is all the more striking because the
title also notes that she committed the work to Mary Fane
"at the houre of hir death ... as a Jewell of health for the
soule, and a perfect path to Paradise, verie profitable to be
used of everie faithfull Christian man and woman" (139). A
deathbed legacy has a particular moral and spiritual force,
helping to sanctify the writer's works and yet also removing
her from consideration as a living woman. Lady Aburgavennie's maternal concern for her daughter's soul can thus
extend to all the faithful who need the help of "fruitfull
praier." And like a true mother, she provides prayers for all
times of the day and all occasions so that her readers will not

ever want for words.[36] Not only does she collect private prayers for grace, remission of sin, and mercy, but also "A godlie praier for the true worshipping of God, which may be used in the Church before common praier" (158), as well as a prayer for use before communion and at burials. Aiming at her male audience, she provides a prayer in battle; more generally, she composes prayers for prosperity, for time of trouble, and in thanksgiving. One of her last prayers attempts to cast the net so wide as to exclude nothing and no one:

> Being tempted by the ghostlie enimie (as all that feare God are) to doubt in anie article of the Catholike faith, to despaire in Gods mercie, to yeeld to melancholie fansies, to be vexed with unkindnes of friends, or the malice of enimies, to be troubled with sicknesse, or anie other waies oppressed with griefe of bodie and mind:saie devoutlie as followeth. ... (191)

In her attempt to compose the complete prayer book, Aburgavennie did not neglect a prayer in meter, choosing like Elizabeth Tyrwhitt and other gospelers, the plain fourteener. "A necessarie praier in Meeter against vices" covers the seven deadly sins as well as such added vices as "scoffing," "backbiting and slandering," and blasphemy. The plain style particularly suits Aburgavennie's clear distinctions between good and evil as well as her final desire that summarizes all the rest:

> Make me so little to esteeme those things that worldlie bee,
>> With hart and voice that I may crave in heaven to be
>>> with thee.   (175)

The final items in Bentley's "Second Lampe" give special emphasis to the Psalms, the fundamental text of Protestant piety. One "godlie harted Gentlewoman" writes prayers taken from the Psalms, particularly for deliverance out of trouble. The "right vertuous and godlie Matrone and Gentlewoman," Dorcas Martin, provides an English translation of French prayers including Psalm verses and the Ten Commandments.

Again, Scripture enabled and authorized a feminine contribution to the Protestant mainstream.

Some of these writers draw attention to their place in the long tradition of women's prayers, suggesting that Bentley correctly assumed the importance of women's past spirituality to his female readers. In her prayer for her soon-to-be-martyred son, John, Mistress Bradford compares herself to Hannah, the mother of Samuel:

> As Hanna did applie, dedicate, and give hir first child and sonne Samuel unto thee: even so doo I deere Father; beseeching thee, for Christs sake, to accept this my gift; and give my sonne John Bradford grace alwaies trulie to serve thee, and thy people, as Samuel did. (215)

Likewise, the "godlie harted Gentlewoman" who draws her prayers from the Psalms denounces herself as a sinner, "a banished woman," and prays that God will look on her "as thou didst looke upon Susanna, and Sarai the daughter of Raguel. Thos holie women trusted in thee, and thou didst deliver them; they hoped in thee, and were not forsaken" (217). To these writers, the women of Scripture are not simply virtuous examples, but evidence of God's special grace for chaste women and pious mothers.

One of these last pieces emphasizes the importance of motherhood, perhaps anticipating the genre of the mother's advice book which was concerned with the spiritual education of the child. Bentley prints a dialogue between mother and child which is, in effect, a catechism concerning communion. The "Lampe" concludes with two "godlie exhortations" against sin and "to holiness of life" written by "a vertuous Gentlewoman." This anonymous figure appropriately concludes Bentley's collection of women's pious writings because she is significant both for the Reformed church and for women writers. The persona of the true Christian woman, whether she was politically prominent like Katherine Parr or Elizabeth, or an unknown virtuous gentlewoman, represented the best Christian virtues for all the faithful: piety, humility, constancy, patience. She was both a visible exemplum and an active force for spreading Reformed doctrine. And through her work for the church, the educated woman discovered her creativity. Some women confined themselves to the dissemination of doctrine and learned to teach and to preach. Some, as the next chapter shows, while teaching and preaching, became poets.

FOUR

PIETY AND POETRY:
ISABELLA WHITNEY,
ANNE DOWRICHE,
ELIZABETH COLVILLE,
RACHEL SPEGHT

WRITING private prayers for the godly conformed to the role of the virtuous and learned woman, perhaps because of the illusion that she herself was absent from the work. But when pious women sought to express their religious calling in more public forms, they at once encountered the limitations on their gender. The problem of moving out of the private into the public sphere concerned writers like Anne Bacon, but it touched even more deeply the women who saw themselves both as spiritual teachers and as poets. Many Reformers regarded poetry as useful to their cause, and wrote much doctrine in verse, some of it good, much of it unskilled and mechanical.[1] In the case of women writers, however, the choice of poetry was highly significant, for in the second part of this period the desire to instruct the godly evolved into a poetic apprenticeship for their sex. To write poetry, a woman had to breach the convention that poets were male: she had to overcome her lack of formal training, the self-inhibiting realization that women poets were a novelty, the attendant fear of censure, and perhaps most difficult, she had to present herself publicly in an authoritative role. The tactics women employed reveal both their doubts and attainments.

– 87 –

Perhaps a poet's most important choice is persona, and this selection posed particular problems for an incipient religious poet who was also a woman. Should the didactic voice be male or female? How much authority, how much learning could she assume? While the conventions of Christian poetry may account for her choices, interestingly, each of these poets adapts the persona of the Christian pilgrim, raising the possibility that a quest is central to her poetry; two poets create dreamers, allowing them to distance themselves from the authoritative stance.

The four writers considered in this chapter are united in their strong Reformist faith and their dedication to poetry; three of them are middle class, and reveal some of the concerns of their class. Together, these women exemplify the development of the woman poet in the sixteenth century. Their authorial stance ranges from the already familiar masquerade and ventriloquism to the assertion, however tentative, that women's own poetic voices belonged legitimately to the mainstream of religious poetry.

ISABELLA WHITNEY (fl. 1567–1573)

The religious renovation of the state did not concern Isabella Whitney whose interests revolved around living the godly life in a middle-class environment. In her works, a series of personae convey the moral vision of a middle-class Protestant woman, a morality protective of women undefended by family structure, working away from home, who had to abide carefully by the restrictions on their virtue. Whitney did not take for granted the learning and virtue proclaimed for upper-class women because she saw an ever-present danger from those who would "procure the shame" of girls in service. Her task as a poet was to teach women, and ultimately men, how to live virtuously during their temporary sojourn in the "infected" world. Although one of the first English women of the period to write about love, her moral earnestness always took precedence, suggesting that she did not, or could not, conceive of herself as a love poet.[2] Indeed, her strong didactic spirit often preceded the poetry itself, halting her verse at a ubiquitous common meter. Whitney's main impulse was to advise, to offer maxims useful to the moral and spiritual welfare of her readers, many of whom she surmised were other young women. Her decision to sermonize in verse reflected the current Reformist concept that poetry was a valuable teaching tool, ensuring the reader's attention to and retention of the matter. But she also clearly recognized that her gender created complications both for her readers and the poet herself.

This self-consciousness appears both explicitly and implicitly. In a verse letter to her married sister, for instance, she admits that a writing woman is different, although she would of course replace her pen with a broom if need be:

> Had I a Husband, or a house,
>   and all that longes therto
> My selfe could frame about to rouse,
>   as other women doo:
> But til some houshold cares mee tye,
>   My bookes and Pen I wyll apply.[3]

The implied deprecation of her literary endeavors, when joined with her continual laments for her lack of success in the world, suggests a deliberate pose designed to modulate her strong vocation as a moralist. In part, she may have been trying to convey through her persona a sense of human inadequacy without God, an idea that reappears in her main didactic work, *A sweet Nosegay*. But the elaborate framework of apologies and letters which surrounds her poetry also indicates the public caution with which Whitney approached the role of teacher, whatever the private satisfaction she may have gained from it.

Little is known of Whitney's life, except that she was probably Geoffrey Whitney's sister, and about him, the author of *A Choice of Emblemes* (1586), we know that he came from Coole Pilate in Cheshire, went to Oxford and Cambridge without receiving degrees, and became a lawyer and underbailiff for Great Yarmouth. Serving the Earl of Leicester, he certainly espoused the Reformist religion and indeed accompanied the Earl to the Netherlands in 1586, where he attended the University of Leiden. Besides Geoffrey and Isabella, there was another brother, Brooke, a sister who became Ann Borron, and two younger sisters, one of whom became Mary Colley.[4] Part of Isabella Whitney's published work consists of letters addressed "To her Brother G.W.," "To Her Brother, B.W.," "to her younger Sisters servinge in London," "To her sister, Misteris A.B.," "To her cosen, F.W.," and to her cousin, "G.W." Both this G.W. and the George Mainwaring to whom Whitney dedicates *A sweet Nosegay* appear as dedicatees for emblems in Geoffrey Whitney's work.

Whitney thus belonged to the minor gentry, to an old family, but one not able to support four daughters, for at least three of them appear to have served in gentle families in London. From Whitney's verse letter to her sisters, which is, of course, not necessarily literal, we might gather that part of this service consisted of housekeeping(D).

If Geoffrey Whitney's education had the advantages of Oxford and Cambridge, from Isabella's works we can only assume a knowledge of some contemporary literature, Scripture, some classical authors, and the rudiments of verse making. Although her poems draw upon Ovid's *Heroides*, George Turberville's 1567 translation, *The heroycall epistles*, and other English sources could have supplied all of Whitney's mythological material.

Whitney's works consist of two poems, published by Richard Jones, probably in 1567, "The Copy of a letter, lately written in meeter, by a younge Gentilwoman: to her unconstant Lover. With an Admonition to al yong Gentilwomen, and to all other Mayds in general to beware of mennes flattery"; and the versified *A sweet Nosegay or pleasant posye. Contayning a hundred and ten Phylosophicall flowers*, published in 1573. In addition to the 110 "flowers," this last work contains "Certain familier Epistles and friendly Letters by the Auctor: with Replies" and a fictional "Wyll and Testament" addressed to the City of London.[5] Almost all Whitney's verse is in ballad measure, a version of the native fourteeners favored alike by Sternhold for his Psalms and by countless other sixteenth-century practitioners of a plain style suitable for conveying basic doctrine to a wide audience.

Her first poem, "The Copy of a letter" reveals that Whitney's subject is not woman's passion, but a vindication of woman's traditional virtues. Her persona is a woman betrayed by a lover who now intends to marry another woman. By fashioning the poem as a letter to the unconstant one, Whitney can castigate him all the more directly and emphatically; but this seemingly naturalistic situation and the advocacy for deceived women should not obscure the main focus of the poem, to endorse the Christian definition of women's characters as chaste and pious and to condemn the basic evil of lust.

The poet begins by contrasting her own goodness and constancy with her lover's fickleness:

> And this (whereso you shal become)
>   full boldly may you boast:
> That once you had as true a Love,
>   as dwelt in any Coast.[6]

By insisting that their former promises are still valid, she underscores that he is as treacherous as Sinon, "Whose trade if that you long shal use,/ it shal your kindred stayn"(A2v). This stanza heralds the poet's moralized reading of classical exempla which occupies most of her remaining verses. Her source is Ovid, principally the *Heroides* but also the *Ars amatoris* and the *Metamorphoses*, probably because these works offered the widest collection of sexual betrayals available. And the poet's theme here, and even more particularly in "The Admonition," is the vulnerability of women to sexual appetite, mostly men's, but occasionally, their own. Accordingly, she notes the falsehood of Aeneas who left Dido, and Theseus who deserted Ariadne, "stealing away within the night,/before she dyd awake." But her main exemplum, over which she lingers for seven stanzas, is Jason's betrayal of "two Ladies," Medea, and the unnamed Hypsipyle. Considering Medea's unsavory reputation for sorcery and murder, which the poet ignores, her insistence on Jason's betrayal of his vows clearly indicates a selective moralization. Her purpose here is in fact to raise the fear that the betrayers of women seem to escape punishment:

> How durst he trust the surging Seas
> knowing himselfe forsworne?
> Why did he scape safe to the land,
> before the ship was torne?   (A3)

Jason is unrepentant, and his falsehood hidden, he passes safely home again. Nevertheless, the poet draws the moral that underlies all her writing, that eventually divine providence will prevail and will favor the virtuous and punish the sinners: betrayers of women in particular will suffer the "perpetual Fame" or rather, "shame" of being known as unfaithful lovers. Her own lover, indeed, may be happy now, but he too risks Jason's fate.

Posing always as restrained and resigned, her faith wholly in divine retribution, the poet wishes only for her lover that his wife will be the ideal woman with all the traditional pious, domestic qualities, with Helen's beauty, Penelope's chastity, Lucrece's constancy, and Thisbe's truth—someone like herself, in fact. By the end of the poem, although still referring to the classical models, her message emanates more explicitly from Christian piety. Recognizing that she can neither predict or alter events, she quietly accepts whatever may occur, asking God to guide her and her lover (A5). She prays for him a life as long as Nestor's, "And after that your soule may rest/ amongst the heavenly crew." For his remaining time, she wishes him the success of riches and somewhat ironically, "With as much rest and quietnesse/as men may have on Mould."

Having asserted her own Christian forgiveness and constancy, the poet turns to the main beneficiaries of her poems, "all yong Gentilwomen" and "al other Maids being in Love," offering them the lesson, "always trie before ye trust." "The Admonition" is a conventionally moral castigation of lust addressed to "Ye Virgins . . . whose hearts as yet with raginge love/most paynfully do boyle" (A5v), warning them of such trickeries as are found in Ovid's *Arte of love*, offering the negative examples of Scylla who betrayed her own father for lust of King Minos; Oenone betrayed by Paris; and Phillis betrayed by Demophon; and the positive example of the "constant, true, and just" Leander who proved his love for Hero many times by swimming the Hellespont. Their love predictably ends, however, with Hero scratching her face and tearing her hair in grief over Leander's death: love is at best evanescent.

Suddenly abandoning the recitation of her classical *exempla*, Whitney concludes the poem with a plain moral presented through the homely emblem of the "little fish," one of whom takes the bait, swallows the hook, and thus quits "the streames/Whereas syr Phebus dayly doth,/shew forth his golden beames" (A8). The folly of the unwary fish contrasts with the wisdom of the cautious fish who "from fisher's hooke did sprint," and "now he pries on every banke,/suspecting styll that pricke:/(For to lye hid in every thing)/wherewith the fishers strike" (A8v). The poet's message is clear: as the fish must beware the fisher's spear, so virgins too must preserve their chastity against "that pricke." Implicit in "The Admonition" is not merely an attitude oriented toward the woman's point of view, but more precisely, to the doctrine defining women as virtuous if they are chaste, pious, constant, and humble, and more practically, careful in the preservation of these virtues.

In a direct style that combines both classical allusion and homely analogy, a suggestion of learning with familiar wisdom, Whitney declares that women are naturally all that convention suggests—simple, virtuous creatures easily betrayed by a wicked world unless they are vigilant. Whitney's morality is itself simple, because she advises women to protect their "vartue" rather than increase their spiritual and moral insight. At base, virtue is virginity; the principal evil is concupiscence.

In these poems, it is difficult to say precisely how Whitney was influenced by decorum, by what was appropriate for a young woman to write about love. Certainly, her concentration on remonstrance and admonition rather than on emotion may have mitigated for herself and for her readers her presumption as a female poet dealing with the most highly charged and commonplace of male poetic subjects. But if advocating virtuous womanhood might be construed as a woman poet's province, so needing no particular apology, in her later work, *A sweet Nosegay*, the assumption of the role of teacher to men and women summons up an elaborate apparatus of authorial apologies and self-deprecation.

In *A sweet Nosegay*, a collection beginning with moral platitudes and ending with a vision of life represented by the worldly city of London, Whitney conveys the doctrine of prevalent sin, human frailty, and godly wariness more directly to a wider audience. In this work, the broad appeal of ballad meter seems entirely appropriate and aligns the poet with a tradition of didactic and religious verse writing.

In her dedication to George Mainwaring, Whitney notes that while she has stepped "into anothers garden for these Flowers ... and though they be of anothers growing, yet considering they be of my owne gathering and makeing," perhaps Mainwaring will protect her from others' spite. Whitney refers here to the original from which she copies her work, Sir Hugh Plat's *The Floures of Philosophie* (1572), comprised of some 883 pseudo-Senecan sentences, what she later calls "*Plat* his Plot."[7] Given the freedom with which sixteenth-century authors borrowed from and imitated one another, Whitney's worries about her extensive cuttings seem exaggerated. In her half-apology to Plat, however, she may be driven by womanly self-consciousness, the fear of presumption, more than by guilt for theft. She imagines Plat raging:

> were she a man,
> that with my Flowers doth brag,
> She well should pay the price, I wolde
> not leave her worth a rag.   (Cv v)

But her high purpose clearly overcame her compunctions, and her dedications emphasize her moral mission. Conceiving of the world in metaphors of "infection" and "pestilent aire," she offers her flowers from a spiritual garden to ward off the evils and temptations besetting her readers. Her address to the reader expands the metaphor of the garden's curative virtues by relating her own spiritual history. Claiming to be "subject unto sicknesse, that/abrode I could not go," she embarks on the familiar topos of searching through various sources for cure and enlightenment, though she "learning lackt." She reads Scripture, but lacks a "Devine" to "resolve mee in such doubts,/as past this head of mine/To understand." She reads histories and discovers human folly past and present; she consults all kinds of poetry—epic, love, and pastoral—in Virgil, Ovid, and Mantuan, but finds she grows weary and "mased." Like the medieval dreamer, or pilgrim, she arises to walk and eventually is guided by "good Fortune" to "*Plat* his Plot," where "fragrant Flowers abound/The smell whereof prevents ech harme,/if yet your selfe be sound" (Avi v). Resting in this medicinal spot for an hour, the poet finally cuts a slip "which might be my defence./In stynking streetes, or lothsome Lanes/which els might mee infect ... " Master Plat's garden becomes a daily habit, and she gathers her own "Nosegay" from his flowers. So unexceptionable a framework for her words might be thought sufficient, but again the poet apologizes for her artistic deficiencies, and notes that her sentences are not in any order, "in a bundle"; yet she claims they will protect her readers' "health" as long as the mind is not already "infected."

Such concern with her readers' spiritual well-being characterizes both Whitney's moral earnestness and the restrictions in subject and form she set for herself as a poet. As her admirer, Thomas Berrie, reports in his praise of the author,

> And for her seconde worke, she thought it meete,
>   sithe Maides with loftie stile may not agree:
> In hoape hereby, somthynge to pleasure thee. ....   (Bv)

Whitney's sense of poetic decorum produces a persona who conforms to a maid's demeanor. She has a meek, devout, charitable mind, and accordingly, her style will not presume to the high and heroic, but express only her humility.

Whitney's choices from Plat range from truisms about friendship to advice not to be covetous, to accept criticism, to love virtuously in youth, to live by truth, to be charitable, and to control the passions. Denunciations of dicing, ambition, and lawyers mingle with advice on relations with friends— to accept their admonitions, to season their blame with praise, to beware of false friends, to try friends before trusting them. As in "The Copy of a letter," and "The Admonition," one must always be wary in dealing with a world full of fickle events and beings:

> Accompt so ever of thy friend,
> as he thy foe may frame
> So beare thee, that in enmytie,
> he thee procure no shame.[8]   (The 56)

Similarly, advice for lovers, while acknowledging love's allure, stresses its folly with many cautions against blows, wounds, and lightness. Whitney finally writes explicitly that "the formost step to wisdom is:/from love to keepe thee free:/The second for to love so close,/that none the same may see" (The 73).

Clearly divided between the godly and the wicked, the poet's world shows the godly being wary, yet charitable; cautious, yet generous; and the wicked being fickle, covetous, and luxurious. If the "vertuous man," fears God, he is safe (The 77) and possesses the chief worldly good, "a well contented mind" (The 81). With his mind on the hereafter, he counts the present day as his last, giving his goods freely to those that deserve them (The 85). By contrast, the wicked man, exemplified by the covetous lawyer, preys upon poor people while he "thrusts/the mony in his purse" (The 104). The wicked may also count on eventual disaster, for when they are "in midst of all their jolitye:/Misfortunes standeth at the dore..." (The 110). Again, Whitney's vision of ultimate divine justice meliorates the difficulties of living in a world beset by human sin and folly. These sentences separate bad from good, negotiate daily life in accord with godliness, with the final goal of arriving at "safety" or salvation.

WHITNEY, DOWRICHE, COLVILLE, SPEGHT

The theme of the poet's own unhappiness, her participation in general human misery, appears again in a series of thirteen "familiar Epistles and friendly Letters by the Auctor: with Replies" appended to the *Nosegay*. In her own letters and in their replies, she appears in the Boethian guise of Fortune's victim, deprived of position and money. Whether or not her grief has an actual autobiographical source—for example, she tells her brother that she has lost her place with "a vertuous Ladye" (Cvi v)—the effect of her complaints confirms her general moral, that it is a fallen, fickle world, well represented by the image of Fortune turning her wheel.[9] To emphasize the doctrine of the *Nosegay*, Whitney composes a special verse epistle for women, a "modest meane for Maides," which is a letter of advice to "two of her yonger Sisters servinge in London," intended to promote their "wealth" and "quietnesse of mynde" (Cvii v). Designing the letter around the working day of the serving girls, she tells them to begin their day with prayer, asking God's protection for themselves and their loved ones,

> so pray you that your ends,
> May be in such a sort,
> as God may pleased bee:
> To live to dye, to dye to live,
> with him eternally.   (Cvii v)

Such living includes doing their assigned duties, and avoiding "all wanton joyes." Recalling her concerns about women's virtue, the poet particularly warns her sisters against those who would "Procure your shame" (Cviii). Their demeanor should not suggest lightness or pride, but they should be modest and "gentyll" to everyone. If wrongdoing should occur, God will avenge.

The sisters should please their employers to the point that after the family retires, the sisters should watch and ward, caring for the family's goods and "safety":

> See that their Plate be safe,
> and that no Spoone do lacke,

> See Dores and Windowes bolted fast
> for feare of any wrack.   (D)

The day should end as it began, with prayer and thankfulness to God.

This commonplace advice indicates how Whitney's poetical voice serves or evolves from her ethics. Her subject, whether it is responsibility for the worldly goods of the "rulers" or concern for the chastity of her sisters, dominates her poetical invention.[10] As in "The Copy of a letter," Whitney's interest seems to lie more in her mission than in developing her poetic voice, which is, after all, quite satisfactory for conveying her doctrine. Only in the last part of her work, the "Wyll and Testament," does she grow as a poet, moving tentatively toward figurative complexity.

In this imaginary "Wyll and Testament," the poet "fayneth as she would die," and names London the executor of her legacies. While her subject probably has roots in Whitney's own life and observations, her interest is neither in auto-biography nor in a naturalistic rendition of sixteenth-century London. The "Wyll" is a vision of worldly life in the *de contemptu mundi* tradition, for London, the "famous Citie" is also the City of Man, which the poet remembers for its "great cruelnes:/That never once a help wold find,/to ease me in distres." But the spirit in which one should leave the world and make a will is not anger but "perfect love and charitie," and this, the poet claims, motivates her to consider the ap-propriate gifts for the citizens of the city. In godly terms, such a persona sees the world clearly for what it is, and so takes her leave willingly and freely.

Doling out her bequests, the poet again recalls the prev-alence of lust, the fear of "infection," and dejection over worldly reversals. But in this poem, Whitney's persona is a seer, allowing her to view earthly woes with a detachment approaching comedy. Her theme and her authorial stance seem to have liberated the poet in Whitney, giving her a new range of tones and even a penchant for satire.

The beginning of the "Wyll" is central to the poet's mean-

ing, for it implies the disparity between the earthly city and
the heavenly one. She echoes the traditional words of departure from the things of the world, a release that allows her
to treat them with the distance of comedy:

> I whole in body, and in minde,
>> but very weake in Purse:
> Doo make, and write my Testament
>> for feare it wyll be wurse.

This turns her attention to a wholly serious matter, the world
to come: commending her soul to God and her body to the
grave, she hopes that they will be reunited at Judgment "to
dwell for aye in joye:/Whereas I trust to see my Friends/
releast, from all annoy" (E3v). Her will, then, is made with
this end in mind.

There follows what at first seems to be a colorful hodge-
podge of bequests to the citizens of the city: butchers and
bakers to provide their food; wool- and linen-makers, gold-
smiths and tailors to provide their clothes; apothecaries, phy-
sicians, and surgeons to heal their ills, all presented with
concrete details of location. But noticing first that churches
occupy one and a half lines, while all the material goods and
pleasures of life appear over the next 100 lines; and second,
that the largest single section of 59 lines is devoted to prisons,
accompanied by a description of her parental Smithfield
which includes the Spitle, Bedlam, and Bridewel, we are
compelled to consider the significance of the poet's organization and presentation of her material. Most notably, Whitney divides her poem along class lines, beginning with a
satirical look at the conspicuous consumption of the lords,
ladies, and gentlefolk. They already possess jewels, plate,
"French Ruffes, high Purles, Gorgets and Sleeves," and if
they desire any other "needeful knacke," "I by the Stoks have
left a Boy,/wil aske you what you lack" (E4). Ironically, a
market stands where once there had been stocks, underlining
Whitney's theme about material goods, but it is the disparity
between rich and poor which provides the true criticism of
such spending. The rich may find apothecaries to cater to

their "daynty mouthes, and stomacks weake" with junkets, but when she turns to "the poore," Whitney can think only of leaving something to the prisons. The lines on the prisons, the Counter, Newgate, Fleet, and Ludgate, and the mention of Holborne hill convey images of a world beset by gamblers, thieves, and murderers as well as by disease, unjust laws, and corrupt officials:

> The Newgate once a Monthe shal have
> a session for his share:
> Least being heapt, Infection might
> procure a further care.
> And at those sessions some shal skape,
> with burning nere the Thumb:
> And afterward to beg their fees,
> tyll they have got the some.   (E5v)

Life may teem here, but it does so without lifting its head above the daily, material demands of food, drink, and shelter. In this London, the rich indulge themselves to excess, and the poor decline into misery; both are spiritually bankrupt. By contrast, the poet gives orders for her own death and burial, significantly asking that there be no earthly markers, no stone, no bells, no feast, but instructing, "Rejoyce in God that I am gon,/out of this vale so vile." Satirically, she offers London the aid of Fortune in executing her will, for Fortune rules the dispensation of all worldly things which fill the City of Man, and her mutability reflects the inconsequentiality of these goods.[11]

In the "Wyll and Testament" Whitney moves beyond verse circumscribed in subject and form by a cautious and apologetic persona to the poetry of open commitment to her cause. Whereas "The Copy of a letter" and "The Admonition" were conventional warnings to young women to protect their virtue against lust, in the "Wyll and Testament" the poet implicitly asks all Christians to examine their worldliness in the face of death. The breadth of vision in the last poem demands a poetic persona only glimpsed in the early poems—a persona whose language is unconventionally feminine in assuming

many tones, from comic to pious, ironic, acerbic, and apocalyptic. In other words, Whitney begins to redefine how a
woman may write by addressing a wide audience without
apology. Her goal is still to teach her readers, but the lively,
metaphorical description of the city suggests that here she
thinks more as a poet creating images than as a preacher
merely using verse as a convenient way to express exempla
and platitudes. Like the prose writers of the early Reformation, Whitney's art evolved from her vocation as a learned
and virtuous woman aiding the godly.

ANNE DOWRICHE (fl. 1589)

Her belief that she too had a vital message to impart to her
readers motivated Anne Dowriche to compose and publish
*The French Historie: A Lamentable Discourse of three of the
chiefe, and most famous bloodie broiles that have happened in
France for the Gospell of Jesus Christ* (1589). Basing her poem
on the English translation by Thomas Timme of Jean de
Serres's *Commentaries* on the French civil wars, Dowriche
follows the arch-Protestant design of that work to condemn
the Catholics and vindicate and comfort the Reformers.[12]
Beginning with her dedication to her brother, Pearse Edge-
combe, Dowriche's pose throughout is merely as a conduit
for the godly matter of her source. She asks him to consider
if not the work's worth, then "the will of the worker," to
read it for the matter, if not the manner, which "I confesse
it is base and scarce worth the seeing." Deprecating her writing talent, she admits, nevertheless, to a great pleasure in
"collecting and disposing" her work, and trusts that if her
brother does not find similar pleasure, he will "remember I
pray, that it is a womans doing."[13]

Like Whitney, Dowriche downplays herself as a writer in
order to emphasize the matter, attempting to appear as a
teacher concerned for the souls of her readers rather than as
a conscious artist. Opening with text from Paul, "Let al things
be done unto edifying," she dedicates herself to the reader's
spiritual health: "my onlie purpose in collecting and framing

this worke, was to edifie, comfort and stirre up the godlie mindes unto care, Watchfulnesse, Zeale, and firventnesse in the cause of Gods truth . . ." (A3v). To do this, she has chosen "singular examples" of Satan's action in the world against the godly as well as presented the "Picture of all the morall vertues most livelie described, in the strange patience, the godlie perseverance, the comfortable orations, sweete speeches, and the constant and famous endings of these sacred Martires" (A3v-A4). The familiar division between God's elect and Satan's forces informs Dowriche's view of history, so much so that, as she here promises, the Devil will actually appear on the scene to hold two councils with the hated French Catholic faction—the House of Guise and Catherine de Medici—in order to plot the downfall of the Reformers.

Despite her unimpeachable desire to edify her readers, Dowriche does at least suggest her literary vocation when she offers three specific reasons for writing her history in verse:

> First, for mine owne exercise, being a learner in that facultie; Secondlie, to restore againe some credit if I can unto Poetrie, having been defaced of late so many waies by wanton vanities. Thirdlie, for the more noveltie of the thing, and apt facilitie in disposing the matter framed to the better liking of some mens fantasies, because the same Storie in effect is alreadie translated into English prose. (A4)

Modestly, Dowriche presents herself as an apprentice poet, but as one who wishes to retrieve poetry from secular abuse. Here she grossly underplays her ambitious and largely successful undertaking to transpose historical narrative into a form that would both teach and delight her coreligionists. At the end of her address to the reader, she cautiously predicts a future for herself as a poet when she promises more works if this one be well accepted. A double message thus emerges from Dowriche's preface: hesitantly and modestly, she presents herself as a poet; yet her artistic goals are no less than to write God's truth, to regenerate poetry, and to move a wide audience with the power of poetry. Certainly her fiery descriptions of the Catholic persecution of the godly would inflame her audience, while details of their eventual punishment would confirm her readers' sense of their own righteousness. But her insistence that her powerful subject alone—not her own skillful treatment of it—will move her readers masks her assumption of the role of poet. The efficacy of her poem, she claims, derives from the action between subject and reader, as if unmediated by the poet:

> To speake without vaine glorie, I thinke assuredlie, that there is not in this forme anie thing extant which is more forceable to procure comfort to the afflicted, strength to the weake, courage to the faint hearted, and patience unto them that are persecuted, than this little worke, if it be diligentlie read and well considered. (A4)

Earnestly, she asks other poets to write only of "the glorie of God, the edifying of his Church, and the salvation of the soules of Gods chosen," thus ensuring their literary immortality (A4v). Perhaps this was an expression of her own wishes.

Dowriche structures *The French Historie* to reflect her poetic self-repression, for she invents two personae, a male author and a "godlie French exile" who bears witness to the three events of French history that constitute Dowriche's evidence against the Catholics and in favor of the Reformers—"The winning of St James his Streete, 1557," the "martyrdom" of Councilor Annas Burgeus, 1559, and the marriage of Margaret, sister of Charles IX, which was shortly followed by the massacre of the Huguenots in August 1572. To transfer her role to a male persona mitigates once more her presumption and completely disguises the knowledge and ability of a woman to write so public a narrative poem.

This male persona, while walking in the woods, overhears the French exile "within a bushie dale" mourning his country's fall because of the persecution of true religion. Declaring the disintegration of the commonwealth to follow upon faithlessness, the exile apostrophizes France in a variation of *ubi sunt*:

Where is the mutuall love that Prince and people had?
Where is the noble Union, that makes the Countrie glad?
Where is the due regard that Princes ought to have;
From all the bands of tyrannie their people for to
    save?   (1 v)

Striking one of the poem's central themes, the exile asserts
that despite present woe, "God will revenge our case,/And
for his chosen when he list provide a dwelling place" (2v).
Behind this lies Dowriche's conviction that Elizabeth's England should be a godly commonwealth, but these very ideas
may have moved her to conceal her feminine presence as
inappropriate for public affairs. Through the exile, Dowriche
characterizes a reformed England as "this pleasant Ile," a
country "which hast the truth established with peace and
perfect rest." The Frenchman subsequently agrees to tell his
story "in verse" to the "Englishman" while enjoying his hospitality. At the end of his narrative, the French exile prays
that England may never deviate from "the Truth," and that
Queen Elizabeth will continue to be a "chiefe Pastor" who
will discover "and hunt with perfect hate/The Popish hearts
of fained frends before it be too late" (37v). France stands as
a warning to the English godly.

   Written in couplets of iambic hexameter and iambic hep-
tameter, the narrative itself dramatically, if unrelentingly,
stresses the doctrine of Catholic evil and Protestant godliness.
Dowriche most successfully brings alive the *Commentaries* and
simultaneously refutes her assumed poetic absence by in-
venting "orations" at key moments for the main participants,
thus making immediate her message to the godly. Dowriche
merely notes in her preface to the reader, "Many of these
orations that are here fully and amplie expressed, were in the
French Commentaries but onely in substance lightly touched,
and the summe set downe without amplifying the circum-
stance, and yet heere is no more set downe, than there is
signified" (A4). Dowriche humbly omits her creative initiative, her own imaginative reconstruction of the moment and
the character, at times considerably amplified from her source.

In the history of Annas Burgeus, councilor to Henry III, for example, Dowriche invents a brief, potent speech for the Devil, inciting the king to eradicate the Reformers' opposition:

> Your Senate favours truth too much, your Judges too
>   remisse;
> They are not sharpe inough to shred appearing ill,
> They suffer impes of *Luthers* sect too much to have
>   their will.   (9v)

Burgeus, in turn, strongly exhorts the king to join the godly:

> What Giant can withstand of *Truth* the piercing might?
> What earthlie force of shining Sunne at noone can
>   quench the light?
> Then leave to love these Popish lies, let whorish Babel
>   fall.   (11v)

Building a dramatic scene from the *Commentaries*, Dowriche stars Burgeus as a Protestant hero speaking the "truth" at the moment of greatest danger from hostile authorities.

Likewise, she makes the Catholic faction irredeemably wicked as they plot the massacre of the Huguenots. Dowriche creates a speech for Catherine de Medici, the queen mother, to echo the worst of Elizabethan villains, Machiavelli.[14] As a "divelish sorceresse," Catherine urges her son, Henry III, to seize the moment when the Huguenot Admiral, Gaspar de Coligny, lies wounded, and the Prince of Condé is in their power:

> What thogh ye do forswear? what thogh ye break your
>   faith?
> What thogh ye promise life, and yet repay it with their
>   death?
> Is this so great a fault? Naie, naie, no fault at all:
> For this we learne we ought to doo, if such occasions
>   fall. ...
> Plucke up therefore your sprites, and play your manlie
>   parts,

Let neither feare nor faith prevaile to dant your
    warlike harts.
What shame is this that I (a woman by my kinde)
Neede thus to speake, or passe you men in valure of the
    minde?
For heere I doo protest, if I had bene a man;
I had myself before this time this murder long began.

                                  (23v-24)

Dramatically imagining what is only briefly hinted in the
Commentaries, Dowriche makes the queen into a vivid Popish
villain, a prototype Lady Macbeth taunting men to possess
her own warlike courage and to embark on ambitious action.
The queen mother's villainy is at the opposite extreme from
the rather colorless, pious "women of great parentage" whom
Dowriche briefly sketches in the affair of "St James his
Streete." In this memorable fictional appearance, Catherine
de Medici may be the first female character created by a
woman writer of this period. That Dowriche chose to develop
a villain indicates her nascent dramatic instinct, and that she
did it in a religious work suggests once again how pious
writing gave women the opportunity to develop their craft.

Fervently committed to the Reformed church, Dowriche
composed 2,400 lines of verse for the cause, but she still
declined to call herself anything but an apprentice poet. To
emerge from behind the mask of feminine inability did not
suit her understanding of her mission. Perhaps to balance her
exempla drawn from recent public events and her open admonition to the entire country, Dowriche decided to maintain
a strictly modest authorial stance.

All the classic signs of female authorship mark the work
of these two pioneering poets, Isabella Whitney and Anne
Dowriche. In Whitney's case, we find an apprenticeship characterized by apology and a careful selection of material appropriate to her sex. Only in the "Wyll and Testament" did
she more daringly try her wings, indicating how she had
developed to the point of thinking poetically. Like Whitney,
Dowriche deprecates her work even as she alludes to the
satisfaction it gives her, and the mask of a male persona seems

her solution to the problem of assuming the role of poet and historian for her sect. Not until the later work of Elizabeth Colville do we find a Reformist poet who, perhaps truly benefiting from the gradual establishment of women as poets, sheds many of her predecessors' fears and circumlocutions.

Elizabeth Colville, Lady Culros (fl. 1603)

Celebrated by her fellow Scots Presbyterians as a "faithfull and vertuous Ladie," as "famous for her piety as for her Dream anent her spiritual condition, which she put in verse, and was by other published"; and as a woman "unwearied in religious exercises," who could also "delite in poesie," Elizabeth Colville demonstrated both her religiosity and her poetic skill in her poem of 480 lines, *Ane Godlie Dreame, Compylit in Scottish Meter* (1603).[15] Its popularity appears to have warranted ten further editions between 1606 and 1737, indicating how accurately Colville expressed the faith of her sect: an almost overwhelming sense of human depravity coupled with the infinitely sustaining mercy of God which will guide the chosen to immortal life. Significantly for women's poetry, Colville does not hesitate to establish her persona at the center of the poem, whether as poet, Christian pilgrim, recipient of God's grace, exemplum, or teacher.

The poem is in three movements: the first ten stanzas record the poet's affliction and misery; the next thirty stanzas narrate her dream in which Christ appears to guide the pilgrim through suffering to the heavenly city; the last twenty stanzas contain her exhortation to the godly to learn from her dream and to prepare for their end.[16] By far the most vivid, accomplished poetry is that of the dream itself where the full force of Colville's faith guides her images and dialogue surely and movingly, and no doubt assures the success of her final homily to the faithful.

Colville's pilgrim persona begins with conventional, yet quite strenuous, declamations of her misery, based both upon her own sin and the vice of the "wretchit warld" in general. Piteously, she cries to God in vivid apostrophe to "mak haist" (stanza iv) and fulfill his promise to come: "Lord Jesus cum and saif thy awin Elect" (stanza vi). Her emblematic tears and the release of prayer lead her to sleep and to dream, where she again finds herself praying and longing for succor.[17]

To her appears "Ane Angel bricht, with visage schyning cleir" (stanza xii), who bids her "ryse up" and offers to be her guide (stanza xv).[18] The angel identifies himself as "thy God for quhom thou sicht sa sair" (stanza xvi), and further elucidates in thoroughly scriptural language:

> I am the way, I am the treuth, and lyfe,
> I am thy spous that brings thee store of grace;
> I am thy luif quhom thou sald faine embrace,
> I am thy joy, I am thy rest and peace;
> (stanza xvii)[19]

Prepared to begin her pilgrimage, and casting herself as a wise virgin meeting her bridegroom, the poet declares herself ready to follow Christ through all the pain and torment that precedes arrival at "that pleasant place" (stanza xix).

The subsequent journey, vividly expressed in images of an unyielding physical landscape, conveys the struggles of the soul to overcome worldly afflictions:

> Throw waters greit wee war compellit to wyde,
> Quhilk war sa deip that I was lyke to drowne;
> Sumtyme I sank, bot yit my gracious gyde
> Did draw me out half deid, and in ane sowne.
> In woods maist wyld, and far fra anie towne,
> Wee thristit throw, the breirs together stak;
> I was sa waik their strength did ding me down,
> That I was forcit for feir to flie aback.
> (stanza xxiii)[20]

In contrast to these heavily alliterative, forceful lines is the sudden vision offered her of the heavenly city, a representation of the aspirations of the godly soul to immortality:

> I luikit up unto that Castell fair,
> Glistring lyke gold, and schyning silver bricht:
> The staitlie toures did mount above the air,
> Thay blindit mee, thay cuist sa greit ane licht.
> (stanza xxvii)[21]

To this shimmering sight the pilgrim eagerly rushes, only to be rebuked for running off without guidance before her afflictions are ended. Still she must journey through hell itself (clearly distinguished from that "Papists purging place"—stanza xxxiii—which Christ forcefully denounces), a black pit "most full of smock, and flaming fyre most fell."[22] Here, Christ encourages the pilgrim to "play the man" (stanza xxxv) as she walks through the fire and torments. Thus glancing at her persona's womanly weakness which now needs manly courage, Colville brings the dreamer safely through "past the paine," at which time she awakes.

The last part of the poem aligns Colville squarely with the preaching poets, for she too is moved to write to aid the salvation of the chosen. Expounding on her pilgrimage metaphor, "Let us learne," she exhorts her readers, and "Prepair your selves," for after suffering comes the reward, "The Land of rest, quhen endit is your strife" (stanza xliv). Specifically following the example of her dreamer, the godly must suffer "the Thornie cairs of this deceitfull lyfe. . . . And thocht ye fall, yit ly not loytring still:/Bot call on Christ, to help you in your need . . ." (stanza xlvi).[23] To avoid pride, to follow Christ "with humbill heart" (stanza lii), to recognize that "your paine is short, your joy sall never end" (stanza liii) is Colville's essential sermon, which she concludes with thanksgiving and praise:

> Lift up your hearts, and praises to him sing,
> Triumph for joy, your enemies ar keilde.
> (stanza lv)[24]

The exultation of heaven's bliss is modulated only slightly by the injunction that "the tyme is neare, be sober, watch and pray . . ." (stanza lix), but the poem ends in the deep affirmation of God's infinite power to save and defend "his awin"[25] (stanza lx).

Ane Godlie Dreame, written with considerable poetic confidence, freely allows the poet to appear as the archetypal godly Christian, journeying through life, experiencing worldly affliction before receiving God's grace to overcome her trouble and entering into the state of blessedness. Rather than efface herself or apologize, the poet creates a persona through whose visionary experience she establishes a strong guiding presence in the poem as witness, example, and teacher. Although her mission is no less urgent than Whitney's or Dowriche's, Colville seems to have trusted her material to legitimize her as a poet as well as a preacher. By using the convention of the dream, she endowed her teaching with the authority of divine vision and authorized her public stance by her claim to inward revelation. Colville's tacit assumption of her poet's role through her pious calling distinguishes her both from Whitney and Dowriche who explicitly compensate for their gender, and also from Rachel Speght, who more openly affirms the role of women as spiritual guides for the "common benefit."

Colville's choice of a pilgrim persona for a Christian poem is not surprising, and yet it also bears an interesting relation to the other works studied in this chapter. Whitney's persona in *A sweet Nosegay* searches for a cure, and in the "Wyll and Testament," she explores the earthly city of London in preparation for her final journey. Dowriche's first persona walks in the woods and finds a witness to the faith who takes him on a spiritual journey to France to reveal God's truth fighting evil. Coincidentally or not, each poet chooses a version of the pilgrimage, the journey over a rocky way to reach the heavenly city. This may only indicate that each poet adapts commonplace Christian typology; but it may also suggest that the spiritual quest is an idea at the heart of women's poetry, involving a search for Christian identity and poetic authority. In her allegory of the search for knowledge, Rachel Speght suggests that the spiritual journey may actually generate women's poetry.

RACHEL SPEGHT (fl. 1617–1621)

Rachel Speght's self-consciousness as a literary woman manifests itself both in the subject of her first work, *A Mouzell for Melastomus* (1617), a defense of women written in direct response to Joseph Swetnam's *Araignment of Lewde, idle, fro-*

– 110 –

ward, and unconstant Women and in the persona of her second,
a poem, *Mortalities Memorandum, with a Dreame Prefixed*
(1621).[26] In the dream portion of this second work, Speght
presents an allegorized version of the struggles of an avowedly
pious woman to gain access to knowledge, whether earthly
or divine. Here Speght composes a countermyth to Eden in
which, instead of following Eve's desire for forbidden knowledge, the poet seeks to banish her own ignorance, find knowledge of good, and use it for the spiritual profit of her godly
audience. As a prose polemicist, Speght had devoted herself
to the cause of women, but as a poet, she commits herself to
the public role of ministering to the souls of all her Christian
readers.

Dedicating *Mortalities Memorandum* to her godmother, the
"vertuous Gentlewoman," Mrs. Marie Moundford, Speght
immediately points to the crucial distinction between women
creating in the private sphere and in the public sphere, and
cites the desire for public good as the most valid reason for
moving from one to the other: "Amongst diversitie of motives
to induce the divulging of that to publique view, which was
devoted to private Contemplation, none is worthy to precede
desire of common benefit."[27] To save souls in the hour of
death, declares Speght, is the only motive for the publication
of this present work. The considerably less controversial nature of *Mortalities Memorandum* results perhaps from her
"having bin toucht with the censures" of "criticall Readers"
of *A Mouzell for Melastomus* and her attendant recognition of
"that apothegme which doth affirme Censure to be inevitable
to a publique act" (A2v). Indeed, Speght's writing career
measures a woman writer's sensitive response to adverse criticism, for she seems to reply to censure by withdrawing from
the open battle of the "woman question," adopting instead
the proven strategy of redeeming Eve by less direct tactics.
Now she aims not for an audience of "ignorant Dunces," but
for the "courteous Reader" who will correct her faults "with
judgement" and approve "what pleaseth thy Minde" (A3v).
Revealing a developing sense of her own literary vocation,
Speght, more than any writer thus far, explicitly ponders the

central issues for a woman selecting and addressing her audience.

As we have seen, the continuous attempts to please, to write what is appropriate, and to avoid censure derive from the woman writer's sense that by being publicly articulate, she simultaneously represents and endangers her sex, and that in the public eye, she must actively prove her virtue. In Speght's case, her self-consciousness results in the creation of a new myth of woman's intellectual experience, which is directly connected to her pious mission to save souls.

The psychodrama that Speght presents in "The Dreame"— a device that objectifies her experience by placing it in an essentially literary rather than a personal context—details the progress, or pilgrimage, from natural ignorance to divine knowledge. At the beginning, the poet describes herself as "disconsolate," stricken by "griefe," "sadnesse," "disease," and the "maladie" of "Ignorance." To the figure of Thought who suddenly appears, she describes her state as not knowing bad from good, and continually falling into unnamed "evils," and she begs Thought "to tell me how my cure I may obtaine" (3). Thought declares herself unable to help in this case and recommends that the poet seek Experience to whom Age will direct her. Experience immediately prescribes the aid of Knowledge, but only the good sort which "by labour is attained," and she in turn directs the poet to *Eruditions* garden" (4), to which she will be guided by Industrie. Unlike Eve, who merely plucked her knowledge from a tree, the poet must labor for hers, guided by worthy Experience rather than by Satan. Yet, a counterforce to this positive progress appears in the figure of Disswasion, who fills the poet with perplexities and fear by offering the hindrances of "dulnesse, and my memories defect;/The difficultie of attaining lore,/My time, and sex, with many others more" (4). To her defense spring Industrie, who promises to cut away all obstacles by encouraging the poet's own diligent labor (*Labor omnia vincet!*) and Truth who denies the poet's sex is a hindrance. Beginning with Biblical authority, Truth cites Paul that both men and women possess the three faculties of "the mind, the will, the power" (5), and that God could not have given women intellect in vain, since "All parts and faculties were made for use." Moving on to examples, Truth names the precedents of Cleobulina, Demophila, and Tilesilla for poetry, Cornelia for eloquence, Hypatia for astronomy, Aspatia for rhetoric, and Areta for art.[28] Turning to the poet, she exhorts her to keep a constant mind to forestall Disswasion, for if she remains steady and industrious in her purpose, she will gain the knowledge she desires.

The climax of "The Dreame," expressed in its most lyric, exalted language, is the poet's arrival in *"Eruditions* garden," where, simply, she learns of matters human and divine:

Where being come, *Instructions* pleasant ayre
Refresht my senses, which were almost dead,
And fragrant flowers of sage and fruitfull plants,
Did send sweete savours up into my head;
And taste of science appetite did move,
To augment *Theorie* of things above.

There did the harmonie of those sweete birds,
(Which higher soare with Contemplations wings,
Then barely with a superficiall view,
Denote the value of created things.)
Yeeld such delight as made me to implore,
That I might reape this pleasure more and more.   (7)

The joyous release of long pent-up frustrations recalls the drive and desire of generations of women before her to know, to reach the restricted source of power. And most notably, the poet's fulfillment occurs in a garden, a counter-Eden where she partakes only of "good" knowledge, the very knowledge, Speght reveals, by which God confers essential humanity. Truth tells the poet, "by it Gods image man doth beare,/Without it he is but a humane shape,/Worse than the Devill . . ." (8). In other words, as the humanists had always agreed, to deprive women of learning only makes them more vulnerable to ill, for "by vertue of it evils are withstood;/*The minde without it is not counted good.*" But going further than the humanists ever did in women's cause, Speght contends even more specifically that "True *knowledge*," "the mother of faith, hope and love" leads to immortality: " 'Tis life eternall God and Christ to *know*." As Eve's Eden introduced death, Speght's new garden leads to Christ and salvation.

But despite its vital role, the lifelong pursuit of knowledge cannot be an occupation for this poet, for without detail, she recounts, "some occurrence called me away." Now she must "rest content with that I had,/Which was but little," and without hope for continuing her study, "I my time must otherwayes bestow" (9). Quietly, she accepts her destiny outside of the realms of thought and scholarship. The history of uncounted women authors exists in these few poignant lines describing the physical and mental circumscription seemingly imposed by the circumstances of sex.

Referring to her previous work, *A Mouzell for Melastomus*, Speght alludes to it as an accomplishment of her brief time of freedom, although she also acknowledges the criticism she received, particularly from Ester Sowernam, whose work, *Ester hath hang'd Haman* continued her own response to Swetnam, to be shortly followed by Constantia Munda's *A Soppe for Cerberus*. While she does call Esther Sowernam a "selfe-conceited Creature" (having a high opinion of her own qualities), Speght modestly accepts criticism and deprecates her own "weake exployt." Speght nevertheless cites her work and that of her successors in the defence of "*Eves* sex" as examples of how knowledge contributes to the proper restoration of women to their full humanity. Admission into the ranks of learning not only redeems the individual soul, but authorizes the rehabilitation of the entire discredited sex.

Such authentication of her knowledge leads Speght to her present task in the common good of all believers, a poetic *memento mori* conceived during a dream-vision of Death who slew "With pearcing dart my mother deare" (10). Waking, she finds her mother is indeed dead "though of her life it could not her bereave,/Sith shee in glorie lives with Christ for aye." Accordingly, to show Death for what it is, the poet proceeds with *Mortalities Memorandum* for the "profit" of her readers.

To trace the genesis of Death in the world, Speght must of course return to the Eden story. Following her evocation of a redeemed *"Eruditions* garden," in which a woman may truly learn, her characterization of Eden is brief, perhaps to avoid the delicate issue of Eve's guilt. Compressing all the historically troublesome parts of Genesis into two lines— "And Sathan thinking this their good too great,/Suggests the Woman, shee the man, they eate,"—Speght concludes, "Thus eating both, they both did joyntly sinne" (13). Death enters the world because both Adam and Eve displeased God, and Speght barely hints that Eve may have started the trouble by listening to Satan. Having redeemed Eve in her "Dreame," she cannot dwell on Eve's traditional role, even if the rest of her poem relies on received doctrine.

While *A Mouzell for Melastomus* and *Mortalities Memorandum* seem to be very different works—the first a prose polemic championing woman's character, and the second a poem describing Death from the traditional Christian perspective celebrating resurrection and immortality—together they reveal in the author's pose and relation to her writing the growth of her consciousness as a woman artist. By responding to Joseph Swetnam's attack, by making woman her subject, Speght courageously assumed that such an assault should be faced openly and refuted openly, but in the resulting work, her topical limits and rhetoric are in fact established by the male author to whom she responds. As radical as this work may seem in publicly defending women, its real roots are in the reactionary language and ideas of Swetnam himself. But in "The Dreame," Speght's garden myth justifies woman's right to knowledge as part of her human inheritance from God, crucial to her individual salvation. As a preamble to the traditional doctrine of *Mortalities Memorandum*, "The Dreame" firmly includes women in the poetic search for salvation.

Speght herself uses her laboriously won knowledge, even if it be "little," for the "common benefit" of all who face death, that is, of all humanity. Her poetry, addressed now to a wider audience, entrenches her, without apology, as a minister to and a teacher of her flock of readers. Contrasting earth with heaven, she emphasizes the "sicknesse, want, and woe," the "maladie" here with the "melodie" there. Joyously, she creates the heavenly scene:

> There Saints are Crown'd with matchlesse majestie,
> Invested with eternall roabes of glorie;
> There Sunne doth shine, and suffers no eclips,
> Earths chiefest joyes are vaine, and transitorie.
> Unconstant, fading, fickle, and unsure,
> But heavens pleasures permanent endure.   (18)

In her ministerial role, Speght retreats from the woman question as defined by men, and instead conceives of herself fully contributing to the Reformed effort to awaken humankind to its plight and potential salvation—in its way, a more radical role to assume.

To juxtapose these four poets is not to claim that they constituted a school of feminine poetry; they wrote over the course of fifty years and no external evidence exists to show that they knew each other's work. They have in common the pilgrimage metaphor, suggesting that their piety was both traditional and articulated in images of searching. The conventions of feminine virtue do seem to have affected their writing, since assuming the role of poet seemed so audacious a step to at least three of these poets that they went to great lengths to defend themselves. In all four cases, piety drove the poet, so that her learning and virtue would serve the "common benefit" of the godly.

Is there evidence of evolution, both for the individual and for the group? Unsurprisingly, they write better the more they write; surprisingly in so small a group, each poet surpasses her predecessor. Whitney's "Wyll and Testament" is superior to her earlier poetry; Dowriche's orations are more able than her narrative, and as doctrinaire as *The French Historie* may be, its creator unleashed a marvelous poetic imagination; Colville's visions surpass her admonitions, and her confident assumption of the role of preacher banishes all apologies. Speght takes overall precedence as a skilled versifier and convincing mythmaker—the combination at the heart of all good poetry.

Such distinctions in poetic ability may not be a chronological coincidence. Time would allow women to evolve poetically because once there was one published woman poet, other women would not only start practicing, they would realize that women could be poets without sacrificing their character. For the significant difference between Whitney and Speght is not poetic smoothness but poetic confidence, the feeling that despite continuing cultural roadblocks, writing pious poetry was an important vocation that actually expressed feminine virtue.

Of course, these were not the only women to write poetry during this period. The next four chapters will consider works that appeared between 1590 and 1621, written by women who not only continued to develop as poets but also to expand the topics and forms appropriate to women's poetry.

PART II

"Mighty towers and
strong bastions"

FIVE

THE DIVINE POET:
MARY SIDNEY,
COUNTESS OF PEMBROKE

*A*s THE FIRST woman in this period who sought a clear literary vocation and who, as a poet, far surpassed any of her predecessors, Mary Sidney, Countess of Pembroke (1561–1621), presents a turning point in the development of the woman writer. While her piety and her commitment to the Reformed cause ally her closely to figures like Katherine Parr or Anne Dowriche, her devotion to poetry and her studied development as a literary artist distinguish her from her precursors and contemporaries. And while the didactic spirit of writers like Whitney and Dowriche brought them apologetically into the domain of public poetry, with each succeeding work, Mary Sidney addressed an ever-widening circle of readers, beginning with private translations, proceeding to an elegy for her brother, Philip Sidney, and concluding with her translation of the Psalms, a text intended narrowly for the devotions of court and queen, and more broadly for the comfort of all the godly. Yet, despite her considerable growth as a poet and despite her widened audience, these "good works" still characterize the Countess of Pembroke as a learned and virtuous woman writer aware of her limitations.

Mary Sidney's most significant achievement was her evolution as a lyric poet. Either because the education of most women did not encourage imitation and composition of lyric poetry or because their weighty subject matter seemed best expressed in plain style, Mary Sidney was the first to embark on a course of imitation and experimentation which led her through varied personae and a wide range of lyrical forms. That she in particular should have progressed beyond the ubiquitous ballad meter or rhymed couplets is probably the result of a combination of circumstances: her talents; her education in French and Italian; a familial environment of humanist parents and two literary brothers, one among the most accomplished writers of his time; the interest of her class in lyric poetry; and the circumstances of her life which led her particularly to the lyrical topics of praise and elegy. While her writing career begins and ends with translation, her final version of the Psalms far surpasses the ingenious literalness of her first efforts in conception, execution, and effect. In the process, she established herself as both a divine poet and a fresh voice for the Reformed cause.

Few writers unwaveringly improve from one work to the next, and where accurate dating is problematic, an overall assessment is even more difficult. With such cautions in mind, we may find in the *oeuvre* of the Countess of Pembroke, if not an absolute progress from apprenticeship to mastery, a clear series of trials in form and voice on the countess's three related interests, the godly life, the relationship between poetry and divine truth, and the role of the pious female poet. Her works include three translations: the doctrinaire prose of Philippe de Mornay's *A Discourse of Life and Death*; Robert Garnier's play, *Antonius*, and Petrarch's *Triumph of Death*; an elegy on her brother, Philip Sidney, "The Dolefull Lay of Clorinda"; the pastoral dialogue, "Thenot and Piers in Praise of Astraea"; two long dedicatory poems, one to Queen Elizabeth, one to Philip Sidney; and her greatest and most self-defining work, a metrical version of the Psalms. Each reveals how she worked to articulate her piety, first by experimenting with the works of others—by ventriloquizing—and then by developing her own literary personae. In the Psalms, she seems to have found the voice most suited to her religious and poetic vocation.

In recent years, Mary Sidney has received renewed critical attention; her works have been reprinted and studied more seriously. Many old assumptions about the all-pervasive influence of her brother, the "school" at Wilton, and the countess's patronage have been corrected, and have given way to appraisals based not on dedicatory imagery but on research into her life and work.[1] This chapter will clarify her writing career by showing how her evolution as a poet relates to the general development of Renaissance women writers.

What has probably most distorted our view of Mary Sidney is the influence of her brother, Philip Sidney. Digging through the accretions of legend, gossip, and speculation that have dogged the Countess of Pembroke's reputation over the last four centuries is particularly difficult because of the ever-present shadow of his greater legend.[2] As in the case of Margaret Roper, we find a woman writer who has been associated at every turn with a close relative, a beloved man who himself represents an important ideology of life and literature. While the influence of her brother is undeniable, Mary Sidney developed intellectually apart from him, unlike Margaret Roper whose father supervised her closely. Only in the late 1570s, as adults, were Mary and Philip reunited. Indeed, her literary apprenticeship may owe more to her humanist parents than to her brother, particularly because of the different education, expectations, and environment accorded to men and women of their class.

Mary Sidney was seven years younger than her brother. When he left for Shrewsbury School, she was a toddler under three, and his subsequent education at Christ Church, Oxford and on his continental travels would not include or even parallel her experiences at home. From her work, we know that Mary Sidney was fluent in French and Italian, and these she may have learned from the tutors of her other brothers, Robert and Thomas. A letter from Sir Henry Sidney to Lady Cecil incidentally recommending to her his French tutor, John Tassel, suggests the presence of resident tutors who might have taught the daughters as well as the sons in the Sidney home.[3] Leaving home in 1575 to attend Queen Elizabeth at court and on progress, as her mother had before her, Mary Sidney would lead a life quite different from her brother's, now burgeoning into that of the diplomat, scholar, and Protestant partisan. On April 21, 1577, she was married to Henry Herbert, a widower old enough to be her father and began her life as the Countess of Pembroke and chatelaine of Wilton House.

During Philip Sidney's first extended return to England, the two Sidneys began their real association, for Philip visited Wilton in August, September, and November of 1577. His most famous sojourn in the spring of 1580, when out of favor with Elizabeth over the Alençon affair and when he began the *Arcadia*, has encouraged much speculation about the role of each in the other's life. Perhaps the countess's own literary beginnings date from this period if she started translating the Psalms, that "coupled worke," with her brother.[4] Sidney's subsequent visits in mid-December 1581, late January 1582, November-December 1582, and the summer of 1583 suggest that he came to Wilton while engaged in serious writing, despite his underplayed reference to the *Arcadia* as an "idle work" written "in loose sheets of paper, most of it in your presence," and imply that as his first reader, the countess found her literary interests actively engaged—perhaps also to the extent of doing her own work.[5] How much the births of her four children during this period (William in April 1580; Katherine in October 1581; Anne in March 1583; Philip in October 1584; Katherine died in 1584) might have affected her writing is mere speculation.

But it was after other significant changes in her life that Mary Sidney dated her translations, allowed her work to be published, and began to edit and publish her brother's. In 1586 both her parents died, and Philip Sidney was killed in battle in the Netherlands. Her children were growing older and she gave birth to no more. This period, between 1586 and 1601, is usually designated as the flowering of the "academy" at Wilton when the countess is supposed to have become the patron of many authors. As Mary Ellen Lamb has convincingly shown, the countess did not patronize every writer who mentions her name in a dedication, nor did she wish to clean up the barbarisms of the English stage as many have suggested. Lamb hypothesizes rather, that the countess wished "to rescue writers whom she believed her brother had befriended and to help them to get started in some career"; and second, and "more important, the Countess probably wished to keep herself amused and intellectually alive," so that she created a "society of her own at Wilton," to encourage the works of herself and men like Samuel Daniel, Thomas Moffett, and Nicholas Breton.[6]

The essential domesticity and privacy of this arrangement accords well with the countess's general reputation as a learned and virtuous lady. But its exclusivity and the legend of her assuming Philip Sidney's role as patron generated a mythology around her that critics fostered for centuries.[7] In the numerous dedications of admirers and flatterers alike, she appears not as a writer, but idealized as the living embodiment of a *donna angelicata letteraria*, a beloved lady and a muse to inspire others. Her identification with such figures as Urania, while nodding at her literary gifts, accentuated more her ability to facilitate and encourage the work of male writers, diminishing her as a fellow writer, but praising her as the glory of the traditional learned and virtuous woman: chaste, distant, inspiring.

Samuel Daniel, for example, was one of the few writers traditionally linked with the countess who actually seems to have associated with her, but his public addresses conform to the mythology. In his dedication of *Delia*, she is "Wonder of these, glory of other times./Great Patroness of these my humble Rymes,/Which thou from out thy greatnes doost inspire. ..."[8] In the preface to his *Cleopatra*, a work apparently suggested by the countess as a companion piece to her translation of Garnier's *Marc-Antoine*, she is the one

Who onely doth predominate my Muse:
The starre of wonder, which my labours chose
To guide their way in all the course I use.
   Shee, whose cleere brightnes doth alone infuse
   Strength to my thoughts, and makes me what I
     am ... (H5)

Modestly deprecating his own efforts to limn Cleopatra, the poet claims, "Yet lightning thou by thy sweet favouring eyes,/ My darke defects which from her sp'rit detract. . . ." Appropriating the language of love to literary inspiration, Daniel accentuates the position the countess was continually placed in by her fellow poets.

Unlike the countess's other admirers, however, Daniel does give us a brief insight into the importance she attached to her version of the Psalms. Implicitly acquiescing in Philip Sidney's view of the Psalms as the highest poetry, in the same preface, Daniel assures the countess that "those *Hymnes* that thou doost consecrate to heaven. . . . By this (Great Lady,) thou must then be knowne." Her home, Wilton, may crumble, but "Heere thou surviv'st thy selfe, heere thou art found," and it is the Psalms that will bring her lasting fame (H6-H6v). Given that he is familiar with her translations of other "noble" works, his extended notice of the Psalms indicates something beyond the empty praise of a patron's deeds and suggests that Daniel recognized how much this writing defined Mary Sidney's being. And despite his previous fulsome gratitude, he seems to be the only admirer to claim immortality for her not because she is a patron, but because she is a writer.

Nevertheless, other dedicators emphasize only the countess's principal role as a female figurehead, and are content to repeat a litany of titles: "Musarum Religionis et Doctrinae decus et praesidium" [glory and help of the Muses of Religion and Learning], "a pearle, that orient is of kind," "vertuous and learned," "pia nympha" [godly nymph]. Chaster and more beautiful than Venus, she is also the generator of the Graces, Muses, and Pallas.[9]

The depiction of the countess as a muse, a grace, a goddess, a star, conforms to current conventions of sycophantic dedication, but also to the patterns seen throughout this period that project the learned, creative woman as primarily an exceptional creature, whose real abilities are obscured by disproportionate praise. She may be idolized and sought after, but as Mulcaster had written, she "may well be alleaged for a president to prayse, not for a patern to prove like by. . . ."

However, Mary Sidney clearly did not conceive of her creative life as fulfilled by being a muse or by editing her brother's works, largely because her religious devotion drove her to find her own poetic voice. Her religious education had placed her firmly in the camp of the Reformed Protestants: the Sidney family as a whole was thoroughly dedicated to "godly" living, Calvinist doctrine, and the politics of the Puritan Earls of Leicester, Warwick, and Huntington (all Mary Sidney's uncles). Mary Sidney's marriage to the Earl of Pembroke cemented an alliance between two Puritan families (as did her brother Philip's to Sir Francis Walsingham's daughter), and their retainers at Wilton, Abraham Fraunce, Gervaise Babington, and Nicholas Breton, were noted for their Calvinist piety.[10] Her upbringing and her social position encouraged her to advance the Reformers' cause; her sex modified what she would do; her woman's training what she could do.

How her coreligionists saw Mary Sidney appears in a work by one of her literary protégés. In his "Countess of Pembroke's Passion," Nicholas Breton creates a role for the countess reflecting the godly piety which was central to her life. In a striking instance of a male author providing a woman with words, Breton characterizes the countess as piously aware of her human depravity and longing for God's grace:

> I sighe to se my infancie myspent,
> I morne to finde my youthfull life misled;
> I weepe to feele my further discontent,
> I dye to trye how love is livinge dead;
> > I sighe, I mourne, I weepe, I livynge dye,
> > And yett must live to shew more misereye.[11]

After the countess meditates on Christ's Passion, Breton's poem concludes with her praising the redeeming mercy of God's love, and the power which "his chosen soules preserveth." In his idealization of his patron as a godly exemplum, probably with a glance at her ongoing translation of the

Psalms, Breton not only creates a pious role for her, but he also speaks for her in a way similar to the borrowed voices she now began to choose for herself. Her translation from Philippe de Mornay, *A Discourse of Life and Death* is dated May 13, 1590, and from Robert Garnier, the *Antonius*, is dated November 26, 1590; the works were published together in 1592.

Perhaps the de Mornay translation paid tribute to Philip Sidney's friendship with this prominent Huguenot; since Sidney himself had partially translated de Mornay's *De la Verité de la Religion Chretienne*, *A Discourse* may be a companion piece; perhaps the countess's own grief at the deaths of her parents, her child, and her brother motivated her to translate it.[12] Such suppositions may be partly true, but a fuller biographical and literary account of this work finds in it a Christian attitude most likely to have been Mary Sidney's own. This work also relates closely to her two subsequent translations of Garnier and Petrarch. *Antonius*, read in conjunction with *A Discourse*, becomes a play illustrating the worldly life against which de Mornay inveighs. The *Triumph of Death* gives us the voice of Laura who teaches de Mornay's final advice, "Die to live, Live to die."[13] The Cleopatra of *Antonius* and Petrarch's Laura thus become opposite poles, the first an exemplum of worldly passion, the second an incentive to divine love, each demanding from the countess a language suitable to her role.

In *A Discourse of Life and Death*, de Mornay condemns a life dominated by the world, manifested in the desire for pleasure, material goods, and worldly position and fame. If a youth follows pleasure, he will find it to be "spent and past in a moment" (A3v). To accrue wealth is equal vanity, for wealth is "vile excrement" (B), and since one cannot persuade materialists "that mortall men have any other good in this world, but that which is mortall," once they lose their goods, "they fall into despaire, out of the which commonly they cannot be withdrawen" (Bv).

Attacking the pride of worldly pomp, de Mornay castigates

both courtiers who forever seek to rise in power and princes themselves who may appear mighty and free of trouble:

> Yet free doubtles they are not when the lightening often blasteth a floure of their crownes, or breakes their scepter in their handes: when a drift of snowe overwhelmes them: when a miste of heavines, and griefe continually blindeth their wit, and understanding. Crowned they are in deed but with a crowne of thornes. They beare a scepter: but it is of a reede, more then any thing in the world pliable, and obedient to all windes: it being so far off that such a crowne can cure the maigrims of the minde, and such a scepter keepe off and fray away the griefes and cares which hover about them: that it is contrariwise the crowne that brings them, and the scepter which from all partes attracts them. (B4-B4v)

The excellent translation here—its impressive phrase making, its stately rhythms composed of pauses between pithy, vivid aphorisms and the balances between negative and positive— suggests that Mary Sidney learned how to use language by imitating in English de Mornay's subject, by finding a rhetoric to express his ideas, so compatible with her own.[14]

Her translation proceeds with a section on the inner struggle, a theme which will continually echo in her own poetry. Merely to flee the external world is not, de Mornay insists, to be saved, for "Retire wee our selves into our selves, we find it there as uncleane as anywhere" (C3). Fundamental human depravity, the spoiling of human goodness at the Fall, cannot even be redeemed by great learning, for "these knowledges ... make him learned, but they make him not good: cunning, but not wise" (C4). The best knowledge can do is to teach a man his ignorance and imperfections, or as Solomon said, "the beginning and end of wisedome is the feare of God." Such doctrine appears in Mary Sidney's occasional poems, in her elegies, and of course, in the Psalms, each time expressed by a different persona.

Another of the countess's constant subjects is death, an obvious concern of Protestant doctrine, and not necessarily her own private obsession.[15] De Mornay observes that even in the face of life's misery, yet human beings fear death:

> Behold, now comes Death unto us: Behold her, whose approach we so much feare. . . . Wee have her in horror: but because wee conceive her not such as she is, but ougly, terrible, and hideous: such as it pleaseth the Painters to represent unto us on a wall. (D2)

By contrast, death should be seen as "the issue of our miseries and entraunce of the porte where wee shall ride in safetie from all windes." Life, not death, brings pain and trouble, and with "quietnesse of mind, constancie, and full resolution, wee shall not finde anie daunger or difficultie at all" (D2v). To die is to see the "Dawning of an everlasting day," to free the soul from "this foule and filthie prison," to "restore us both life and light" (D3v-D4). Nevertheless, the injunction against suicide stands, for "the Christian is ordained by God to fight ... and cannot leave his place without incurring reproch and infamie" (E2). He ought not to feel despair or cowardice at the approach of death, but "constantly and continually waite for her comming, that shee may never finde us unprovided" (E2v-E3). Such doctrine teaches the Christian to view life as a continual battle for righteousness against humanity's fallen nature, and to possess patience and constancy in the hope of God's grace. This viewpoint informs all Mary Sidney's other works, and every time, she explores a new mode of expression.

In this first published expression of the doctrine that influenced her life, Mary Sidney relied on the ideas and organization of another writer, yet her translation is neither slavish nor unskillful. The common themes in this work and in her subsequent translations, occasional poems, and the Psalms suggest that she may have planned a conscious development for herself from prose to poetry. More than any other woman writer to date, Mary Sidney embarked on a course similar to that of her male peers, a training by imitation and exercise in the arts of poetry. That her most skillful, most successful, and final work was a version of the Psalms probably indicates both the goals and the limits she consciously set upon her writing career.

When she turned to Robert Garnier's play, *Marc-Antoine*, Mary Sidney found a compatible moralist who vividly presented a drama of passion, attended by the grief and remorse of both Antony and Cleopatra.[16] Here, as in the exposition of de Mornay, Mary Sidney found a drama of the ambitions of great princes, their confrontation with death, and also the insufficiency of the pre-Christian world. By translating Garnier's alexandrines into blank verse, she provided convincing lyric voices for the laments of a despairing Antony now well past his prime, for the passionate avowals of a vigorous but wayward Cleopatra, and for the philosophizing of Philostratus, Lucilius, and Agrippa.

The play shows Antony acting out his passionate, worldly life with its inevitable end in reproach, guilt, and despair. After Actium, in resonant but plain terms, he mourns his former glory, his lost honor, and Cleopatra's faithlessness:

> Returned loe, dishonoured, despisde,
> In wonton love a woman thee misleades
> Sunke in foule sinke: meane while respecting nought
> Thy wife *Octavia* and her tender babes,
> Of whom the long contempt against thee whets
> The sword of *Caesar* now thy Lord become. (F4)

Now "cag'd," Antony knows his occupation is gone and he succumbs to blaming Cleopatra and denouncing his own crimes. The first chorus provides the appropriate perspective, echoing de Mornay's words about "our woe" beginning with our life and ever increasing; there is

> No stay in fading states,
> For more to height they retch,
> Their fellow miseries
> The more to height do stretch. (G)

The sombre, didactic style of the chorus suits its lesson about humanity's "thousand thousand woes," and is followed by Philostratus who catalogues the disastrous results of passion, as Antony had enumerated those of ambition. Philostratus details how "bloudie, murdring, hellish love" has destroyed Egypt as it destroyed Troy before, and the chorus underscores the extremity of his lament.[17]

Ironically juxtaposed here is Cleopatra's expression of continuing passion, as she declares that Antony's love is "more deare then Scepter, children, freedome, light" (H). While acknowledging that human beings are free to control their passions, she chooses to follow Antony, despite Charmian's admonition to consider her duty to "children, frends, and to our countrie soile" (H3v) and to beware how "with so strong charmes doth love bewitch our witts ..." (H4). Cleopatra's essentially pagan perspective betrays itself to the Christian moralist by her decision to deceive Antony yet again by pretending death. But Cleopatra's fickleness is only an instance of general earthly mutability, detailed by the chorus to Act II in its account of the inevitable fall of Egypt and Rome itself, for "Everything *Time* overthrowes,/Nought to ende doth stedfast staie" (I3v).

De Mornay's insistence on the slavery of pleasure echoes in Antony's last scene as he reiterates his bondage to Cleopatra, comparing himself to the sick man who thirsts and drinks "albee the drinke he still desires/Be nothing else but fewell to his flame ..." (Kv). At last he admits to Lucilius that the search for pleasure has destroyed him:

> Nay, as the fatted swine in filthy mire
> With glutted heart I wallow'd in delights,
> All thoughts of honor troden under foote.   (L)

Pleasure, confirms Lucilius, is the particular vice of kings, who thereby invite disorder and rebellion; in this submission to pleasure, Antony ironically fulfills his descent from Hercules. This passage indicates some of Mary Sidney's skills as a translator and poet, although it is not without the weaknesses of experimentation. From a faltering line like "Alone hath me this strange disastre spunne," based on Garnier's half line, "M'a filé ce desastre," Sidney works up to a pointed rendition of his image, "Ains comme un porc ventru touillé dedans la fange,/A coeur saoul me voitray en maints salles plaisirs,/Mettant dessous le pied tous honnestes desirs" (*Two Tragedies*, ll. 1148-55). Her alliterative "fatted swine in filthy mire" vividly conjures the gross image of the original and conveys precisely the moral degradation implied by "la fange" ["vivre dans la fange" = live in vice or degradation]. "Glutted" and "wallow'd" continue the swine metaphor, and are perfectly placed for emphasis in the English line.

The subsequent meditation on death by the chorus, while scorning "this dastard feare of dieng" (L3v), can only offer the pagan version of death as the sole means to restore personal honor; it must be left to the Christian to recall that, as de Mornay teaches, death is not an end but a beginning.

In the character of Caesar, Sidney also found de Mornay's type of the ambitious prince boasting of his worldly conquests and looking for more. Censuring Antony for his "presumptuous pride" in confronting Rome, in cold, plain language Caesar plans to eradicate his own opposition:

> Murther we must, untill not one we leave,
> Which may hereafter us of rest bereave. (M2v)

Unsurprisingly this self-styled master of the world ends the act by planning a sordid lunge for Cleopatra's treasure, fulfilling the doctrine that the ambitious and the covetous are never satisfied.

The drama concludes with Cleopatra's lament for her fall with Antony, and with it, the fortunes of her country and children. She berates herself for ensnaring Antony and feels only self-reproach and heartbroken grief. Antony himself, lying dead in her tomb, is an image of the fall of princes, and all Cleopatra can envision for them is that they journey together "to the hellish plaine" (O2) and wander as shades "Where brookes of hell do falling seeme to mone" (O2v). Her final act is to confirm her earthly passion with desperate kisses on Antony's dead lips:

> I spent in teares, not able more to spende,
> But kisse him now, what rests me more to doe?

Then lett me kisse you, you faire eies, my light.
Front seate of honor, face most fierce most faire!
O neck, o armes, o hands, o breast where death
(Oh mischief) comes to choake up vitall breath.
A thousand kisses, thousand thousand more
Let you my mouth for honors farewell give:
That in this office weake my limmes may growe,
Fainting on you, and fourth my soule may flowe.   (O2v)

Cleopatra's language is highly impassioned, even moving, but it nonetheless expresses a woman lost in her earthly passions. The drama mirrors spiritual emptiness in a world devoted to the material and the passionate, to avarice and ambition. When reading and translating Garnier's drama, the Countess of Pembroke probably found her moral view of literature confirmed, and could combine her piety with a poetry that attempted to express the "truth" about fallen human nature. Garnier's moral version of history, which generates the choruses, the downward spiral of the structure, and the monolithic aspect of the characters, provided Mary Sidney with a proving ground for both the poetry of impassioned outburst and of moral judgment. As the play ends by being more Cleopatra's than Antony's, and as the countess showed her particular interest in Cleopatra by asking Daniel to write Cleopatra's final scenes in a sequel, she was probably interested in learning how to create the langue of the passionate, worldly woman—unlike many pious writers before her who concentrated their art solely on sermonizing. Ultimately such ability to express the passions contributed to the success of her version of the Psalms, where the sinner stands before God.

To counterpoint the worldliness of *Antonius*, the countess turned to the spirituality of Petrarch's *Trionfo della Morte*. Here, she reveals her already keen poetic judgment and skill by retaining the terza rima of the original, so rendering Petrarch with remarkable fidelity; yet, by still relying on iambic pentameter, she also achieves a smooth, flexible English sound. Compared with previous English translations by Lord Morley

(1554) and William Fowler (1587–1588), both longer versions in iambic pentameter couplets, Mary Sidney's version is much more in tune with Petrarch's vision. Already she was becoming a sensitive, capable poet.

Laura, "questa leggiadra e gloriosa donna," clearly defines a spiritual plane as Cleopatra represented a worldly one. Where Cleopatra's "weapons" were her "winning partes" which were "nothing else but fiers, fetters, dartes" (717-18), Laura conquers Love, "il gran nemico," "the mightie foe" not with arms—"not with sword, with speare or bowe,/But with chaste heart, faire visage, upright thought,/wise speache, which did with honor linked goe."[18] Unlike Cleopatra who incites passion, Laura epitomizes the chaste, virtuous woman defeating lust, as represented by her emblem, the "snowy Ermiline."

Recalling the theme of life's frailty in *A Discourse of Life and Death* allows us to see even more clearly what may have drawn Mary Sidney to Petrarch. In the *Triumph of Death*, Petrarch represents both in Laura's life and in the figure of Death a poetical expression of Christian doctrine compatible with de Mornay's. Death, the black-garbed female figure, comes to claim the young and beautiful Laura, and inspires the poet with a vision of "a never-numbred summe" of the dead. Represented are temporal rulers, "All naked now, all needie, beggars all," their crowns, their "roabes, and purple dye" all gone (I, 79-87).

But given this consciousness of universal human frailty, marked out in brief images rather than in extended moralizing like Garnier's, the poet's focus is on the death of Laura, a loss of intense personal magnitude, yet rendered not histrionically, but with attention to the ghostly beauty and holiness of the moment when the spirit is free of the body:

> Not as great fyers violently spent,
>   But in them-selves consuming, so hir flight
>   Tooke that sweete spright, and past in peace
>   content,
> Right lyke unto som lamp of cleerest light,

Little and little wanting nutriture,
　Houlding to end a never changing plight.
Pale? no: but whitelie: and more whitelie pure,
　Then snow on wyndless hill, that flaking falles:
　As one, whom labor did to rest allure.
And when that heavenlie guest those mortall walles
　Had leaft: it nought but sweetelie sleeping was
　In hir faire eyes: what follie dying calles
Death faire did seeme to be in hir faire face.
　　　　　　　　　　　　　　(I, 160-72)

The rendition of Petrarch's rhyme "bel seno . . . ciel sereno" as "bosome deare . . . heavens clear" retains both the musicality and the association of Laura's heart with heaven, preparing us for the moving, lyrical finale. The sanctified hush of Petrarch's lines created by "non come fiamma," "un soave e chiaro lume," "un dolce dormir" echoes in the countess's understanding of the significance of the moment not as a struggle but a blithe return to the maker. Her "sweet spright," "peace content," "cleerest light," and particularly the rendition of "ma più che neve bianca,/Che senza vento in un bel colle fiocchi" as "whitelie: and more whitelie pure,/Then snow on wyndless hill, that flaking falles" capture Laura's death as a natural, effortless passing.

The beauty of this translation suggests how carefully Mary Sidney sought the perfect lyric articulation for her theme. In Chapter Two, Laura's instruction to Petrarch receives equal attention, for here Laura expresses ideas central to the countess's ongoing work on the Psalms, and we may suppose that achieving lyric preciseness here prepared her for the greater work ahead. For example, answering the poet's question about whether death is painful, Laura acknowledges that the fear of damnation may make it so for some:

But when the panting soule in God takes breath;
　And wearie heart affecteth heavenlie rest,
　An unrepented sighe, not els, is death.
　　　　　　　　　　　　　(II, 49-51)

Here Sidney transforms Petrarch's straightforward "pur che l'alma in Dio si riconforte" to a metaphor of exhausted longing receiving life support, and extends the connotation of "un sospir breve" to the more highly charged and devout "un-repented sighe." This terzina, an exhalation of simultaneous physical and spiritual release, heralds the concise style of so many of the countess's Psalms, where a single metaphor may convey the whole history of the soul's quest for God.

The role of Laura in Chapter Two is to teach Petrarch how to live and how to love free of the "flames" that had tormented him. Turning on him a beneficent aspect, "that gentle smile . . . the Sunne of my woe-darkned skyes," Laura acknowledges their mutual love, "Onelie thy flame I tempred with my cheere;/This onelie way could save both thee and me" (90-91), so reinterpreting for her lover as care for his soul what might have appeared as cold disdain. Her reason bridled her will, and her virtue tempered her love, so that "I have thee brought/wearie, but safe to my no little joye" (119-20).

Such idealized virtue, as it often does in Renaissance poetry, leads the male poet to salvation, fulfilling Laura's Easter role; for Mary Sidney, it also opposes the chaotic worldliness and despair of Cleopatra's guidance. Laura radiates the spiritual sense of chastity as an expression of God's will and the path to blessedness, and redeems her lover rather than destroys him. Like the Virgin and Eve, Laura and Cleopatra are op-posite types of womanhood, and in the Countess of Pem-broke's subsequent poetry and in the poetic role she ultimately affirmed for herself, both Cleopatra's worldliness and Laura's divinity are placed clearly in their Christian perspective.

Probably the first of Mary Sidney's occasional poems was her fine elegy for her brother, published in Spenser's collection of elegies for Philip Sidney which included his own "Astro-phel."[19] Generally known as "The Dolefull Lay of Clorinda," it is a pastoral with obvious classical antecedents, but also a pastoral with specific Christian connotations. As the grieving shepherdess, Clorinda not only inhabits an earthly rural land-scape but translates that landscape into a vision of heaven.

Her poetry encompasses the mutable, fallen world and the bliss of the eternal, redeemed one, because the pastoral traditionally represents both.[20] The death of the shepherd Astrophel provokes her "impatient griefe" and "inward paine" (stanza 1) and causes her to look both to heaven and to earth for consolation. However, realizing that heaven ordained her loss and that men "like wretched bee" (stanza 3) and are themselves in need of comfort, Clorinda is forced to confront herself and her landscape. Through the description of a "desolate" pastoral world, she presents a cleareyed vision of fallen nature, now clarified for her by the immediate presence of death. In hollow, echoing lines, "all the fields do waile their widow state,/Sith death their fairest flowre did late deface" (stanza 5), and "shepheards lasses" must break their garlands and wear "sad Cypres" and "bitter Elder" (stanza 7). Following such vivid images of "Death the devourer," Clorinda asks the crucial question: what has become of Astrophel? "Can so divine a thing be dead?" (stanza 11).

Her answer, while no immediate remedy for those left behind in the fallen world, affirms the hope of "blisfull Paradise" in the life to come. Astrophel, that spirit from the "hevenly quires select" will be serenaded by celestial birds, "In bed of lillies wrapt in tender wise./And compast all about with roses sweet, / And daintie violets from head to feet" (stanza 12). The delicate beauty of the celestial pastoral, expressed in soft sibillants and balanced lines, represents Astrophel's initiation into immortality through divine love, and contrasts with the mournful appearance and hollow laments of earthly nature, where love is finite and therefore painful.

By adopting the persona of the grieving shepherdess, Mary Sidney can make pastoral convention convey both her view of human beings "that here in dole are drent" and the hope of immortal life. In this poem, she begins with the heavy rhetorical grief of "Ay me, to whom shall I my case complaine ..." but finds consolation only in understanding the real source of her woe, human sin and helplessness, and the ultimate remedy for human misery in God. The identification of herself as the shepherdess sister of the shepherd Astrophel suggests several poetic connotations. Spenser had introduced her as "most resembling both in shape and spright /Her brother deare" (F4v), and her guise as shepherdess might confirm her succession to Astrophel's role as poet. But more significantly, in the context of Christian pastoral, the role of shepherd designates the follower of Christ, and so the persona of Clorinda expresses not only a poetic identity but a religious one. Mary Sidney ends her poem as a true Christian, not by lamenting her brother, whom she believes is now a divine soul, but by mourning for all those left on the wretched earth. Here, her assurance of Philip Sidney's divinity is crucial to her assertion of faith; in future poems, it will also give her a way to define her poetic mission.

In light of Mary Sidney's devotion to the Reformed cause and her experiments with poetic voice, her two poems to Queen Elizabeth, "A Dialogue betweene two shepheards, Thenot and Piers, in praise of Astraea" and the dedication of the Psalms, "Even now that Care which on thy Crown attends," are noteworthy for their presentation of the queen and their further experiments with persona. Both draw on current mythology to glorify Elizabeth at a time when many English Reformers identified their country as the militant champion of the Protestant cause.[21] Many writers had associated Elizabeth with Astraea the virgin, and the return of a golden age of justice; just as insistent was the Reformist propaganda that identified her as the ruler of the new Israel, an England redeemed from the Catholic Antichrist. In this guise, she was equally a Deborah, a David, and a Solomon, but for Mary Sidney the queen's association with the divine virgin, Astraea, and with David—king, poet, and forefather of Christ—were the most significant.[22]

In each of these poems, Sidney uses the occasion of praise to explore the poetic expression of divine or ineffable truth. Developing the idea of the divine lady, whom she cannot address as Petrarch did his Laura, she seeks nevertheless a voice and a language appropriate to her sense of mission. The solution in the "Dialogue betweene two shepheards, Thenot and Piers, in praise of Astraea," is to present two contrasting voices which articulate the problems inherent in poetry about divine truth.[23] Certainly the poem flatters Elizabeth, but more important, it depends on the exalted connotations of "divine Astraea" to demonstrate how the praiser needs "the truth" but can only use words that fall so far short of divinity as to prove him "so oft a lier" (stanza 1). Because the fallen world and heaven are so completely divided, whenever Thenot praises Astraea's divinity by relating it to something on earth, he will fail to express her:

> Thenot. Then say, she is so good, so faire,
> With all the earth she may compare,
> Not *Momus* selfe denying.
> Piers. Compare may thinke where likenesse holds,
> Nought like to her the earth enfolds,
> I lookt to finde you lying.
> (stanza 3)

Even to praise her by saying that "*ASTREA* sees with Wisedoms sight,/*Astrea* workes by Vertues might" (stanza 4) is to reverse the reality, because both Wisdom and Virtue emanate from the divine and do not exist as independent earthly entities. Comparison itself becomes an impossible technique because the divine Astrea is unique, "to us none else but only shee." Like the sonnet-lover, Thenot uses all his rhetorical techniques in an attempt to define his lady and his love. Like Clorinda, Piers emphasizes the chasm between worldly and heavenly vision by pointing out that darkness often clouds light, but "*Astreas* beames no darknes shrowdes. ..." The inadequacy, of course, extends to language, and Piers's final verse explains to Thenot why his words lie, and "strive in vaine to raise her":

> Words from conceit do only rise,
> Above conceit her honour flies;
> But silence, nought can praise her.

The human imagination must suffer too from the Fall which totally cut off humankind from its original divinity. Thenot may sense what he wants to say, "my meaning true," but nothing in human experience is now adequate to express that understanding. Although Elizabeth would still be pleased by a poem asserting how far beyond mortal expression Astraea was, nevertheless, for a poet, the problem remained of finding the words to convey the nature of divinity.

To pose this artistic and religious problem, Mary Sidney chose two male voices in dialogue, reminiscent perhaps of Sidney's Arcadian Eclogues, and even more of Spenser's *Shepheardes Calender* where both a Thenot and a Piers appear. In the February, April, and November eclogues, Thenot, the old commentator, represents experience from which the younger shepherds can learn, as revealed by his parable of the Oak and the Briar, by his upbraiding of Colin's foolish love, and by his encouragement of Colin's true poetry. The countess's Thenot reverses this role by learning through his attempts at praise of the insufficiency of human "conceit" and language. But more significantly, Spenser's Piers, appearing in May and October, heralds the specific concerns of Mary Sidney's Piers. In May, pitted against the Catholic priest, Palinode, he is the Protestant pastor inveighing against the pastors or shepherds who care for worldly pleasure and not their flocks. A "shepheard muste walke another way,/Sike worldly sovenance he must foresay" (81-82); he must act righteously to be ready to account to Christ, the "great Pan." In the October eclogue, in dialogue with Cuddie, "the perfect paterne of a Poete" who laments the age's contempt for poets and poetry, Piers confirms the argument that poetry is a "divine gift and heavenly instinct," despite its present degeneracy, and he praises the kind of love that lifts mankind's mind "up out of the loathsome myre ... above the starry skie." The countess's Piers closely resembles the May Piers, advocating as a good Protestant that Thenot "the truth but plainely tell" and "speake in measure"; and if he denies the ability of Thenot's poetry to express the divine, he, like the October Piers, may only be admitting the failure of contemporary poets.[24]

But more important, at its core, the dialogue expresses disappointment in the insufficiency of human language, or the sense of fallen inadequacy, to express faith. But while she composes a poem about the failure of poetry in two male voices, thus distancing her personae from herself in number and gender, Mary Sidney reserves the celebration of poetry for a persona who more nearly resembles Clorinda, sister of Astrophel, who is actually enabled as a poet by her perception of the divine. The two poems she wrote to dedicate the Psalms, one to the queen, one to her brother, indicate how she achieved her vocation as poet of the truth.

In her second poem to Queen Elizabeth, "Even now that Care which on thy Crown attends," the speaker is the poet, now defining herself as the faithful and reverent subject praising her queen as God's chosen ruler, the present-day analogy to David himself. Addressing the queen first as the earthly prince bound by the unending cares of state, she at once strikes the theme of Elizabeth's divine right:

> What heav'nly powrs thee highest throne assin'de,
> assign'd thee goodnes suting that Degree:
> and by thy strength thy burthen so defin'de,
> To others toile, is Exercise to thee.
> (stanza 2)[25]

The analogy between Elizabeth and David follows, justifying the presentation of his "English denizend" Psalms to the woman synonymous with England, "what English is by many names is thine" (stanza 6).

However, the comparison of Elizabeth to David is not merely the witty conceit or flattery of a dedicator. For Sidney's belief that Elizabeth is a David builds a vision of England as the new Israel, a vision fervently espoused by other godly writers. Indeed, the countess may have remembered a text like Thomas Bentley's *Monument of Matrones*, the third part of which clearly makes David Elizabeth's archetype, as he was of her father, Henry VIII. In "The Kings Heast, or GODS familiar speech to the QUEENE: Collected out of the holie Psalmes of good king DAVID, as they are learnedlie expounded by THEODORE BEZA," God speaks to Elizabeth "as he sometimes did unto David, though not in so mysticall maner," declaring how Providence guided her preservation from her enemies, and promising to bless her and her realm.[26] In "The Queenes Vow, or selfe-talk with GOD," also collected out of Beza's Psalms, we hear how "the Queenes Majestie, after a most Christian maner, even with Davids spirit, his sweet words, and divine sentences, first inciteth and prepareth her hart and mind to devotion" (320).

In carefully balanced clauses, Mary Sidney herself draws the analogies between David's rule and Elizabeth's:

> For ev'n thy Rule is painted in his Raigne:
> both cleere in right: both nigh by wrong opprest:
> And each at length (man crossing God in vaine)
> Possest of place, and each in peace possest.
> Proud Philistines did interrupt his rest,
> The foes of Heav'n no lesse have beene thy foes;
> Hee with great conquest, thou with greater blest;
> Thou sure to winn, and hee secure to lose.
>
> (stanza 9)

This remarkable phenomenon of a woman ruler extending her power over male heads of state, "Kings on a Queene enforst their states to lay ... Men drawne by worth a woman to obay" (stanza 11), derives its legitimacy from her ordination by God himself. Elizabeth's sacred right is in fact demonstrated by her great success as a ruler, although the poet claims that such workings of divine providence are too exalted a topic for her muse. But what her muse can contribute is an English voice for an English queen. The poet's legitimacy as a divine maker comes, not because she herself is God's chosen, but because she provides a song for the chosen, for God's new David, Elizabeth. Her belief in the queen's divine right, her "thrice sacred" nature, underpins her own vocation as *vates*, the divine poet. For Mary Sidney the problem of how a woman poet may sing divine truth is solved first by recasting King David as Queen Elizabeth:

> And who sees ought, but sees how justly square
> his haughtie Ditties to thy glorious daies?

> How well beseeming thee his Triumphs are?
> his hope, his zeale, his praier, plaint, and praise,
> Needles thy person to their height to raise:
> (stanza 8)

And second, she offers the English Psalms to be the queen's voice, so that Elizabeth may "Sing what God doth, and doo What men may sing"—praise God and enact her subjects' praise of her.

If she believed as fervently as the other Reformers that England was the new Israel, then no greater task existed for the poet than glorifying Israel's and England's God. By rendering the Psalms in English verse, Sidney would be simultaneously following divine authority and identifying herself as a true poet. Significantly, she was also following the authority of all the Reformed commentators who gave the Psalms vital importance in the new faith, suggesting that her decade of writing and revising may have been motivated by more than a desire to finish her brother's work.

From Thomas Becon's *Davids Harpe* (1541) to the key commentaries of Calvin and Beza, both of which were available in English, the English Reformers took the Psalms to be a text central to the new spiritual life of their church. They were the source and inspiration of private meditation available for every Christian to use, and the most applicable scriptural text representing an unmediated path to God: as a record of human suffering, conflict, guilt, repentance, faith, and joy, they were particularly appropriate to the Reformers' perception of fallen humankind in continual war against itself, with only God's grace to offer the hope of salvation.[27]

Addressing Katherine, Countess of Huntingdon (Mary Sidney's aunt), Anthonie Gilbie, translator of Beza's *Paraphrase and Commentary on the Psalms*, invokes the Psalms as a path to righteousness at a time when he trembles for the safety of England beset by "general plagues" and the threat of God's wrath for her sins. All English people need to pray for mercy, "that so by earnest praiers, either we may turne away his fearce wrath from us altogither, or at the least with our

Hezekias (our gracious Queene I meane) to obteine that it come not in our daies." Every Christian must daily "meditate them in their hearts," in order to learn "what we shal saie unto God."[28]

Expressing the goal of the Reformers to purify the Church of England and to universalize the new faith, these writers turn to the Psalms as an all-encompassing text to aid private prayer and pubic renovation. By translating the Psalms into a wide range of verse forms, experimenting with meter and rhyme to find the most apt expression of emotion and faith for each song, Mary Sidney sought to play her part in the encouragement of godliness among her peers. To provide them with more memorable forms than might be found, for instance, in the Sternhold-Hopkins Psalter, was to subscribe to the ancient dictum, *utile et dulce*, and to make the songs even more attractive to an audience whose ears were attuned to the variety and subtlety of lyric poetry.

At the same time that she was creating the language of Antony and Cleopatra, Laura, and Clorinda, Mary Sidney worked on her version of the Psalms, editing the first 43 by her brother, and composing Psalms 44 through 150 herself. The seventeen extant manuscripts reveal a long process of writing and revising over ten years, suggesting that the countess considered this work worthy of considerable serious effort in order to accomplish her goals.[29] And if her other poetry had ranged through passion, divine love, grief, and praise, in the Psalms, all these were placed in the perspective of "what we shal saie unto God," an attempt to express both human fallibility and the longing for God, to recognize the gulf between humanity and the divine, yet attempt to bridge it through praise.

Basing her version on a variety of contemporary sources, from the glosses of the Geneva Bible to Marot's translation to the commentaries of Beza, Mary Sidney embarked on a pious work that was essentially scholarly, and yet still poetically inventive. All readers of the Sidneian Psalms have remarked upon the variety of verse forms—Rathmell notes only four instances in all the Psalms that exactly repeat the same stanza pattern and rhyme scheme—suggesting that both Sidneys, but to a greater extent, Mary, saw the fulfillment of their task to lie in conveying received doctrine through the individual expression of the poet. To write "heavenly poesy" required not only theological knowledge to make readers think about doctrinal matters, but appropriate forms to make them feel the griefs and joys the poet-prophet experiences.[30]

This chapter permits but a brief focus on how the countess handled one of the central subjects of the Psalms as interpreted by the Reformers, but it will clarify the continuities between her other poetry and this work, and confirm the direction of her growth as a poet. In the countess's other work, the central Reformist doctrine of the insufficiency of humankind unaided by God's grace appears both as a theme and as a technical problem of language. In the Psalms, however, instead of clinging to her Biblical text or authorities, she uses metaphor and stanzaic form to convey doctrine; in other words, by marrying form and content, her writing escapes the safety and disguise of being mere doctrine, and becomes poetry. While clearly not the first time that a woman poet has recognized the importance of form, still it is the first time that form has been elevated to the central role of moving readers' minds and penetrating their consciences.

In the countess's Psalm 51, for example, a penetential psalm that has received some attention for its merits,[31] the fourth stanza enlarges upon verse 7 of the Psalter, "Purge me with hyssope, and I shal be cleane: wash me, and I shalbe whiter then snowe," and verse 8, "Make me to heare joye and gladnes, that the bones, which thou has broken maie rejoyce."[32] Adopting the Geneva gloss of hyssop as a cleanser of leprosy (Leviticus 14:6), Sidney introduces the image of leprosy, thus doubling the significance of whiteness and intensifying the joy of cure:

Then as thy self to leapers hast assign'd,
   With hisop, Lord, thy Hisop purge me soe:
And that shall clense the leaprie of my mind;
   Make over me thy mercies streames to flow,
   Soe shall my whiteness scorn the whitest snow.

To eare and hart send soundes and thoughts of gladness,
That brused bones maie daunce awaie their sadness.

The repetition in the second line of "hisop, Lord, thy Hisop,"
emphasizes the teaching that the cure of such a deadly diseased
soul is all God's. Connotative of purification and also of a
lowly plant, the hyssop reminds the reader that redemption
is possible and that humility is the way. And the following
image of the dread white scabs of leprosy miraculously van-
ishing in the healing waters, leaving instead the pure whiteness of natural health, vivifies and dramatizes the simpler
scriptural "wash me, and I shal be whiter than snow." Implied
in "mercies streames to flow" is the abundance of God's grace
and its immediate ability to turn *in malo* to *in bono*, human
deformity into divine beauty.[33] Such miraculous cure prompts
the final prayer of the stanza, that the sinner may rejoice in
salvation. Adding "thoughts" to the "soundes" of gladness of
the Biblical text marks the improvement from "leaprie of my
mind," while the image of "brused bones" now dancing
underlines the joy of spiritual regeneration for which the
sinner longs. The weak endings of the couplet provide a final
lift to the stanza, a lighter touch indicative of the poet's hoped-
for gladness.

A more dramatic example of the function of stanza form
in the countess's Psalms is Psalm 57. In the Geneva version,
verse 1 reads, "Have mercie upon me, o God, have mercie
upon me, for my soule trusteth in thee, and in the shadow
of thy ways wil I trust, til these afflictions overpasse." Mary
Sidney's stanza appears:

> Thy mercie Lord, Lord now thy mercy show,
>   On thee I ly
>   To thee I fly
>   Hide me, hive me as thine owne,
>   Till these blasts be overblown,
> Which now doe fiercely blow.

Here, the urgency of the sinner's plea for mercy evolves from
the short, intense lines, from the staccato rhymes of "ly" and
"fly" and the near-rhyme of "Hide" and "hive," and the

explosiveness of "blasts . . . overblown . . . blow." Building on the Geneva gloss, "He compareth the afflictions, which God layeth upon his children to a storme, that commeth and goeth," in this brief stanza, Sidney's diction conveys both the vehemence of the sinner's woes which "fiercely blow" and the close protection sought with God, "Hide me, hive me as thine owne." Everything seems in chaotic motion, except the implied still point of safety—and salvation—within the hive, thus evoking the distance between the mutable world and the unchanging heavens.

Such attention to language and form typifies much of Mary Sidney's writing in the Psalms. Although they were never published in her lifetime, the wide currency of manuscripts in court circles suggests that they did indeed fulfill a need and achieve some measure of success. The Psalms may be seen, then, both as a public act of devotion and a private dedication of Mary Sidney to the role of divine poet. The prefatory address to the queen confirms the first, and the dedication to her brother bears witness to the second.

The intense fervor of "To the Angell spirit of the most excellent Sir Phillip Sidney" might suggest a "sincere" outpouring of the countess's personal grief, but its emotional energy should not obscure its essential elegiac and self-dedicatory purposes. Like "The Dolefull Lay of Clorinda," this poem is an elegy and displays Mary Sidney's awareness of the elegy's classical components of praise, lament, and consolation. But while Clorinda found consolation in believing that Astrophel was immortal, she also emphasized the insuperable division between paradise and earth. In "To the Angell spirit," however, while the poet still laments her terrible loss—"Deepe wounds enlarg'd, long festred in their gall/ fresh bleeding smart; not eie but hart teares fall:"—and still acknowledges the gulf between his "pure Sprite" and earth dwellers, almost all her praise concerns Sidney the poet, and thence evolves her consolation and her inspiration (Rathmell, *The Psalms*, xxxv-xxxviii). As an elegy that is also a dedication, praise is the dominant mode, but it does not simply arise from fraternal and personal affection. Instead, the belief in her brother's divinity allows her to find a bridge between earth and heaven through the "sacred Hymnes" which he began and which she has finished:

> So dar'd my Muse with thee it selfe combine,
> as mortall stuffe with that which is divine,
> Thy lightning beames give lustre to the rest.
>
> (stanza 1)

If this is "presumption too too bold/if love and zeale such error ill-become," yet her act grows from "zealous love, Love which hath never done,/Nor can enough in world of words unfold" (stanza 4). "Zeal" is, of course, a key word in the Puritan lexicon for the devotion of the elect to God, and the repetition here with "Love" suggests that Sidney composed her Psalms as a direct response to divine love, represented by her apotheosized brother. In addressing her brother's celestial being as "fixt among thy fellow lights" where "Thy Angell's soule with highest Angells plac't/There blessed sings enjoying heav'n-delights/thy Maker's praise," she herself imitates the divine, likewise singing God's praise, albeit with the shadowy language of earth. Her Psalms echo heavenly music, praising God to whom Sidney is near, and so simultaneously erecting a monument to her brother's "ever praised name." The Psalms will be both God's "Hymnes" and Sidney's "obsequies," because her belief in Sidney's divinity makes hymns and obsequies identical in the poet's mind.

If the countess consulted Sidney's discussion of *vates* in *The Defence of Poesie*, she would have found his definition of the poet as "diviner, foreseer, or prophet," and his designation of David's Psalms as a "divine poem" or a "heavenly poesy, wherein almost he showeth himself a passionate lover of that unspeakable and everlasting beauty to be seen by the eyes of the mind only, cleared by faith." In response, she took up a role for herself hitherto unique among women writers, to become that divinely inspired poet, legitimized by a divinely ordained queen and a sanctified brother.

In the context of Mary Sidney's poetic development, "Thenot and Piers, in praise of Astraea" and "Even now that

Care which on thy Crown attends" seem not merely flattery of Elizabeth, but rather the poet's expression of her true lyrical subject. Similarly, the poems about Philip Sidney reveal little about the actual sibling relationship; instead, they are metaphoric celebrations of Mary Sidney's idea of her brother, animated by his death. Poetically, Queen Elizabeth and Philip Sidney share the greatness that Petrarch attributed to Laura, the function of leading the poet to a divine vision and dedication to God's Word. Mary Sidney wrote good, and sometimes very fine, lyric poetry partly because she created in her brother and her queen rich emotional and intellectual sources of language and imagery, and clearly defined her poetic personae in relation to them. Instead of merely translating doctrine into verse, she trained herself as a poet devoted to her sovereign's rule and worthy of her brother's immortality.

Unlike Anne Dowriche or Rachel Speght, Mary Sidney did not write prefaces apologizing for or defending her sex. More like Elizabeth Melville Colville, she devoted herself entirely to the writing itself. She was both innovative and conservative. On the one hand, she considerably extended the range of women's literary accomplishments by following less the conventions of humanist education for women and more the path of her own experiments with language and persona; on the other hand, she by no means broke with feminine literary decorum, but indeed represented to her own and succeeding generations the essence of learning and virtue. By choosing wisely her subjects and points of view, from the de Mornay translation and *Antonius*, through Clorinda to the Psalms, she could write about a variety of situations, locations, and characters without challenging the implied limitations on women's writing. Because the essence of her work was her piety, she could transcend the treatise writers and versifiers without sacrificing her legitimacy.

SIX

THE MAKING OF
A FEMALE HERO:
JOANNA LUMLEY AND
ELIZABETH CARY

QUEEN ELIZABETH's lofty stature as revered monarch, embodiment of the national destiny, and epitome of chaste virtue might suggest that English authors would fill their poems and plays with similarly heroic female characters. But beyond the representations of Elizabeth herself and the usual catalogues of exceptional types—the Biblical Deborah and Judith or the classical Cornelia—most writers only exalted women as paragons of the private virtues. Indeed, those female characters who defy their conventional bounds are more likely to be literary villains.[1] In effect, the emphasis on Elizabeth's unique, divinely ordained position isolated her as a special case, and her public authority seems to have exerted little influence either on the private lives of her female subjects or on male writers' characterization of women in English literature, unless to make them affirm more than ever the traditional virtues.[2]

As Chapter Five suggests, however, Elizabeth was an important aspect of at least one woman's poetry. Elizabeth, the heir to David's throne, appeared as an alter ego of Mary Sidney, the heir to David's lyre. Superficially, the queen's poetic importance for Mary Sidney may resemble Elizabeth's symbolic enablement of Spenser's *Faerie Queene*, Peele's *Arraignment of Paris*, or Davies's *Hymns of Astraea*, but Sidney's poetic treatment of the queen seems to have emanated from a different source, the woman writer's desire to create a true female hero.

Toward the end of the sixteenth and in the early seventeenth century, a small but important group of women writers appear to find the heroic woman an increasingly significant focus of their interrelated attempts to redeem Eve and to establish their own literary presence. Female heroism had no one definition for every woman writer, although these women often tended to transform the traditional private virtues into a more public role. Women writers did not, however, merely copy masculine ideals of feminine heroism like Griselda or Lucrece.[3] Rather, they raised traditional feminine virtues from their subordinate, private status, and emphasizing their quintessential Christianity, they established women's spiritual experience independently of men, and at the very heart of human existence. Paradoxically, their conservative ideals engendered a radical exposition of feminine character.

The next three chapters will present drama, poetry, and prose by writers whose concepts of women diverge from masculine conventions. In their dramas, Joanna Lumley and Elizabeth Cary center their works on the spiritual heroism of their female characters, exalting the feminine archetype of the Christian soul. In her poem, Aemilia Lanyer creates women of past and present as exemplary Christians, praising contemporary English women as the epitome of all virtue. In her prose romance and sonnet sequence, Mary Wroth creates Pamphilia, a character who bridges the worlds of politics, love, and divinity, demonstrating her heroic virtue in each sphere. These writers determined that literature could transform women's apparently private and passive virtues into public, active attributes and that women should contribute significantly to the conduct of the commonwealth. This belief nourished their art, although it could not erase the paradoxes and uncertainties inherent in female authorship.

While Mary Sidney's translation of Garnier's *Marc-Antoine* permitted her to express her beliefs and to practice the poetic creation of diverse characters and moods, it could hardly be said that the drama responded to events of her personal life. Indeed, to assume that a play represents an author's inmost feelings and ideas is always to risk misinterpretation. Even in the unperformed Elizabethan and Jacobean closet drama, personal feeling does not seem to be the playwright's central concern, for the genre is by nature impersonal.[4] Yet, in the very first play to be translated into English by a woman, Euripides's *Iphigenia* by Joanna Lumley (c. 1550), and in the first English play known to be written by a woman, Elizabeth Cary's *The Tragedie of Mariam* (published 1613), personal connections seem to be involved both in the genesis of the works and in the characterization of the protagonists. Whereas Mary Sidney translated *Antonius* on the way to her greater goal of becoming a poet, Joanna Lumley, whose work was confined to youthful exercises, seems to have translated *Iphigenia* in direct response to a work by her husband; and Elizabeth Cary appears to have used the drama to represent and symbolically resolve conflicts in her own life. While Lumley's work is notable for its heroic subject, more important to women's writing is Cary's *Mariam* in which the playwright modified the impersonality of a literary genre to express her own ideas and emotions. A brief look at *Iphigenia* as an early indication of interest in the female hero will precede a detailed examination of *Mariam* as a more fully developed glorification of woman. Since neither of these plays was designed for public performance, the playwright, unconfined by stage conventions, may have felt more able to represent her own ideals.

JOANNA LUMLEY (1537?–1576/1577)

Joanna Lumley's teenage years were a humanist's delight, for a holograph manuscript includes her Latin versions of five orations by Isocrates, two Latin letters to her father, the Earl of Arundel, and "The Tragedie of Euripides called Iphigeneia translated out of Greake into Englisshe."[5] In one of the letters to her father she noted that following the recommendation of Cicero, she was devoting herself to Greek literature and that she derived "incredibilem voluptatem," wonderful pleasure, from reading "Evagoras," Isocrates' fourth oration to Nicocles.[6] Herself the owner of at least fifteen books, Lumley was fortunate to have a father who collected a large library and to marry John, Lord Lumley, who possessed "probably the largest private library in Elizabethan England," having inherited both his father-in-law's library and that of Thomas Cranmer.[7] Sharing his wife's interest in learning, in 1550, John Lumley translated Erasmus's *Institutio Principis Christiani* as *The Education of a Christian Prince*, dedicating the work to his father-in-law. At about the same time, using Erasmus's Latin translation, Joanna Lumley was translating *Iphigenia*, raising the possibility that the two works were companion pieces.

Married shortly after John Lumley's matriculation at Cambridge in 1549, Lord and Lady Lumley remained Catholic, and were prominent at Queen Mary's coronation. However, they also survived the Protestant reigns before and after hers, despite John Lumley's spending at least a year and a half in prison under suspicion of complicity in plots involving Mary, Queen of Scots. Camden memorializes him as a "person of entire virtue, integrity, and innocence, and in his old age a complete pattern of true nobility."[8] Little else is known of Joanna Lumley, except that in 1575–1576, Sir Nicholas Bacon, Lord Keeper of the Great Seal, sent "at her desire" an illuminated manuscript of the classical *sententiae* which decorated the long gallery at Gorhambury.[9] Besides indicating Lumley's continuing interest in the classics and something of her taste for moral statement, the gift suggests a possible acquaintance between her and Sir Nicholas's learned wife, Anne Cooke Bacon.

Joanna Lumley's principal work, the translation of *Iphigenia*, is illuminated by her particular circumstances and by consideration of the genre she chose. She seems to be not only the first woman, but also the first person, to translate a Greek drama into English. Perhaps the Lumleys shared a scholarly interest in translation and so each chose to prepare a work by Erasmus. But what drew Joanna Lumley to *Iphigenia* in particular? It may be that using Erasmus's Latin, as copy text or as aid, assured an entirely "safe," impersonal voice for a play about female heroism. Drama, especially a translated drama, might indeed have interested a young woman because of its very impersonality. Built on conflict, a play may present several sides to a question, so that seeking the playwright in one character or opinion becomes difficult or impossible. As a mask, it is highly satisfactory because it even precludes the need for a persona; thus, Joanna Lumley appears not as the creator of the play, but as an English voice for Euripides.[10]

The action of *Iphigenia at Aulis* evolves from Agamemnon's terrible dilemma between patriotism and paternal love, for he must decide whether to sacrifice his daughter Iphigenia to Diana to ensure the Greek forces' safe passage to Troy. But it is Iphigenia herself who finally assumes the burden of decision—and a hero's stature—for after overcoming her initial fear and horror, she decides to sacrifice herself for the benefit of her country:

I wolde counsell you therfore to suffer this troble paciently, for I muste nedes die, and will suffer it willingelye. Consider I praie you mother, for what a lawfull cause I shalbe slaine ... if this wicked enterprise of the Trojans be not revenged, than truly the grecians shall not kepe neither their children, nor yet their wives in peace: And I shall not onlie remedie all thes thinges withe my deathe: but also get a glorious renowne to the grecians for ever. Suerlie mother we can not speake againste this, for do you not thinke it to be better that I shulde die, then so many noble men to be let of their journye for one womans sake? for one noble man is better than a thousande women. Besides this seinge my deathe is determined amongste the goddes, trulie no mortall man oughte to withstande it. Wherfore I will offer my selfe willingly to deathe, for my countrie. (fol. 91v-92v)[11]

Significantly, the theme here, subordination of the self for the good of one's country, echoes a central theme of the work John Lumley completed in 1550, Erasmus's *Education of a*

Christian Prince. The fundamental assumption of Erasmus's work is that it is morally, ethically, and spiritually "the duty of a good prince to consider the welfare of his people, even at the cost of his own life if need be. But that prince does not really die who loses his life in such a cause."[12] The prince must imitate Christ's humility, so that Erasmus advises, "if you cannot look out for the possessions of your subjects without danger to your own life, set the safety of the people before your very life!" (154-55). Erasmus advises the prince's instructor to create the picture of a perfect ruler for the prince to emulate:

> a sort of celestial creature, more like to a divine being than a mortal: complete in all the virtues; born for the common good; yea, sent by the God above to help the affairs of mortals by looking out and caring for everyone and everything. . . . (162)

In response to John Lumley's interest in such teaching, Joanna Lumley produced a text featuring a noble princess, a female version of the selfless prince. Just as Erasmus's *Education* continually insists on the prince's need of Christianity ("He should be taught that the teachings of Christ apply to no one more than to the prince," 148), his Latin *Iphigenia* suggested to Joanna Lumley that Iphigenia was a crypto-Christian imbued with the spirit, if not the knowledge and grace, of a Christian. When Erasmus renders the Greek with implicitly Christian diction, Lumley provides English parallels. In the renunciation speech to her mother quoted above, numerous phrases resonate with Christian connotations: "I wolde counsell you therfore to suffer this troble paciently, for I muste nedes die, and will suffer it willingelye. . . . And I shall not onlie remedie all thes thinges withe my deathe . . . . I shall not only leave a perpetuall memorie of my deathe. . . ." The chorus at once responds, "Suerlie you are happie O Iphigeneya, that you can suffer so paciently all this troble." To Achilles who offers to help her to live, Iphigenia says, "suffer me rather to save all grece withe my deathe," and to her grieving mother, "Be of good comforte mother I praie you" (fol. 93). Iphigenia believes that "with my deathe I shall purchase unto them a glorious victorie..." (fol. 94v). After her miraculous assumption by Diana, the Nuncius tells Clitemnestra, "this daie your daughter hath bene bothe alive and deade," and the chorus remarks that she is indeed "taken up into heaven" (fol. 96v), so recalling the words of St. John in Revelation 1:17-18, "I am the first and the last: I am he that lives and was dead; and behold I am alive for evermore." By choosing a Greek play about a heroic woman and by selecting those passages from Erasmus with Christian resonance, Lumley composed a version of the play which would pay tribute to a woman's Christian spirit, courage, and eventual sanctification.[13]

Elizabeth Cary (1585–1639)

In 1641, Clarendon remarked that Elizabeth Cary was "a lady of a most masculine understanding, allayed with the passions and infirmities of her own sex. . . ." In 1962, Douglas Bush wrote that "Lucius Cary was the son of . . . a devoutly Catholic mother of literary, masculine, and eccentric character."[14] The attribution of masculinity that has haunted Elizabeth Cary's intellectual achievements may explain why women so carefully guarded or apologized for their abilities. For many reasons, Cary—a scholar, dramatist, poet, religious polemicist, wife, and mother—encountered difficulties in practically every aspect of her life; a source of continual conflict was her attempt to live the "masculine" life of the mind while devotedly carrying out the role and duties of a woman.

The full-length biography of Elizabeth Tanfield Cary, Viscountess Falkland, written by one of her daughters, enriches interpretation of her work, because there are clear parallels between her experiences as a woman and wife and the content of her play, *The Tragedie of Mariam, The Faire Queene of Jewry*. In this respect, *Mariam* seems atypical, if not unique, among Elizabethan and Jacobean closet dramas, and suggests that a woman writer actually modified conventional forms to express her particular subject. As the study of Aemilia Lanyer's treatment of poetic praise and Mary Wroth's use of romance and sonnet sequence in the next two chapters will also suggest, late Renaissance women writers may indeed have been striving to create their own distinctive literature from existing traditions.

Written by one of her four daughters, all of whom became nuns at Cambrai, *The Lady Falkland: Her Life* (c. 1655) is complicated by the author's reverence for her mother and by her own piety. The daughter's central interest is her mother's conversion to Catholicism, and so the biography becomes a spiritual history verging on hagiography of Lady Falkland who withstood persecution from her husband and her society for decades. Nevertheless, the account of Elizabeth Cary's early years seems relatively free from bias and accurate when compared to other sources, and if the biographer sympathized strongly with her mother, by no means does she cast her father as a villain.[15] What the biographer does consistently reveal is that all her life, Elizabeth Cary struggled with established authority, whether it was that of her parents, the Protestant church, her mother-in-law, or her husband. She wrote *Mariam* sometime during the first decade of her marriage, when she was beginning to live under her husband's authority; juxtaposed to *The Lady Falkland: Her Life*, *The Tragedie of Mariam* seems to be closely related to the life of its author as a young married woman.[16]

Mariam is also unique as a drama in two other respects: it is the first English play about the private lives of King Herod the Great and Queen Mariam, and it is the only early play on the subject in which the drama centers on Mariam's tragedy.[17] Cary drew her material from Lodge's 1602 translation of Josephus' *Jewish Antiquities* which provides a detailed account of Herod's career. But Cary's protagonist is Mariam, around whom she designs a drama relevant to Cary's own time and indeed to her own life. With countless other writers of the sixteenth and seventeenth centuries, Cary treats the question of obedience to authority, and in particular, the obedience of a wife to the authority of her husband. Through the characters and choruses, she presents both the orthodox view of wifely obedience and a challenge to that tradition. In the end, this conflict gives way to a Christian allegory, by which the drama is resolved.

Elizabeth Cary's unwillingness merely to endorse accepted attitudes is startling, considering how social theory, law, religion, and custom upheld a husband's authority. In Renaissance England, the authority of a husband over his wife was a principle constantly uttered in pulpit and press. Indeed, a wife's obedience was as strongly urged as the subject's obedience to the monarch or the Christian's to the church. The Elizabethan additions to the *Homilies* included one "Of the state of matrimony" advocating wifely obedience, and in *Basilikon Doron*, James I instructed his son in the authority of a husband as in the authority of a king.[18] In the early seventeenth century, the two famous divines, Dr. William Gouge and William Whately, preached and later published their advice on marriage which centered on the wife's duty to obey.[19] St. Paul was everywhere quoted as the authority for domestic arrangement: "Wives, submit yourselves unto your husbands, as unto the Lord." In the face of such strictures, Elizabeth Cary's independent spirit seems all the more extraordinary, and her conflicts all the more understandable.

Elizabeth Cary was brilliant, pious, energetic, and talented. If her biographer is correct, she was one of the most prolific literary women of her time. Before she was seventeen, she translated Ortelius, and later wrote two plays and a life of Tamburlaine, translated Cardinal du Perron, and composed verse lives of St. Mary Magdalen, St. Agnes Martyr, and St. Elizabeth of Portugal, as well as many lesser verses. She is also the possible author of a history of the reign of Edward II.[20] At the same time, she led the life of a daughter of the upper gentry: she married the man chosen by her parents and had eleven children. If it were not for her daughter's biography, Cary's image would be that of the well-born, well-educated Renaissance woman who was a wife and mother, and author of classical or pious works as well—a "learned and virtuous" woman like Margaret More Roper, Anne Cooke Bacon, or Mary Sidney Herbert. But the *Life* is a disturbing document that details the many conflicts and emotional crises that Elizabeth Cary experienced during much of her life. Many of her troubles came from her early attraction and final conversion to Catholicism, an act that caused spiritual, familial, and political struggles. Some of the biographer's information suggests that certain of Cary's problems also stemmed from the continual, internal clash between her desire for intellectual independence and achievement and the requirements of her position as daughter, wife, and mother.

She was the only child of Sir Laurence and Lady Elizabeth Tanfield of Burford Priory, Oxford. Her stern parents bore a reputation in the county for hardness and arrogance. Lady Tanfield in particular was disliked by the inhabitants of Great Tew who complained that "she saith that we are more worthy to be ground to powder than to have any favour showed to us...."[21] Whether Elizabeth Cary's mother was harsh at home, the biographer does not say; but Cary seems to have been an isolated child who without teachers learned French, Spanish, Italian, Hebrew, and Latin, and who "was skilful and curious in [needle] working, never having been helped by anybody" (*Life*, 5). Elizabeth, without siblings "nor other companion of her age, spent her whole time in reading, to which she gave herself so much that she frequently read all night" (6). In an attempt to discipline this intellectual thirst, her mother forbade the servants to give her candles, but Elizabeth bribed her attendants to bring her the necessary light. Her father was totally devoted to his work as a judge, and is mentioned in other contexts in the *Life* only when he gave Calvin's *Institutes* to the twelve-year-old Elizabeth (the biographer claims she found Calvin wanting) and when he married her to Sir Henry Cary. Although the biographer's glimpse of Elizabeth Cary's childhood is brief, she describes a solitary, precocious, independent spirit who would circumvent or even challenge authority when her quest for knowledge demanded it.[22]

The Tanfields contracted the alliance to Sir Henry Cary in June 1602, the marriage took place in the autumn, and the seventeen-year-old bride continued to live at home for the first year or more, perhaps until the autumn or Christmas of 1603. The biographer claims that "about that time" Henry Cary went to Holland "leaving her still with her own friends." It was the conventional arranged marriage, for the *Life* records that Henry Cary married Elizabeth "only for being an heir, for he had no acquaintance with her (she scarce even having spoken to him) and she was nothing handsome, though then very fair" (7). The biographer does not directly reveal Lady Cary's attitude except to note that while living at home and separated from Sir Henry, her letters to her husband were written by others under her mother's orders. In view of Cary's precocious ability, it is possible that her mother did not approve of what she would send to Sir Henry, or that the new wife was not inclined to write.

Sometime in the second year of marriage, Sir Henry's mother insisted that Elizabeth come to live with her. The young bride did not get along well with her mother-in-law and Lady Katherine Cary, vested with the power of a parent, treated her daughter-in-law strictly. Lady Katherine was

> one that loved much to be humoured, and finding her not to apply herself to it, used her very hardly so far as at last to confine her to her chamber, which seeing she little cared for, but entertained herself with reading, the mother-in-law took away all her books, with command to have no more brought her. (8).

Those books, catalogued near the end of the *Life*, reveal Cary's prodigious appetite for learning:

> She had read very exceeding much; poetry of all kinds, ancient and modern, in several languages, all that ever she could meet; history very universally, especially all ancient Greek and Roman historians; all chroniclers whatsoever in her own country, and the French histories very thoroughly; of most other countries something, though not so universally; of the ecclesiastical history very much, most especially concerning its chief pastors. Of books treating of moral virtue or wisdom (such as

Seneca, Plutarch's Morals, and natural knowledge, as
Pliny, and of late ones, such as French, Mountaine, and
English, Bacon), she had read very many when she was
young, not without making her profit of them all....
(113)

So habitual and dedicated a reader would find peculiar frustration in the removal of her books, and at this point the *Life*
notes that Cary "set herself to make verses" (8).

Again, she appears as an isolated figure, persecuted by her
mother-in-law, and visited only in secret by one of her husband's sisters and a waiting gentlewoman. But Sir Henry's
return ended her captivity and "from this time she writ many
things for her private recreation, on several subjects and occasions, all in verse...." (9). Life with Sir Henry was difficult,
however. Later, summing up her parents' relationship, the
biographer depicts her father as a stern figure whom her
mother was able to please only through the exercise of enor-
mous self-discipline. Like many other young women of her
time, Elizabeth Cary, joined to a man she did not know, had
to curtail her independent impulses to suit his wishes:

> He was very absolute; and though she had a strong will,
> she had learned to make it obey his. The desire to please
> him had power to make her do that, that others could
> have scarce believed possible for her; as taking care of
> the house in all things (to which she could have no
> inclination but what his will gave her), the applying
> herself to use and love work. (14)

For his sake, although she feared horses, she rode; she dressed
well, although "dressing was all her life a torture to her" and
in fact, she went only so far as to let others tend her "while
she writ or read."

Nevertheless, Cary continued to follow her own interests.
Most notably, the biographer records that "when she was
about twenty years old, through reading, she grew into much
doubt of her religion" (9). The biographer thought that reading Hooker in particular caused her to question her Protestant

faith, but for personal or political reasons, Cary waited another twenty years before breaking openly with her husband, Church, and State.

Elizabeth Cary's conflicts arose because she was both an independent intellectual and also very much a woman of her time, with a strong sense of duty as a wife and later as the mother of eleven children. The biographer emphasizes her strict principles:

> she did always much disapprove the practice of satisfying oneself with their conscience being free from fault, not forbearing all that might have the least show or suspicion of uncomeliness or unfitness; what she thought to be required in this she expressed in this motto (which she caused to be inscribed in her daughter's wedding-ring): *Be and seem*. (16)

This insistence on the conformity of appearance and reality may help to explain how, despite her intellectual cravings and religious troubles, Cary could be a diligent housekeeper and teacher of her children—but not, apparently, without inner conflict and considerable psychic cost.

Symptoms of mental stress did not appear at once, but in later years they would include long bouts of sleeping to escape depression. Sleeping was "her greatest sign of sadness." This "she was used to say she could do when she would, and then tad most will to when she had occasion to have sad thoughts waking...."[23] When she was pregnant with her second and fourth children (Lucius, 1609–1610; Lorenzo, 1612), she "had some occasions of trouble" and became subject to such melancholy "that she lost the perfect use of her reason" (16). The biographer suggests that "it is like she at first gave the more way to it at those times, thinking her husband would then be most sensible of her trouble, knowing he was extraordinarily careful of her when she was with child or gave suck, as being a most tenderly loving father" (17). That Elizabeth Cary used her pregnancies to attract her husband's attention to her "trouble" suggests a pathetic call for affection. But they were an ill-matched pair: he was a soldier and courtier, an active, worldly man of severe and stubborn temperament; she was an introspective, unworldly woman of deeply religious bent. Their relationship deteriorated with time, and much later in 1625, a final rift was caused by Lady Falkland's open conversion to Catholicism. At this point, Henry Falkland cut off her allowance, removed everything he could from the house, and took away her children and all but one servant. Hasty judgment and some vindictiveness, rather than religious indignation, characterized his actions, and only a Privy Council order restored to Lady Falkland a subsistence maintenance.[24]

In *The Tragedie of Mariam*, Cary seems to have used the figures of the drama to represent some of the problems and contradictions which were surfacing in her early married life, and to place her struggles in a wider context. The play may be seen as a psychomachia, one that Elizabeth Cary resolved by extending the limits of her personal conflict.

No contemporary notice of *Mariam* survives. While early criticism tended to belittle Cary's subject matter and poetic skills, more recently, critics have given closer attention to what Cary actually achieved. Leonora Brodwin noted that "however inferior her poetic and dramatic talents may be, Cary's treatment of Herod does show a remarkable perception of one of the most complex of psychological types." Nancy Cotton Pearse has suggested that the "sentiments expressed in the play are autobiographical," and that Cary's ambivalence about her life is reflected in the contrasting characters of Mariam and Salome. Sandra Fischer thinks *Mariam*, based on Cary's own experience, reveals "how a woman handles tyranny and maintains her own integrity."[25] What is indeed remarkable about this play is the unusual prominence given to a virtuous woman's psychological conflicts, the carefully balanced polemic on the question of woman's place, and the extraordinary fifth act in which the female protagonist becomes a type of Christ. If not a great work, if not poetically brilliant, *The Tragedie of Mariam* is created from a strong conflict intelligently understood and sometimes eloquently expressed.

Mariam is based on material in Chapters 15 and 16 of Lodge's translation of Josephus's *Jewish Antiquities*. Strictly maintaining the unity of time, Cary collapses years of Josephus's account into the events of a day. While Herod, King of the Jews, is away making peace with Octavius Caesar after Actium, his prolonged absence provokes a rumor of his death. In the first three acts, the main characters respond to the news: Herod's brother, Pheroras, thinking he is now free of the king's prohibition, plans to marry the low-born Graphina; Salome, Herod's sister, decides to divorce her husband, Constabarus, in favor of her lover, Sylleus; Constabarus in turn frees the sons of Baba whom he has been hiding from Herod for twelve years. Queen Mariam, at first mourning Herod, recalls that he had ordered her death in the event of his own, and this knowledge, together with his previous execution of her grandfather and brother, initiates her own rebellion. In Act 4 Herod returns to find treason everywhere and his wife cold and accusatory. Salome, Mariam's inveterate enemy, convinces Herod that the queen had plotted with her guardian Sohemus to poison him, and also betrays Constabarus and the sons of Baba. Herod orders the execution of all his enemies, including his wife. Mariam dies nobly, leaving Herod to bitter regret and "Frantike passion for her death."[26]

The historical context is vital to Cary's characterization. Josephus's narrative covers 29–28 B.C., and if the imminence of the Christian era were not already obvious, the margins in Lodge's 1602 translation note the number of years remaining until the birth of Christ.[27] Cary would thus be continually reminded as she read the *Antiquities* that these were the last years of the old dispensation, and she would surely recall Herod the Great as an archetypal villain of the old law and a common symbol of envy, wrath, cruelty, and murder, chiefly remembered for the Slaughter of the Innocents.[28] Believing a new era to be at hand to replace the laws of Herod's kingdom, Cary reinterpreted Josephus's history, and through the workings of Christian allegory, Mariam's defiance of Herod takes on an entirely different aspect. In one sense, she is rebelling against order, but in another, she is heralding the new law.

The most crucial differences between *Mariam* and its source are in Cary's Christian perspective and in her understanding of Mariam's character. Josephus thinks that "nothing more grieved Mariam" in her relationship with Herod "but that she had not any hope to live after him, if so be he should happen to die, especially for the order he had left as concerning her" (*Josephus*, 396). Josephus's Mariam is a schemer who bribes Sohemus to reveal Herod's order with "pretty presents and feminine flatteries"; and Josephus finds all of Mariam's "incredible and apparent hatred" for Herod to have its source in her anger at this order (397). And while he finds her "chaste and faithfull unto him; yet had she a certaine womanly imperfection and naturall frowardnesse, which was the cause that she presumed too much upon the intire affection wherewith her husband was intangled; so that without regard of his person, who had power and authoritie over others, she entertained him oftentimes very outrageously . . ." (397). Josephus consistently disapproves of Mariam's outspokenness, even when she complains of her father's and brother's deaths, for from Herod "she received nothing that might discontent her," yet "she presumed upon a great and intemperate libertie in her discourse" (399).

By contrast, Cary's Mariam is psychologically more complex: from the first scene, her Mariam thinks less about Herod's order for her death than about the conflicting passions in her heart; she thinks about Herod's jealousy destroying her love, but also about her own early love for him. Cary's Sohemus is "mov'd to pitie by Mariam's distrest estate," for her Mariam is incapable of using feminine wiles in any situation and is, if anything, naive about her powers. In other words, the one character flaw that explains Mariam for Josephus is insufficient for Elizabeth Cary, who creates new problems of private and public behavior for her protagonist and probes more deeply into her character.

Indeed, Cary structures the play to make Mariam's conflict between obedience to and rebellion against Herod's authority the central concern. Since Herod does not appear until Act

4, the first three acts mainly elucidate Mariam's position through soliloquy and through the other characters' acting out her psychomachia. We find that Mariam gradually turns away from the influence of Herod's rule, a rule of passion and irrationality, but that her way is beset with inner turmoil and outer conflict. She begins the play torn by her emotions, identifying herself primarily as a woman in love. Eventually, however, she finds she must conquer passion with reason, and learns that she must defy Herod's authority whatever the consequences.

Marriage is the battlefield of the play. Virtue and vice collide through Mariam's and Salome's opposing views on marriage; two minor characters, Graphina and Herod's ex-wife, Doris, provide still other perspectives on wedded life. At the same time, Salome and Graphina dramatically represent the opposing sides of Mariam's dilemma. A philosophical commentary is provided by the choruses—particularly the chorus to Act 3 which considers a wife's duties—and by Constabarus's long last speech on womankind.

Both Mariam and Salome state their positions in Act 1. Mariam is as chaste, loyal, and naive as Salome is promiscuous, inconstant, and scheming. Mariam's heart is "too chaste a Scholler ... To learn to love another than my Lord," while Salome lusts after a new husband as soon as she tires of the old. This time, Salome's means are wholly unorthodox, as she plans to use divorce, a right given only to Hebrew men, to rid herself of Constabarus:

> Why should such priviledge to men be given?
> Or given to them, why bard from women then?
> Are men then we in greater grace with heaven?
> Or cannot women hate as well as men?
> Ile be the custome-breaker: and beginne
> To shew my Sexe the way to freedomes doore,
> And with an offring will I purge my sinne,
> The law was made for none but who are poore.[29]   (B3)

Salome's seizure of male prerogative, accompanied by so cynical a view of law, shakes the proper order of things, for Cary does not allow such female rebellion to go unanswered. Imaging the ancient world in terms of traditional medieval and Renaissance order, Constabarus articulates the orthodox response to impending disorder:

> Are Hebrew women now transform'd to men?
> Why do you not as well our battels fight,
> And weare our armour? suffer this, and then
> Let all the world be topsie turved quite.
> Let fishes graze, beastes, [swine], and birdes descend,
> Let fire burne downewards whilst the earth aspires:
> Let Winters heat and Summers cold offend,
> Let Thistels growe on Vines, and Grapes on Briers,
> Set us to Spinne or Sowe, or at the best
> Make us Wood-hewers, Waters-bearing wights.
>
> (B4v-C)

In a deeply offended tone, underlined by anaphora and oxymoron, Constabarus raises the specter of the "mannish woman" and the "womanish man," both signs of divinely arranged order turned upside down. He reacts both to Salome's vociferousness and to her sexual aggression, the reverse of traditional feminine silence and chastity.[30] Cary writes most vividly here, perhaps an indication of the importance she attached to this war between the sexes. That she should have created a dialectic between husband and wife is interesting, but it is even more noteworthy that she does not allow the conventional pro-husband response to dominate in either poetic form or content. At the same time, authorial approval cannot easily be assigned to Salome, the villain, and Constabarus's argument bears all the weight of tradition. Tensely, the two sides balance, partly because the even match between Salome and Constabarus foreshadows the difficult situation soon to face Mariam, and partly because Cary may have been unwilling to resolve the conflict.[31]

Salome expresses Mariam's rebellious tendencies, although Mariam herself is no villain. The slave, Graphina, represents Mariam's purity at the very time when the queen intends to disobey her husband. As Salome's opposite, Graphina is the epitome of traditional female virtue: she is chaste, obedient, and silent. In the scene Cary invents between Graphina and her lover, Pheroras, Graphina is modestly silent, speaking only when addressed and then with humility and gratitude for Pheroras's having chosen her. She promises "steadfast love/And fast obedience." The word "silence" is associated with Graphina five times in less than thirty lines, making her a significant foil to the vociferous Salome and even to Mariam's "unbridled speech." Compared to Salome, Graphina is feeble and lackluster, but literary virtue often appears less interesting and lively than vice, and requires the reader to distinguish the truth. Cary may have given Salome better lines because dramatic villains customarily reflected the attractiveness of vice; or it may be that she enjoyed articulating Salome's impudence much more than Graphina's pious orthodoxy.

More important, Cary here represents the dilemma which continually faced women writers themselves: in a culture that associated silence with feminine virtue, the articulate woman, whether her message was Salome's or Mariam's, risked all the opprobrium reserved for "lewde, idle, froward, and unconstant women."[32] The writer's problem, like Mariam's, was to prove that her utterance did not make her an unnatural woman nor preclude her virtue.

The extremes that Salome and Graphina physically embody also exist in Mariam's mind. By the middle of Act 3, Mariam, though chaste and virtuous, finds she must disobey Herod. Discovering that he is, after all, alive, Mariam feels the prison walls closing around her again. Her love turns to hatred, and rather than fear Herod, she now rejects their old relationship:

> I know I could inchaine him with a smile:
> And lead him captive with a gentle word,
> I scorne my looke should ever man beguile,
> Or other speech, then meaning to afford.
>
> (E2v-E3)

The once-submissive Mariam determines to stand against her husband, identifying herself with the forces of innocence and good against those of evil. Abjuring the temptations of power and position and having sworn "solemne vowes" to forsake Herod's bed, she staunchly concludes, "Let my distressed state unpittied bee,/Mine innocence is hope enough for mee" (E3). It is not enough for Elizabeth Cary, however; against this ringing declaration, she sternly casts a Third Chorus which ponderously recites the code of laws for Judea's wives:

> Tis not enough for one that is a wife
> To keepe her spotles from an act of ill:
> But from suspition she should free her life,
> And bare her selfe of power as well as will.
>
> (E3v)

Wives belong to their husbands body and soul, so much so that even "their thoughts no more can be their owne" (E4v). Not only total loyalty to her husband, but total lack of desire for public recognition must govern the true wife's actions. In the judgment of such authority, Mariam stands guilty both because of her confidential talks with Sohemus and because of her rebellion against Herod. In the dramatic structure of the play, the Third Chorus ensures that there is a complete separation between Mariam and established authority.

The extent of Mariam's isolation is marked by her final, brief confrontation with Herod, late in the play. Quietly defying her husband, Mariam returns his passionate declarations with sober accusations that he has killed her relatives. Her stance is like that of an early Christian martyr—an analogy that may well have been in Cary's mind.[33] While Josephus's unequivocal moral is that disobedience means death, even for the otherwise virtuous Mariam, Cary goes on to create an elaborate mechanism by which Mariam can be both rebel and virtuous woman. She begins by making the very voice of order, Constabarus, into Mariam's eulogist.

Constabarus, also betrayed by Salome, goes to his execution cursing all womankind except Mariam. According to Constabarus, the world that destroys Mariam is thoroughly evil, peopled by women who are "Tygers, Lyonesses, hungry Beares," the fallen Angels, the scourge of mankind, the second flood, destroyers of order and laws: "Your best are foolish, froward, wanton, vaine,/Your worst adulterous, murderous, cunning, proud" (G). Evil entered the world with women and is maintained by them, particularly those who deny their proper place and take upon themselves men's roles. This vituperation, reminiscent of many literary attacks on women, should theoretically apply to Mariam herself. But Cary uses it here to effect Mariam's complete separation from her environment by making her "alone of all her sex," the virtuous exception. While Constabarus claims women caused the first fall, Mariam with whom he associates "grace," is gradually being established as the atoner for that fall. After this assertion of Mariam's uniqueness, her death cannot be an execution, but a sacrifice.

In her last soliloquy, Mariam praises humility, implying her own abandonment of worldly pride. The Third Chorus detailed her breach of fealty to Herod, the old law; Constabarus distinguished her from all other women; and her final speech separates her from the world: "And therefore can they but my life destroy,/My Soule is free from adversaries power" (G4). Although Salome and Herod are responsible for Mariam's death, ironically they free her from themselves, from malice, passion, wrath, and pride.

At the climax of the play is the transfiguration of Mariam: her death is an allegory of the Crucifixion, for she foreshadows redemption from the old law, typified by Herod's kingdom. By transcending his earthly authority, she points to a higher and final authority.

A Nuntio describes Mariam's death to Herod in a speech filled with analogies to the death of Christ. In the second line of Act 5, the Nuntio already refers to Mariam as "your heavenly selfe," and he reports on going

> To see the last of her that was the best:
> To see if death had hart to make her stoop,
> To see the Sunne admiring *Phoenix* nest. (H2)

The resurrection of the phoenix traditionally symbolized the resurrection of Christ, and the death of Mariam mirrors that event.[34] She was calm and mild, her look keeping "the world in awe." But her mother, Alexandra, turned on her to "loudly raile" and revile her, recalling the multitude reviling Christ. Even Herod is shocked at this treatment of the "worlds delight." But Mariam "came unmov'd with pleasant grace,/As if to triumph her arrivall were." Herod asks, "But what sweet tune did this faire dying Swan/Afford thine eare: tell all, omit no letter" (H2v). To the Christian ear, Herod's metaphor recalls the bird who sings joyfully at its imminent death, for it knows that death leads to eternal life. Mariam's last words to the Nuntio allude to the resurrection: "By three daies hence if wishes could revive,/I knowe himselfe would make me oft alive" (H3). Finally, the Nuntio records that she prayed silently, "And thus to heav'n her heav'nly soule is fled." In his darkness, Herod indeed wishes for Mariam's resurrection, but cannot understand how this might occur, other than to hope for some sort of magic trick.

In a clear allusion to the suicide of Judas Iscariot, the Nuntio then reports that he found the butler who betrayed Mariam hanging himself on a tree.[35] Realizing Mariam's innocence, Herod knows "She was my gracefull moytie, me accurst,/To slay my better halfe and save my worst" (H3v). The Nuntio in fact identifies Mariam with Abel, a traditional type of Christ: "If sainted *Abel* yet deceased bee,/Tis certaine *Mariam* is as dead as hee" (H3v). Herod himself intensifies the allusion by representing himself as worse than Cain. As Mariam's light surpasses Herod's darkness, like Christ, she surpasses all classical comparisons. More beautiful than Venus, more clever than Mercury, chaster than Cynthia, Mariam is the reality next to which "the/*Greekes* but dreame." They are but the shadow, she the real substance.

By raising Mariam to spiritual heroism at the end of the play, Cary removes her protagonist from the earthly problems that beset her to a transcendant state. The idealization of Mariam changes her from a disobedient wife and subject to a prophet of Christianity. With Mariam's death, the play becomes a triumph of the spirit over the flesh, of patience over passion.

This reading of Mariam emphasizes concerns that appear to have their spiritual roots in Elizabeth Cary's own life. While Cary seems to have accepted the tradition of male authority, her own experience living under its rule was difficult and often painful. Her biographer claims that her mother consciously made Sir Henry the arbiter of all her actions, even though her own instincts directed her elsewhere. Whether Salome speaks for Cary's rebelliousness or Graphina articulates her ideas on obedience is unclear; significantly, the first four acts of the play consider both duty and individual need and reveal Cary's concern with the difficulties of obedience in an authoritarian marriage, especially in matters of individual conscience.

While viewing a play through the playwright's life is often problematic, to do so in this case allows insights not possible from a simple dramatic analysis. For instance, the play may indeed echo something of Herod's medieval heritage, or of Salome's similarity to popular stage villains; using Graphina and Salome to represent Mariam's two sides may recall the medieval Virtue and Vice, the Good and Bad Angels of *Dr. Faustus* or even Desdemona and Iago in *Othello*. But more crucial to the play is the character of Mariam, who is an unusual balance of virtue and error, of chastity and pride, crowned by a final sanctification. No stereotyped Castiza or Castabella, nor yet possessing the dramatic power of a Webster heroine, Mariam serves Cary's purpose by undergoing her own conflicts and then becoming a divine symbol. Current dramatic conventions, with which Cary was certainly familiar, may account somewhat for the shape of the play, but give little help in understanding Mariam's character or the ending.

Certainly, the coincidental parallels between the lives of Mariam and Elizabeth Cary are striking: an isolated woman, an ill-matched marriage, an authoritarian husband who dominates even from afar, a cold and unsympathetic family. These analogies alone may have drawn Cary to choose her subject from Josephus. But if the play began with the author's attraction to a historical figure, it developed into a discussion of woman's place, of marriage, and the strong identification of a female character with the Christian ethic. Mariam's heroic martyrdom may also have been Cary's attempt to justify the way she chose to live her own life.

In this respect, the fifth act assumes considerable interest. While the idealization of Mariam as a spiritual hero certainly seems to evolve from a historical context in which Mariam represents the new religious dispensation, her glorification may also have psychological roots. The playwright's double perspective on Mariam, which results from sympathizing with her problems and yet knowing she defies proper authority, is simplified by redesigning her death. Cary makes Mariam a purely symbolic figure who does not appear at all in Act 5. The emotional crises evaporate and we are left with a repentant Herod and a final chorus seeking a "warning to posteritie" in the play's events.

To Elizabeth Cary, problems, whether in art or in life, could be solved by glorifying the specifically Christian virtues of patience, fortitude, and unselfishness. Certainly in the early stages of her marriage, she attempted to live by this creed, suppressing self-interest and patiently guiding herself to submit. The biographer cites her mother's rule, "that wherever conscience and reason would permit her, she should prefer the will of another before her own" (*Life*, 13). Similarly, her play, after four acts of rampant self-assertion by the characters, ends with heroic self-abnegation, making the protagonist a precursor of Christ's self-sacrifice. Perhaps Cary's own religious longings prompted her to give a female character such a role. Her attraction to Catholicism included particular devotion to the Virgin Mary; the biographer recalls that she

> bore a great and high reverence to our blessed Lady, to whom, being with child of her last daughter (and still a Protestant), she offered up that child, promising, if it were a girl, it should in devotion to her bear her name, and that as much as was in her power, she would endeavour to have it to be a nun. (18)

Earlier, while still struggling with the form of her faith, Cary drew the Mariam of Act 5, perhaps to create a model of the divinely inspired woman, an ideal of patience in adversity, of fortitude under oppression.

Mariam may have meant even more to Cary, because she also dramatizes the problems of the woman writer struggling between the private sphere of silent feminine virtue and the public world of masculine discourse. When Mariam speaks to someone besides her husband, she breaks the rules governing feminine utterance; when she reasons and argues with Herod, she compounds her disobedience by expressing it eloquently. Cary specifically shows how Mariam's "unbridled speech" precipitates her condemnation. But even if she speaks publicly, as the virtuous exception in Constabarus's misogynist attack, Mariam also resembles the learned and virtuous Renaissance woman, the atoner who devoted herself to redeeming her sex from Eve's guilt. On one hand, Mariam's death punishes her outspokenness, so warning women to be silent; on the other hand, it makes her a martyr. Mariam's Christian triumph may well reflect Cary's optimism for her own art by detaching her surrogate from earthly oppression. By affirming Christian values, Cary modified the challenge her writing posed to traditional feminine boundaries. And significantly, she designated woman's Christian heroism as an important subject for the woman writer.

Cary's intense religious devotion offered her a way to understand her position and to live her life, but not without intellectual conflict and mental anguish. In her play, however, she could create a fictional resolution for her dilemmas and a triumph for her highest ideals. Cary deliberately ends the play with Mariam calm, dignified, and victorious, while Herod is half-mad with grief and despair. Not only do they appropriately represent the new law and the old, but Elizabeth Cary may also have fulfilled her own wishes in the triumph of Mariam over Herod. The end of the play, where history, allegory, and pyschodrama merge, certainly alters the perspective of Josephus's narrative, and perhaps also on the nature of authority itself. In the end, Herod's authority as husband and king is supplanted by the power of Mariam, to whom Cary gives the higher authority of Christian doctrine.

It is tempting to suggest that the identification of a female protagonist with the Christian ethic is Cary's way of superseding male authority, which she otherwise seems to support. In her own life, she always deferred to Henry Cary, and taught her children to revere him, although her Catholicism and their incompatibility brought about a bitter separation lasting from 1625 to just before his death in 1633. In her account of her parents' marriage, the author of the *Life* clearly wished her mother to be remembered not as a rebel, but as a pious woman who recognized a hierarchy of duty: her first priority was God, and she sacrificed to her faith not only physical comfort and material needs, but also a conventional marriage and family life.

As a writer, Cary dramatized the dilemmas of a virtuous woman whom she developed as a Christian hero. Like other women writers, she introduced a feminine type, an allegorical figure like the wise virgins or brides of Christ to emphasize the transcendant power of feminine spirituality; but for the first time, evidence exists that this allegory actually emanated from the writer's perceptions of her own life as well as from her literary and religious education. If feminine images and symbols were important in the works of earlier writers, here they seem to be inextricably linked to the complex process of becoming a writer.

SEVEN

THE FEMINIZATION
OF PRAISE:
AEMILIA LANYER

T HE IMPETUS to glorify virtuous women, whether manifested in Mary Sidney's consecration of Elizabeth or in Joanna
Lumley's and Elizabeth Cary's idealization of fictional heroines, was crucial to the development of women's poetry. In
creating such images of beneficent feminine power, these
women writers justified their own literary endeavors: whether
in the person of a Virgin Queen or a feminine type of Christ,
a redeemed Eve who spoke and acted wisely and well authorized their own virtuous intentions as writers. By ransom-
ing women's knowledge and speech from the suspicion of
subversion and shrewishness, they could themselves attempt
more as writers and gently woo an audience to read their
works. Nowhere is this process more evident than in the work
of Aemilia Lanyer, the first woman seriously and systematically to write epideictic poetry, the poetry of praise, about
women.

Until Lanyer wrote *Salve Deus Rex Judaeorum* (published
1611), the Renaissance praise of virtuous women, both as real
people and as ideal figures, was almost entirely in the hands
of men and so had accrued many conventions appropriate to
men addressing women. Dominant were the language of
courtship and the assumption that the woman praised was
an exception to her sex. Often, male praise evolved from the
poet's own amorous, political, religious, economic, or poetic
interests rather than from the woman herself.[1] Even the trend

which Barbara Lewalski has called "the Christianization of the poetry of praise," while it might alter the virtues for which the lady was praised, did not ultimately focus on the woman's spirituality but on the poet's.

For instance, in her study of Donne's *Anniversaries*, Lewalski argues that in his treatment of the fifteen-year-old Elizabeth Drury, Donne's "praise does not celebrate Elizabeth Drury as an individual or her personal merit as a Catholic saint, but rather God's image in her, God's grace working upon her, which causes her to exhibit to us the paradigm of regeneration. The focus is not upon God but upon Elizabeth, yet upon her as she is recipient of the grace of regeneration and thereby able to symbolize the apex of human goodness in the orders of nature, grace, and glory."[2] In some respects, Donne's poems of praise expanded greatly the possibility of feminine symbolism, much as women writers would themselves wish. But his choice of Elizabeth Drury reflects the male point of view as much as does Ben Jonson's projection onto Lucy, Countess of Bedford of the ideal woman "I could most desire/To honor, serve, and love; as *Poets* use."[3] Donne's praise is thoroughly Protestant, as Lewalski shows; but this includes his clear acceptance of traditional views about women and concupiscence ("One woman at one blow, then kill'd us all,/ And singly, one by one, they kill us now"—*The first Anniversary*, ll. 106-107), which also explains why he saw the image of a chaste, virtuous girl as the perfect poetic representation of the regenerate soul:

> She, of whom the Ancients seem'd to prophesie,
> When they call'd vertues by the name of *shee*;
> Shee in whom vertue was so much refin'd,
> That for Allay unto so pure a minde
> Shee tooke the weaker Sex; shee that could drive
> The poysonous tincture, and the staine of *Eve*,
> Out of her thoughts, and deeds; and purifie
> All, by a true religious Alchymie;
> Shee, shee is dead;[4]

It is Elizabeth Drury's very "virgin white integritie" that encourages Donne to explore through her the redemption of all humanity; in this sense, her sex is useful, but it is only her chastity that is essential.

Aemilia Lanyer probably wrote *Salve Deus Rex Judaeorum* a few months before Donne began his first poem on Elizabeth Drury, the "Funerall Elegie."[5] While both poets were concerned with the ideal Christian woman, it is important to distinguish Donne's praise (and Jonson's too) of the Christian woman from Lanyer's, because Lanyer's work evolves from a quintessentially feminine poetic consciousness. Whereas Donne and Jonson developed their images of virtuous women "as *Poets* use," hoping to reveal a truth about human nature (and revealing much about the poet himself), Lanyer wrote specifically to praise women, and more precisely, to redeem for them their pivotal importance as Christians.

To accomplish her task, Lanyer called upon her considerable knowledge of English poetry, her scriptural reading, and a familiarity with traditional debate material on the woman question. Whether or not she had read the works of other women writers—she does refer to Mary Sidney's Psalms—like many of her predecessors, she found particular value in the feminine allegories of Scripture. The parable of the wise virgins and the Songs of Songs provided images central to Lanyer's attempts to place women at the heart of Christianity, and she developed their potential with new intensity and completeness.

To this point, the only other feminine work of praise to develop the image of the brides of Christ was an elegy on Marguerite de Navarre, published in 1551 and written by Anne, Margaret, and Jane Seymour, the three young daughters of Edward Seymour, Duke of Somerset and Anne Stanhope, both ardent Reformers. In their 104 Latin distichs, the Seymours present Marguerite, the "Sacra Regina," as the example of feminine purity and piety while on earth and like the wise virgins, as the bride of Christ in heaven. Marguerite is ready with her oil-filled lamp when the bridegroom comes ("Foelix quae SPONSO vigilans veniente reperta est/Lampada non oleo dificiente suam"—13); she strives to lead a pure life in order to die well ("Quaeris cur studuit puram bene ducere vitam?/ Ut bene supremum posset obire diem"—

39); and she burns with Christ's delicious kisses ("Ussit, et exarsit: quidni? libabat amica/Oscula, sed CHRISTO deliciosa suo"—55).[6]

In the preface to their book, the sisters themselves were the subject of much praise for their "learned and chaste" efforts, including a conceit by Ronsard that if Orpheus heard these "Vierges de renom," these English sirens play, he would have broken his pagan lyre and become a disciple "Dessous leur chanson Chrestiene."[7] Their admirers' insistence that virtue and chastity engendered the sisters' divine poetry actually reflects their own theme that Marguerite de Navarre's perfect virtue prepared her for marriage with Christ. The sisters and their subject, Marguerite, share a virtue which promises salvation after death, or "a second life." By so praising the great woman—and of significance for English Protestants, a woman identified with the French Reformation—the Seymours glorified feminine virtue and glimmeringly suggested the lines that Aemilia Lanyer would later develop to praise the whole sex.

As shadowy as Aemilia Lanyer's life may be today, as a writer she emerges with the color and sound of a vivid personality. Claiming to be motivated by misogynist disparagement of women, in her one published work, *Salve Deus Rex Judaeorum* (1611), Lanyer presents a single-minded, fervent argument for the importance of woman's virtue. Viewing women's history from Eve to the present, Lanyer represents her sex as the heroic protectors of the Christian spirit. In her work, she infuses the image of the true Christian woman, already so important to women writers, with a dramatic new scope. Ranging from Genesis to Gethsemane to the present, her generous imagination successfully unites the most sacred moments of Scripture with figures of contemporary life.

Establishing women's spiritual prominence demands a poetry of praise rooted in women's qualities, and this Lanyer creates more fully and skillfully than any writer before her, partly by extending the conventional exempla to invent her own panegyrics for contemporary ladies, and partly by exploiting imagery representing women's continued reception of God's grace. But Lanyer's devoted praise of women, from her apology for Eve to her encomia for the Countess of Cumberland, does not derive solely from anger or even a desire for justice. Rather, it evolves from her own piety and her poetic calling as a Christian visionary who yearns for a world greatly different from the one she knows. Continually, her poem opposes the fallen, ungodly world with a vision predicated upon Christian ideals, manifested first by Christ himself, and then by women—the Virgin and the Daughters of Jerusalem in the past, and women like the Countesses of Pembroke and Cumberland in the present. Although she has been censured for exaggerating women's qualities and toadying to the great, Lanyer is better understood as a millenarian advocating the establishment on earth of God's will through the particular agency of women. But while her poem begins optimistically enough with the symbols of triumph and communion, and proceeds to celebrate women at the heart of Christian doctrine, it concludes when she painfully recognizes the vast gulf between human wishes and their realization.

Little positive information about Lanyer survives. She has been identified as the daughter of a court musician, Baptist Bassano and his common-law wife, Margaret Johnson; on her title page "Mistris Aemilia Lanyer" appears as the wife of Captain Alfonso Lanyer, who had both a commission and a position as a court musician from 1594 to 1613.[8] Lanyer's text reveals only that Susan, Duchess of Kent had been "the Mistris of my youth,/The noble guide of my ungovern'd dayes"; that Margaret, Countess of Cumberland was something of a patron; and that Lanyer knew about the manuscript of the Countess of Pembroke's Psalms, "written newly."[9] When Captain Lanyer died in 1613, he left her his patent for weighing hay and straw coming to the city of London, but she assigned it to his brother Innocent, with half the profits to go to her. In 1635, she was petitioning for fifty pounds a year, describing herself "in great misery and having two grandchildren to provide for." In subsequent suits against Clement Lanyer who had obtained the monopoly, Lanyer asked for twenty pounds a year, but then refused his proffered five pounds for two quarters. No further references exist after 1640.[10]

Lanyer's poetry reveals that she was ardently Protestant, knew Scripture well, and drew on both Christian and classical tradition to mix scriptural narrative, meditation, and theological allegory with pastoral, encomium, and elegy. While she refers to misogynist tracts and knew their traditional rhetorical devices, as well as those of women's defenders, the core of her argument evolves not from repeating and reversing the old terms of the woman question, but from her admiring portraits of living women praised as the descendants of a redeemed Eve, the daughters of Jerusalem, and the Virgin. In Lanyer's poem, the image of the brides of Christ assumes a new prominence as a way of declaring women's spirituality. By praising such women as the Countesses of Kent, Cumberland, and Pembroke, Lanyer attempts to realize Christian virtue in living women, to warn misogynists of their impiety, and to inspire other women. Particularly in her treatment of the Countess of Cumberland, Lanyer merges her Christian vision and her concept of ideal womanhood.

Salve Deus Rex Judaeorum is divided into three parts: more than 800 lines dedicating the work to Queen Anne, Princess Elizabeth, seven other virtuous ladies, and "To all Vertuous Ladies in generall"; the poem of over 1800 lines, *Salve Deus Rex Judaeorum*, divided into four parts, "The Passion of Christ," "Eves Apologie in defence of Women," "The Teares of the Daughters of Jerusalem," and "The Salutation and Sorrow of the Virgine Marie"; and a poem of 211 lines, "The Description of Cooke-ham," an early example of a country-house poem. These three divisions overlap and interweave in theme and image, creating an integrated vision: the dedications present the essential Christian virtues in the figures of contemporary ladies; *Salve Deus* narrates the central experience of their lives, Christ's passion, and justifies the importance of women to Christianity; "The Description of Cooke-ham" is an elegy for a feminine, Christian paradise.[11]

Although she composed on the well-explored subject of

Christ's Passion, Lanyer's particular perspective results in a distinctive poem. Like other such poems, Lanyer's "Passion"embraces both encomium and elegy, but it also becomes the model for both the subject and form of her poetry on women. In her direct praise of Christ, Lanyer actually reveals Him as the true source of feminine virtue: He appears not as a masculine warrior-hero, but "he plainely shewed that his own profession/Was virtue, patience, grace, love, piety" (109).[12] In the dedications and in her praise of the Countess of Cumberland, Lanyer follows the epideictic mode to glorify virtue imitating that of Christ. In "The Description of Cookeham," she echoes both the death and resurrection (temporal loss and consolation in immortality) of Christian elegy. As a result, her superficially digressive poem develops along single lines of thought, imagination, and execution, all emanating from meditation on the meaning of Christ's life and death. Continually, Lanyer emphasizes this integrity by repeating images of Christ the bridegroom and the Christian triumph, and by developing the Countess of Cumberland's multiple functions as imitator and bride of Christ, patron of Christian poetry, and divine mother-figure.

The dedications may seem at first to be the most dubious part of Lanyer's work, sounding to twentieth-century ears like fulsome, self-serving flattery of potential patrons.[13] Like readers of Jonson's "To Penshurst" or "Elegy on Lady Jane Pawlet," the reader of so much praise must wonder why Lanyer presents her subject as such a paragon of virtue. But seeking to answer that question leads to the poem's central purpose: to reveal the ultimate reality behind the virtuous life, or as Lanyer proposes, "To write of Christ, and of his sacred merits. ..." In her dedications, Lanyer concentrates on the spiritual gifts of women, expressing her intention most clearly in the image of the wise virgins prepared for the bridegroom who will indeed come in the central section of her poem. Unlike many defenders of women, Lanyer implies that her dedicatees are precedents for other women, not mere "blazing comets," and as she intends her "little booke for the generall use of all virtuous Ladies and Gentlewomen of this

Kingdome," she also designs her "commendation of some particular persons of our owne sexe" to prove that "all women deserve not to be blamed." Indeed, this is an understatement, because Lanyer attempts to eradicate centuries of blame with a burst of encomium. In the dedications, each woman's spirituality dominates her portrait, and she joins an ideal gallery devoted solely to Christian virtue.

The persona Lanyer creates to perform this task also emerges in the dedications as a humble soul, apparently self-deprecating like other women writers, yet wholly dedicated to her important task. In the first dedication to the queen, she refers to herself as "dejected," "feeble," "rude," and "unpolished," and continually describes herself as a troubled unfortunate tied to a miserable world, yet yearning for the "happy rayne" of the next. Linked closely to this traditionally Christian affliction is the confession of her inability as a writer, particularly as a divine poet:

> Vouchsafe to view that which is seldome seene,
> A womans writing of divinest things
> (stanza 1)

> My weake distempered braine and feeble spirits,
> Which all unlearned have adventur'd thus
> To write of Christ, and of his sacred merits. . . .
> (stanza 24)

But by redefining the inability topos as human inadequacy before God, Lanyer can identify the poet as a true Christian and underscore the piety of her attempt to praise Christ and to clarify the nature of women.

Exerting negative influence are, she implies, both men who defame women and male poets:

> Not that I learning to my selfe assume,
> Or that I would compare with any man:
> But as they are Scholers, and by Art do write,
> So Nature yields my Soule a sad delight.
> (stanza 25)

Naming the source of her creativity as Nature, Lanyer seeks to circumvent the "Art," the conventions and rhetoric with which men commonly represent women, but "since all Arts at first from Nature came,/That goodly creature, Mother of perfection. ... Why should not She now grace my barren Muse,/And in a Woman all defects excuse" (stanza 26). Like her contemporaries, the poet defines Nature as what God gives humankind, the prime essence, as opposed to Art, what mankind does to nature, the imitation that is often false. Just as she seeks to redefine women's spirituality, the poet wishes to find her poetic voice "At the well head [where] the purest streames arise."[14] This poet, accurately perceiving how she is blocked from masculine Art, wants to create a feminine "natural" poetry not to be judged by men's standards but to be read, delighted in, and used by women. Lanyer does not mean to abandon literary tradition: her poem, although it diverges from masculine conventions of praise, cannot reject all precedents. Instead, mixing form and genre, Lanyer forges a new context and direction for poetry about women.

One of the important aspects of Lanyer's work is the inclusiveness by which she tries to interest a wide feminine audience in its long spiritual history. Not only does *Salve Deus* narrate the Passion, but it turns to the past to exonerate Eve and to the future to praise the Countess of Cumberland. Likewise, in her dedications, she embraces the first lady of the body politic, the queen, "all vertuous Ladies in generall," seven prominent aristocratic women of her day, and the anonymous "Vertuous Reader," thus implying a whole commonwealth of women—or city of ladies—learned and virtuous, to whom she may appeal.

Beginning appropriately with the most prominent, Lanyer addresses Queen Anne, and by themselves these 27 stanzas might seem to conform to the style of florid overstatement common to Renaissance dedications:

> For you have rifled Nature of her store
> And all Goddesses have dispossest
> Of those rich gifts which they enjoy'd before. ...
> (stanza 2)

THE FEMINIZATION OF PRAISE

But in the context of the whole, this language conforms to the poet's exalted style when she considers the qualities of virtuous women. Contributing to this heightened manner are three images drawn from conventional rhetoric, yet used to dignify and enhance women's spirituality. The triumph, the mirror, and the feast appear continually in the dedications, and reinforcing one another, they express the elevation of each woman's virtue.

First, Queen Anne appears in triumph. Like "great Eliza" before her, she displaces the goddesses in the Judgement of Paris and wins the golden ball, gaining State and Dignities from Juno, Wisdome and Fortitude from Pallas, and "all her Excellencies" from Venus. In her "fair triumphant Chariot," she is attended by the Muses, all the Artists, sylvan gods and satyrs, Cynthia and her nymphs.[15] The poet hopes that the splendid light of Anne's triumph will "light on me/That so these rude unpolisht lines of mine,/Graced by you, may seem the more divine" (stanza 6). Holding up a mirror "where some of your faire Virtues will appeare," the poet invites the queen to behold the source of true royalty, "that mightie Monarch both of heav'n and earth/He that all Nations of the world controld" (stanza 8), he who is "Crowne and Crowner of all kings" (stanza 9). In the Passion of Christ that will pass through the mirror, Anne will view "through a glass darkly" the reality of Christian virtue which her own virtues imitate, as do those of the other great ladies whom the poet asks to gaze into the "dim," but true steel.

The third and most important image that Lanyer introduces is that of the feast, to which the queen is "the welcom'st guest." Designating it as a Passover feast, for which she has "prepar'd my Paschal Lambe,/The figure of that living Sacrifice," the poet recalls the Last Supper and its symbolic promise of resurrection. In subsequent dedications, the other virtuous ladies are also bidden to "grace this holy feast" until the poet has completed a female communion: all the seats are for virtuous ladies who act as the new apostles attending Christ. No other image in the poem expresses so powerfully Lanyer's conviction of the unity of women with the central

doctrines of Christianity. To ask the Countess Dowager of
Kent or the Countess Dowager of Pembroke or the Countess
of Dorset to come "unto this wholesome feast" is to praise
them as exemplary Christians in the context of a religious
poem which will examine the very roots of faith. If this is
mere flattery, one suspects that it would not please women
of such piety as Margaret Russell or Mary Sidney.

Lanyer separates her praise of the queen and a brief dedication to her daughter, the Princess Elizabeth, from the dedications to the other seven women with a dedication "To all
vertuous Ladies in generall." While continuing the image of
the triumph, the poet concentrates on representing such ladies
as the wise virgins well prepared for their bridegroom, Christ.
Although this parable had appeared regularly in women's
writing, in her dedications and in her praise of the Countess
of Cumberland, Lanyer exploits the full poetic force of lover
and beloved. The fate of virtuous ladies in poetry had always
been to exist as the idealized, and often deceased, beloveds
of male poets who were principally interested in finding their
own way to heaven. But in this poem, these living women,
because of their own virtues, have a direct relationship with
Christ, their only lover. Having put on their "wedding garments," filled their lamps "with oyle of burning zeale," and
decked themselves with lilies, the ladies may mount in Titan's
"shining chariot" guided by "simple Doves, and subtill ser-
pents" (representing love of the Holy Ghost and Wisdom)
and "come swifter than the motion of the Sunne,/To be trans-
figur'd with our loving Lord": for "In Christ all honour,
wealth and beautie's wonne." Leaving behind "dull and sen-
suall earth," they will undergo "second berth" so that their
"blessed soules may live without all feare,/Being immortall,
subject to no death." As Lanyer develops the metaphor expressing the direct communion of virtuous women with the
resurrected Christ, she simply circumvents masculine poetry
which treated such figures as extraordinary or as mediators
for the poet. Her poetry insists that this is woman's true
nature. Appropriately, in the final stanzas of this dedication,
Lanyer alters the function of Fame who usually heralds the

achievements of great men in the world. Instead, Fame commends the "very best" of these ladies to the poet's particular notice, and their "glorious Trophies" will be a litany of womanly virtue.

Lanyer's ensuing subjects of praise are no less than the most prominent noblewomen in England, all of whom she lauds for their learning and virtue: Lady Arabella Stuart; Susan Bertie, Countess Dowager of Kent; the Countess Dowager of Pembroke; Lucy Harington Russell, Countess of Bedford; Margaret Russell, Countess Dowager of Cumberland; Katherine Knyvet, Countess of Suffolk; Anne, Countess of Dorset.[16] Although the British Museum copy includes dedications to only three women in addition to the queen and princess, suggesting there may have been a difference in presentation copies, there are seven women in the complete dedications and nine if the queen and princess are counted. Both numbers are probably significant, for seven would remind Lanyer's readers of the familiar series of the seven spiritual virtues which emanate from the seven gifts of the Holy Ghost and lead to the seven beatitudes. Nine was the number of the Nine Worthies, a literary commonplace featuring nine heroic conquerors. In *Love's Martyr* (1601), Robert Chester had included Nine Female Worthies.[17] As Rosemond Tuve has noted, the series of spiritual virtues is one of the great commonplaces of the Middle Ages and the Renaissance, "as ordinary in devotional books and moral treatises as it is in iconography," and Lanyer's summoning it now enhances still further her entrenchment of women at the heart of Christianity.[18] While Tuve notes some fluidity in the arrangement of the series, in general the gifts of the Holy Ghost are fear of God, piety, knowledge, fortitude, counsel, understanding, and wisdom; the corresponding virtues are humility, benignity, discretion, strength, mercy, chastity, and sobriety.[19] Lanyer's dedications are not so schematized as to assign one gift or virtue to one lady, and indeed this would defeat her conception of each as an ideal Christian. Rather, taken together, the seven ladies compose a picture of the virtues which befit the brides of Christ. Thus, Lady Arabella is "great learned

Ladie," "Rare *Phoenix*" and "Beauteous Soule"; the Countess of Kent's gifts and virtues include "love and feare of God," "Humilitie," a "mind so farre remote/From worldly pleasures," and "Faith"; the Countess of Bedford and the Countess of Cumberland both possess knowledge and understanding; the Countess of Dorset goodness, bounty, grace, love, piety, a pure and godly heart, and love and fear of God.

The virtues of the Countess of Pembroke, to whom the longest and central dedication is addressed in the form of a dream-vision, are first expressed by a parade of mythological figures whom the countess greets and subsumes: the Graces (gifts of God), Minerva (Wisdom and Chastity), the Muses (who with "Harps and Vialls in their lilly hands" are distinctly angelic), Bellona ("a manly maid which was both faire and tall"—Fortitude and Wisdom), Dictina (Chastity), and Aurora (Beauty). In her presence, Art and Nature are encouraged to dwell together in a new union, for in this pastoral setting of woods, flowers, and a sacred spring, Nature inspires Art to sing "holy hymnes." Perhaps recalling Mary Sidney's "Lay of Clorinda," Lanyer reiterates that Nature is the source of feminine Art. More precisely, she implies that women accurately translate Nature, God's book, into sacred poetry. Envy is banished because of the countess's piety and benignity, witnessed by the assembled ladies who sing her Psalms. Surpassing even her brother, Philip Sidney, "for virtue, Wisedome, learning, dignity," Mary Sidney "in virtuous studies of Divinitie,/Her pretious time continually doth spend." She predominates because she is a contemplative and because her poetry enlightens others:

> Shee fils the eies, the hearts, the tongues, the eares

> Of after-comming ages, which shall reade
> Her love, her zeale, her faith and pietie;

Her knowledge, which she uses to illuminate God, and her wisdom, which produces harmony, the "heavenli'st musicke ... That ever earthly eares did entertaine," qualify the Countess of Pembroke as a divine poet. Lanyer, attempting to relocate the source of feminine virtue in God rather than in man, creates in her dream-vision a centerpiece of feminine beauty, wisdom, and harmony more immediately potent than conventional symbols because of its attachment to a living woman writer.

Although she had disclaimed learning, Lanyer repeatedly raises the subject of knowledge in her poem. As we have seen, feminine knowledge posed problems for both men and women writers, but Lanyer's positive emphasis on women's learning, knowledge, and wisdom as attributes contributing to their spirituality and virtue foreshadows her impassioned defense of Eve. Well beyond her peers, she asserts the power of knowledge and still continues to praise it as a feminine virtue.

In each of these dedications, the poet apostrophizes the lady, asking her to meditate upon the Passion and to ready herself to accept Christ as her lover, "That in his dying armes he might imbrace/Your beauteous Soule, and fill it with his grace"; or "Whom your faire soule may in her armes infold:/Loving his love, that did endure such paine,/That you in heaven a worthy place might gaine." In the Countess of Suffolk's dedication, the poet describes Christ as the perfect spouse, "a Lover much more true/Than ever was since first the world began," the possessor of "all that Ladies can desire," such as "Beauty," "Wisedome," wealth, honor, fame, and more, "zeale," "grace," "love," "pietie," "constancie," "faith," "faire obedience," "valour," "patience," "sobrietie," "chast behaviour," "meekenesse," "continence," "justice," "mercie," "bountie," "charitie." Here, Lanyer confirms that the spiritual virtues, those conventionally assigned to women, have their source and perfect expression in Christ.[20]

In her final prefatory address, a prose piece "To the Vertuous Reader," Lanyer clearly articulates her purpose in praising women. Castigating women who criticize other women and the "evill disposed men" who defame them, Lanyer identifies the latter as those who also "dishonoured Christ his Apostles and Prophets, putting them to shamefull deaths." Insisting that the same hatred produces both misogyny and

AEMILIA LANYER

anti-Christian deeds leads the poet to the positive association of women and the Christian faith. Not only have "wise and virtuous women" been God's scourges to punish evil men, but most important, they surrounded Christ in his ministry:

> As also in respect it pleased our Lord and Saviour Jesus Christ, without the assistance of man, beeing free from originall and all other sinnes, from the time of his conception, till the houre of his death, to be begotten of a woman, borne of a woman, nourished of a woman, obedient to a woman; and that he healed women, pardoned women, comforted women: yea, even when he was in his greatest agonie and bloodie sweat, going to be crucified, and also in the last houre of his death, tooke care to dispose of a woman: after his resurrection, appeared first to a woman, sent a woman to declare his most glorious resurrection to the rest of his Disciples.

Advocating the restoration of women to their rightful place necessitates not only praise of great ladies, but a recitation of the deeds of Christ and of women, to show how the one imitates the other. This task Lanyer fulfills in the second part of her work, the poem, *Salve Deus Rex Judaeorum*.

Lanyer organized *Salve Deus* to unite women's piety with the principal story of Christianity. Of the 230 stanzas, the central 123 (stanzas 42-165) relate the main events of the Crucifixion drawn from Scripture; woven in and around this narrative is extended praise of God and Christ and a related series of seven encomia on the Countess of Cumberland. Indeed, fully one quarter of the stanzas praise the Countess, a number that might seem inappropriate to a poem on Christ's Passion had the dedications not already established the links between God and woman. The Countess's spiritual life is sketched in her stanzas: her understanding, her contempt for the world, her love of God and his creation, her devotion to the Bridegroom, her imitation of Christ, and her apotheosis.

Notably, Lanyer's encomia do not celebrate the military deeds, power, or public virtue appropriate to men, but the piety, humility, charity, faith, patience, and constancy of women. The Countess of Cumberland, who played little part in the politics and powermongering of the day, who, unlike some great ladies, influenced no great actions, who patiently endured her afflictions, who retired from court to country— surely the most uneventful life for encomium—appears instead as the perfect Christian. Her great drama is the Passion of Christ itself, and to Lanyer her participation in it surpasses any possible worldly achievement.

Why Lanyer chose the Countess of Cumberland as the pivotal personality in the poem may relate to the protection the countess gave the poet in her youth. Her daughter, the Lady Anne Clifford, whose companionship Lanyer professes to have enjoyed, attests to the pious and constant character of her mother, who

> was endowed with many perfections of mind and body. She was naturally of a high spirit, though she tempered it well by grace; having a very well-favoured face, with sweet and quick gray eyes, and of a comely personage. ... She had a discerning spirit. ... She had a great, sharp, natural wit, so as there were few worthy sciences but she had some insight into them; for though she had no language but her own, yet were there few books of worth translated into English but she read them; whereby that excellent mind of her's was much enriched, which even by nature was endowed with the seeds of the four moral virtues,—prudence, justice, fortitude, and temperance. She was a lover of the study and practice of alchemy (chemistry), by which she found out excellent medicines, that did much good to many. She delighted in distilling of waters and other chemical extractions, for she had some knowledge in most kind of minerals, herbs, flowers, and plants. And certainly the infusion which she had from above, of many excellent knowledges and virtues, both divine and human, did bridle and keep under that great spirit of hers, and caused her to have the sweet peace of the heavenly and quiet mind, in the midst of all her griefs and troubles, which were many.[21]

According to the seventeenth-century inscription on the Great Picture at Appleby Castle, "the death of hir two sonns died soo much afflict hir as that ever after the booke of Jobe was her daly companion." It also notes how the Lady Anne "was blessed by the education and tender care of a most affectionate deare and excellent Moother, who brought hir up in as much Religion, goodnes, and knowledg, as hir seakts [sex] and yeares weare capabell of."[22] The countess seems to have inspired a similar veneration in Lanyer, who presents her as a perfect Christian, a living woman to admire and emulate. Not only will she appear as a bride of Christ, but also as a mother-figure similar to the Virgin Mary and as an inspirer of divine poetry.

Adapting the conventions of praise to the entirely spiritual qualities of her subject, in her first address to the countess, Lanyer strikes the theme that will echo throughout the poem: how the countess's life subjects earth's temporary afflictions to heaven's immortal beauties. The poet exalts the countess by placing her in succession to the now-canonized Elizabeth, "ascended to that rest/Of endless joy and true Eternitie ... Where Saints and Angells do attend her Throne,/And she gives glorie unto God alone" (stanza 1). Contemplating the countess's virtues, the poet apologizes in the standard inability topos, yet proceeds to emphasize the countess's understanding, her "Eagles eyes" which see God reflected in the world's beauty, but recognize earth as a mere shadow of heavenly reality: "With his sweet love, thou art so much inflam'd/As of the world thou seem'st to have no part" (stanza 6). The countess appears here and later as one who has suffered, but her afflictions actually prepare her for glory at the Day of Judgment when "thou as the Sunne shalt shine; or much more cleare" (stanza 7). Because the countess possesses a truly Christian soul, meditating on her brings the poet to contemplate God's power and justice which must reward the righteous and punish sinners. In a passionate attack against "wicked worldlings," the poet assails the "ungodly" whom the Lord will "root" out, raining down "fire and brimstone from above,/Upon the wicked monsters in their berth/That

THE FEMINIZATION OF PRAISE

storme and rage at those whom he doth love:" (stanza 18). The deep division between good and evil, between the "blest" countess and the godlessness around her, thematically unites the poet's praise of the lady and her praise of Christ to which the poem is progressing.

The second encomium on the countess (stanzas 19-23) pursues her rejection of the world, founded on her "constant faith" which scorns equally "base affliction" and "prowd pomps." Her retirement from court to country represents her "leaving the world, before the world leaves thee" and reveals the countess as "the wonder of our wanton age," serving heaven's king before earth's. Her life teaches others to love virtue rather than the world, "that great Enchantresse."

That the countess's praiseworthy attributes are not her beauty or position, but her gifts of character, her spiritual virtues, leads Lanyer to a topic often considered by male poets, an "Invective against outward beuty unaccompanied with virtue." Physical beauty, "that pride of Nature" brings only danger for it causes men to "seeke, attempt, plot and devise,/ How they may overthrow the chastest Dame." Lanyer's examples range from Helen of Troy and Lucrece to Cleopatra, Rosamund, and Matilda, all betrayed by their outward beauty. But like the martyred Matilda, the countess is filled with the grace of God who is the "Husband" of her soul and "dying made her Dowager of all;/Nay more, Co-heire of that eternall blisse." In this third encomium, which establishes the primacy of the spirit, she figures as the bride of Christ, one of the faithful whom he died to save, bringing the poet to her central meditation on the Passion.

To praise fully the Christian soul, Lanyer must return to its source, Christ Himself, and it is at this point in the poem that she clearly dedicates herself as a divine poet. To introduce her exalted theme, she spends eight stanzas consulting with her muse and gathering her forces, continually expressing her weakness for the task. While comparing herself to the overreachers, Icarus and Phaeton, nevertheless, the poet asks for God's grace to give her "Power and Strength to write" (stanza 38). Fully aware of the authority vested in "most holy Writ," she insists her language will not venture beyond the limits of doctrine; nor does she seek poetic fame, but rather writes for God's glory, "in plainest words to showe,/The Matter which I seeke to undergoe." Like other Reformist writers who chose the "plainest words" to convey scriptural truth, Lanyer's "unworthy" persona wants a crystal-clear style to convey Christ's story. Thus, she asks God "t'illuminate my Spirit," announcing her vocation as a preacher of the Word, guided by divine inspiration.

Lanyer's insistence that she will adhere strictly to doctrine rationalizes her feminine perspective on the Passion, for although Christ is the central hero of the next 123 stanzas, he is surrounded primarily by women: by the visionary wife of Pilate, by a redeemed Eve, the Daughters of Jerusalem, the Virgin Mary, and the Countess of Cumberland. Through her vivid retelling of Scripture, Lanyer makes her case for women's essential place in Christianity.

The narrative begins on the dark night in the garden of Gethsemane, and adhering closely to the gospels, Lanyer feelingly recreates the betrayals and the torments of Christ that ultimately lead to human redemption. She particularly details how the disciples abandon Christ: protesting that they will never forsake him, "They do like men, when dangers overtake them" (stanza 79). Although "men" may well be the generic term here, it recalls men's betrayal of women earlier cited, and in light of Lanyer's subsequent praise of the Daughters of Jerusalem, her intention may well be to criticize the sex. She deepens the disciples' disgrace by passionately praising Christ, listing His names and attributes, from "beauty of the World, Heavens chiefest glory," to "Water of Life," "Guide of the Just," and "Ransomer of Sin" (stanza 81). Here Lanyer reveals the source of all praise in her work and contrasts His glory with the cruel behavior of the judges, particularly Caiaphas and Pontius Pilate.

Just before the drama of Pilate's decision, in a vivid and arresting passage, Lanyer introduces the voice of his wife who pleads with her husband not to condemn Christ, specifically because such a fault far overshadows Eve's sin, and she cautions, "Let not us Women glory in Mens folly,/Who had power given to over-rule us all."[23] Pilate's wife, arguing that such cruelty to "thy Saviour" surpasses anything women have ever done, and liberates them from their "former fault," launches into an apology for "Our Mother Eve." This section, balanced between blame for men, particularly Adam, and praise for Eve and her daughters, shows how Lanyer assigns the sexes distinct characteristics, as did the patristic commentators, but by contrast exploits that tradition to redeem women and to refurbish them as Christians. The defense of Eve relies on the classic definition of woman as the lesser creature, one who "was simply good, and had no powre to see" (stanza 96). Her "undiscerning Ignorance and Weaknesse" allowed the serpent to deceive her, although her pure heart intended no ill. Adam, by contrast, must accept blame, because he had strength and knew God's commandments even before Eve was created. While Lanyer follows traditional interpretation in admitting Eve's deception, she insists that Eve sinned "for knowledge sake" but that Adam sinned for the worse motivation, only because "the fruit was faire." Deliberately omitting any rationale for Adam, such as St. Augustine's admission of Adam's "social love" for Eve, Lanyer intends through Pilate's wife, to exonerate Eve "whose fault was onely too much love,/Which made her give this present to her Deare." And in an ironic twist, Pilate's wife remarks, "Yet Men will boast of knowledge, which he tooke/From Eves faire hand, as from a learned Booke." Thus locating the origin of all knowledge in a woman's act, even if it does corroborate her inherent weakness, Lanyer attempts to undermine the male stranglehold on learning by suggesting that men owe it all to women.

More important, in the moral realm, Lanyer distinguishes between Eve's simplicity and the malice with which Pilate will betray Christ. Although Eve is blameworthy, Pilate's deed will be the worst sin of all time, so bad that men can no longer declare themselves superior to women, and "your fault beeing greate, why should you disdaine/Our beeing your equals, free from tyranny?" Almost imperceptibly, the voice of Pilate's wife merges into the poet's, as Lanyer vigorously attacks Pilate, using traditional material to bolster her case for women. Beginning by exonerating all women from this male betrayal of Christ, "To whiche (poor soules) we never gave consent,/Witnesse thy wife (O Pilate) speakes for all" (stanza 105), in angry apostrophes, the poet blames Pilate for his weakness in appeasing the crowd; she compares him with Barrabas the Thief, naming Pilate as the baser; she implies a comparison with Christ "which right Judgement ever gra-ceth"; she castigates his evil deeds as a judge because he condemns the innocent, and she decries his immoral character because he refused to listen to his own conscience. As a rep-resentative man, Pilate can bring no credit to his sex, precisely serving Lanyer's enthusiastically biased purpose.

Sharply contrasted to this extended vituperation is the de-scription of Christ going to His death, His attributes humanly mirrored in the "teares of the daughters of Jerusalem" and in "the sorrow of the virgin Marie." Christ professes "virtue, patience, grace, love, piety"—a list already familiar to readers of treatises on women's education, but here placed firmly in context at the very heart of Christian doctrine. The lesson of the Cross is "how by suffering he could conquer more/Than all the kings that ever liv'd before" (stanza 120), a doctrine that exalts spiritual strength over physical might, and that in Lanyer's view gives women their particular prominence. She represents this idea in the poem by immediately introducing the weeping women, the only ones in the multitude to pity Christ and to receive from their Lord, Love, and King "mer-cie, grace, and love." Lanyer images the women's "Eagle eyes" looking into "this Sunne," praise indicating their spiritual power and ability to see clearly, reminiscent of Margaret Russell's unclouded vision. In vivid contrast are the "spightfull men" who whip, spurn, and tear the hair of Christ, and who "see" so badly that their hearts are harder than flint or marble. Completing the picture is the grieving Virgin Mary, a *Mater Dolorosa*, "All comfortlesse in depth of sorrow drowned," and again the poet exalts womankind in her praise of Mary, extended in an apostrophe of over fourteen stanzas to include all the main events of Mary's life.

Mary's stature derives from her essential femininity as "Mother of our Lord," and "most beauteous Queene of womankind." Although the Virgin had long been an important image for Christian women, Lanyer avoids Catholic doctrine but still designates Mary as a shining example for her sex. She asserts an acceptably Protestant role for the Virgin as the archetypal true Christian woman: chaste, obedient, humble, pious. Lanyer dwells mainly upon Mary's chastity—her pure thoughts, "modest cheere," "chast eares," "virgin thoughts," "chaste desire"—and pointedly recalls that "Farre from desire of any man thou art,/Knowing not one, thou art from all men free." The very chastity that liberates her from obedience to a man qualifies the Virgin for the superiority of spiritual submission as "Servant, Mother, Wife, and Nurse/To Heavens bright king, that freed us from the curse" (stanza 136). Like Christine de Pisan's Virgin, she appears as the supreme example of a woman empowered by chastity in a male world.

Through Mary, Lanyer moves to her depiction of Christ's death, vividly painted and decried. And at this most painful and dramatic moment, Lanyer turns again to the Countess of Cumberland, inviting her as the "Spouse of Christ" to view the Passion with "the eie of Faith," to feel both grief and joy as "thy Love" dies, "his count'nance pale, yet ... sweet" (stanza 147). By summoning the countess here, the poet makes her an analogy to the Virgin Mary, an example to all women, and brings her into complete sympathy with the love and self-sacrifice of Christ.

The narrative proceeds with the effects of the Crucifixion on earth, the descent from the Cross, the Entombment, and the coming of the Marys to discover the Resurrection. Lanyer's allegory at this point reminds her readers of the female imagery attached to the Church:

> And now those pretious oyntments he desires
> Are broght unto him, by his faithfull Wife
> The holy Church; who in those rich attires,

Of Patience, Love, Long suffring, Voide of strife,
Humbly presents those oyntments he requires:
  The oyles of Mercie, Charitie, and Faith,
  Shee onely gives that which no other hath.

(stanza 162)

While this image is fundamental in Christian theology, in this context it is notable that the Church and the ideal woman possess many of the same qualities and that both belong to patriarchal systems that mirror each other: the marriage of Christ to the Church is the model for human marriage. But the only "human" marriage Lanyer celebrates here is that of the countess and her Bridegroom, Christ, a marriage that attempts radically to redefine the importance of female spirituality. Most naturally, Lanyer turns to the Canticles as a source of imagery, for the Song of Songs had long been allegorized as the love of Christ and the Church, or Christ and the individual soul, or even Christ and the Virgin Mary. Combining direct quotations ("His head is likened to the finest gold"; "his cheekes are beds of spices"; "His lips like Lillies, dropping downe pure mirrhe") with her own interpretation of the verses, Lanyer recreates the image of Christ the bridegroom. Quite startlingly, she then declares herself "unable" to continue with such beauty, and instead, leaves "His perfect picture" in the Countess of Cumberland's heart, "where it shall stand,/Deeply engraved in that holy shrine,/ Environed with Love and thoughts divine" (stanza 166).

Echoing here are the conventions of the sonnet sequences in which women figure as the beloved object, often "sanctified" in the lover's heart. In *Salve Deus*, though, the perfect lover is Christ, beloved and enshrined by a woman who is the perfect Christian. Her love, described in the next five stanzas, is unlike the usual sonnet story: contemplating the Crucifixion, the countess understands the love that prompted such sacrifice and so may receive grace; her love gives her faith to withstand all worldly afflictions; her love allows her to open her soul to Christ in whatever manifestation He appears; her love makes her follow in Christ's footsteps, tend-ing the "naked, poore, and bare," diseased, sick and wounded; such mercy makes the countess particularly loved by God, and, says the poet—once more asserting Margaret Russell's special vision—"Thy faith, thy prayers, and his speciall grace/ Doth open Heav'n, where thou behold'st his face." The traditional Christian allegory of the Song of Songs opens up a source of imagery to Lanyer that allows her more literally to glorify a Christian woman as the particular beloved of Christ, not only because of her spiritual beauties but for what she does in the world—caring for others and dispensing charity. Praise devolves on her not only for contemplating the Passion, but for her *gestae*, for performing works of mercy.

In the inevitable comparisons with famous examples of the past, the countess exceeds Deborah, Judith, Esther, Susanna, and the Queen of Sheba. At the head of the list, somewhat surprisingly is Cleopatra, the very mention of whom in such company may seem eccentric. But Cleopatra represents the male version, perhaps fantasy, of great worldly power and glory, and so really the world's frailties and inconstancy:

> Her Love was earthly, and thy Love Divine;
> Her Love was onely to support her pride,
> Humilitie thy Love and thee doth guide.
>
> (stanza 177)

Cleopatra has beauty and riches; the Countess of Cumberland has "inward virtues"; to her "deerest Love," Christ, the countess presents faith and good deeds, and "beares his crosse." She lives "chaste as the Turtle dove" and "his flock she feeds." If Cleopatra's death was "worthy," the Countess's "virtuous life" exceeds it. Acknowledging the possible accusation of flattery, Lanyer admits that the countess herself thinks "these prayses overmuch"; yet the poet claims that destiny has charged her to build "Th'everlasting Trophie of thy fame." Her task is not to flatter a patron, but to memorialize "Heav'ns beauty" in this human soul whose daily adherence to Christian teachings and continual war "against that many headed monster Sinne" make her worthy of eternity.

Once again, praise of the countess leads to praise of Christ, pictured in glory, the images now drawn from Revelation (stanzas 205-209). The countess participates in this vision, for her praises are taken up by the saints and angels who "to their Heav'nly Lord doe daily sing/Thy perfect praises in their lowdest voyce." Here prayers are brought directly to "that spotlesse Lambe," whom the poet continues to glorify. Finally, in the company of all the martyrs, saints, and apostles, in "whose worthy steps you doe desire to tread," the poet feels her muse weakening, and all the beauties of the blessed retreat into the countess's breast. In her last encomium, Lanyer credits the countess with inspiring her to write "what my thoughts could hardly apprehend," and of being the "Articke Starre that guides my hand." From the beginning of the poem, Lanyer felt sure of the countess's immortality, here expressed in the most exalted imagery. Now ending her work, the poet reveals that the countess's "excellence hath rais'd my sprites to write," that she has inspired a poem on immortality and enabled the poet to overcome her insufficiency. In this respect, the countess again acts as a mother-figure, giving birth and nurture to poetry itself.

Salve Deus Rex Judaeorum ends with a beatific vision, an apotheosis of the beloved countess, but this is not Lanyer's final conclusion. She had already praised the countess for her withdrawal from court to country, a theme that was almost an obsession with Jacobean poets. But the retreat to the estate of Cookham, which had a long association with noble women, is not merely a sign of the countess's contempt for the worldly city; in light of Lanyer's concept of nature, it also expresses the countess's virtue and divinity.[24]

Nature had a significant function in the dedications to *Salve Deus*. In her dedication to Queen Anne, Lanyer had quite conventionally described Nature as the creation of God and as the source of Art; but it was also the "Mother of perfection" and Lanyer particularly claimed its protection for her own work. In her praise of the Countess of Pembroke, she had created a perfect natural setting, a woodland spring where Art and Nature existed equally in "sweet unitie," and she had designated it as the place where the countess's holy Psalms might appropriately be sung. In the last part of her poem, "The Description of Cooke-ham," Lanyer retrieves these earlier allusions in a poem that transforms a literary landscape into a redeemed Eden inhabited by three women: the countess, her daughter, and the poet. The countess's presence blesses the landscape, her daughter, and the poet, who is enabled to write her poem in praise of divine virtue. Again, Lanyer draws an analogy between nature sanctified by a godly woman and the creation of art. The poem is, however, retrospective, a farewell to Cookham, and so its prevailing tone is elegiac. It seems that the vision of paradise, of a redeemed nature, is at best momentary, and when her redeemed Eve withdraws, the landscape and the poet must alter radically.[25]

Implicitly comparing the pastoral landscape to Eden, Lanyer composes a parable of the Fall: at first, the landscape reflects an earthly paradise, but a special one where the female virtues flourish; however, unnamed outside forces, represented by Fortune, inevitably bring change, and the type of those virtues, the countess, must leave. Unlike the poet's exalted mood at the end of *Salve Deus* when she celebrated the countess's virtue from a celestial perspective, the mood here suits the insufficiency of the world to sustain grace, and in the last part of "The Description," both Nature and the poet mourn the passing of such perfection, the poet hoping that at least its memory may live for future ages in the poem itself.

From the beginning of the poem, Lanyer couches her description of Cookham as a farewell, both to the source of her poetic inspiration and to a place of pleasure, grace, and virtue. But the place's pleasures, she reminds the countess, are as "fleeting worldly Joyes that could not last:/Or as divine shadowes of celestial pleasures,/which are desir'd above all earthly treasures" (ll. 14-16). These images dominate the poem, urging the reader to see the beauty of this world as a testament to its Creator, and yet to recognize the evanescence of the earthly realm. From the beginning, too, the countess, "Mistress of that Place," represents the source of grace; through the course of the poem, Lanyer clarifies its Christian foundation, which echoes the first two parts of *Salve Deus* by imaging the beneficent and nurturing influence of the countess upon the landscape and its occupants, her daughter and the poet. Her departure defaces and desolates the setting and leaves the poet to mourn, suggesting the spiritual death of a world devoid of such grace and virtue.

"The Description of Cooke-ham" combines the poetic traditions of the *locus amoenus*, pastoral, and praise of a patron; it offers a serious challenge to Jonson's "To Penshurst" as the first English example of a country-house poem.[26] Like Jonson, Lanyer recalls classical precedents and creates an idealized and moralized landscape as part of her praise. She, however, proceeds beyond encomium to a vision of absence and loss because earth cannot possess the Edenic perfection of virtue represented by the countess.

The *locus amoenus* appears in lines 17 through 74, with its constituent "cristall Streames" and brooks, trees providing shade from the sun, fruits and flowers, "pretty Birds" singing, and "gentle Windes." Lanyer imagines the landscape actively exerting itself to please and delight its mistress:

The Walkes put on their summer Liveries,
And all things else did hold like similies:
The Trees with leaves, with fruits, with flowers clad,
Embrac'd each other, seeming to be glad,
Turning themselves to beauteous Canopies,
To shade the bright Sunne from your brighter eies: ...
The gentle Windes did take delight to bee
Among those woods that were so grac'd by thee.
And in sad murmure utterd pleasing sound,
That Pleasure in that place might more abound:
The swelling Barkes deliver'd all their pride,
When such a *Phoenix* once they had espide.

But the idyllic beauty and harmony of this paradise are not allowed to mask its earthliness, and natural description gives way to a spiritualized landscape. The poetic transition between the worlds of nature and grace is the image of the "stately Tree" to which the countess habitually resorts to meditate. It is an oak far taller than all surrounding trees, and is at once "like a comely Cedar ... Whose beauteous stature farre exceeded all" and "like a Palme" spreading its "armes" to welcome the countess, "Desirous that you there should make abode." The two similes suggest that the oak is not merely a notable item of landscape, but the representation of an idea, since only figuratively or allegorically can an oak resemble both a cedar and a palm. In their Biblical contexts, the cedar is the building material for the temple of God, and the palm is the symbol of spiritual victory. Patristic commentary interpreted both trees as the Church and the disciples of Christ.[27] Because it describes the countess so appropriately, the most probable context here is that of Psalm 92: "The righteous shall flourish like the palm tree: he shall grow like a cedar in Lebanon. ... Those that be planted in the house of the Lord shall flourish in the courts of our God. ..." The righteous countess is welcomed into the "coole fresh ayre" of the Christian spirit as she sits beneath the tree, observing "Hills, vales, and woods, as if on bended knee/They had appeared your honour to salute." Echoing the Psalms here and in her reiteration of the "brookes and christall springs,/ A Prospect fit to please the eyes of Kings," Lanyer pictures the countess meditating in an entirely Christian way upon the landscape, seeing in the Creation the power of the Creator:

> And in their beauties did you plaine descrie,
> His beauty, wisdome, grace, love, majestie.
> In these sweet woods how often did you walke,
> With Christ and his Apostles there to talke.

The countess accompanies three Biblical patriarchs—Moses on Mount Zion, "lovely David," and "blessed Joseph"—in performing God's will, singing His praises, and accomplishing her acts of charity. With her is her daughter Anne, "in whose faire breast true virtue then was hous'd." Anne's presence again recalls the countess's role as spiritual mother, showing here how she has multiplied her own virtues in those of her daughter.

But realizing a Christian vision means relinquishing earth's beauty, facing death, and believing in immortal life. Though momentarily distracted by unconstant Fortune that separates the great ones of the earth from the humble, the poet remembers, "although we are but borne of earth,/We may behold the Heavens, despising death." The pleasures of Cookham retreat into "Memorie" and the poet keenly feels their loss. However, the purpose of the poem is not self-pity, but praise of the countess, and through her, of God. This the poet accomplishes by the "nature reversed" *topos* revealing a landscape that mourns the departure of the countess and her daughter. The abundance and fertility of spring and summer that characterized nature in the presence of divine virtue earlier in the poem die into a winter landscape, wrinkled, shrunken, and dried:

> The trees that were so glorious in our view,
> Forsooke both floures and fruit, when once they knew
> Of your depart, their very leaves did wither,
> Changing their colours as they grewe together . . .
> Their frozen tops, like Ages hoarie haires,
> Showes their disasters, languishing in feares:
> A swarthy riveld ryne all over spread,
> Their dying bodies halfe alive, halfe dead.

In the single dramatic event of the poem, the countess leaves a "chaste, yet loving" parting kiss on the great oak, which the poet immediately steals for herself, as if trying to absorb the countess's love and spirit. All nature mourns with the oak, and in the best passage of the poem, Lanyer creates metaphors of age and death to fulfill her warning that these were but mutable earthly joys:

> The Flowres that on the banks and walkes did grow,
> Crept in the ground, the Grasse did weepe for woe.
> The Windes and Waters seem'd to chide together,
> Because you went away they knew not whither:
> And those sweet Brookes that ran so faire and cleare,
> With griefe and trouble wrinckled did appeare. . . .
> Each arbour, banke, each seate, each stately tree,
> Lookes bare and desolate now for want of thee;

Turning greene tresses into frostie gray,
While in cold griefe they wither all away. . . .
The house cast off each garment that might grace it,
Putting on Dust and Cobwebs to deface it.
All desolation then there did appeare,
When you were going whom they held so deare.

(ll. 180-205)

Because she is a vessel for God's grace, when the countess withdraws, she leaves behind an unregenerate world, filled with images of death. Cookham without the countess reflects a world without God's love and grace to redeem it. While *Salve Deus* drew an ideal picture of a world blessed by women's Christian virtue, "The Description of Cooke-ham" shows not only the ideal but the misery of its absence.[28]

Only in the poet's "unworthy breast" will the countess's virtues live on, "tying my heart to her by those rich chaines." And when the poet dies, it may be only her poem that memorializes the Edenic Cookham. In her final lines, Lanyer does not offer much hope that her exultant vision of woman's Christian virtue will hold sway in the fallen world.

"The Description of Cooke-ham," like the dedications and *Salve Deus Rex Judaeorum*, is a poem densely packed and intensely written. As avowals of the importance of feminine virtue, the three works succeed not through reasoning, but through the poetry of faith and revelation. And poetry is central to Lanyer's piety and her attempts to establish the spiritual preeminence of women. Only by availing herself of a rich range of poetic forms, images, and allusions could she create a canvas large enough to impress and convince her readers. Her great centerpiece, the Passion of Christ, serves as both doctrinal and poetic pattern for the rest of the poem, presenting as it does the archetypal subject of praise, the image of perfect virtue. By her mix of genres, Lanyer achieves an effect similar to that of a monumental triptych: the large central panel conveys the crucial doctrine by revelation of a divine event; each side panel relates that divine image to the human landscape and to particular lives.

In this light, Lanyer's adherence to a "natural" poetry can be more fully understood. Having found that male "Scholers" "by Art do write," she identified the source of her own work as Nature. Considering that she must use conventional poetic forms and figures, her meaning may not at first be clear. Both poetically and philosophically, Lanyer wished to circumvent masculine thinking and writing about women, and to return to what she envisioned as the source. To redeem women, she claimed the innocence of the first woman, and identified feminine virtue with Christ's virtues. To alter the traditional separation between woman and God, as a poet she mixed genres, interrupted sequence, and juxtaposed high matter with low. As a result, her poem cannot easily be classified according to conventional kinds. In other words, in following Nature as the source of her Art, the poet used what she needed at the moment to convey her doctrine, whether it was encomium, narrative, or elegy, or whether she wished to move from a Christian's love for Christ to Cleopatra's love for Antony in one stanza. If this far from seamless method does violence to Renaissance poetic decorum, and may even annoy the modern reader, Lanyer gains the power of surprise and drama in her attempts to reach and teach her audience. One may view her as she conveys herself at the beginning as a naive writer "of slender skill," and "all unlearned," or by contrast, as a fit contemporary of John Donne and Ben Jonson. The poet who married the Countess of Cumberland to her bridegroom, Christ, with the language of Canticles, and who may be responsible for initiating the country-house poem in English is, after all, a woman who, despite her disavowals, did not fear to tread where angels walked.

EIGHT

HEROIC VIRTUE:

MARY WROTH'S *URANIA* AND

PAMPHILIA TO AMPHILANTHUS

*A*T FIRST GLANCE, Elizabeth Cary's *Mariam*, Aemilia Lanyer's *Salve Deus Rex Judaeorum*, and Mary Wroth's *Urania* and *Pamphilia to Amphilanthus* seem to be widely differing works. Wroth's secular settings, her concern with chivalry, statecraft, war, and love suggest a very different temperament and literary orientation from those of her fellow authors. As the first English woman to write a romance and a sonnet sequence, Wroth did indeed break new ground, but her work participates no less in the attempts of women writers to restore the spirituality and redeem the virtue of their sex.

Indeed, the spirit in which Lanyer glorified the Countess of Cumberland's active virtue or in which Cary apotheosized Mariam's patience is very much like the spirit in which Wroth develops constancy as the preeminent virtue of her main character, Pamphilia. Constancy, long associated with woman's chastity, piety, and obedience, reappears in the *Urania* and in *Pamphilia to Amphilanthus* as the heroic virtue capable of transforming a lovelorn woman into a great queen, a poet, and finally, a transcendent image of divine love.

Born in 1586 to Robert Sidney and Barbara Gamage, Mary Sidney Wroth acquired a formidable social and literary inheritance, one she seems to have borne willingly and well. Sidneys, as dedicators always reminded her, were literary giants; they were also public servants. Her uncle, Philip Sidney, had died fighting for England and was among the foremost Elizabethan writers; her aunt, the Countess of Pembroke, exalted for her piety, learning, and virtue, had served in the Elizabethan court; her father was continually occupied, to his own financial ruin, on Queen Elizabeth's and King James's business, and was also a poet. Philip Sidney's romance, *Arcadia*, his sonnet sequence, *Astrophil and Stella*, the Countess of Pembroke's translations, occasional poetry, and her Psalms, and Robert Sidney's sonnet sequence are all variously reflected in Mary Wroth's work, particularly in her choice of genre.

Although the picture is incomplete, information about Wroth appears in the Sidney family letters and in state papers.[1] The eldest of four girls and two boys, she grew up at Penshurst in a close-knit, happy family. Her mother, memorialized for her hospitality in Jonson's "To Penshurst," was greatly attached to her children and household, and despite her own probable illiteracy, seems to have supervised her daughter's education.[2] In 1599, his faithful steward, Rowland Whyte, wrote to Robert Sidney that

> Mrs. *Mary* is grown so tall, and soe goodly of her Yeares, as that your Lordship cannot beleve yt, unles you saw yt; and surely will prove an excellent Creature. My Lady sees them well taught, and brought up in Learning, and Qualities, fitt for theire Birth and Condicion.[3]

By 1602, Mary Sidney was appearing at court, dancing before the queen.[4] In 1604, she married Sir Robert Wroth and continued to move in court circles; however, a letter from Robert Sidney to his wife suggests that the marriage may not have been an early success, and Ben Jonson later remarked to William Drummond that "My Lord Lisles daughter, my Lady Wroth is unworthily maried on a Jealous husband."[5] In 1614, Dudley Carleton wrote to his wife that "Sir Robert Wroths lady after long longing hath brought him a sonne," but one month later he writes that Sir Robert had died of "a gangrene *in pudendis* leaving a younge widow with 1200^{li} joynter, and a young sonne not a moneth old: and his estate charged with 23000^{li} debt."[6] Wroth's son died in 1616, leaving her alone and bereft even of her husband's estate which went to the next heir. Further references to her indebtedness exist through 1628.[7] Such difficulties were probably intensified by Wroth's unconventional behavior, for as Josephine Roberts's research has shown, Wroth had an affair with her cousin, William, Earl of Pembroke, by whom she had two children. Roberts suggests that the characters of Pamphilia and Amphilanthus may reflect Wroth's portrait of herself and Pembroke, although she rightly cautions against a strictly autobiographical reading.[8]

What Wroth's actual patronage of writers—another Sidneian activity—may have been is unclear, particularly given her husband's impecunious estate. Every dedication revolves around her Sidneian identity, from Nathaniel Baxter's designation of her as Agape, "Chaste, holy, modest, divine and perfect,/Arcadian *Sydney* gave thee this aspect . . ." to Robert Jones's insistence that "It is hereditarie to your whole house, not onely to be truely Honourable in your selves, but to be the favourers and furtherers of all honest and vertuous endevours in others. . . ."[9] Baxter's 1606 work, *Sir Philip Sydneys Ourania*, while exploiting references to all Sidney relatives, specifically gives Mary Wroth a "Heroycall disposition." Whether or not he intended anything beyond flattery, Baxter associates Wroth at a very early date with her own particular literary theme. Although she may have begun earlier, not until 1613 does a dedication imply she is a writer.[10]

Wroth's relationship with Ben Jonson seems to have been one of mutual admiration. She appeared in his 1605 *Masque of Blacknesse* and 1608 *Masque of Beautie*; he dedicated *The Alchemist* to her; and to her he addressed two rather conventional epigrams praising her as the "faire crowne of your faire sex," a worthy bearer of the Sidney name, and as the possessor of all the virtues of "a *Nymph*, a *Muse*, a *Grace*." In one of his rare sonnets, Jonson praises her sonnets, claiming the unlikely truth that since he has copied them out, "I . . . am become/A better lover, and much better Poet."[11] The instruction may well have gone the other way, however, for some key Jonsonian themes, steadfastness, and "the centered self" may have influenced Wroth's conception of heroic virtue.[12]

In 1621, just after her mother and her aunt died, Wroth's prose romance, named after her cousin Philip Herbert's wife, *The Countesse of Montgomeries Urania*, and the sonnet sequence, *Pamphilia to Amphilanthus*, were published together. But a scandal blew up over the volume, and in December of the same year, Wroth withdrew the book from sale. Lord Edward Denny claimed she had slandered him, his daughter, Honora, and his son-in-law, Lord Hay, in the episode concerning the drunken and abusive Sirelius. Denny and Wroth exchanged insulting verses, and in a letter, Denny advised her to "redeem the time with writing as large a volume of heavenly lays and holy love as you have of lascivious tales and amorous toys; that at the last you may follow the example of your virtuous and learned aunt."[13] Although Denny's charges probably had some foundation, Wroth denied them; but perhaps lacking support, she backed down from her vigorous self-defense and withdrew the book. If the *Urania* does contain other contemporary portraits, few courtiers would have come to her aid, but Wroth had by this time retired from the court. She seems to have lived the rest of her life in the country, and died around 1640.

How much Wroth's rather difficult life may have spurred her on to her brief but prolific writing career is conjecture. While it is tempting to imagine her feverishly writing more than a hundred sonnets, a romance that would fill 558 folio pages (plus a manuscript continuation), and a pastoral drama to occupy her lonely hours of widowhood, she may well have begun her work much earlier, perhaps as an alternative to an unhappy and, for a long time, childless marriage. How much the romance reflects her experiences at court, her relationships with Wroth and Pembroke, and her family life is less relevant here than a consideration of how she actually tackled problems that had beset literary women throughout this period. By her choice of genres, she was able to solve them rather well. Because she imagines Pamphilia, a fictional character who is chaste, obedient, and patient, she appears to support the traditional conditions of woman's virtue; and yet this same character is heroic, transcending all the injunctions to privacy, domesticity, and silence. In Wroth's sonnet sequence, Pamphilia becomes her poetic persona, through whom she successfully adapts the hitherto exclusively male love sonnet.[14]

In choosing to write a prose romance, Wroth had the guidance of her uncle's work and the tacit blessing of her learned and pious aunt: it was, after all, *The Countess of Pembroke's Arcadia* and she had been its first editor and publisher. But more important, Wroth selected a form that freed her from the woman writer's biggest limitation, the adherence to a feminine decorum that demanded only pious forms to express pious subject matter. Aemilia Lanyer had partially escaped her limits, but Wroth breached the wall.

The conflict between romance and feminine decorum had been explicitly recognized by Margaret Tyler who in 1578 translated from Spanish the prose romance, *The Mirrour of Princely Deeds and Knighthood*. Tyler felt impelled to defend her choice of "a story prophane, and a matter more manlike then becometh my sexe."[15] Its "manlinesse" she challenges, first, because her interest is less in war itself than in the virtues of magnanimity and courage displayed in battle; and second, because both the fear of war and armed victory concern women as well as men. Critics might suggest "divinitie" would more suit her years and "matters more easy and ordinary in common talke" her situation as a "gentlewoman," but Tyler has nevertheless bowed to the familiar pressure of "friends" and translated a Spanish romance. If men dedicated works of fiction, war, medicine, law, government, and divinity to women, she reasons, women may read them; and if they read them, why not write on these subjects?[16] Her critics, she hopes, would not offer the alternative "either not to write or to write of divinitie" (Aiv v). But not until Mary Wroth would a woman writer take up the matter of romance as a potentially "feminine" genre. This meant, of course, that the work would not be entirely secular, and indeed, in her main character, Pamphilia, Wroth created another variation on a familiar figure, the true Christian woman.

Sidney's *Arcadia* had earlier confirmed the romance as a

serious genre, for like pastoral poetry, which "underneath the prettie tales of wolves and sheepe can enclude the whole considerations of wrong doing and patience," romance could convey a whole range of moral and spiritual issues.[17] Almost forty years later, Wroth recognized it as a genre giving her the scope to write literally about women's thoughts, feelings, and deeds as no woman had before, and even to extend their sphere of action; in addition, she could still convey a serious doctrine, the importance of constancy in all aspects of human affairs.

That both the romance and the sonnet sequence were out of vogue by 1620 is significant here. Worn-out forms may encourage knee-jerk imitation and engender parody, both of which appear in Wroth's versions. More to the point, their demise meant that the first woman to write in these genres had greater freedom to adapt them to her special perspective than if she had followed a current fashion.[18]

While Wroth exploits the conventions of the Elizabethan prose romance—a huge number of characters, many of them stock figures of the pastoral, dozens of locations, flexible time sequence, parallel scenes, debates, the interweaving of poetry—she also develops in her romance a way to see woman as hero outside of the normal masculine standards of heroism, which she challenges. Elizabethan romance offered a variety of stock female characters, from the Amazonian warrior (whether legitimate or cross-dressed) to the faithful, domestic Penelope, from the scheming lustful queen to the innocent lovelorn shepherdess, from the beloved court lady to the nymph of Diana. In almost all cases, these characters are stereotyped idealizations if virtuous, and stereotyped vilifications if not. Writers had devoted most of their energy to developing the adventures of men, limiting the range of feminine behavior, and relegating women to subordinate, reactive, or symbolic roles. Few writers developed their narrative around active feminine virtue.[19] Similarly, the conventions of sonnet sequences had been built around the male experience of loving a shadowy Stella, Coelia, Phillis, Chloris, or Parthenope, with all the attendant rhetoric and imagery of passion, praise, desire, guilt, despair, or fulfillment. The sonnet lady may have radiated virtue and chastity, or perhaps faithlessness and cruelty, or represented an ineffable truth or idea; few poets associated constancy of any kind with the lady, preferring to keep that attribute for themselves, and if anything, to accuse her of change.[20]

It is notable that given romance conventions, Wroth rejected the option to give the starring role to an Amazonian hero, a woman warrior who could fight and win her way through knightly adventures. Perhaps the shadow of Spenser's Britomart was too long, or perhaps the associations with Sidney's Pyrocles-Zelmane too undermining. Instead, she created the noble Pamphilia, Queen of Pamphilia, virtuous monarch, constant lover, and poet. Pamphilia appears in a range of situations from the plighting of her lifelong faith to her country, to expressing friendship for other women, to feeling jealousy, to being an allegorical figure of Constancy itself. Most important, Pamphilia is also a poet and her moments of deepest feeling inevitably come forth in verse. Wroth exploited both the dynamism of the romance to develop the heroic ideal of constancy, and the contemplativeness of the sonnet to make constancy divine: in these works, Pamphilia acts a double role, performing her virtuous deeds and then as Wroth's surrogate, transforming her experiences into art.

THE COUNTESSE OF MONTGOMERIES URANIA

The genre of romance not only gave Wroth imaginative scope, but fiction also provided the freedom to explore men's and women's behavior in a setting where almost anything could occur. Although partly bound by her own conservative conception of the nature of woman, Wroth gave her subject a vivid and sometimes comic treatment by offering frequent debates, parallel episodes, and contrasting characters. And if Wroth's own opinions on men and women may not be extrapolated from every action of every character, by listening to the narrator's voice, by considering the placement and tone of an episode, and by looking at the romance as a whole, we can reach some conclusions about the world she portrays. Moreover, in Pamphilia we have the stimulus of reading the first extended fictional portrait in English of a woman by a woman, and of trying to understand the mixture of psychological "realism" and fantasy that makes up her character.

But before plunging into the *Urania* itself, a brief look at the influence of Philip Sidney's *Arcadia* will highlight Wroth's concept of the female hero. The complicated relationship of *Urania* to the *Arcadia* deserves a full-length study; here, only two of the most relevant connections are considered.[21]

First, Wroth's hero, Pamphilia, descends from two of the more complex female characters in Elizabethan romance, Pamela and Philoclea; indeed, her very name recalls theirs. In the *Arcadia*, Pamela and Philoclea reflect the archetypal opposition of Diana or armed chastity and Venus or love. Through the character of Kalender, Sidney reveals that "love plaide in *Philocleas* eyes and threatened in *Pamelas* ... *Philoclea* so bashfull ... so humble, that she will put all pride out of countenance ... *Pamela* of high thoughts, who avoides not pride with not knowing her excellencies, but by making that one of her excellencies to be voide of pride; her mother's wisdome, greatness, nobilitie, but ... knit with a more constant temper."[22] Pamela displays a virtuous self-sufficiency, while Philoclea invites relationship. When Pyrocles, disguised as the Amazon Zelmane, first sees the two sisters, he marks Pamela's "riche *Diamond* set but in a blacke horne, the worde I have since read is this; *yet still my selfe*" (I, 90). Of his beloved Philoclea, he claims she is "the ornament of the Earth, the modell of heaven, the Triumphe of Nature, the light of beauty, Queene of Love ... her haire ... drawne up into a net, able to take *Jupiter* when he was in the forme of an Eagle..." (I, 90). While Philoclea is sweet, soft, and humble, Pamela is majestic and stern, likely to become "angry Love, and lowring beautie, shewing disdain" (III, 355) for Musidorus who attempted to kiss her. Pamela's severest test is resisting the wicked Cecropia, when, despite physical and mental tortures, she reveals the virtues of chastity, fortitude, patience, righteous anger, piety, and constancy (III, Chapter

10).[23] Partly for plot, partly for the contrast between passive and active virtue, Sidney created two opposing female characters as sisters. In the *Urania* Wroth draws on his creations, but unites them in one female character, Pamphilia, thus giving birth to a philosophically complex, emotionally conflicted, and more varied, more profound, more significant female hero.

Second, Wroth named her eponymous character after Sidney's Urania, a character who never actually appears in the *Arcadia*. She is a "fair shepherdess," a "heavenly beauty" whose offstage appearance to the shepherds, Strephon and Claius, as she embarked on the seas inspired immediate love and devotion. Her picture appears later in the tournament procession as

> a young mayd, which sate pulling out a thorne out of a Lambs foote, with her looke so attentive uppon it, as if that little foote could have bene the circle of her thoughts; her apparell so poore, as it had nothing but the inside to adorne it; a shephooke lying by her with a bottle upon it. But with al that povertie, beauty plaid the prince, and commanded as many harts as the greatest Queene there did. (I, 104)

Significantly, she draws to her cause the meekest and poorest, including the half-naked shepherd boy, Lalus. The clear Christological references—the thorn, the lamb, the sheephook, her poverty, her charity, her humble, devoted followers—indicate that Sidney conferred considerable significance on his Urania. In Wroth's romance, despite the title, Urania appears not as the central heroic figure, but perhaps in deference to Sidney, as the embodiment of a spiritual principle conceptually close to his. While she first appears as a poor shepherdess, Urania soon takes her rightful royal position as a princess, sister of Amphilanthus and cousin of Pamphilia, and attempts to dissuade her relations from passionate love and to teach the doctrine of divine love. Her role and her influence on Pamphilia's constancy will appear later in this chapter.

The intricacy, richness, and sheer cumulative weight of the *Urania* cannot be contained in one chapter, and thus only those scenes which best reveal Wroth's unique development of feminine heroic virtue will be discussed here. But since, as Charlotte Kohler once said, "the firmest mind could not keep disentangled all the countless manicoloured threads of the innumerable plots, which spread out, one from another, fanwise, and enmesh all in their tangles," and because the work is not widely known, the immediately necessary details of plot and character will be provided.[24]

If we step back from the many characters and events of the *Urania*, the dizzying images of activity and the unceasing shifts in location begin to resolve into the larger theme of change. Change occasions the romance's countless unhappy love affairs, whether they fail through fickle emotions or through death. Change produces political revolutions, veering alliances, and the eternal alternation between peace and war. Indeed, late in the romance, the unhappy Pelarina refers to the source of all her woes as "I know not what Devill, but the great one himselfe, Change."[25] At certain points in the narrative, Wroth invites the reader to consider mutability as characteristic of humankind itself, but in particular, she consistently blames the male characters for inconstancy and deviation from reason.

Against this chaos, Wroth develops Pamphilia as the embodiment of constancy. Continually, Wroth reveals her not only as a virtuous woman in love, but also as a woman who transcends love to devote herself to the public good. On one hand, Pamphilia's constancy to her beloved Amphilanthus appears to be active and all-consuming, rooted in high principles of selflessness and love of virtue, and only because of the essentially mutable nature of the world does it doom her to continual unhappiness. Pamphilia's constancy to her kingdom, on the other hand, brings peace and happiness, recalling the "golden age" of the late Elizabeth I, whose best public attributes Pamphilia echoes.[26]

Constancy is a recurrent theme in Renaissance art and literature, appearing as an active means to transcend the woes

of a mutable world seemingly ruled by fortune. In explaining
an impresa "Of Resolution and true Constancie," Henry Peacham writes that "though Fortune frowne," the constant soul
"stands irremooved streight,/Laughing to scorne, the paper
blastes of Fate."[27] This concept is close to Ben Jonson's ideal
of the virtuous soul "that is round within himselfe, and
streight," who "Need seeke no other strength, no other
height;/Fortune upon him breakes her selfe, if ill,/And what
would hurt his vertue makes it still." Those men and women
whom Jonson praises reject the "turning world ... Giddy
with change" and "keeping a just course," withdraw to their
own spiritual centers.[28] Wroth's constancy evolves from similar principles, but her main interest seems to be in the specific
conflicts experienced by the constant soul in the mutable
world. Anatomizing woman's constancy in ways uncommon
to literature—in love, in the public sphere, in poetry, and in
divinity—Wroth goes to some lengths to show a woman's
particular internal dilemmas when she loves, rules, writes,
and believes with unwavering constancy.

To emphasize that constancy is the cornerstone of Pamphilia's character, Wroth, early in the romance, composes an
allegorical episode that defines the later course of events.
Wroth shows the complexity of constancy here by developing
three simultaneous aspects of the virtue: Pamphilia appears
with Amphilanthus as a constant lover; dressed in a style
strongly reminiscent of Elizabeth I, she is a constant queen;
and finally, she appears as an emblem of the constancy of
divine love.

By the end of Book I, many of the characters find themselves shipwrecked on the Isle of Cyprus, Venus's kingdom,
where is found the Throne of Love, and where lovers are
magically enchanted by love's power. Only the most constant
lady and the most valiant knight can free them: Amphilanthus
arrives first, followed by Pamphilia, and they prepare to end
the enchantment. Pamphilia appears

> in a Gowne of light Tawny or Murrey, embrodered with
> the richest, and perfectest Pearle for roundnesse and

URANIA AND PAMPHILIA TO AMPHILANTHUS

whitenes, the work contrived into knots and Garlands; on her head she wore a crowne of Diamonds, without foiles, to shew her clearenesse, such as needed no foile to set forth the true brightnesse of it: her haire ... was prettily intertwind betweene the Diamonds in many places, making them (though of the greatest value) appeare but like glasse set in gold. Her necke was modestly bare, yet made all discerne, it was not to be beheld with eyes of freedome: her left Glove was off, holding the king by the hand, who held most hearts. He was in Ashcolour, witnessing his repentance, yet was his cloake, and the rest of his suite so sumptuously embroidred with gold, as spake for him, that his repentance was most glorious. ... (141)

Here, Pamphilia closely resembles the elaborate glory and careful symbolism of Elizabeth's portraits, and if we also recall the conceit of certain entertainments that Elizabeth could break spells, Pamphilia's likeness is even more pronounced.[29] Elizabeth herself drew on the tradition of the constant ruler with her motto, *Semper eadem,* and in the emblems of the phoenix and the crowned pillar associated with her in portraits and entertainments.[30] But as Pamphilia is a constant queen, so is she a constant lover, and Wroth clearly differentiates her from Amphilanthus throughout this episode by accentuating her constancy and his repentance, in this case for loving another woman, Antissia; and by distinguishing her constancy from his valor or "worth." He is conspicuously not constant, and indeed, later in Book II, we find that his name actually "signifieth the lover of two" (250).

Pamphilia and Amphilanthus proceed to the three towers of the House of Love. On the first "Desire" is written in gold, and when Amphilanthus knocks, the gate opens and they proceed through to the next tower. This one displays "Love" written in rubies, and they open the gate to the next tower. Here, "*Constancy* stood holding the keyes, which *Pamphilia* tooke; at which instant *Constancy* vanished, as metamorphosing herself into her breast" (141). The very virtue itself now has its seat in Pamphilia's heart, inextricably tying her future course to its precepts. She hands the keys to Amphilanthus who opens the last gate into the gardens where the imprisoned lovers stand. A voice intones, "Loyallest, and therefore most incomparable *Pamphilia*, release the Ladies ... and thou *Amphilanthus*, the valliantest and worthiest of thy sexe, give freedome to the knights ... and thus is *Love* by love and worth released." Here, constancy is attached to women and valor to men, and often the *Urania* will describe a world ruled by valiant but changeable knights and princes who initiate most of the loves and wars; the ladies and princesses are more often endowed with a constant, steadfast disposition. This is certainly not to say that the female characters are merely reactive, and there are indeed some constant male characters and some faithless ladies. But apart from Cyprus, Wroth continually draws attention to the changeable nature of her male characters, as in passages like the following, describing a book Pamphilia reads:

> the subject was Love, and the story she then was reading, the affection of a Lady to a brave Gentleman, who equally loved, but being a man, it was necessary for him to exceede a woman in all things, so much as inconstancie was found fit for him to excell her in, hee left her for a new. (264)

Even stronger are the later words of a lovelorn lady, describing the other sex:

> the kindliest, lovingst, passionatest, worthiest, loveliest, valiantest, sweetest, and best man, will, and must change, not that he, it may bee, doth it purposely, but tis their naturall infirmitie, and cannot be helped. (375)

With some humor, Wroth seems to reverse the conventional literary attributes of the sexes, reinforcing her view with a sometimes satiric perspective on male valor. Describing the difficulties mounted knights are having going uphill, Wroth remarks: "Here with much difficulty and paine (which to adventurous knights is called pleasure, their life being a mere vexation, wilfully disguised to content) they got downe . . ." (324). That knightly adventures may not in deed define true valor, but rather lead to disruption and chaos—especially when seen from a woman's point of view—is a perspective that the *Urania* invites the reader to take. The romance's glorification of constancy suggests that a less martial virtue demands as great a dedication and discipline, and more important, ultimately spreads peace rather than war.

To return to the Cyprus episode, the religious aspect of the scene evolves during a series of feasts to celebrate the release of love's prisoners, the last feast being given by the king of Cyprus himself. He, impressed by such worthy Christian princes, decides to convert and is christened with his wife, daughter, and son by Amphilanthus, "and so became the whole Island Christians" (142). Allegorically, the conversion of the ruler of Venus's stronghold represents the transformation of worldly love to the love of God, and such a metamorphosis foreshadows the evolution to occur in Pamphilia herself during the course of her sonnet sequence. During the action of *Urania*, however, Wroth depicts in Pamphilia the plight of the constant soul enmeshed in an inconstant world, examining Pamphilia's roles as lover and as queen.

Such episodes in which Pamphilia performs specific deeds, or in which the iconography vividly depicts her nature explicitly convey Pamphilia's heroic constancy. More subtle and perhaps more psychologically modern are Wroth's adaptations of conventional tropes to reveal the inner conflicts of a virtuous woman who is as majestic and self-sufficient as Pamela, yet as desirous to love as Philoclea.

Despite Amphilanthus's attachments to other women, Pamphilia remains entirely faithful, and so must suffer absence, jealousy, and the alternation of devotion and abandonment that Amphilanthus proffers her. Wroth dissects Pamphilia's woes in minute detail, showing scene after scene in which Pamphilia probes her love, her sufferings, her lover's actions, and inevitably concludes with a mournful poem to express her sorrow. In a typical scene, early in the romance, before Amphilanthus knows she loves him, Pamphilia wanders into a conventional poetic landscape of trees and a brook, realizes that the scene reflects her own state of mind, and "Seeing this place delicate without, as shee was faire, and darke within as her sorrowes, shee went into the thickest part of it . . ." (74).

Musing on Cupid's cruelty, she regrets her modesty in not telling Amphilanthus openly that she loves him, "but soone was that thought recalled, and blamed with the greatest condemnation, acknowledging her losse in this kinde to proceed from vertue" (75). In language that Pamphilia herself will use in her sonnets, the narrator tells us that she is "the most distressed, secret, and constant Lover that ever *Venus* or her blind Sonne bestowed a wound or dart upon." To herself, Pamphilia soliloquizes, "for all these disorderly passions, keepe still thy soule from thought of change . . . and let me rather hate my selfe for this unquietnesse; and yet unjustly shall I doe too in that, since how can I condemne my heart, for having vertuously and worthily chosen?" (75). She concludes by carving a sonnet on the bark of an ash tree, as have melancholy lovers throughout all literature.

Pamphilia's quandary, expressed in the trope of Venus and blind Cupid wounding her heart, is that passion disrupts the order of a virtuous soul and challenges Pamphilia's principles to the core. Entering the grove, she journeyed into the darkest part of herself, and can acknowledge that her own virtue—her modesty, constancy, and silence—have caused much of her grief; but to regret her fall into passion is also to regret loving the virtue and worth she recognizes in Amphilanthus. Pamphilia resolves to seek solace in art, to write sad sonnets to confirm her constant spirit. Perhaps at this point the male hero of romance would dedicate himself to wooing the beloved or at least to performing valorous deeds. Or he might decline into melancholy. Wroth rejects such paths for Pamphilia, choosing not to make her a Britomart seeking her Artegall, nor yet to immobilize her by lovesickness; instead, she reinforces Pamphilia's adherence to patience and fortitude, reiterates her dedication to poetry, and gives her a kingdom to rule.

Consistently, Wroth returns to Pamphilia's queenliness as the best representation of her heroism. She probes the nature of Pamphilia's rule not only by imagining adventures for her, but by introducing parallel episodes involving other characters. One such narrative, perhaps one of the best, is the story of another queen, Nereana of Stalamina, who is an instructive contrast to Pamphilia's virtue. Nereana visits Pamphilia to seek redress against Steriamus who has rejected her love because he loves Pamphilia. Pamphilia tells Nereana that she is

> the first that ever I heard of, who take so knight-like a search in hand; men being us'd to follow scornefull Ladies, but you to wander after a passionate, or disdainefull Prince, it is great pitie for you. Yet *Madam* so much I praise you for it, as I would incourage you to proceede, since never feare of winning him, when so many excellencies may speake for you: as great beauty, high birth, rich possessions, absolute commend, and what is most, matchlesse love, and loyaltie ... (163)

Pamphilia's praise proves to be misplaced, however, and may indeed have been ironic, for Nereana, resuming her search, assumes "the part of an adventurous lover, as *Pamphilia* in jest had call'd her ..." (165). But the narrator seems to disapprove fully of women acting like men, for she plunges Nereana into nightmarish experiences meant to strip her and the reader of illusions about women playing men's roles, and to reveal the source of Nereana's adventurousness not as constancy, but as its opposite, pride.

Leaving Pamphilia, Nereana is cast by a storm onto Sicily, where the love-maddened Allanus attacks her, recreates her as a parody of the buskined Venus, and hounds her through the landscape of love ("a cleere spring ... in the middest of a faire meadow, the ground painted over with all sorts of dainty flowers...") so that now the pursuer is pursued, knowing no rest or peace (166). Eventually her ordeal expunges her former "masculine" assurance. Living alone in a cave, eating herbs and roots, Nereana grows "as humble, as before proud," and "extremity forcing her, contented with patience, and patiently contented . . ." she returns to essential womanliness by merely contemplating her love (287).

But Wroth still wants to show the important difference between love rooted in constancy and love based on pride. In the next twist of her story, the virtuous king Perissus rescues Nereana, but mistaking his courtesy for passion, she rushes headlong into another delusion. Once again dressed as a queen, "she began to grow to her wonted accustomed humours; like a garden never so delicate when well kept under, will without keeping grow ruinous" (289). Conceiving of herself as the "favorite of the loving Gods, and Goddesses," Nereana returns to her kingdom of Stalamina, but unlike the noble queen, Pamphilia, beloved of her people, Nereana finds her sister chosen queen in her absence; she is imprisoned and fed meagerly to "keepe downe her fancy."

As Pamphilia's alter ego, Nereana reveals Pamphilia's nature as a woman, a lover, and a queen. Having in the past imprisoned her sister and threatened her with death, Nereana taught her people to fear her rule. When she returns, some of her subjects wish to restore her, but eventually because "pride could not gaine obedience, nor scorne, command," and because they feared her revenge, her people choose to violate the law rather than risk her retribution, and Nereana is deposed. Nereana's pride links her behavior as a woman, a lover, and a ruler, just as Pamphilia's constancy guides the varied aspects of her life. Wroth opposes pride and constancy by showing in her narrative that at the root of Nereana's pride is love of the self, while at the root of Pamphilia's constancy is love of another, a selflessness that appears continually in the *Urania* until it is finally consecrated in *Pamphilia to Amphilanthus*.

While drawing a pointed moral from Nereana's story, Wroth eventually allows it to end happily. Her subjects realize the importance of honoring the succession, and recanting their treason, they restore Nereana to the throne. She, having been truly humbled by "poore living and neglect," exhibits the appropriate gravity and demeanor for her station and becomes "an excellent Governess, and brave Lady, being able to over-rule her old passions ..." (421). The change in Nereana from "adventurous lover" to "excellent Governess" reflects Wroth's view of a woman's potential, which is not to become manly, but actively and publicly to exercise her best womanly qualities.

Part of Wroth's technique is to develop her ideas in such parallel stories and characters, but she also relies on another romance convention, the debate. The nature of Pamphilia's constancy, its foundation in humility and selflessness, and its resulting misery for her, do not go unchallenged in the *Urania*. At times, she wanders into self-doubt, asking herself whether she was born to suffer because of her "rare excellent qualitie of constancy" (395). But when questioned directly, Pamphilia always defends her constancy and her love. However, in Book III, her cousin and Amphilanthus's sister, Urania, criticizes Pamphilia for loving at all. Pamphilia remarks that all the stories show how even the "most excellent men have been lovers and are subject to this passion" (399). With some acerbity, Urania counters that she considers "it was a blemish to their other excelling vertues." When Pamphilia wonders why Urania is so bitter, Urania responds with the classic argument against passion, one that enlarges upon the very problem Pamphilia had always recognized about falling in love. Urania is not passion's "slave," and indeed scorns Cupid for "a proud, then puling Babe"; she believes that only "want of courage and judgement" subjects the lover to such a deity (399-400).

To this critique, Pamphilia justly remarks that such clear-eyed reason cannot rule love and its attendant despair and martyrdom. More important, she loves Amphilanthus because of his virtues, independently of whether he loves her. Idealistically, Pamphilia asks nothing for herself but to be able to love virtue, and to "still maintain a vertuous constancy." Even more caustically, Urania returns

> Tis pittie ... that ever that fruitlesse thing Constancy
> was taught you as a vertue, since for vertues sake you

will love it, as having true possession of your soule, but understand, this vertue hath limits to hold it in, being a vertue, but thus that it is a vice in them that breake it, but those with whom it is broken, are by the breach free to leave or choose againe where more staidnes may be found; besides it is a dangerous thing to hold that opinion, which in time will prove flat heresie. (400)

The narrator directs the reader here by remarking, "Thus did the divine *Urania* againe by her excellent wit conquer . . . ," so that what we will eventually realize is not that Pamphilia's whole devotion to constancy is "fruitlesse," nor that Urania is encouraging her to abandon Amphilanthus for another man. (This becomes clear when we hear a shepherd comically praise variety in love, for constancy is "the foolishest unprofitable whining vertue," 484.) Rather, Pamphilia should indeed "choose againe where more staidnes may be found" and only in this way may she avoid "flat heresie." The meaning inherent in Urania's words is that constancy to Amphilanthus suffers the limits of ordinary human mutability and will naturally bring Pamphilia unhappiness. Something more "staid" to love is the divine, and the heresy is to love and be constant to man before God, to set up blind Cupid as deity instead. The full force of Urania's words does not register in Pamphilia until the meditative atmosphere of her sonnets which distill the experience of loving Amphilanthus and redirecting her constancy to divine love.[31]

Shortly after this exchange, Wroth again accentuates the importance of Pamphilia's virtue by providing her with a regal procession, reminiscent of an Elizabethan progress. But here, she intertwines Pamphilia's roles as lover and queen, thus emphasizing both the importance of Pamphilia's existence beyond her love for Amphilanthus and the momentary nature of any of their encounters. While all her subjects come "from all parts to see her, and joy in her presence," Pamphilia's unhappiness prevents her from enjoying anything, "yet she lost not her selfe; for her government continued just and brave, like that Lady she was, wherein she shewed her heart was not to be stur'd, though her private fortunes shooke round about her" (411). Even when threatened by the King of Celicia who attacks her kingdom to win her love, her strength as a queen never falters, so that "her Counsell admired her magnanimity ..." (429). They also admire her practicality in sending for Amphilanthus to rescue the country. Naturally, he defeats the invading king in single combat, and the lovers enjoy a brief interlude of love, hunting together and wandering through yet another landscape of love.

On one of these excursions, they meet a shepherd who, not recognizing Pamphilia, unabashedly delivers his opinions of her as a monarch and a woman, again setting off her one aspect against the other. She is, he says, beloved by the humble and feared by the great, "curteous, affable," and wise; and yet, she has fallen in love:

> shee is upright and just, in her government mild, and loving to her subjects, she loves all good exercises as well abroad, as at home; shee hath indeed they say, a brave and manlike spirit, and wonderous wise shee is; yet for all these good parts, shee could not keepe out of *Cupids* clawes. ... (483)

The shepherd concludes by remarking tartly that as Pamphilia's beloved has "as it is said, a prety humour of changing, wee doe not wish him to her, least wee should loose her" (494).

Here again, as if to reinforce the importance of Pamphilia's constancy beyond her love for Amphilanthus, Wroth provides details, echoes, and allusions to associate her with the past glory of Elizabeth I. Emphasizing the love of her people, Wroth echoes the adulation Elizabeth received in her lifetime as well as her posthumous veneration. The legend surrounding Elizabeth claimed she always placed her country first, especially when the question of love and marriage arose, and that as she loved the commoner so was she feared by the noble. "I know I have but the body of a weak and feeble woman; but I have the heart of a King, and of a king of England too," she claimed at Tilbury, and her justice was proclaimed in her iconography as Astraea.[32] All these attributes Pamphilia reflects, but it is Elizabeth's love for and constancy to her subjects that resonate most clearly in the Queen of Pamphilia.

It is significant that throughout the long course of the *Urania*, Pamphilia and Amphilanthus never marry. As early as Book II, Pamphilia reveals that her idea of marriage has little to do with knights, but everything to do with her position as queen. To her father she explains why she will not marry:

> his Majestie had once married her before which was to the kingdome of *Pamphilia* from which Husband shee could not bee divorced, nor ever would have other, if it might please him to give her leave, to enjoy that happinesse; and besides, besought his permission, for my Lord (said shee) my people looke for me, and I must needs be with them. (218)

This is a clear allusion to Elizabeth, who spoke of herself as England's wife. According to Camden's *History*, when asked if she would marry, Elizabeth replied:

> Yea, to satisfie you, I have already joyned my self in Marriage to an Husband, namely, the Kingdom of England. And behold (said she) which I marvell ye have forgotten, the Pledge of this my Wedlock and Marriage with my Kingdom. (And therewith she drew the Ring from her Finger, and shewed it, wherewith at her Coronation she had in a set form of words solemnly given her self in Marriage to her Kingdom.)[33]

Wroth found in the late queen the model of an ideal ruler and woman of virtue, and perhaps her nostalgia for that "golden" age of Elizabeth also influenced her choice of forms, the romance and the sonnet sequence, both so inextricably identified with the Elizabethan era. Certainly, the image of Elizabeth shadowing Pamphilia throughout the romance reinforces the significance of Pamphilia's constancy beyond her devotion to Amphilanthus.[34] If Pamphilia is "already bestowed upon her people and had married herselfe to them"

(220), she cannot also be united to Amphilanthus, and in fact, their love belongs to a lesser sphere, quite separate from Pamphilia's consecration as a queen, and eventually its worldliness demands its purgation.

Near the end of the romance, Wroth provides a momentary view of the ramifications of Pamphilia's constancy and Amphilanthus's infidelities with two parallel scenes, experienced in turn by both lovers, featuring the "hell of deceit" and the two witches, Musalina and Lucenia, with whom Amphilanthus had been involved previously. Shortly after their love interlude, Amphilanthus disappears during a stag hunt, and though Pamphilia searches for him, significantly all she finds is a black-clad huntress, a faithful older woman whose lover has left her for someone younger. Going into the most deserted part of the woods, Pamphilia finds a trail of blood that leads her to a dead boar and to a place "made round like a Crowne of mighty stones" (493). On the biggest stone is Amphilanthus's battered, bloody armor, and his sword struck deeply into the rock. Sure that Amphilanthus is dead, Pamphilia succumbs to grief, but then seeing a ring in the rock, she pulls it and discovers inside "a place like a Hell of flames and fire, and as if many walking and throwing pieces of men and women up and downe in the flames, partly burnt, and they still stirring the fire, and more brought in ..." (494). And there stands Amphilanthus, with his chest ripped open and "Pamphilia" written on his heart, and a crowned and enthroned Musalina about to raze that name with a sword. Though eager to save Amphilanthus, and though she burns with "as hot flames as those she saw," Pamphilia is helpless because "Faithfull lovers keepe from hence/None but false ones here can enter." Her torment is to see his nature, but to be powerless to assist him or change him. She has no choice but to return to court where "more like a religious, then a court life, she lived some yeares."

The parallel episode, Amphilanthus's alternate version of this adventure, follows some time later and is related by the squire of the Duke of Burgundy, one of Amphilanthus's allies. In his account, when separated from Pamphilia at the stag hunt, Amphilanthus was told that she had been stolen by thieves. Searching for her, he reaches an obscure part of the wood and the "Crowne of mighty stones." Killing an attacking boar, Amphilanthus is immediately set upon by many armed men who magically vanish when he has killed the one "young man unarm'd" who had most vigorously attacked him. Amphilanthus hears Pamphilia's voice cry, "Farewell, Amphilanthus," and instead of a young man "hee saw to his thinking *Pamphilia* slaine" (553). Despite his efforts, she is carried into the rock, and when he strikes the stone, his sword sticks there. Pulling a ring in the rock, he finds Pamphilia dead "lying within an arch, her breast open and in it his name made, in little flames being like pretty lamps which made the letters, as if set round with diamonds, and so cleare it was, as hee distinctly saw the letters ingraven at the bottome in characters of bloud ..." (554). Unable to enter the cave to rescue Pamphilia, Amphilanthus sees only the words, "This no wonder's of much waight,/'Tis the hell of deepe deceit" (554). But whose deceit becomes clear when suddenly Musalina materializes, calling for help, and "she must be followed, *Pamphilia* is forgotten, and now may lie and burne in the Cave, *Lucenia* must bee rescued also, her hee saw madly carried by a savage man. ...." Completely enchanted by the two witches, yet protected from mortal danger by "the divine powers" (554), Amphilanthus follows the ladies to Tenedos, becomes unenchanted, and lives there "in much pleasure" (555).

In these two "magical" or allegorical episodes, Wroth encapsulates the story of Pamphilia's faith and Amphilanthus's perennial infidelity, but indicates that more is at stake than mere disappointment in love. These scenes completely reverse the trope of the beloved raising the lover to a vision of heavenly love and vividly show the moral and spiritual peril implied both by inconstancy and continued constancy to a mutable being. In Pamphilia's version, she realizes the horrors that lie beneath the surface of her love. Inconstancy is betrayal of the beloved (whose name or image is engraved on the heart) and even death itself, since Musalina's sword will ensure "his heart as the wound to perish." Because she is forbidden to enter the hellish world of deceit, Pamphilia's constancy is reaffirmed as a moral and spiritual state, providing her with the strength to maintain faith, to resist change, and to continue to love virtue.

But Wroth only clarifies the danger of her continued attachment in Amphilanthus's account of the scene. His vision includes his murdering Pamphilia, her descent into the hell of deceit, and the portrayal of his name written on her heart in letters of flame fed by her blood. As the victim of inconstancy, yet maintaining her own constant love, Pamphilia risks spiritual death. Her constancy, as Urania warned, will become a "dangerous thing" and, in time, "flat heresie."[35]

Wroth does not rescue her characters from their spiritual hell, nor does she resolve their problems. Much more about constancy appears in Pamphilia's sonnet sequence, but the printed *Urania* concludes with a highly ironic reunion between the lovers, particularly considering its juxtaposition to the scenes of hell. Since Amphilanthus has just promised his regent and council to return to Germany very shortly, it is obvious that he will not remain long with Pamphilia. Nevertheless, Wroth designs their rendezvous on an ironic background of "sweet Ayre, pleasant Fields, Brookes; Meddowes, Springs, Flowres," and a "dainty Spring" into which Pamphilia weeps medicinal tears (557).[36] Almost parodying a farewell scene, the narrator claims, "never was such affection exprest, never so truly felt, to the company, they together, returned, he leading her, or rather imbracing her, with his conquering armes, and protesting the water he dranke being mixed with her teares, had so infused constancy and perfect truth of love in it, as in him it had wrought the like effect ..." (557-58). Fifteen lines later, he is leaving for Germany, and Pamphilia is to go only as far as Italy with him to visit his mother. The narrator reminds us that words are only air to Amphilanthus by wryly noting that the lovers return briefly to the wood to revisit the hell of deceit, "but now no more to be abused." Amphilanthus destroys the "Crowne of mighty stones," the monument to his "former ficklenes," but the problem does not lie in a pile of stones, but in the morality which they represented. The journey of Pamphilia and Amphilanthus, if they adhere to their present course, will only be a continuation and repetition of what has already passed. As she first conceived of these characters, Wroth could never unite them.

In Pamphilia, Wroth achieved the most detailed portrait yet drawn of woman's constancy. Her picture is not simple, largely because Pamphilia is not merely the stereotyped helpless lovelorn lady: she is a queen, a poet, and a strong woman. In what Wroth defines as women's terms, she is heroic in her duty and obedience to the state, despite private grief, and in her devotion, despite suffering, to constancy. Ironically, her virtue is also her flaw, and this conundrum is the main subject of her sonnets, where Wroth eventually proposes yet another role for her hero, that of the divine poet.

Pamphilia to Amphilanthus

In this revival of the Elizabethan sonnet sequence, Wroth used much of the conventional language and imagery of sequences from the 1590s, yet she radically changed the tradition by making her sonneteer a woman. Wroth's choice of genre raises a number of interesting problems about poetry and gender. Because sonnet sequences had been written so exclusively by male poets, Wroth cannot ignore the conventions established by the male poet-lover, and, as in other sequences, she directs sonnets to love, night, sleep, the stars, day, hope, grief, and absence, and uses familiar images like "night's blacke Mantle," "my woe-kild heart," "the fires of love," "Loves swift wings," "that Sea of teares," "such store of sighes," as well as the ubiquitous oppositions of the *petrarchisti*:

> Can pleasing sight misfortune ever bring?
>   Can firme desire a painefull torment try?
>   Can winning eyes prove to the hart a sting?
>   Or can sweet lips in treason hidden ly?
>   (Sonnet 5, 87)[37]

But while *Pamphilia to Amphilanthus* resembles the Elizabethan sequences, its contexts make it significantly different. Unlike the poems of many other sonneteers, Pamphilia's sonnets are not designed to woo and win her lover nor to express attachment to his physical charm. Instead, Pamphilia's sequence explores the nature of constancy, her own greatest attribute, to the almost complete exclusion of poetry directly concerning her beloved. Here are no *blasons*, indeed, almost no mention of Amphilanthus's physical presence; after the title, his name is not mentioned again. Such an omission means the customary language of courtship is absent from most of the sequence; only in the last sonnets, in which Pamphilia redirects her love and constancy to the divine, does that language, refurbished and renewed, appear.

Our understanding of this sequence is increased by studying it from several different perspectives: its immediate literary context as companion piece to the *Urania*; the poetic innovations required to adapt the genre to a female sonneteer; its relationship to the tradition of women's writing now a century old; its belated relationship to the Elizabethan sequences; and the possible familial influences.[38] On all accounts, through her sonneteer (Pamphilia), Wroth expands the possibilities of a female poetic voice to encompass passion, purgation, and vision. The first half of the sequence records Pamphilia's already familiar sufferings for love, while in a crown of fourteen sonnets near the end of the sequence, she fulfills Urania's exhortation by directing her constancy beyond Amphilanthus to the divine. If she explores the psychology of woman's passion to a much greater extent than her aunt, the end of her sequence finds an appropriate analogy in the Countess of Pembroke's Psalms.

As an integral part of the *Urania, Pamphilia to Amphilanthus* reflects the characterization of Pamphilia as constant, chaste, and modest, and underscores her heroic adherence to these virtues. In the sonnet sequence appear both extremes of Pamphilia's experience, a vision of the hell of deep deceit and the promise of divine love, as well as Pamphilia's parallel realization that the true home for her constancy is not inconstant man but the God of Love. The structure of the sequence reflects these two different modes and the changes in Pamphilia's poetic vision. For the first 48 sonnets and 7 songs, the design is perfectly regular: 6 sonnets followed by a song. These sonnets include the most familiar images of Elizabethan sonnet style and numerous Sidneian echoes. Such careful arrangement suddenly dissolves into scattered songs and sonnets, and wholeness only reappears with a crown of 14 sonnets, a perfect circle dedicated to praising love, and then the sequence concludes with Pamphilia's acknowledgment of her true poetic vocation.[39]

The sonnets arranged in eight groups of six anatomize the heart and mind of the weeping Pamphilia, mourning the absent Amphilanthus, yet ever constant to her love. The regular ordering of the sonnets is ironic, belying the disorder of Pamphilia's mind in the throes of grief, jealousy, and despair. Here, the very Cupid about whom Urania had warned Pamphilia ranges freely, imaging the fires of passion controlling Pamphilia's life and art. This is yet another version of Astrophil's "murthering boy," and his "babish tricks" and "Purblinde charmes" recall the woes of a whole tradition of long, but self-inflicted, suffering in love.

Detailing the psychology of passionate and unrequited love, Pamphilia makes wholehearted use of the familiar paraphernalia of lovesickness. Over and over again the verbs reveal her suffering: "I for mercy cry" "I groaned," "I suffer'd," "All night I weepe," "Sorrow Ile wed," "I weepe, I cry, I sigh, I mourne, I grieve." Yet with this agony is the clear self-consciousness of a poet-lover who will obey love's "charmes . . . but love nott want of eyes" (Sonnet 7, 90). She is knowingly enthralled to this Cupid, the blind, imperious, playful, "fond Childe" responsible for burning hearts and servitude to love, who is also the tyrannical power capable of protracted cruelty (Sonnet 11, 92). In the very first sonnet of the sequence, echoes of the hell of deep deceit resound as Pamphilia describes a dream of her fall into love. Venus appears in her chariot "drawne by wing'd desire," accompanied by Cupid who adds fire to the burning hearts she holds. "Butt one hart flaming more then all the rest" is placed in Pamphilia's breast and "martir'd my poore hart."

What Pamphilia insists on here, as she did all the way through the *Urania*, is her constancy, her decision to be faithful to love despite all vicissitudes. In the first song, sung by a constant shepherdess, Pamphilia transfers the expression of passion to a persona who articulates an extreme that Pamphilia projects for herself, dying for love. The shepherdess asks for the epitaph, "She who still constant lov'd/Now dead with cruell care,/Kil'd with unkind dispaire,/And change, her end heere prov'd" (89). The scenes of hell in the *Urania* have already portrayed the danger of obsessive devotion, and in these early sonnets a despairing Pamphilia actually contemplates death "since you will nott save" (Sonnet 6, 88).

But if such a pose and such language recall other sonnet lovers, Pamphilia differs from her male predecessors. First, she does not woo. The title may be *Pamphilia to Amphilanthus*, but she addresses sonnets not to him but to sleep, night, grief, shades, time, or Cupid. Amphilanthus lives in her imagination, in shadows, but Pamphilia never mentions his name, never describes him, never considers his physical attractions. The only reward she desires exists totally within the bounds of a chaste love: the transfer of his heart to her, where it will "see the sacrifises made/Of pure, and spottles love . . ." (Sonnet 26, 102). She explicitly rejects a love manifested in "fond, and outward showes/Of kissing, toying . . ."; initiated by "face and lookes"; maintained by "sighes, or teares"; lasting only as long as "favors" are dispensed (Sonnet 40, 110). As in the *Urania*, Pamphilia declines to assume the male role of courtship, and bound by the ideals and decorum of womanly modesty, humility, and chastity, she uses her poetic art to present these virtues and to reveal what happens when they are wounded by passion. In Sonnets 34 and 36, for instance, her modesty and silence cause her to hide her love, and then suffer pain for concealing it.

Second, while Pamphilia's imagery echoes her predecessors, she resembles neither traditional sonnet ladies nor their lovers, for she is a woman *and* a poet, who, possessing and believing in the virtues of constancy and chastity, expresses how she suffers in a world subject to time, fortune, and mutability; and it is indeed a man's world, in which she cannot hope for a requited constancy and chastity from him. But because the story emanates from the woman's point of view, she does not merely present idealized female virtue, but reveals what it is like to bear that virtue when in love with inconstant man. Here is no simple reversal of male and female roles, but an attempt to define how a woman's poetry can reveal her passions and predicaments.

At this point, the sequence disintegrates formally and psychologically with a new series of sonnets increasingly dark and confined, reminiscent of the hell of deep deceit. Shadows and a constriction of spirit appear when the poet contemplates "bace jealousie;/O in how strang a cage ame I kept in?" (Sonnet 4, 121); and when she calls herself a "Tombe for sad misfortunes spite" (Sonnet 5, 122). Claustrophobia threatens when she images how "my paine, still smother'd in my grieved brest,/Seekes for some ease, yett cannot passage find/To bee discharg'd of this unwellcome ghest" (Sonnet 6, 122). Evoking near-panic from the simile of a ship sinking deeper in the sand "the more she strives," Pamphilia's verbs to convey her state of mind are "Sunk, and devour'd, and swallow'd." Once, the poet had imagined that she could never be tied by love, but yet she finds herself in "lovers slaverie" and "bound" not to try to free herself (Sonnet 10, 124). Her state of mind grows more desperate, more in need of release.

In the last two songs before the crown of sonnets, Pamphilia presents the source of her captivity, the conventionally moralized blind boy Cupid. Song 16 details his tricks and flattery, and his pleasure in deception (125). Song 17 underlines Cupid's danger with an insistent refrain, "So though his delights are pritty,/To dwell in them would bee pitty" (126). Such warning of the "pitty" resulting from worldly pleasure becomes in the last stanza a fervent exhortation, "Doe not dwell in them for pitty." But the last sonnet before the crown marks the turning point, for having exhausted the poetry of suffering, Pamphilia suddenly curses the thought and hand which first wrote against Cupid, and now "that hand shall guided bee aright,/And give a crowne unto thy endless prayse,/Which shall thy glory, and thy greatnes raise,/More then thes poore things could thy honor spite" (126).[40]

Here, Wroth evokes the familiar iconography of two Cupids, one to represent sensual love, the other the love of virtue—a traditional opposition she could have learned from many sources. Alciati explains the antithesis of the two figures in the emblems concerning the triumph of Anteros over Eros, identified respectively as love of virtue and love. In the first emblem, Anteros denounces voluptuousness, and while wearing the wreath of wisdom, kindles instead the fires of learning. In the second emblem, Anteros binds Eros to a tree, consuming his fire with a new fire.[41] While the interpretation of Anteros as the opposite and destroyer of Eros was an anomaly in the main classical tradition of Anteros as mutual love, it was a departure known well to Renaissance scholars and to such diverse writers as Marguerite de Navarre and Ben Jonson.[42] Although the convention in sonnet sequences was to present Cupid only as an image of voluptuous love, Wroth uses the two opposing Cupids to illustrate the extraordinary turn which Pamphilia's love takes.[43]

Although Pamphilia had never succumbed to lust, she was enchained to the love of an earthly being. She gains her release only by rejecting blind Cupid and by turning to praise the divine Cupid; by rejecting old sonnet language and becoming the poet of divine love. It almost goes without saying that other sonneteers have moved from the entanglements of sublunary love to contemplation of the divine. But in each case, the beloved lady performs an important function for the poet: loving Laura eventually brings Petrarch to love God. The poet's language of love for a lady may ironically mask "higher" love, or by rejecting earthly love for his lady, the poet may strive to love the divine. On her part, the lady can offend, torment, inspire, teach, or turn the poet's attention inward or upward.[44] In Wroth's sequence, however, the beloved man is not there at all. Sonnet language does not exist here to woo him or even to reject him, but almost as if to show its own tiredness and inefficacy. In Sonnet 39, Pamphilia had described "My owne fram'd words, which I account the dross/Of purer thoughts, or recken them as moss/While they (witt-sicke) them selves to breath imploy" (110). So far, conventional sonnet language has not measured up to Pamphilia's ideas, nor expressed her true identity.

As a chaste, constant woman, Pamphilia finds her vocation as a lover and a love-poet limited; she needs a role and a language less trammeled by considerations of gender, less worn by the century-long experiences of male sonneteers. Innovating by extending the crown of sonnets to a full fourteen, Wroth uses the unmistakable connectedness of the form to reveal a new integrity within Pamphilia. Rather than anatomize her constancy in continual conflict with fortune, time, and mutability, Pamphilia will now reveal its origins in "true virtue," in divine love. In the crown, there is no language of discord or suffering, only the language of harmony and joy, because her constancy now exists in its true, timeless, unchangeable setting.

The first sonnet marks the transition from love poet to divine poet, encapsulating the dark, constricting, even hellish experience of the last sixty sonnets in the image of the "strang labourinth." Disorienting, thwarting, isolating, the labyrinth represents the world of continued doubt and woe from which she has come. But now she will "leave all, and take the thread of love," which in Sonnet 2 "straite leades unto the soules content" (128). Suddenly all those sonnets of night, shadows, absence, and despair disappear and the world, guided by chastity, gleams with light, fire, plenitude, and hope:

> Love is the shining starr of blessings light;
> The fervent fire of zeale, the roote of peace,
> The lasting lampe, fed with the oyle of right;
> Image of fayth, and wombe for joyes increase.   (128)

Briefly recalling the wise virgins with their lamps filled with oil, Pamphilia vividly contrasts this love with blind, peevish boy-Cupid; more, this love is an essence "Cleere as th'ayre, warme as sunn beames, as day light/Just as truthe, constant as fate . . ." (Sonnet 3, 129). This love does not inflict pain by its momentary meetings, but its heavenly fires will last until the end of the world. And so, "although, itt pierce your tender hart,/And burne, yett burning you will love the smart" (Sonnet 4, 130).

Unlike its earthly shadow, the fire of divine love abolishes sin, and possesses "vertues which inspire/Soules with devine love—which showes his chaste art." This love has salutary effects, for "He may our profitt, and owr Tuter prove" (Sonnet 5, 130).[45] More, while earthly fire destroys—as does the fire of the hell of deep deceit—"this doth aspire,/Increase, and foster all delights above" (Sonnet 7, 131). This love transcends the "briers/Of jelousie" so troublesome to Pamphilia earlier, and more important, distinguishes (as many male sonneteers do not) mere coldness from true chastity which indeed moves "vertuouse love" (Sonnet 8, 131).

Measuring how far the sequence has come is Sonnet 9 which rejects "*Venus* follyes" and praises "her sunn; wher sinn/Never did dwell" [1621, "her Sonne"]. The Christological echoes are deliberate, for Pamphilia excoriates the false Cupid, that "Monster" of lust; and rejecting the ills of "fraile, dull earth" and fading blossoms, she urges lovers to choose the "fruit" which repairs or redeems the loss. To envision the divine Cupid, an essence of light and fire, is to be moved by God, also the "lord commander of all harts," and to him, the poet offers her constant soul, her poetry of praise and "all that I have more" (Sonnet 13, 134). In the final sonnet, Pamphilia gives her constancy its proper home, for she offers up to divine love her "faith untouch'd," and her heart "where constancy beares sway." Unlike the first sonnet in the sequence, this one attests to her freedom from the pangs of earthly desire.

But the vision must end, and it is time to move out of the circle of the crown, back into time and mutability. Emerging from heavenly contemplation, the poet recognizes the foes of divine love lying in wait, like "Curst jealousie." The last couplet, while it repeats the first lines of the crown, also adds the word "fervently": "Soe though in Love I fervently doe burne,/In this strange labourinth how shall I turne?" The question in Sonnet 1 concerned "burning" in love for Amphilanthus, and so blindly seeking her way through the twisting labyrinth. But in Sonnet 14, the poet burns fervently in divine love and, poetically inspired by that love, wonders how she will ever readjust to life in the labyrinthine world.

In the last few songs and sonnets after the crown, we too must ponder how her divine vision has affected Pamphilia as poet and as lover. While the first song after the crown is not overtly divine, its diction clearly resonates of the spiritual: "Sweet," "injoye," "bright," "sunn," "spring," "delight," "pleasures," "bliss," "faithfull," "just," "joyes," "gladnesse," "flames of faith," "burne," "life," "blessed," "light"—all the language of the crown of sonnets, but apparently in the quite different context of a traditional song from lover to beloved, "Sweet, lett mee injoye thy sight. . ." (135). Perhaps Pamphilia has learned that divine love may be shadowed in sublunary love, so that the language itself is deliberately ambiguous, meant to refer both to mortal love, and more secretly, to love of the divine.

The first song may be yet another expression of faithful love, but coming after the crown, its last three lines are arresting:

> And grant mee lyfe which is your sight,
> Wherin I more blessed live,
> Then graced with the sunns faire light.   (135)

Clearly a spiritual reading is possible here, and is reinforced later by the couplet of Sonnet 4 which suggests that "the truer Image" lies unseen in her heart (140). If all the forces of jealousy, that is, the powers that work against selfless or true virtue, are massed against her, the solution is to preserve her "true love" hidden within her heart and under her apparent meaning. Perhaps the most convincing example of such doubling of language is in the seventh sonnet, which follows two sonnets referring to hidden meanings: "Soe wrong may shadow mee, till truth doe smile,/And justice (sun-like) hath those vapors tyde" (140); "To mee itt seems, as ancient fictions make/The starrs all fashions, and all shapes partake/While in my thoughts true forme of love shall live" (141). The sonnet to "deere love" begins by expressing both love and pain, but concludes with language connotative of much more:

> When all alone, I thinke upon thy paine,
>> How thou doest traveile owr best selves to gaine;
>> Then howerly thy lessons I doe learne,
>
> Think on thy glory, which shall still assend
>> Untill the world come to a finall end,
>> And then shall we thy lasting powre deserne.
>
>> (Sonnet 7, 141)

This could just barely refer to Cupid, but again the Chris-tological echoes dominate and recall the apocalyptic vision of crown Sonnet 4 which precedes the establishment of the King-dom of Love.

By suggesting that the reality at the core of Pamphilia's language is divine love, Wroth creates a poetry that expresses not merely woman's love for man, but the wise virgin's love for her bridegroom. Having seen how this parable inspired the imaginations of so many women writers, we should not be surprised to hear it echo at the heart of the first real love poetry by a woman.

Having purged her love and her language in the crown of sonnets, Pamphilia's subsequent poems include her love of God. Yet the poetry of those fourteen sonnets seems to have been both a beginning and an end. The last sonnet in the sequence, "My muse now hapy, lay thy self to rest," is a farewell without regret to the poetry of passion:

> Leave the discource of Venus, and her sunn
>> To young beeginers, and theyr brains inspire
>> With storys of great love, and from that fire
>> Gett heat to write the fortunes they have wunn.
>
>> (Sonnet 9, 142)

Instead her muse will study "those thoughts adrest/To truth, which shall eternall goodnes prove." In the past, Pamphilia's poems have shown how truly she could love Amphilanthus. Now, and for the future, she has found the true source of her constancy, and recalling that divine virtue, she instructs her muse, "Now lett your constancy your honor prove."

In *Pamphilia to Amphilanthus*, Wroth glorifies a love which affirms and sanctifies the primacy of woman's virtue, for chastity, modesty, and constancy, so afflicted in the world, triumph in the celebration of divine love. If Wroth was influenced in many of her sonnets by other sequences, like those of her father and uncle, she finally gave her homage to divine poetry, as did her aunt in the Psalms.

Perhaps Wroth's most important accomplishment in the *Urania* and *Pamphilia to Amphilanthus* was to expand the possibilities open to women writers. Her generous imagination and her sheer stamina produced two big works that are almost encyclopedic in their treatment of love and virtue. In particular, by seriously projecting women's actions, feelings, and dilemmas, Wroth developed a female hero without equal in Elizabethan romance. That this character is a poet only adds to her significance, for in her name, Wroth composed lyric poetry as no English woman had before.

And yet, despite her innovations, and contrary to Lord Denny's bitter opinion, Wroth preserves important aspects of traditional feminine literary decorum. If, for instance, her romance treats love affairs, they are not merely as Denny claimed, "lascivious tales and amorous toys," but rather, images of the mutable world, placed clearly in a moral framework acceptable to Renaissance concepts of order. Like the Countess of Pembroke in her translation, *Antonie*, Wroth vividly represents passion and violence at least partly to clarify their nature and their proper place in human affairs. The fact that Pamphilia's very heroism grows out of her adherence to the traditional feminine virtues indicates that Wroth elaborates rather than contravenes the conventions.

But Pamphilia is fundamentally an Elizabethan heroine, not only because she is modeled after Queen Elizabeth, but because through her Wroth evolved a feminine perspective on themes, images, and genres that defined the literature of the preceding era. Wroth's references to the past also indicate closure, the final evolution of the female hero whose poetic beginnings may be seen in the Countess of Pembroke's Clorinda and Elizabeth. In fact, the lyric impulse to praise, glorify and apotheosize women, and the fictional treatment of heroic virtue, appear not to have concerned Wroth's Jacobean sisters who instead took up the basic issues of the woman question and women's essential feminine roles.

PART III

_____

"Lofty walls all around"

NINE

REDEEMING EVE: DEFENSES
OF WOMEN AND MOTHER'S
ADVICE BOOKS

*I*N THIS FINAL chapter, works concerning female rulers, their adventures in love, and their devotion to poetry will seem very distant. Mary Wroth's book does not appear to have influenced other women writers, either in content or form, perhaps because she withdrew it, perhaps because her work might appear as a nostalgic version of an aristocratic past. Indeed, the times seemed not to elicit concern for the virtuous woman's ability to rule kingdoms and to write sonnets, but instead, for the very fundamentals of traditional feminine identity. Rather than continuing the expansion suggested by Cary, Lanyer, and Wroth, other women writers from 1600 to 1625 wrote prose works to provide explicit evidence of women's Christian virtue. They differed from most of their sixteenth-century predecessors, however, because by writing defenses of women and by developing the uniquely feminine genre of the mother's advice book, they self-consciously defined their personas as exclusively and specifically feminine.

At first glance, the defenders of women and the writing mothers seem to have little in common. The authors of defenses of women seem outspoken, raucous, even rude, while the authors of mother's advice books seem conventional, restrained, and pious. Yet both are inspired by their faith, the writing mothers describing themselves as teachers seeking salvation for their children, and the defenders of women emphasizing the divine mission of the virtuous Christian woman to spread the word. Both groups are essentially conservative in their espousal of traditional female virtue, and both attempt to redeem woman by idealizing her. The differences in their style and voice are significant only insofar as they reflect the different audiences which these writers overtly addressed and the different personas they developed. The defenders of women set out to answer their masculine detractors, to redeem Eve by argument, to use words as their weapons; in the process they discovered both a new verbal power and a new source of anxiety in the clash of language with decorum. The writing mothers assumed the role of redeemer—Mary rather than Eve—and ostensibly instructing only their children or other women, they found a voice that could properly absorb and render all the feminine virtues.

Defenses of Women

Responding to specific misogynist attacks, four women came to the defense of their sex: Jane Anger answered a pamphlet by a "late Surfeiting Lover" with her *Protection for Women* (1589); Joseph Swetnam's *Araignment of Lewde, idle, froward, and unconstant women* (1615) sparked Rachel Speght's *A Mouzell for Melastomus* (1617), Esther Sowernam's *Ester hath hang'd Haman* (1617), and Constantia Munda's *The Worming of a mad Dogge* (1617). The titles of the last three suggest an unusually aggressive pose for the woman writer; however, the three pseudonyms indicate not simply the writer's chosen role, but her underlying anxiety about publication of her response. Each of these works attempted something stylistically and formally new for the woman writer, although they did not represent the birth of a feminist consciousness. Rather, adopting a genre that had long been exclusively masculine, these women modified its main characteristics to suit their own goal, the vindication of women's Christian virtue. In the process, each created a persona who could argue, assume for herself a hitherto prohibited authority, and develop a strategy of confrontation. To take responsibility for defending them-

selves called for an active, inventive wit which quickly chal-
lenged the author's conventional apologies for her inability.
The legacy of the defenses of women may lie not so much
in what these writers said, but more in how they said it.

Considering how many women writers implicitly or explicitly strove to demonstrate the virtues of their sex, one
might expect them to have joined the debate on the "woman
question" at an early stage. They did not do so, however,
until relatively late in Jane Anger's case, and very late in the
case of Speght and her successors. The question of why they
entered the discussion at all is best explained by examining
specifically what these defenders accomplished.

Perhaps women did boil with rage at misogynist insults
for so long that eventually they had to speak; perhaps they
were "sincerely" angry. More likely, "Jane Anger" was a
useful and appropriate persona to begin the task, just as "Constantia Munda" was an appropriate pseudonym for the defender of women's fortitude under oppression. Once more, it
is important to understand the choice of genre.

Woodbridge argues convincingly that the formal controversy over women had developed as an elaborate rhetorical
game, a series of conventional arguments for or against
women, allowing, for example, one ingenious author to argue
both sides.[1] It is almost impossible, however, to imagine
Rachel Speght, Ester Sowernam, or Constantia Munda arguing the case against women, surely because of the woman
writer's continual struggle for her virtue and her literary
identity; instead, these women belatedly took up an old genre
specifically to undermine the game and to discredit its per-
petrators.[2] Both Jane Anger, who responded to the work of
a "late Surfeiting Lover," and her successors took the opportunity to reply to a relatively weak attacker. For the later
women, Joseph Swetnam was the perfect target. His attack,
lacking wit, skill, polish, and even the rhetorical ingenuity of
earlier works, demonstrated how debased the genre had become by 1615.[3]

In its tired state, the controversy provided Speght and her
followers with the opportunity to alter its fundamental tone.

If it had always been a masculine game—accompanied by many old jokes—to attack women and then to defend them with similar material, by contrast, these writers perceived the subject and its treatment as a serious task. About the female defenders of women, Woodbridge observes both that Christian beliefs bar them from making feminist arguments and that they either missed the jokes or in Ester Sowernam's case, made the "tactical error" of trying "logical analysis on old jokes" (92, 96, 99). Indeed, these two perceptions belong together: *because* of their Christian beliefs, these women argue seriously about feminine virtue; and to discredit their opponents' style and views, they do not participate in the joshing, but concentrate on a rhetorical response. The importance of this step should be emphasized, that women used the arts of language not only to redeem their sex, but to inflict damage on the methods of the masculine debaters. And if they do not have much new material to contribute to the defense of women, they do assume the more dramatic pose of self-defense, as well as provide the first occasion in this period when women writers attack men in print. While these defenders of women had no sense of humor about antifeminist jokes, fortunately they did cultivate a highly energetic style of attack that enlivens and sharpens their own work.

Jane Anger (fl. 1589)

Although Jane Anger is known only for one work, she is a significant figure. As the first woman to write a defense of women, she added to feminine literature the persona of a woman angry on behalf of her whole sex.

Choosing to launch her *Protection for Women* (1589) with a direct attack on a pamphlet by a "late Surfeiting Lover" and so on "all other like Venerians," Jane Anger quickly defines her perspective as that of the virtuous woman outraged at the insults of lecherous men and determined to show that men are false while women are constant, chaste, and honest.[4] The terms are familiar, drawn from rhetorical tradition rather than life, and Jane Anger supports her claims with classical references, exempla, and apothegms. But her style differs profoundly from the almost universal restraint of women's works that preceded hers, because rather than pious and disciplined, it conveys the fertility of a mind whizzing from idea to idea, excited, determined, willing to use any means to make the point. Exclamation and rhetorical questions mark the dedication "to all women in generall, and gentle Reader whatsoever":

> Fie on the falshoode of men, whose minds goe oft a madding, and whose tongues can not so soone bee wagging, but straigt they fal a railing. Was there ever any so abused, so slandered, so railed upon, or so wickedly handeled undeservedly, as are we women? Will the Gods permit it, the Goddesses stay their punishing judgments, and we ourselves not pursue their undoinges for such divelish practises? ... and shall not *Anger* stretch the vaines of her braines, the stringes of her fingers, and the listes of her modestie, to answere their Surfeitings? (Title page v)

The jingling of rhymes, parallel constructions, and climactic arrangement bespeak a writer who labors for a style to match the persona of Anger, a startlingly new character in the female canon.

Although she herself uses rhetorical techniques, she attacks them as the very heart of misogynist tracts: women's enemies are "so caried away with the manner, as no care at all is had of the matter: they run so into Rethorick, as often times they overrun the boundes of their own wits, and goe they knowe not whether" (B). And with amused irony she comments particularly on the work of the "late Surfeiting Lover" as a triumph of style over substance, "So pithie were his sentences, so pure his wordes, and so pleasing his stile" (B).

Anger's own style is an entertaining mix of supposition, learned glosses of Latin tags, expostulation and "proofs" of woman's virtuous character and man's folly, intended to justify women rather than change their lot. For instance, she notices, as others had, that the virtues tend to be represented by female figures. Ironically, she wonders why the gods had not assigned some of the moral virtues to men, "except their Deities knewe that there was some soverainty in us women, which could not be in them men." Further, to rationalize the clear supremacy of men in religion and society, she suggests that this is a way to prevent women's "wonderfull vertues" from turning into mere pride, thus leaving only men to Lucifer (B2v). The tone here and the "arguments" (no better or worse than many found in contemporary pamphlets) suggest that while Anger admits that men dominate, they do so only to compensate for their own faults and women's strengths; that is, she is not admitting to anything, least of all the natural ability of men to rule.

That she is interested in a moral victory is suggested by Anger's determined rehabilitation of Eve. Near the end of her work, Anger considers creation and concludes that as the creation of man from dust was a process of purification, so the creation of woman from man indicates "how far we women are more excellent than men." Women are "fruiteful, whereby the world encreaseth," and they preserve the race. Most important,

> From woman sprang mans salvation. A woman was the first that beleeved, and a woman likewise the first that repented of sin. In women is onely true Fidelity (except in her) there is no constancie, and without her no Huswifery. (C-Cv)

Omitting any mention of Eve's guilt, Anger insists instead on women's adherence to the ideals embodied in the Virgin Mary, the first to receive grace. Since "ther is no wisdome but it comes by grace," women are wise, and more, because the first is the best, "therefore women are wiser than men" (C2).

Ignoring the contradictions in her own principles, Anger depends on a witty restatement of conventional defenses to create her position. Believing also in the usefulness of attack to a defense, she castigates men for their *Dishonestie and unconstancie*," promising that they will be the cause of their own downfall. Trotting out exempla as easily as the misogynists did, Anger notes that men like Paris have ruined women, but that women like Artemisia and Portia have been models of virtue.

Her final advice to women is to be skeptical, to avoid the worst fault of their sex, credulity, when dealing with male flattery which is directed solely at depriving women of their "virtue." This seems to be a mixture of practicality and literary stereotyping, and marks the general toning down of style as the work progresses. The persona of Anger proves hard to maintain, perhaps because the author recognized the need to modulate her voice in order to argue convincingly. In the closing verses to the Reader, an admirer even appears to blame her anger for any offense given, "For ANGERS rage must that asswage,/as wel is understoode."

What Jane Anger initiated, however, was a generic adaptation in which women could represent themselves and try out a new literary role. The literary stance implicit here is that of a virtuous, chaste sex, maligned and mistreated by wicked men: this siege mentality produces a vigorous, sometimes entertaining work, but one that is finally flawed by a cramping single-mindedness. Later writers managed to diversify both form and content, perhaps learning to build on Jane Anger's foundation.

Rachel Speght (fl. 1617–1621)

In her dedication of A Mouzell for Melastomus (1617) "to all vertuous Ladies Honourable or Worshipfull, and to all other of Hevahs sex fearing God," Rachel Speght, "though yong, and the unworthiest of thousands," claims to have been moved to defend women by Joseph Swetnam's defamations in The Araignment of ... women.[5] Excusing her own "insufficiency in literature and tendernesse in yeares," as she would also do in Mortalities Memorandum, she addresses great ladies as well as commoners because Swetnam had slandered "all Hevahs sex," rich and poor, learned and illiterate. She promises them "this Antidote, that if the feare of God reside in their hearts, maugre all adversaries, they are highly esteemed and accounted in the eyes of their gracious Redeemer, so that they need not feare the darts of envy or obtrectators" (A3v). To carry out her Christian purpose, Speght's main tactics to restore women's character are first, to castigate Swetnam's unchristian attack on God's creatures, his blasphemy and misuse of Scripture, and second, to compose portraits of a redeemed Eve and her idealized descendants.

Speght's largely *ad hominem* attack on Swetnam is characterized by the new feminine literary mode of sharp language and name-calling. She calls him the "pestiferous enemy," a "monster," his work an "illeterate Pamphlet," and she fortifies her aggressive tone with descriptions like "your mingle mangle invective," bolstering her own authority with learned phrases like "contagious obtrectation" and "this my Chirograph." But Speght's tract gathers its real substance from her discussion of the creation of Eve, again an attempt to return to the beginnings to restore women's image. One by one, she considers the objections of women's detractors: that Eve listened to Satan and brought death and misery to the world; that ony Eve, not Adam, was deceived; that St. Paul said it is not good to touch a woman; and that Solomon could not find a faithful woman.

In response, Speght argues that Eve cannot bear the full burden of guilt and that women have been a source of good in the world. At the same time, her assumption, like that of other defenders of women, is still that women are weaker than men, physically and morally. For this reason, Satan attacked her first. "Yet we shall find the offence of *Adam* and *Eve* almost to parallel: For as an ambitious desire of being made like unto God, was the motive which caused her to eate, so likewise was it his" (4). And Speght reasons, if Adam did not approve of Eve's deed, he should have reproved her; one cannot blame "the bellowes that blowed the fire" if one burns one's hand. To remove further the full burden of guilt from Eve, Speght notes that Eve's punishment was "particular to her owne sex, and to none but the female kinde: but for the sinne of man the whole earth was cursed" (5). On the contrary, Eve becomes, by God's promise, the source of salvation, for woman will bring forth a Saviour. Expanding here, Speght calls Christ the "Saviour of beleeving women, no lesse of men, that so the blame of sinne may not be imputed to his creature, which is good; but to the will by which *Eve* sinned, and yet by Christ's assuming the shape of a man was it declared that his mercie was equivalent to both Sexes" (7). Despite its long antifeminist history, this was no more than Christian tradition allowed, for Paul himself affirmed "that male and female are all one in Christ Jesus." But if Speght insists on the unqualified acceptance of this doctrine, she does not affirm what was argued by the polemicists at the end of her own century, that women and men are simply equal. Like so many of her contemporaries, she separated her insistence on women's spiritual equality from her acceptance of women's social and political inferiority, and she colored the rest of her argument accordingly.

Ingeniously and fervently, she responds to misogynist defamation. Like Protestant women writers of the century before her, Speght relies heavily on her reading of the Biblical text, weighting her exegesis in favor of women as much as Swetnam does against them. Consistent with her whole argument, she claims that Adam too was deceived (1 Cor. 15:22); that St. Paul's injunctions to the Corinthians against women must be put in the particular historical context of the persecutions against the early Christians; and that Solomon's diatribe must be seen in the light of his 700 wives and 300 concubines who turned him from God.[6] But Speght's central discourse focuses on women's initial creation, neatly presented in traditional terms of efficient, material, formal, and final causes. Speght argues first that woman must be good, since God made her; second that she was created from Adam's side, "neare his heart, to be his equall; that where he is Lord, she may be Lady": for as Genesis 1:26 tells, God makes "their authority equall, and all creatures to be in subjection to them both" (10). Third, woman resembles only man, for she too is created in the image of God, and fourth, the end of her existence is "to glorifie God, and to be a collaterall companion for man to glorifie God." Indeed, citing the examples of those women who served Christ—Mary Magdalen, Susanna, Joanna, and the Virgin Mary—Speght claims women's central purpose is to serve God. Part of this service does include helping man, but in one of the more emphatic passages, she explains that helper means *helper*, that women should not bear the "whole burthen of domesticall affaires and maintenance" by themselves. Since the husband is stronger, he should bear the most weight.

Because she accepts male strength and authority, Speght can more easily emphasize spirituality for women, rather than concur with traditional fleshliness and domesticity. When she considers marriage, the traditional analogy to Christ's love for the Church and the Chosen serves her purpose very well. Acknowledging that man is woman's head, Speght argues convincingly in scriptural terms that this supremacy gives man "no authoritie . . . to domineere, or basely command and imploy his wife, as a servant . . ." (16). Indeed, following in Christ's footsteps, *"Men must love their wives, even as Christ loved his Church"* (17). She pictures a marriage in which the husband loves, honors, and teaches the wife, and the wife obeys and learns from the husband. Paradoxically, Speght's repetition of traditional doctrine, couched in traditional rhetoric, is meant to aid in the restoration of women's credit and position.[7] Her argument may even be a quid pro quo: men are dominant if women are virtuous.

By studying, recapitulating, and reinterpreting Scripture in favor of women, Speght would best convince her selected audience of God-fearing women, and perhaps even men, to consider women's worthiness. She allied herself with the highest authority, associated women with important moral attributes, and found an acceptably Christian way to rationalize their subjection to men. Her approach is quintessentially Protestant in its emphasis on individual reading of Scripture and spiritual self-determination, although she does not overstep the bounds of decorum appropriate to a minister's daughter. While accepting women's worldly inferiority, she also asserts the spiritual worth and social value of the "weaker vesel," and in her writing, she appears to find no conflict in her position. She directs all her aggressiveness at Swetnam, finding little to attack in her society.

Beyond her careful stance, Speght may have gained further acceptance from her audience through the continual insistence on her youth and attendant purity. Any vigorous language or assertiveness might be saved from indecorousness or unnaturalness by characterizing the author as a chaste and virtuous young woman bent on a pious mission; thus, both the author and her supporters repeat the conventional motif of the woman writer as chaste and private. Speght allies herself with the female stereotype by citing her "imperfection in both learning and age" as reasons for seeking the patronage of great ladies. More explicitly, the praisers of the author and her work, "Philalethes and Philomathes," characterize her as a David fighting Goliath and the champion of the so-called "feeble women" slandered by Swetnam. Verses by "Favour B" set out most precisely the qualification of Speght's chaste innocence as the accompaniment to her education and her position as women's defender: she is "a Virgin young," not yet twenty, whose wit, learning, and magnanimity have triumphed over women's detractors (B4v). The implication is that only such a paragon as this could be an accredited public voice for women. Swetnam, of course, needed no such qualities in order to be heard, nor did he have to establish the virtue of his sex. To redeem hers, Rachel Speght chose to appear as an exemplary woman reasoning and arguing from Scripture for the justice of her cause.

Ester Sowernam (fl. 1617)

Speght's obeisance to men, whether genuine or politic, was firmly rejected by her successor, aptly self-created as "Ester Sowernam." Also motivated by Joseph Swetnam's *Araignment*, this writer combines her defense of Eve with a frontal attack on misogyny and an "arraignment" of Swetnam himself, thus fulfilling her name as Ester, the redeemer of her people and "Sowernam," the bitter antithesis of Swetnam. Anger certainly lies at the heart of Ester Sowernam's work, yet she depends less than her predecessors on vituperation to color her position. Instead, through the down-to-earth, knowledgeable voice of the bourgeoise, she argues as teacher and preacher to strengthen women and correct men. While her description of women follows the familiar idealization, she labors diligently to establish the seriousness of her defense. Less successful is her attack on men, because it merely reverses misogynist terms.

The author appears briefly at the beginning of her work in her dedication "to all Right Honourable, Noble, and worthy Ladies, Gentelwomen, and others, vertuously disposed, of the Foeminine Sexe."[8] Having arrived in London the previous Michaelmas term, at supper one night she hears about Swetnam's work, and having read it the next day, she denounces it for condemning all women, not just the "lewde, idle, inconstant" women it purported to pillory (A2). Clearly accustomed to action, Ester Sowernam at once begins a reply, but hears that a minister's daughter, Rachel Speght, had already written an apology for women which was ready for press. Sounding rather annoyed, Ester Sowernam claims that the "Maidens Booke" is too short, that Rachel Speght is too young to argue effectively, and actually condemns women; she decides to proceed with her own work.

In laying out the plan of her book, Ester Sowernam emphasizes, as others had, the divinely ordained mission of women in the world: "I doe in the first part of it plainely and resolutely deliver the worthinesse and worth of women, both in respect of their Creation, as in the worke of Redemption" (A2v). Examples from both Testaments support her claims for women "as gratious instruments to derive Gods Blessings and benefits to mankinde." With such authority for support, she then cites ancient and modern authorities who have valued women; responds to their detractors; and finally arraigns "lewd, idle, furious and beastely disposed" men. She aims to praise God through his work, woman; to encourage women to live up to their divinely ordained purpose; and to castigate those who have fallen away from the nature of true womanhood: "in Creation, noble; in Redemption, gracious; in use most blessed" (A3).

While Ester Sowernam assumes that middle-class women will read her book, she also addresses the group of men most likely to affect their lives, "All Worthy and Hopeful young youths of Great-Brittaine." Even more specifically, she aims at "the best disposed and worthy Apprentices of London." At the other end of the spectrum from Lanyer's exaltation of the female aristocracy, Ester Sowernam's interest is in the quality of marriages to be made among the men and women of the middle class. To educate potential husbands, to encourage them to admire and respect women is as much part of her plan as to establish women's virtue in their own eyes. Advocating a kind of chivalry in these "worthy youths," she urges them to defend women's reputations, not to believe Swetnam's slanders, and encourages them "to be joyned in marriage with a Paraditian Creature. Who as she commeth out of the Garden, so shall you finde her a flower of delight, answerable to the Countrey from whence she commeth" (A4). To Ester Sowernam, freeing women from the burden of Eve's sin is not only an intellectual or theological concern, but also a practical aspect of the status of women in marriage. She not only points out that "there can be no love betwixt man and wife, but where there is a respective estimate the one towards the other," but also suggests how to attain this state.

While echoing the Puritan recommendations for marriage, Ester Sowernam's motive, like Rachel Speght's, is to restore women's dignity, rather than to exalt marriage itself. She thus foreshadows the work of the late seventeenth-century feminists, although she ultimately remains circumscribed by the cautions and limitations of her own time. But as a self-conscious writer, Ester Sowernam is aware that her subject, her method, and her mood are engendering a new kind of writing for women, for she comments that she may "use more vehement speeches then may seeme to correspond the naturall disposition of a Woman," although the provocation demands this or more. Her awareness that she is defending her sex and taking a stand against a battery of male opinion results in a style that employs ingenious (and sometimes ingenuous) argument, careful rhetoric, and a confident tone. For instance, if Joseph Swetnam attributes women's crooked disposition to her creation from a rib, Ester Sowernam trumps him by responding that man was made from dust and clay and so has a dirty, muddy disposition, that woman's spirit is from God, and that man has more crooked ribs than woman. Rejecting Swetnam's tired old jokes, though sometimes not offering much in return, Ester Sowernam composes an essay that wins the argument largely by not copying his abusive style: she develops a strong, convincing voice that counters Swetnam at every turn and consistently proposes an alternate and serious vision of women as "chosen to perform and publish the most happy and joyful benefits which ever came to man-kinde" (4). She counters the conventional myth of Eve by claiming that woman was made in Paradise, so that she "neither can or may degenerate in her disposition from that naturall inclination of the place, in which she was first framed, she is a Paradician, that is, a delightfull creature, borne in so delightfull a country" (6). Woman's subsequent history evolves from her fundamental nature, deviations from which are caused, as they were in the beginning, by a "Serpent of the masculine gender" (7). Having redeemed women, Ester Sowernam prepares to mount her full attack on the evils perpetrated by men.

As Scripture may be quoted for almost any purpose, Ester Sowernam finds as many texts in support of women as the misogynists do against them; it is all a matter of interpretation, and like Rachel Speght, Ester Sowernam is unafraid to leap in where many women had hesitated to enter before. Ecclesiasticus 25 may say that "Sinne had his beginning in woman," but this only means, she is sure, that sin had its fullness in man. More, St. Paul himself says that "By one mans sinne death came into the world" and that "All die in Adam," clearly exonerating Eve from the burden, says Ester Sowernam. And if woman is commanded to obey man, "the cause is, the more to encrease her glorie. Obedience is better than Sacrifice: for nothing is more acceptable before God then to obey" (9). Armed with these texts, Ester Sowernam strides on in Chapter 3 with more than a dozen texts from the Old Testament supporting her claim that women are God's instruments, not man's bane. And inevitably this argument culminates with the "blessed mother and mirrour of al womanhood, the Virgin *Marie*."

Like Aemilia Lanyer, Ester Sowernam contends that women are close to the source of Christianity, being thus endowed with a spiritual as well as a physical fruitfulness. She claims that "in all dangers, troubles, and extremities, which fell to our Saviour, when all men fled from him, living or dead, women never forsooke him" (13), that Jesus said woman's faith and devotion were incomparable, that the promise of a Messiah was brought to a woman, his birth was by a woman, and "the triumphant resurrection with the conquest over death and hell, was first published and proclaymed by a woman." Like other women writers, Ester Sowernam finds that the search for female heroes inevitably leads back to the scriptural sources which authorize a beneficent view of women in both religious and secular history. The most honored women are the members of the early church, the saints and martyrs, but in her sweeping vision reminiscent of Christine de Pisan's catalogue, Ester Sowernam includes homage to classical deities, and ancient and modern women of history, concluding with Elizabeth I, "the glory of our Sex," "a patterne for the best men to imitate," and "the mirrour of the world" (21). Moving from belief to the fanciful attribution of beneficial inventions to classical goddesses (Bellona invented sword and armor; Ceres corn and tillage, Diana hunting, etc.) to praise of the women who stand behind men (Queen Elenor, wife of Edward I who saved his life; Margaret, wife of Henry VI, who had the foresight her husband lacked; Margaret of Richmond, mother of Henry VII, noted for "heroicall prudence and pietie" and for her support of the universities), Ester Sowernam envisions a world in which women are highly valued for their "womanly" qualities, and play active roles in maintaining social and political stability.

Establishing women's virtue at every level is the necessary

prelude to the most dramatic part of Ester Sowernam's work, the "Arraignment of Joseph Swetnam," because in order to sit in judgment of a man, women must be proven worthy and credible judges. The two "Judgesses" are Reason and Experience, and the prosecutor is Conscience. Since the jury must be Swetnam's peers, it is composed of his five senses and the seven deadly sins.[9]

The gist of Ester Sowernam's indictment of Swetnam is that the root of all evil is man himself. The whole war against women, she claims, has been manufactured by malcontent writers who had nothing better to do than slander women. But in a fundamental sense, men have been the source of all women's ills, because Eve herself was betrayed first by the Serpent and then by Adam who taught her to flee God, argue with God, and blame God (34). Adam, says Ester Sowernam, has been the model bad husband throughout history. And if women are said to be the cause of so much of men's woe, men must be weak creatures to begin with—"are men so idle, vaine, and weake, as you seeme to make them?" According to Ester Sowernam, they are indeed lustful, vain, and inconstant, and have only themselves to blame for their problems.

Though ingeniously supported and manipulated, and intended to discredit women's detractors, such arguments merely reverse those offered by the misogynists, thus implicitly accepting their terms. But at this point, such an attack constituted a step forward for a woman writer's self-definition, because it entailed experimenting with a new language and persona, derived from the liberating rejection of female responsibility for the world's evil. But Ester Sowernam is still very much of her time in that these assertions are counterbalanced with her apparent acceptance of women's worldly inferiority. With a disposition "milde, yielding, and vertuous" (43), woman is still "the weaker vessell," still to be governed by men once the male sex has corrected its faults and vices. Perhaps the markedly unyielding disposition of her own persona casts some doubt on her credibility here, but more likely, women were still not ready to challenge received order, at least in print.

Indeed, Ester Sowernam's desire to justify women results not primarily in her attack on men, but in her very affirmation of the traditional feminine virtues. Rather than presenting a revised model of active feminine behavior, she develops the conventional version of idealized woman as the alternative to Eve the sinner. If Swetnam never paused to consider the exaggerated, unrealistic nature of his attack, Ester Sowernam gives only slightly more attention to real women. In effect, she is swept away by the rhetorical drive of her own argument, so desirous of redeeming women's good name that her exempla, maxims, and authoritative quotations create an icon of perfect virtue, a Mary to replace Eve.

Constantia Munda (fl. 1617)

These defenders of women did know, however, that strictly speaking their works contravened the very virtues they lauded in their sex: modesty and silence, the hallmarks of chastity. The paradox might be eased by assurances of the author's pure soul and by explicit obeisance to male superiority, but the contradiction still existed, hampering the free development of a feminine persona and limiting to name-calling what a woman would publish. Of all the defenses of women, none displays the conflict more vividly or uses it to better effect than the brief work of "Constantia Munda" whose beneficent pseudonym belies the angry title of her response to Swetnam, *The Worming of a mad Dogge* (1617). Praising Rachel Speght for having "Wisely layed open [his] singular ignorance," and for refuting much of Swetnam's calumny, Constantia Munda concentrates on a "sharpe Redargution" of the "bayter of Women" in order to destroy Swetnam as a credible author and to dispel the assumption that women will passively allow his slanders.[10]

Constantia Munda establishes her own credibility through a pious dedication to her mother, "Lady Prudentia Munda," whom she describes "in perpetuall *Labour* with me, even untill/The second birth of education perfect me."[11] With deceptive quiet she confronts the key issue, whether women may publicly defend themselves, and she resolves that "though feminine modesty hath confin'd our rarest and ripest wits to silence, wee acknowledge it our greatest ornament, but when necessity compels us, tis as great a fault and folly," to be silent (5). The necessity that compels Constantia Munda to abate her modesty and end her silence is indeed an attack on divinely blessed woman, "the second Tome of that goodly volume compiled by the great God of heaven and earth ..." (2). Joining her predecessors, she makes her case for women by exalting their "matchlesse beauties and glorious vertues shining together," and rhetorically asking men whether women have not been memorialized for "charitable deeds" as often as "couragious Potentates?" In particular, she commends women's "bountifull exhibitions to religious uses and furtherance of pietie" (10).

Having established her imperative need to speak out, Constantia Munda can proceed to her task to mock, to denounce, and to destroy Swetnam. She fashions a persona who at first speaks loudly and clearly, sometimes bitterly, sometimes learnedly, and always with conviction:

> you surmized, that inveighing against poore illiterate women, we might fret and bite the lip at you, wee might repine to see our selves baited and tost in a blanket, but never durst in open view of the vulgar either disclose your blasphemous and derogative slanders, or maintaine the untainted puritie of our glorious sexe: ... The sinceritie of our lives, and quietnesse of conscience, is a well of brasse to beat backe the bullets of your vituperious scandels in your owne face. (14)

Here, Constantia Munda abandons the decorous phrases of her sex and announces a new verbal power for women. From now on, she cries, not only will women rely on their virtue to defeat their detractors, but "Ile take the paines to worme the tongue of your madnesse, and dash your rankling teeth downe your throat ... our pens shall throttle you, or like

Archilochus with our tart Iambikes make you *Lopez* his god-
son: we will thrust thee like *Phalaris* into thine owne brazen
bull, and baite thee at thy owne stake, and beate thee at thine
owne weapon ..." (16).[12] If women must accept an inferior
position in all traditional hierarchies, Constantia Munda is a
writer who will verbally challenge and defeat men who slander her sex.

The Worming of a mad Dogge is a paradigm of the woman
writer's experience with conflicting impulses: to assert her
abilities and her verbal power, while yet insisting on chaste
decorousness as "our greatest ornament." In vociferously redeeming Eve, she risks her status by becoming too much like
the traditional stereotype of her impudent foremother, causing
her to defend even more strongly the alternative stereotype
of the idealized woman. But her angry persona chooses a
rhetorical outburst rather than a demand for change, an attack
on a single misogynist rather than an analysis of a cultural
problem. She does suggest, however, that woman's virtue, her
constancy, must not ignore the unpleasant task of "worming"
and that even the virtuous ideal must discover a language to
do the job.

This new language is Constantia Munda's attempt to shock
her audience into accepting the seriousness of her defense of
women, to end once and for all the debate game by impressing
upon her readers that even modest, virtuous women, the
daughters of "Lady Prudentia," must vigorously oppose the
likes of evil Joseph Swetnam.

Constantia Munda brings to a climax this brief spate of
women explicitly defending their sex. By taking to an extreme
Jane Anger's tactic, she may have succeeded in subverting
readers' assumptions about the levity of the debate genre.
Assuming for herself a persona (one now understands why
she would not have used her own name) whose language
violated the very modesty she claimed for her sex was at the
least a paradox and at the most a device that risked failure;
however, it may well have encouraged readers to sit up and
listen. The Christian tradition of righteous anger in the cause

of good against evil would perhaps have worked in Constantia Munda's favor.

Torpedoing an old masculine genre and creating a new uniquely feminine one are tasks requiring radically different approaches; and the defenders of women indeed diverge widely in style and tone from the authors of mother's advice books. It is important to emphasize, however, that the defenders and the mothers espoused the same cause, to prove women's spiritual worth, whether manifested in pious deeds or literary acts.

MOTHER'S ADVICE BOOKS

Although they differ one from another, all the mother's advice books diverge markedly from the angry and argumentative voices of the defenders of woman. Five of these books appeared in the early seventeenth century, written by Elizabeth Grymeston, Elizabeth Jocelin, Dorothy Leigh, Elizabeth Clinton, the Countess of Lincoln, and M.R. Four of the five mothers present their work as a legacy to their children, offered as a deathbed last will and testament, so that their voices offer restrained, pious exhortations to the godly life. Preceding Jocelin's and Leigh's works are elaborate attempts to legitimize the entry of the woman writer into the public sphere, reflecting both the authors' doubts as well as their publishers' concerns.

As mothers, these writers acknowledge their primary identity in a uniquely feminine role, and recognize that this places them in the private sphere and under the jurisdiction of men. But each recognizes that to write, ostensibly for the eyes of her own children, brings her public notice, particularly as she assumes the authority of a preacher. Jocelin, Leigh, and the Countess of Lincoln express their anxiety over this infringement, but find various means to rationalize it and do not let it prevent them from writing down their motherly advice. While the role of loving mother instructing her children may seem to be a safe persona for a woman writer, instead it highlights the conflict between private and public status, and

since publicity always endangered chastity and modesty, ironically a mother who wrote threatened the essence of her
womanly virtue. In their defense, then, these writers identify
themselves as possessors of spiritual worth, impelled by their
calling as Christian women into the role of writer. In the
process, three of these mothers attain a more general ministry
for the salvation of souls. Elizabeth Grymeston writes to advise her son to live virtuously, but her handbook was widely
consulted. In the case of Elizabeth Jocelin, and even more of
Dorothy Leigh, whose work was continuously republished,
their vocation for public preaching bursts through their doubts
and self-deprecation. But at the close of this period, in their
quite different works, the Countess of Lincoln and M.R.
defuse their public roles by insisting throughout on traditional
feminine domestic virtue.[13]

Elizabeth Grymeston (c. 1563–1603)

In her *Miscelanea, Meditations, Memoratives*, Elizabeth
Grymeston introduces herself as physically weak, a dying
mother. Yet, her book reveals a strong mind, one that cleverly
resolves the woman writer's chronic dilemma, how to possess
"masculine" knowledge and use "masculine" language without sacrificing feminine virtue.

Grymeston dedicates her book to her single surviving child,
Bernye, revealing her affectionate concern for his future happiness, and summoning images of close family ties. Yet in
almost the same breath, she laments her own mother's "undeserved wrath so virulent, as that I have neither power to
resist it, nor patience to endure it, but must yeeld to this
languishing consumption to which it hath brought me. . . ."[14]
And as she now feels herself "a dead woman among the
living, so stand I doubtfull of thy fathers life; which . . . God
hath preserved from eight severall sinister assaults . . ." (A3).
In other words, Bernye may soon be alone in the world and
the need grows imperative for his mother to write something
for his future guidance.

Many of Grymeston's familial difficulties and fears may

have derived from her Catholicism.[15] Her faith seems to have motivated her to provide for her son, justifying the writing of her book, and perhaps even its posthumous publication. Certainly the work was popular enough to have had four editions before 1618, indicating that Grymeston's pious meditations were widely acceptable.

In her dedication, Grymeston specifically proposes to aid Bernye with her own learning:

> My dearest sonne, there is nothing so strong as the force of love; there is no love so forcible as the love of an affectionate mother to hir naturall childe: there is no mother can either more affectionately shew hir nature, or more naturally manifest hir affection, than in advising hir children out of hir owne experience, to eschue evill, and encline them to do that which is good. (A3)

Reminding him of her impending death, and breaking "the barren soile" of her "fruitlesse braine," she offers him "this portable *veni mecum*" which will show him "the true portrature of thy mothers minde," and give him spiritual support and instruction. (A3-A3v).

What she offers Bernye is an extraordinary collection, perhaps more interesting today for its revelations about Grymeston's intellectual substance than for its original purpose. Quite openly acknowledging, like Isabella Whitney, that she has gathered all her material from other writers, she humbly asserts "Neither could I ever brooke to set downe that haltingly in my broken stile, which I found better expressed by a graver authour" (A3v). Grymeston here describes the outline of her book, which is a mixture of paraphrase, straight, and altered quotation of authors from Ambrose to Spenser, from the divine poets, Robert Southwell and Richard Verstegan, to lines from *Englands Parnassus*. She summarizes her own literary method in her advice to Bernye to be a "wits Camelion,/That any authours colour can put on." If she thus recalls the long history of women writers' ventriloquism, she also announces something new: her "passion and hir paine" to give her son sufficiently compendious advice to substitute for her own living presence. She is an intellectual gatherer who turns all "the fruitfull flowing of hir loftie braine" into "a mothers matchlesse care."[16] She devotes her learning, which apparently included Latin, Greek, Italian, the Church Fathers, the classics, and contemporary poetry to the cause of her son's salvation. By doing so, she explicitly unites two main themes in women's writing in the Renaissance: the desire to reach out for all knowledge, to escape intellectually from domestic, private constraints; and the search for an appropriately feminine persona, subject, and form. For other writers, these appeared as conflicting impulses, expansion followed by constriction; but for Elizabeth Grymeston, they are quite remarkably assimilated in the apparently autobiographical persona of the dying mother.

In her prose, interspersed with her reworking of contemporary poetry, Grymeston offered her son examples of the ways she transformed her reading into thoughts about life and death. She taught him by the time-honored method of providing a model to imitate. A brief example of her procedure must suffice here.

In Chapter Three, titled "A patheticall speech of the person of *Dives* in the torments of hell," using the voice of "Dives," the rich man, Grymeston assembles lines from contemporary poets, taken from *Englands Parnassus* and weaves them together with prose derived from scripture and patristic commentary. Recounting his unexpected death, Dives speaks the memorable stanza from *The Faerie Queene* which compares Marinell's fall to the death of the "sacred oxe."[17] Even though she alters the last line, thus weakening the vivid drama of Spenser's lines, Grymeston's purpose seems to be to exploit the power of Spenser's simile in order to express her theme of the pride of life instantly cut down. Catapulted before the "tribunall seat of God," Dives describes it in the words of Edward Fairfax, Tasso's translator, and goes on to an extended description of his present surroundings in hell. Fortifying prose details like "this sinke of the world" and "this Chaos of confusion" are Sackville's famous lines from the Induction to *A Mirror for Magistrates*, which strongly reinforce the horror of Dives' state.[18] Since Dives' final purpose is to preach a warning, nothing could be more spiritually or imagistically appropriate. Citing, and altering, Drayton, he warns "Your blesse is brittle, like a broken glasse," and proceeds with Latin quotations, exegesis, and renderings of Lodge, Spenser, Harington's translation of *Orlando Furioso*, as well as the original, and Daniel to exhort those that "carelesse live" to "learne while you are in your growth, to sway the right way" (C2). For, "what you sowe that you reape, either a crowne of glorie, *quam nemo scit nisi qui accepit*, or a chaos of confusion, *in qua sempeternus horror habitat . . .*" (C2).[19]

The message and the method here are typical of Grymeston's book. Consulting *Englands Parnassus* which anthologizes poetic extracts under headings like "Soule," "Pleasure," "Death," "Good Deeds," or "Life," Grymeston sought those sections appropriate to the doctrine of each chapter and selected verses from the most eminent of England's poets to convey her message. Sometimes she altered or omitted lines to suit her own text, but generally, her borrowings are intact. While the modern reader would consider this plagiarism, Grymeston's contemporaries would see it as a way to bring all knowledge to the service of God. Grymeston's own self-description as a "wits Camelion" is particularly apt because it connotes an intellectual flexibility and the ability to move easily among diverse authors, adapting the subject and form of each to her own purposes.

This thoroughly intellectual method of discovering in books the prescription for living begins to realize what many women had known about the importance of knowledge to their development as writers. The image of a disobedient and talkative Eve reaching for the apple had threatened all women, so that their first task had been to redeem her. Now at least one woman had created an acceptable way to possess jealously guarded masculine knowledge and language by making it a quintessentially feminine gift, a mother's advice to her son. Perhaps the effort of gathering and weaving together the words of other writers also confined Grymeston's own literary development; but perhaps her particular talent lay in making a whole cloth out of others' threads. Certainly, to Bernye she bequeathed a startling, beautiful book in which he could indeed behold "the true portrature of thy mothers minde."

Elizabeth Jocelin (1595–1622)

Both Elizabeth Jocelin's death in childbed and her irreproachable advice in *The Mothers Legacie to her unborn Childe* (1624) might be thought to remove many of the publisher's usual worries about female authors, but at the beginning of the work appear both an "Approbation" of the book and a biography of the author attesting in the most conventional terms to her chaste and virtuous life. Drawing on legal terms, one Thomas Good acknowledges that while a woman cannot dispose of her "temporall estate," still she may bequeath her "morall spirituall riches," for "vertue and grace have power beyond al empeachment of sex or other debility, to enable and instruct the possessor to employ the same unquestionably for the inward inriching of others. . . ."[20] And to preserve her virtuous instruction for all time, it is of course necessary to place it "among the most publique Monuments" (A4v), that is, to publish it. Jocelin's life clearly merited such attention, combining as it did, "the duty of obedience unto Parents," "her true and unspotted love" for her husband, a "constant temper of patience, and more than womanly fortitude" in affliction, as well as considerable education.

Jocelin's own mother died when she was six, leaving her to the care of her father, Sir Richard Brooke, and to the tutelage of her grandfather, Dr. Chaderton, master of Queen's, Cambridge, Professor of Divinity, Lord Bishop of Chester and Lincoln. Under him, she was "carefully nurtured, as in those accomplishments of knowledge in Languages, History, and some Arts, so principally in studies of Piety" (av). Before marriage, Jocelin spent her time studying "morality and history, the better by the helpe of forraine languages, not without a taste and faculty in Poetry: wherein some essay shee hath left ingenious, but chaste and modest, like the Author. Of all which knowledge shee was very sparing in her discourses as possessing it rather to hide than to boast of" (a3v). This paragon of female privacy, praised for the decorous concealment of her ability, also had a brilliant memory that enabled her to repeat more than forty lines of English or Latin after reading or hearing them only once. Characteristically, she would write down the words of a sermon later in her own chamber, indicating, by the way, the confinement and solitude of her intellectual life. In the years before her early death at age twenty-seven, she had devoted herself entirely to the study of divinity, and the publisher lauds her "piety and humility," the submersion of her secular learning in favor of lighting her candle "from the lamp of the Sanctuary" (a2v).

The insistence on Jocelin's piety, learning, humility, and privacy reaches a climax in the description of the preparations for her death. She buys her winding sheet, then "undauntedly looking death in the face, privatly in her closet betweene God and her, she wrote these pious Meditations" addressed to her unborn child. On October 12, 1622, she bore a daughter, and nine days later she died, leaving her good name and her book.

Such careful preparation of the reader for a woman's teaching is even more pronounced in Jocelin's dedication of the work to her husband. Despite her exceptional ability, Jocelin rather tremulously describes how she came to write her book, but the hesitancy which she feels about even writing down her thoughts is not merely the conventional self-deprecation found in so many Renaissance dedications. She refers specifically to her sex as the source of her self-doubt. Concerned that her death would deprive her children of education, she reveals that she thought of writing, but from a sense of inferiority, "durst not undertake it." Eventually, because this was the only way to express her "motherly zeale," she rationalizes her decision:

> First, that I wrote to a Child, and though I were but
> a woman, yet to a child's judgement, what I understood

might serve for a foundation to better learning. Againe, I considered it was to my owne, and in private sort, and my love to my owne might excuse my errours. And lastly, but chiefly I comforted my selfe that my intent was good, and that I was well assured God is the prosperer of good purposes. (B2v-B3)

Jocelin professes a strong sense of her own ignorance and the lack of the "naturall endowments" needed to write; but then excuses herself by claiming that she is only sending her treatise to a loving husband and to an unborn child. Later, she adds that even if the work should "come to the worlds eye, and bring scorne upon my grave" (11), still, working for her child's salvation is the greater concern.

Jocelin's adoption of a humble, self-deprecating demeanor combined with her pious fervor perfectly fulfills the humanist ideal of the educated woman. But whereas Vives and More claimed that learning itself would lead to virtue, Jocelin declares that only the virtuous, wise woman should be educated. Her attitude seems to reflect her own fear that somehow the publication of her work might be thought to advocate the unheard of step of universal education for women. While she does not recommend this, Jocelin does deliver an ambiguous message when she leaves instructions for the upbringing of her own daughter:

I desire her bringing up may be learning the Bible, as my sisters doe, good housewifery, writing, and good workes: other learning a woman needs not: though I admire it in those whom God hath blest with discretion, yet I desired not much in my owne, having seene that sometimes women have greater portions of learning, than wisdome, which is of no better use to them than a mainsaile to a flye-boat, which runs it under water. But where learning and wisdome meet in a vertuous disposed woman, she is the fittest closet for all goodnesse. Shee is like a well-balanced ship that may beare all her saile. She is—Indeed, I should but shame myselfe, if I should goe about to praise her more. (B6-B6v)

The progress of this paragraph may mark Jocelin's ambivalence about herself as a scholar and writer, because while she begins with the orthodox attitude toward women's education, "though" marks her unwillingness quite to scuttle learning for women, while "yet" is a hasty retreat into humility, for *sometimes* even learned women are foolish. But then she lights upon a safe expression of the dilemma: learning and wisdom in a virtuous woman result in goodness, and she caps her conclusion with a triumphant simile. She reveals that this is finally her own identity in the last self-deprecating sentence in which she eschews self-praise.

Finally, she leaves the matter to her husband, and somewhat wistfully, her language reflecting how important the issue was, she concludes that "if" he wants a learned daughter, she prays "God give her a wise and religious heart, that she may use it to his glory, thy comfort, and her owne salvation" (B6v). The syntax of this sentence suggests that while Jocelin will broach the subject of a girl's education, she will not make a statement or come to a conclusion about it. The issue of learning inevitably cedes to the matter of piety, and a "wise and religious heart" becomes the source of salvation rather than "learning."

Jocelin clarifies the continual self-doubts of the woman writer even though she composed an irreproachable work, apologizing for the "disordered" structure of her book and for her lack of learning; she is sure her "Treatise" will betray her ignorance, but comforts herself that only "a most loving Husband" and a beloved child will read it (B10v-B11). Only once does Jocelin explicitly consider wider publication and then she seems to dread "the worlds eye," fearing that her book may "bring scorne upon my grave"; yet, ultimately, like Elizabeth Grymeston, she will not be deterred from working for her child's salvation (11).

In the midst of her protestations, Jocelin projects onto herself the censure of a world hostile to women writers, revealing the inescapable anxiety women felt about publication. It is small wonder then that she and other women writers attempted to offset Eve's threat as breaker of bounds and destroyer of humanity's salvation by assuming the role of Mary, agent of that salvation.

In the treatise itself, Jocelin offers comprehensive advice for living a godly life, including prayers for her child to repeat and exhortations to avoid sloth, pride, drunkenness, and disobedience, and to practice charity, keep the Sabbath, and to love other people. The distinctions between the sexes, already so clear in the dedication, are reflected in Jocelin's instructions for a son as opposed to a daughter. For him, she hopes he will become a minister, for ministers are the "most truly happy" of all men. Her daughter's way, however, must not be to lead, but to follow the examples of virtuous and religious women like Anne, Elizabeth, Esther, and Susanna, all of whom are seen in the light of their feminine virtues of service and chastity. Even Esther appears primarily as "religious," having "taught her maids to fast and pray, Est. 4.15" (39). Later her daughter is also reminded, "thou art a Maid, and such ought by modesty to bee, that thou shouldst scarce speak, but when thou answerest . . ." (69).

The clear instructions of the manual itself, dividing the lot of a son from that of a daughter, while yet earnestly hoping for the salvation of either, are less ambivalent than is the dedication in which the author both affirms women's privacy and silence and yet would herself be heard. When she assumes the role of teacher, Jocelin retires safely behind conventional doctrine; only when she speaks as a woman writer does she perceive the essential conflicts between tradition and the individual woman.

Dorothy Leigh

Like Jocelin, Dorothy Leigh was an educated gentlewoman who recognized the conflicts in her role as a writing mother, but attempted to resolve them by redefining the mother's role to include an authorized public voice. Her book, *The Mothers Blessing* ran to fifteen editions between 1616 and 1630, attesting to the appropriateness of her doctrine and the success of her self-presentation. Part of the attraction, as in the case of Elizabeth Jocelin, might have been that this was a deathbed composition, and death conveyed a sanctity to their words and insured that the authors would remain everlastingly private. The title page itself advertises first Leigh's death and then her "good exhortations and godly admonition profitable for all Parents."[21]

Leigh provided two dedications, both revealing her as a highly self-conscious writer and suggesting she was carefully preparing the reader for the directions her treatise would take. The first to her three sons expresses her motherly love and the second to Princess Elizabeth suggests the image of a more general nurturance and protection in female form.

Knowing that she is about to die, Leigh recalls that before he died, her husband had directed her to care for the "spirituall and temporall good" of their sons (A5v). To fulfill her duties as "a loving Mother and a dutifull Wife," she determines to write, even if it means publicly displaying her "imperfections" (A6). The unimpeachable propriety of her stance, increased by her widowhood–there was no father to care for the boys–cannot completely mask this woman's intense creative energy. Her advice will run to 269 pages and she follows her modest self-introduction with a versified parable, "Counsell to my Children," which, in ballad measure, teaches the benefits of industry over sloth. Perhaps also in her address to Princess Elizabeth, when she admits to the relief of being able to write down her guidance for her sons, her release is as much from a creative burden as from a spiritual one.

By dedicating her work to Princess Elizabeth, King James's daughter, Leigh may well have hoped to insure the safety and success of her book, and her high praise of a great lady may be simple flattery. But it may also indicate that Leigh wished early to establish the type of a divine protectoress as prelude to her sanctification of motherhood and the accompanying praise of the Virgin Mary. Looking up to heaven, Leigh claims, she sees the "Joy of England," the great princes of the land apotheosized, yet looking down to care for their people and "then, even then, Princely Lady, I beheld your milde and courteous countenance, which shewed your heart was bent to doe good to all ..." (A3v-A4). Naming the princess the "Protectoresse of this my booke," Leigh believes that with her patronage "all the wicked wind in the world could not blow it away" (A4).

Her fear of public hostility toward the work of a woman surfaces throughout the first nine chapters in which she defensively amasses seven causes for writing. On the theory that for one cause alone she "would not have changed the usuall order of women," Leigh offers up every reason from motherly affection to encouraging more women to care for their children's salvation, to advocating Bible reading for all children, to advising on the proper naming of children. She even anticipates the wonder of her own sons why she writes rather than speaks, breaking "the usuall custome of women." Motherly affection is her answer, manifested in her desire to write "but one sentence, which may make you labour for the spirituall food of the soule" (5).

Continually moving beyond the immediate audience of her children, Leigh gradually unfolds her perception of the traditional lot of women and proposes her own remedy. Noting first that her sons have received "the great mercy of God toward you, in making you men, and placing you among the wise," and second, that as men they may write and speak Scripture with offense to none, Leigh encourages women

> not to bee ashamed to shew their infirmities, but to give men first and chief place: yet let us labour to come in the second; and because wee must needes confesse that sinne entred by us into our posterity; let us shew how carefull we are to seeke to Christ, to cast it out of us and our posterity, and how fearefull we are that our sinne should sinke any of them to the lowest part of the earth; wherefore, let us call upon them to follow Christ who will carry them to the height of heaven. (16-17)

Here, Leigh envisions the act of writing precisely as a means for redeeming women from the sin of Eve so that they may become the source of redemption for their children. To legitimize this undertaking, Leigh must show that women are not inherently crippled by Eve's disobedience, but that they are essentially good creatures bent on saving humankind. And here, despite her strongly expressed Puritan belief against the images of saints in church, Leigh centers her argument on the Virgin Mary.

Leigh has several principal obsessions in this treatise, if the five long chapters among scores of short ones mark topics in which she was particularly interested. The first of these long chapters, written in a gripping, forceful style, is the ninth, on female chastity. If this seems an unlikely topic in a mother's instruction to her three sons, by the end of the chapter when she explicitly addresses other women, we know that her interest in educating her boys has expanded to a discourse on her own and other women's vocation.

The chapter begins gently enough with the advice to give children "good" names, preferably those of saints, as Philip, Elizabeth, James, Anna, John, and Susanna. The mention of Susanna inspires an unexpectedly protracted essay on chastity, its meaning, importance, and glorification in the Virgin Mary. Her discourse recalls many of the highlights of Vives' advocacy of chastity for women and his glorification of Mary as the supreme woman. But while Vives represented chastity as the source of all the other domestic qualities he projected onto women, Leigh tries to define chastity as a state of mind and being that is particularly and essentially feminine, while yet authorizing a public role for women. As in other cases of "feminizing" their virtues, Leigh redefines chastity to suit the goals of women rather than of men.

Leigh relates that both Christian and pagan writers thought "that a woman that is truly chaste, is a great partaker of all other vertues," but more, "whoso is truly chaste, is free from idlenesse, and from all vaine delights, full of humility, and all good Christian vertues; whoso is chaste, is not given to pride in apparell, nor any vanity, but is alwaies either reading, meditating, or practising some good thing which she hath learned in the Scripture" (30-31). Her motivation should be to bear a "humble, loving and obedient heart" to God and his work. While Leigh's chastity clearly embraces sexual chastity, she represents it as the quintessential Christian virtue, associated most particularly with Mary, "as if or GOD should ... in briefe comprehend all other vertues under this one vertue of chastitie." For Mary's primary title was Virgin, a great inspiration to all women to be chaste; "to whom for this cause God hath given a cold and temperate disposition, and bound them with these words: *Thy desire shall be subject to thy husband*" (37-38). Echoing familiar material from the debate on women, Leigh claims that women are destined by nature to be chaste, and while they must take second place to men, women may also follow the redemptive example of Mary who is a particular blessing God sent to women "to take away the shame, which Eve our grandmother had brought to us."

Now, indeed, instead of cursing womankind, a man may say that women brought salvation, and Leigh believes, "Heere is the great and woefull shame taken from women by GOD working in a woman; man can claim no part in it: the shame is taken from us and from our posteritie forever" (38). Leigh retains the emphasis on woman and on Mary by concluding that it is only through woman, through "the seede of the Woman," that men will find salvation. Her true audience for this chapter is clearly other women, for her purpose here is to rally her sex to their ultimate vocation as vessels for the redemption of humankind. The last sentence of the chapter is in fact an exhortation that above "all other moral Vertues, let women bee perswaded by this discourse, to embrace chastity; without which, wee are meere beasts, and no women" (43). Even while she pays obeisance to women's traditionally inferior status, Leigh nevertheless opens up the role of the mother-teacher to embrace the saving of all the faithful. If her education has shown Leigh how constantly women are blamed for all evil and how much guilt they have to expiate, she indicates how it has also provided her with the means to restore their integrity and virtue.

Elizabeth Jocelin and Dorothy Leigh are the last writers of this era to advocate the extended importance of women's traditional virtue. Like the early Reformers and like Aemilia

Lanyer, they identify feminine virtue with Christian virtue and so legitimize their own vocation for teaching the faithful. Their particular contribution was to develop an impeccable persona, a quintessentially feminine figure with unassailable motives for writing and preaching. The determinate nature of this persona, while guaranteeing her limited literary usefulness, nevertheless provided Jocelin's and Leigh's works with a clear focus and a strong interest.

But contemporary with the attempts by Leigh and Jocelin to widen the legitimate range of feminine influence were two treatises more prophetic of the next thirty years of women's writing, *The Countess of Lincolnes Nurserie* (1622) and *The Mothers Counsell* by M.R. (1624). Both authors were concerned with defining feminine virtue and offered advice specifically to women, but their recommendations resolutely returned women to the private sphere, involving them with daily domesticity rather than intellectual endeavors or extraordinary spirituality. Their city of ladies is a closed circle of constricted feminine interests, withdrawn from the surrounding world.

Elizabeth Clinton, Countess of Lincoln

While the Countess of Lincoln's express purpose in writing her book was to exhort women to breast-feed their babies, the framework in which she placed her argument grew from traditional attitudes toward women's virtue, that its best expression was wholly within the domestic sphere. In a key passage, as the countess answers the objections of women to nursing, that it is troublesome, "noisome to ones clothes," or ages the body, she calls such women uncomely and unchristian, for "they argue *unmotherly affection, idlenesse, desire to have liberty to gadd from home, pride, foolish finenesse, lust, wantonnesse*, and the like evils."[22] To turn her terms around, breast-feeding is synonymous with domesticity, diligence, humility, modesty, and chastity, the litany of virtues dear to Vives and his successors. The particular qualities required to carry out this function are those for which the countess praises her daughter-in-law Briget, "to be full of care to please God, and of naturall affection, and to bee well stored with humility, and patience" (A2v). Indeed, since God ordained breast-feeding in the natural order of things, not to do it defies God and endangers a woman's conscience. Woman's essential piety and virtue can thus be simply expressed and understood as the carrying out of her biological function, a view that has certainly held fast in men's and women's minds to the present. Such an attitude allows the countess a rather odd redemption of her sex, particularly in her scriptural glosses. Eve, for example, is not condemned as a temptress, but praised for suckling Cain, Abel, and Seth "gladly" (3). As a nursing mother, Sarah also took "delight therein" and not to emulate Sarah is to "want her vertue, and piety" (4). Likewise, Hannah, mother of Samuel, and the Virgin Mary reveal themselves as God's servants. And should a woman defy the mother's affection implanted in her by God, then clearly God is not working in her and she is little more than a cruel beast—"yea monstrous unnaturalnesse" (11).

The countess somewhat explains the vehemence of her argument when she admits that she herself did not suckle her eighteen children and that she wrote this treatise in expiation of her sin, to "redeeme my peace" (16). She conveys much personal grief in the few, ambiguous details of her own experience, explaining that she was "overruled by anothers authority," received bad advice, and did not do her motherly duty (16).

But so deeply did the countess believe that she had betrayed both her biological function and her womanly virtue that she was driven to act, to redeem herself by writing. Her uneasy conscience and her suffering draw her to an unusually sympathetic perception of the victims of her behavior, the lower-class wet nurses. She advises her aristocratic peers not to force a poor woman to abandon her own child in favor of a rich woman's, concluding, "Wee have followed Eve in transgression, let us follow her in obedience" (19).

In the *Nurserie*, the Countess of Lincoln offers a closed feminine world predicated on the inescapable links she sees between biology and destiny, anatomy and virtue. Men appear only briefly in the text: the standard approval and praise of the work is offered by Thomas Lodge, and the countess's only reference is that she will "leave the larger, and learneder discourse hereof unto men of art, and learning"; she writes only from her own experience, and "in modestie." Like the other mothers, she fears the scorners, but persists in her self-appointed office (12). To those who will listen to her, she offers an older woman's wisdom to her younger friends, her advice and support to other women unknown to her, and her beneficence to those women below her in station. The moving admission that her own unhappiness has motivated her to try to save the souls of other women is a statement of concern for her sex that had previously been more implicit than explicit in women's writing. In its way, though the doctrine is rigid and "puritanical," the countess's short treatise participates in the woman writer's traditional identification and explication of women's concerns for other women.

M.R.

The least self-conscious of the mother's advice books is M.R.'s *The Mothers Counsell, or, Live within Compasse*. Noting in her preface that this is "the last Will and Testament to her dearest Daughter, which may serve for a worthy Legacie to all the Women in the World, which desire good report from men in this world, and grace from Christ Jesus in the last day," M.R. goes on to analyze the four attributes that bring a woman to "live within compass": chastity, temperance, beauty, and humility.[23] In opposition, bringing her out of compass are wantoness, madness, odiousness, and pride. Vividly diagrammed on the title page, this scheme contributes a feminine voice to the principle of confinement for women. Dressed in the sober garments of a decent bourgeoise, holding a Bible, the mother points to the equally restrained figure of her daughter. The word "Modesty" hangs over their heads, the Bible is at the center of their enclosed space. The concentric circles around them name the desired attributes and offer pithy definitions for each, as "Chastity of body is the key to Religion." This representation of a woman's ideal character differentiates M.R. from other women writers who had created from traditional attributes a way to expand women's intellectual and spiritual lives, and perhaps indicates some of the new problems women were to face in the seventeenth century.

In her treatise, M.R. delivers a series of definitions in a sententious style which is imposing, formal, and distant. Like Elizabeth Grymeston, she intersperses verses taken from *Englands Parnassus*, but M.R. makes no attempt to weave together poetry and prose as Grymeston had done so successfully. Without authorial comment, she merely announces, for instance, "Frugalitie is the signe of Chastitie" (2), or "If Chastity bee once lost, there is nothing left prayse-worthy in a woman" (4). Concluding the chapter are verses taken from the section on "Chastitie" in *Englands Parnassus*, poetry by Daniel, Drayton, and Harington.[24]

The center of the tract is an apology for Puritan doctrine, and reveals how fully it attempted to circumscribe women's lives and attitudes. While extolling "faithfull matrimony," and so perhaps increasing the value placed on feminine roles, the core of this work is the restricted, encompassed figure who is aptly summarized at the end of the section on Temperance in M.R.'s conflation of verses by Drayton and Harington:

Let Wolves and Beasts be cruell in their kinds,
   But women meeke, and of faire temperate mindes.
Though men mindes can cover with bold sterne lookes,
   Pale womens faces are their owne faults bookes,
Those vertues that in women praise doe win,
   Are sober shewes without, chaste thoughts within;
True faith and due obedience to their make,
   And of their children honest care to take.
                                                    (14)[25]

Just how much this advice relates to a cramping of education and imagination is implied by sections castigating "Madnesse," the opposite of temperance, and pride, the opposite of humility. For example, "It is a great madnesse in any woman to amuse upon those things which are farre beyond her understanding" (18). Or, "That kinde of fantasticke contemplation which tends to solitarinesse, is but a glorious title to proud idlenesse. The proud conceit of young women, is, that they can speake wisely, when they cannot understand themselves" (38). No poets allowed here.

Indeed, comparing *The Mothers Counsell* with what was probably a companion piece, *Keepe within Compasse or, The worthy Legacie of a wise father to his beloved Sonne*, makes it very clear that M.R.'s advice is not simply pious, but designed specifically to create a restricted woman's world.[26] The wise father counsels his son on religion, conversation, apparel, and diet, and even his categories announce the differences. "Conversation" means the manner of conducting oneself in the world [OED], and the father assumes that the son will need to know how to choose virtuous friends ("The love of men to women is a thing common and of course: but the friendship of man to man infinite and immortall"—B2); how to choose clothes "sutable for thy place and honour" (B7); and how to "curbe his vaine desires" in order to gain the "wealth of the world" (C8v). Most important, where the father places religion itself as "the ground of all other vertues" (A4), M.R. places chastity of body, calling it the very "key to Religion"; to her, woman's chastity precedes all other qualities necessary for salvation: "The first felicitie that a chaste woman shall have after this life, is the rest of her Soule in Christ" (4).

If she is responding to the father's advice, M.R. does so by distinguishing masculine and feminine spheres as profoundly—but as conservatively—as possible.[27] The extreme nature of her response perhaps indicates how greatly women writers were influenced by men and by conventional attitudes toward women. Her endorsement of women's limitations and her curtailment of any intellectual or creative endeavor—no "getting" for women—distinguish her from Elizabeth Jocelin and Dorothy Leigh who may accede to woman's secondary status, but find in her a unique spiritual strength that fosters creativity and worth. Haunted by the ghost of Eve, M.R.

seems to return to Vives's straitjacket of prevention as a way to deal with the burden of being female. If a woman lives within compass, there is less opportunity for independent and dangerous thought and action. Rather than the redeemer longed for by Jocelin and Leigh, M.R. projects a woman who is the archetypal "keeper" of her chastity, beauty, temperance, and humility, and no other advice seems necessary.

From the work of Jane Anger who introduced into the feminine canon a new persona possessing the rhetoric of a new emotion, to the work of M.R. who resolutely confined her matter and her language, the defenders of women and the writing mothers displayed both the development and the limitations characteristic of women's writing in this period. Each group recognized that women's traditional virtue had to be accommodated in her public utterances. For the defenders, their subject, the redemption of women's virtue, certainly legitimized their literary endeavors, even if their language and imagery often broke bounds. They also reflected the ability of women writers to capitalize on their very circumscriptions, to adapt the defense of feminine virtue into an energetic burst of language hitherto unknown to women writers. But if they made gains in feminine expressiveness, they also wrote themselves into a theoretical corner by conserving the ideals of traditional feminine virtue and perfection. From their somewhat different perspective, the authors of mother's advice books solved the problems of feminine learning and virtue by developing a genre unique to women. Elizabeth Grymeston, Elizabeth Jocelin, and Dorothy Leigh suggest the strengths of this strategy, its legitimization of feminine values in the public domain, while the Countess of Lincoln and M.R. indicate its limitations and ultimate inability to advance feminine art.

AFTERWORD

$\mathscr{C}$ HRISTINE DE PISAN's vision of women building their city was in many ways fulfilled by these five generations of women writing in England. Some devoted themselves entirely to regenerating the image of women; some pondered the influence women's spirit might have on the commonwealth; others wrote to comfort and cheer all humankind. Most seem to have been driven by their ideals and all overcame many obstacles in order to contribute their voices to the cause.

How much influence these writers had on their contemporaries and on succeeding generations is still to be determined. But even now, we should recognize that the Renaissance includes writers like Jane Grey, Isabella Whitney, and Aemilia Lanyer. As new documents come to light, as more writers are unearthed, the canon will continue to grow.

ABBREVIATIONS

Journal abbreviations follow *PMLA* annual bibliography.

AN&Q   *American Notes and Queries*
BSUF   *Ball State University Forum*
CJ   *Classical Journal*
CSPD   *Calendar of State Papers Domestic*
DNB   *Dictionary of National Biography*
ELR   *English Literary Renaissance*
JWCI   *Journal of the Warburg and Courtauld Institutes*
MLR   *Modern Language Review*
N&Q   *Notes and Queries*
PLL   *Papers on Language and Literature*
PMLA   *Publications of the Modern Language Association*
RenQ   *Renaissance Quarterly*
RES   *Review of English Studies*
SAB   *South Atlantic Bulletin*
SEL   *Studies in English Literature, 1500-1900*
ShN   *Shakespeare Newsletter*
SP   *Studies in Philology*
SQ   *Shakespeare Quarterly*
TSLL   *Texas Studies in Literature and Language*
TSWL   *Tulsa Studies in Women's Literature*
YES   *Yearbook of English Studies*

NOTES

INTRODUCTION

1. ~~Christine de Pisan,~~ *~~The boke of the cyte of ladyes~~*, tr. Bryan Ansley (London, 1521), Bb-Bbii. Hereafter cited in the text.

2. Diane Bornstein remarks, "After all the heroic examples, this ending seems like an anticlimax. Nevertheless, it is a pragmatic acknowledgement of the status of women in the real world." *Distaves and Dames: Renaissance treatises for and about women*, facs., intr. Diane Bornstein (Delmar, N.Y.: Scholars Facsimiles and Reprints, 1978), p. xvii.

3. In his recent translation, Earl Jeffrey Richards notes, "This strong religious element may not appeal to some modern critics, but it is an historical fact that Christine saw in Christianity a means of overcoming oppression. ... Christine's title for *The Book of the City of Ladies* alludes directly to Augustine's *City of God*. By juxtaposing the two cities, Christine did not intend that her City of Ladies rival the City of God, but that her political vision be understood as participating in a Christian tradition of political philosophy." *The Book of the City of Ladies* (New York: Persea Books, 1982), p. xxix. See Joan Kelly, "Early Feminist Theory and the *Querelle des Femmes*" (1982), rpt. in *Women, History, and Theory: The Essays of Joan Kelly* (Chicago: The University of Chicago Press, 1984), pp. 65-109, for an analysis of Christine's work as a feminist critique of patriarchy and an assertion of women's ability to learn and to govern. See also Susan Schibanoff's "Comment" on Kelly's essay in *Signs* 9 (1983), 320-26, which stresses Christine's support for women's own experience in defiance of male authority.

4. As every chapter of this book will show, praise of individual women writers followed a formula, always coupling learning and virtue, and often adding chastity, modesty, and piety. When commentators praised learned women as a group, they often did so to demonstrate the superiority of English women over French and Italian women, or of the present over the past, thus inclining themselves to hyperbole for the cause. In 1548, in his dedication to Katherine Parr of *The First Tome . . . of the Paraphrase of Erasmus*, Nicholas Udall claimed that learned noblewomen in England far outnumbered those of antiquity, and that "it is now no newes in Englande to see young damysels in nobles houses and in the Courtes of princes, in stede of cardes and other instrumentes of idle trifleing, to have continually in theyr handes eyther Psalmes, Omelies, and other devoute meditacions, or els Paules epistles or some booke of holy Scripture matiers, and as familiarlye both to reade or reason thereof in Greke, Latine, Frenche or

NOTES TO INTRODUCTION

Italian as in Englishe." In the seventeenth century, William Wotton wrote in *Reflections upon Ancient and Modern Learning* (1694) that "It was so very modish, that the fair Sex seemed to believe the *Greek* and *Latin* added to their Charms: and *Plato* and *Aristotle* untranslated, were frequent ornaments of their closets. One would think by the Effects, that it was a proper way of Educating them, since there are no Accounts in History of so many truly great Women in any one Age, as are to be found between the Years 15 and 1600" (pp. 349-50). In the eighteenth century, George Ballard commemorated the learning and virtue of many Renaissance women in *Memoirs of Several Ladies of Great Britain, Who Have Been Celebrated for Their Writings or Skill in the Learned Languages, Arts and Sciences* (Oxford, 1752). Dorothy Gardiner uses "The Tudor Paragons" as the title of a chapter in *English Girlhood at School* (London: Oxford University Press, 1929), drawing the allusion from Richard Mulcaster's *Positions* (London, 1581), in which he claims the superiority of English ladies "even to the best *Romaine* or *Greekish paragones* be they never so much praised: to the *Germain* or *French* gentlewymen, by late writers so wel liked: to the Italian ladies who dare write themselves . . ." (p. 168).

5. Ruth Hughey, "Cultural Interests of Women in England from 1524 to 1640. Indicated in the Writings of the Women. A Survey." Diss. Cornell University, 1932; Charlotte Kohler, "The Elizabethan Woman of Letters: The Extent of her Literary Activities." Diss. University of Virginia, 1936.

6. See *The Woman's Part: Feminist Criticism of Shakespeare*, ed. Lenz, Greene, Neely (Urbana: University of Illinois Press, 1980). In *Still Harping on Daughters* (Totowa, N.J.: Barnes and Noble Books, 1983), Jardine offers a cogent summary and critique of the principal feminist criticism of Shakespeare (pp. 1-8).

7. I agree for the most part with Hilda Smith's thesis in *Reason's Disciples: Seventeenth-Century English Feminists* (Urbana: University of Illinois Press, 1982). Smith argues that the first group of modern feminists did not appear until the second half of the seventeenth century, and defines "feminists" as "individuals who viewed women as a sociological group whose social and political position linked them together more surely than their physical or psychological natures" (p. 4). She shows how these women "fitted these two major points—intellectual restriction and domestic subordination—into a general system of protest against men's total control of the public and private institutions of English society. These women desired to change the sexual balance of power. They did not simply criticize women's position in society, but saw social change as necessary to restoring women's rightful opportunities" (p. 5).

8. See Elizabeth Hageman's invaluable bibliography, "Recent Studies in Women Writers of Tudor England," *ELR* 14 (1984), 409-25. Anthologies have made more early women writers available to teachers: *The Paradise of Women: Writings by Englishwomen of the Renaissance*, ed. Betty Travitsky (Westport, Ct.: Greenwood Press, 1981); *First Feminists: British Women*

- 289 -

Writers 1578–1799, ed. Moira Ferguson (Bloomington: Indiana University Press, and Old Westbury, N.Y.: The Feminist Press, 1985); Katherine Usher Henderson and Barbara F. McManus, *Half Humankind: Contexts and Texts of the Controversy about Women in England 1540–1640* (Urbana: University of Illinois Press, 1985). Two recent critical anthologies are basic reading on women writers: *Silent But for the Word: Tudor Women as Patrons, Translators, and Writers of Religious Works*, ed. Margaret Hannay (Kent, Ohio: Kent State University Press, 1985); *Women in the Middle Ages and the Renaissance: Literary and Historical Perspectives*, ed. Mary Beth Rose (Syracuse: Syracuse University Press, 1986). See relevant chapters for recent editions and critical studies of individual writers.

9. Linda Woodbridge, *Women and the English Renaissance: Literature and the Nature of Womankind 1540–1620* (Urbana and Chicago: University of Illinois Press, 1984).

10. In her monumental and seminal work, *Doctrine for the Lady of the Renaissance* (Urbana: University of Illinois Press, 1955), Ruth Kelso provides analysis and a bibliography of the flood of sixteenth-century treatises pertinent to the instruction of women. For a survey of Renaissance authoritative texts and commentaries on the nature of woman in theology, science, philosophy, and law, see Hugh Maclean, *The Renaissance Notion of Woman* (Cambridge: Cambridge University Press, 1980).

11. In a popular sixteenth-century prayer book, *The Pomander of prayers*, Thomas Becon instructs maidens to pray: "There is nothing that becommeth a maid better than silence, shamefastnes, and chastitie of both body and mind. ... I therefore most humbly besech thee (O mercifull father) ... that thou wilt so order my tong, and dispose my talk that I speake nothing but that becommeth my state, age, and person, neither that I delight to heare any talk, that mighte in any poynte move me to lewdnes, seeing that evil words corrupt good maners" (pp. 23-24). Wives are bidden to pray: "Give me grace I most entirely beseeche thee to walk worthy of my vocation, to knowledge my husbande to be my head, to be subject unto him, to learne thy blessed worde of hym, to reverence hym, to obey him, to please him, to be ruled by him, peaceably and quietly to live with him ..." (pp. 29v-30).

12. Rachel Wiegall, "An Elizabethan Gentlewoman," *Quarterly Review* 215 (1911), 125-26. Wiegall published extracts from Mildmay's journal which is still in manuscript.

13. See Joan Kelly, "Did Women Have a Renaissance?" (1977), rpt. in *Women, History, and Theory*, pp. 19-50. Kelly answers with a social historian's "no"; I would give a literary critic's much qualified "yes." Kelly's important perception that the labels and periods that describe men's culture may not suit women's deserves further interdisciplinary study and definition.

CHAPTER ONE

1. Studies on the Renaissance education of women include Mary Agnes Cannon, *The Education of Women During the Renaissance* (Washington, D.C.: National Capitol Press, Inc., 1916), pp. 97-123; Myra Reynolds, *The Learned Lady in England, 1650–1760* (Boston: Houghton-Mifflin, 1920), pp. 1-45; Gardiner, *English Girlhood at School*, pp. 141-97, which recognizes the elite nature of an education which "tended to produce paragons rather than to raise the general average of female attainment" (197); Kelso, *Doctrine for the Lady of the Renaissance*, Chapter 4, which begins by describing the "atmosphere of doubt, timidity, fear, and niggardly concession" surrounding the question of women's education; Walter J. Ong, "Latin Language Study as a Renaissance Puberty Rite," *SP* 56 (1959), 103-24, which connects learning Latin, an almost exclusively masculine pursuit, with the teaching of courage and the assumption of power; and Katherine Usher Henderson and Barbara F. McManus, *Half Humankind*, pp. 81-98, which surveys the effects of education on women writers.

2. See Kelso, *Doctrine*, p. 72. STC 24856-24863.

3. Juan Luis Vives, *A very frutefull and pleasant boke called the Instruction of a Christen woman* ... tr. Richard Hyrde (London, 1540), Aii v-Aiii. All further references will be cited in the text.

4. The superiority of chastity to marriage was a commonplace of theology, largely based on Paul, 1 Cor. 7:7-8, and taken up by Jerome; but in misogynist texts it evolved into a debased doctrine that woman represented the flesh, man the spirit. See Jo Ann McNamara, "Sexual Equality and the Cult of Virginity in Early Christian Thought," *Feminist Studies* 3 (1976), 145-58, for a survey of opinions and appropriate texts, and her thesis that assuming the ascetic life brought spiritual equality to early Christian women, making them less womanly and more redeemable. Woman's inherently voracious sexuality was a medieval commonplace surviving in the Renaissance both in medical texts and popular culture. See Hilda Smith, "Gynecology and Ideology in Seventeenth-Century England," *Liberating Women's History: Theoretical and Critical Essays*, ed. Berenice A. Carroll (Urbana: University of Illinois Press, 1976). Smith recognizes the dilemma "of those who accepted the view of women's greater sensuality while advocating a chaste and modest womanhood" (p. 104). Natalie Zemon Davis, in "Women on Top," relates how her internal disorderliness, the lower desires ruling the higher, was taken to forecast women's desire to rule those above her. The "proposed remedies" for such inherent defects were "religious training that fashioned the reins of modesty and humility; selective education that showed a woman her moral duty without enflaming her undisciplined imagination or loosing her tongue for public talk; honest work that busied her hands; and law and constraints that made her subject

to her husband." *Society and Culture in Early Modern France* (Stanford: Stanford University Press, 1975), p. 126.

5. See Gloria Kaufman, "Juan Luis Vives on the Education of Women," *Signs* 3 (1978), 891-96, in which she corrects the assumption that his advocacy of feminine education made Vives a feminist. See also Valerie Wayne, "Some Sad Sentence: Vives' *Instruction of a Christian Woman*," in *Silent But for the Word*, pp. 15-29. Wayne appraises both Vives's restrictions and his innovations, and suggests how such an education might affect potential writers. On women's reading, see Josephine Hull, *Chaste, Silent & Obedient: English Books for Women 1475–1640* (San Marino: Huntington Library, 1982).

6. Richard Brathwait, *The English Gentlewoman* ... (London, 1631), p. 90.

7. George Puttenham, *The Arte of English Poesie 1589*, facs. rpt. (Menston, England: The Scolar Press Ltd., 1968).

8. Thomas Elyot, *The Defence of Good Women 1540*, rpt., ed. Edwin Johnston Howard (Oxford, Ohio: The Anchor Press, 1940), pp. 64-65. All further references will be cited in the text. Elyot's earlier work, *The Boke named the Governour* (1531), instructed men and boys in the virtues necessary for public service and rule.

9. In "Feminism and the Humanists: The Case of Sir Thomas Elyot's *Defence of Good Women*," *Renaissance Quarterly* 36 (1983), 181-201, Constance Jordan suggests that Zenobia "incarnates the central paradox so often generated by the introduction of humanist ideals into the context of an essentially Christian antifeminism" (p. 194).

10. Richard Mulcaster, *Positions Concerning the Training Up of Children* (London, 1581), p. 167. All further references will be cited in the text. Mulcaster (1530–1611) was the first headmaster of the Merchant Taylors School, and later high-master of St. Paul's school; "his memory was revered by some of his greatest scholars" (*DNB*).

11. One woman who taught herself was Elizabeth Cary, Viscountess Falkland, who as a girl ran up a substantial debt to the family servants for candles by which to study at night. Without teachers, she learned French, Spanish, Italian, Hebrew, and Latin. See Chapter Six below.

12. *The Necessarie, Fit, and Convenient Education of a yong Gentlewoman. Written Both In French and Italian, and translated into English by W. P.* (London, 1598), F8. All further references will be cited in the text. The English translation faces the French and Italian "for the better instruction of such as are desirous to studie those Tongues." Thomas Salter's translation of Bruto had appeared in 1579, indicating that a midcentury Italian text against women's intellectual development had some currency for the rest of the century. See Janis Butler Holm, "Thomas Salter's *The Mirrhor of Modestie*: A Translation of Bruto's *La Institutione di una Fanciulla Nata Nobilmente*," *The Library*, 6th ser. 5 (1983), pp. 53-57. Holm speculates that

W. P. was William Phiston or Fiston, who did other French and Italian translations for English publishers (n. 10).

13. Richard Hyrde, Preface to *A devout treatise upon the Pater noster* (London, 1524), aiv v.

14. Contemporary opinions will receive more attention below, but even those hostile to Thomas More admired his daughters. The Protestant historian, Holinshed, while criticizing More for not using his reason rightly, says that "God had extraordinarily blessed his children, and namelie his three daughters, to whome he had given an admirable dexteritie in the science of toongs and arts. . . ." In the eighteenth century, in his *Memoirs of Several Ladies of Great Britain*, Ballard describes the three sisters as famous all over Europe for learning, and Roper in particular "seems to have had all things that either art or nature could give to make her perfect. She had a ready wit, a quick conception, tenacious memory, a fine imagination, and was very happy in her sentiments and way of expressing herself upon all occasions" (p. 29). In the nineteenth century, Roper is particularly admired for her filial piety, as in Emily Owen, *The Heroines of Domestic Life* (London, 1861), pp. 53-87; and Agnes Stewart, *Margaret Roper, or The Chancellor and his Daughter* (London, 1874). In the twentieth century, Roper continues to appear as the model pupil and daughter, as in a full-length biography by E. E. Reynolds, *Margaret Roper: Eldest daughter of Saint Thomas More* (London: Burns and Oates, 1963).

15. William Roper, *The Life of Sir Thomas More, Knight* in *Lives of Saint Thomas More*, ed. E. E. Reynolds (New York: Dutton, 1963), p. 48.

16. Nicholas Harpsfield, *The Life and Death of Sir Thomas More, Knight, Sometime Lord High Chancellor of England* in *Lives of Saint Thomas More*, p. 97.

17. Thomas Stapleton, *The Life and Illustrious Martyrdom of Sir Thomas More, formerly Lord Chancellor of England* (Part III of *Tres Thomae*, Douai, 1588), tr. Philip E. Hallett (London: Burns Oates and Washbourne, 1928), p. 97.

18. The tendency to exaggerate women's intellectual achievements derived partly from their relative novelty and partly from the current opinions of women's abilities. Germaine Greer articulates a similar problem in the case of women painters: "The unreliability of the classic references when it comes to women's work is the consequence of the commentators' condescending attitude. Any work by a woman, however trifling, is as astonishing as the pearl in the head of the toad. It is not part of the natural order, and need not be related to the natural order." Again, "even men who regarded themselves as responsible critics felt no shame in debasing all their standards in order to flatter a woman's work . . . for compliment is the recognised commerce between the sexes." *The Obstacle Race: The Fortunes of Women Painters and Their Work* (New York: Farrar, Strauss, Giroux, 1979), pp. 4, 68.

19. *Saint Thomas More: Selected Letters*, ed. Elizabeth Frances Rogers

(New Haven and London: Yale University Press, 1961), p. 148. All further references will be cited in the text and designated, *Letters*.

20. Women's practice of medicine from the early Middle Ages is documented by Joan Ferrante in "The Education of Women in the Middle Ages in Theory, Fact and Fantasy," in *Beyond Their Sex: Learned Women of the European Past*, ed. Patricia H. Labalme (New York: New York University Press, 1980), pp. 18-19. Roper's schoolmate, Margaret Giggs Clement, was also noted for her medical skill.

21. In a letter from court to his children, More advises them to "first write the whole in English, for then you will have much less trouble and labor in turning it into Latin; not having to look for the matter, your mind will be intent only on the language ..." *Letters*, p. 151. Stapleton records the habit of double translation in More's "school," a process also recommended by Vives and Ascham.

22. In "Margaret Roper's English Version of Erasmus's *Precatio Dominica* and the Apprenticeship Behind Early Tudor Translation," *RES*, 13 (1937), 257-71, John Archer Gee gives an extended appraisal of Roper's translation, judiciously remarking how the work is certainly more than a schoolgirl exercise, and suggesting that Roper had undergone "a considerable apprenticeship in the art of vernacular translation" (p. 264). He notes what is immediately apparent to the reader, that "the translation proceeds straightforwardly from one clause to another of the often long and somewhat involved sentences of the original" and yet, as Gee goes on to point out, "it rarely follows the Latin ordering and structure to the extent of being slavishly literal. At times, to be sure, an absolute-participle construction reveals its Latin source, and there is a tendency for adjectives to succeed nouns and for verbs to gravitate towards the ends of clauses. ..." But, "in general the Latin construction is treated with felicitous freedom which combines scholarship and art. The diction is also praiseworthy, a Latin word being seldom expressed by its English derivative. Likewise observable now and again is a pleasing rhythm, attained in part by skillfully transposing the Latin order ... the translation is to be regarded as a mature achievement of its kind" (p. 265). Gee also reminds us that this translation "belongs to the early history of an important movement, one which did much to establish modern English literary prose" (p. 259). Translation was a valued art in the sixteenth century, practiced by scholars like Tyndale and poets like Chapman.

In "Margaret More Roper's Personal Expression in the *Devout Treatise Upon the Pater Noster*" in *Silent But for the Word* (pp. 30-42), Rita M. Verbrugge analyzes Roper's "care and concern for a responsible translation that belonged to the ideals of the early humanists" (p. 39), giving examples of her "simple, straightforward, and unpretentious" vocabulary (p. 40), and the "mature independence" of her rhetoric (p. 41).

23. *The workes of Sir Thomas More Knyght ... wrytten by him in the Englysh tonge* (London, 1557), p. 1434. All further references will be cited

in the text and designated "More." The letter is reprinted in *The Correspondence of Sir Thomas More*, ed. Elizabeth Frances Rogers (Princeton: Princeton University Press, 1947), pp. 514-532.

24. R. W. Chambers says that "the speeches of More are absolute More; and the speeches of Margaret are absolute Margaret. And we have to leave it at that." *On the Continuity of English Prose from Alfred to More and His School* (London: Early English Text Society, 1932), p. clxii. However, Louis Martz decides that "the arguments in this letter are so circumstantially given, and the language has such a resonance of his own style, that I think that one ends up with very little doubt that this letter is primarily More's own composition. One can imagine More and Margaret planning it out together and speaking much of it aloud in More's Tower room. But its art seems to me all More's." "Thomas More: The Tower Works," in *Saint Thomas More: Action and Contemplation*, Proceedings of the Symposium held at St. John's University, 1970, ed. Richard Sylvester (New Haven: Yale University Press, 1972), p. 63. In "Tragic Perspective in Thomas More's Dialogue with Margaret in the Tower," *Cithara* 17 (1978), 3-12, Walter M. Gordon agrees that it is a collaboration, assuming that "More's thought so dominates the dialogue and Margaret's feelings so color it that the participation of neither can be safely ruled out" (n. 2).

25. Chambers, *English Prose*, p. clxii.

26. The story is cited by Ballard, *Memoirs*, pp. 38, 42.

CHAPTER TWO

1. Immediately after her death, Askew proved her value to the Reformers' cause. The Protestant apologist, John Bale, claimed a thousand converts were made, and even discounting for propaganda, we may suppose that many were swayed by her faith and fortitude. A Latin epitaph for her rejoiced that her truth was not shaken by fetters and that eternal life crowned her ashes. Askew's reputation lived on in the seventeenth century. In "An Essay to Revive the Ancient Education of Gentlewomen" (1673), Bathsua Makin attributed the English Reformation itself to women, particularly like Anne Askew, "a person famous for learning and piety, who so seasoned the Queen and ladies of the Court, by her precepts and examples, and after sealed her profession with her blood, that the seed of reformation seemed to be sowed by her hand." *The Female Spectator: English Women Writers Before 1800*, ed. Mary Mahl and Helene Koon (Bloomington: Indiana University Press and Old Westbury, N.Y.: The Feminist Press, 1977), p. 134. The legend continues, enshrined in two novels, Anne Manning's *The Lincolnshire Tragedy: Passages in the Life of the Faire Gospeller, Mistress Anne Askew* (London, 1866; New York, 1867) and Alison Macleod's *The Heretic* (Boston: Houghton-Mifflin, 1966). Both books reflect the power of Askew's writing to spark the sympathy and admiration of her readers, for

both quote at length from the *Examinations* and find in them the imaginative source of Askew's character.

2. *The first examinacyon of Anne Askewe, lately martyred in Smythfelde, by the Romysh popes upholders, with the Elucydacyon of Johan Bale* (Wesel, 1546). Bale's Preface "to the Christen readers," p. 9v. All further references to this work appear in the text and are designated "I."

3. In *John Bale: Mythmaker for the English Reformation* (West Lafayette, Indiana: Purdue University Press, 1976), Leslie P. Fairfield argues for the pivotal position of Bale in changing the English conception of sainthood. In the case of Askew's *Examinations*, "the main point of Bale's commentary was to show that Anne Askew's faith had been biblical and her martydom valid, and therefore that her judges and interrogators had been agents of the devil" (p. 132).

4. The two examinations were published separately at Wesel in 1546 and 1547 with Bale's elucidation. Four editions combining the two examinations were printed in England during Edward VI's reign, three of which omitted Bale's commentary. Fairfield speculates that there might therefore have been 3,500 copies in circulation (p. 135). The examinations also appeared in John Foxe's *Actes and Monuments* (London, 1563) without Bale's commentary.

5. Fairfield calls *The vocacyon of John Bale* a "fragment of autobiography" in which, describing the years 1552–1553, "Bale cast himself as a Protestant saint . . . [drawing] on his own experience for examples of good and evil" (p. 141). *The Book of Margery Kempe* is usually taken to be the earliest example of spiritual autobiography, to which genre Askew's work also belongs. Fairfield speculates that Bale was encouraged to write his own because he "had seen how successful Anne Askew's accounts of her examinations had been" (p. 142).

6. Writing about the religiosity of the thirteenth-century nuns of Helfta, Caroline Walker Bynum shows that "the mystical union these women achieved, which was sometimes expressed in visions of themselves as priests, enabled them to serve as counselors, mediators, and channels to the sacraments—roles which the thirteenth-century church in some ways increasingly denied to women and to laity." "Women who grew up in monasteries were less likely to be influenced by the contemporary stereotype of women as morally and intellectually inferior. Such women were more likely to see themselves as functioning with a full range of male and female, governing and comforting roles, paralleling the full range of the operations of God." *Jesus as Mother: Studies in the Spirituality of the High Middle Ages* (Berkeley and Los Angeles: University of California Press, 1982), pp. 184-85. Deep religiosity, whether in the thirteenth-century cloistered Catholic or the sixteenth-century Protestant martyr, may indeed have modified women's internalization of narrow definitions of their sex.

7. Helen White, *Tudor Books of Saints and Martyrs* (Madison: University of Wisconsin Press, 1963), p. 12.

8. John King, "The Godly Woman in Elizabethan Iconography," *RenQ* 38 (1985), 41-84. King notes that the martyr's palm and "a book (an ancient Christian symbol for the Four Evangelists)" associate Askew with "the apostolic traditions of the early church" (54). In *English Reformation Literature: The Tudor Origins of the Protestant Tradition* (Princeton: Princeton University Press, 1982), King associates Askew's radiance with the Woman Clothed with the Sun (Revelation 12:1), who "represents the beleaguered church in general as well as each individual Christian" (p. 73).

9. *The lattre examinacyon of the worthye servaunt of God mastres Anne Askewe* (Wesel, 1547), p. 15v. All further references to this work appear in the text and are designated "II." Bale details how Sir William Askew and "olde mastre Kyme" arranged the marriage: "the seyd Sir Wyllyam covenaunted wyth hym for lucre, to have his eldest doughter marryed with hys sonne and heyre (as an ungodly maner it is in Englande moche used amonge noble men) And as it was her chaunce to dye afore the tyme of marryage, to save the moneye he constrayned thys [Anne] to supplye her rowme. So that in the ende she was compelled agaynst her wyll or fre consent to marrye with hym" (p. 15).

10. See Derek Wilson, *A Tudor Tapestry: Men, Women, and Society in Reformation England* (London: William Heineman Ltd., 1972), pp. 155-67, 180-97, 203-37, for a biographical narrative that mixes fact with informed, but imaginative, recreation of Askew's life.

11. A. G. Dickens notes that before she came to London, Askew may have known the Nottinghamshire Reformer, John Lascelles, who had become a sewer of the King's Chamber and "the leading spirit" of a Reformist group at court. *Lollards and Protestants in the Diocese of York 1509-1558* (London: Oxford University Press, 1959), pp. 33-34. See John King, "Patronage and Piety: The Influence of Catherine Parr," in *Silent But for the Word*, p. 45.

12. See Wilson, *Tudor Tapestry*, p. 188.

13. John Lascelles, with whom Askew was burned, wrote a letter from prison wholly concerned with his sacramentarian beliefs. See Foxe, *Actes and Monuments*.

14. With considerably more color, Bale says of Rich, "Without all dyscressyon, honestye, or manhode, he casteth of hys gowne, and taketh here upon hym the most vyle offyce of an hangeman and pulleth at the racke most vyllanouslye" (II, p. 45v).

15. In Coverdale's Bible (1537), the passage reads: "For we wrestle not against fleshe and bloud, but agaynst rule, against power, namely agaynst the rulers of the worlde, of the darknesse of this worlde, agaynst the sprete of wyckednesse under the heaven. For this cause take ye the armour of God, that ye maye be able to resyste in the evell daye, and stonde perfecte in al thynges.

"Stonde therfore, and your loynes gyrded aboute with the treuth, havyng on the prestplate of righteousnesse, and shode upon youre fete with the

Gospel of peace, that ye may be prepared. Above all thynges take holde of the shylde of fayth wher with ye may quench the fyrie dartes of the wicked. And take the helmet of salvacyon and the swearde of the sprete, whiche is the worde of God."

16. Coverdale's Bible (1537), Jeremiah 22.

17. In *The Native Tongue and the Word: Developments in English Prose Style 1380–1580* (Chicago and London: University of Chicago Press, 1984), Janel Mueller analyzes "the stylistic impact in early modern English prose of the combined conceptual position and compositional process" which she defines as Scripturalism: "a writer's molding of his thought and language forms after a recognizable mode or model from the Old or New Testament" (pp. 245-46). Mueller's analysis of a wide range of sixteenth-century prose has been valuable in clarifying scriptural influence on the women writers studied here.

CHAPTER THREE

1. Anne [Locke] Prowse, tr., *Of the markes of the children of God, and of their afflictions. To the faithfull of the Low Countrie. By John Taffin* (London, 1590), A4. Anne Locke Dering Prowse is discussed below.

2. The dedication of women to the Reformed faith appears not only in the narratives concerning Jane Grey and Elizabeth Tudor, but in the records of women martyrs from the lower and middle classes. Foxe documents the deaths of 46 such women in 1556 and 1557 alone. See *Actes and Monuments*, pp. 1451-706. Women had also given considerable help to the spread of lollardy. See Claire Cross, " 'Great Reasoners in Scripture': The Activities of Women Lollards 1380-1530," in *Medieval Women*, ed. Derek Baker (Oxford: Blackwell, 1978), pp. 359-80, in which she documents how lollardy fulfilled the spiritual needs of middle- and lower-class women in a way that the church did not. She also notes that "much learning of lollard scriptures by heart went on in this community, and here women indisputably dominated the scene" (p. 371).

3. See Barbara K. Lewalski, *Protestant Poetics and the Seventeenth-Century Religious Lyric* (Princeton: Princeton University Press, 1979). Chapter 7, "Art and the Sacred Subject," is particularly helpful in clarifying the range of styles thought to be appropriate for pious expression; and in showing how Protestant preachers appealed to "Biblical texture and style as the model for, or at least as a determinant of" their sermons (p. 219). In *English Reformation Literature*, pp. 138-44, John King discusses the origins of the plain style in "biblical English," quoting Nicholas Udall, "For divinitie, lyke as it loveth no cloking, but loveth to be simple and playn so doth it not refuse eloquence, if the same come without injurie or violacion of the truth" (p. 141).

4. Anne Wheathill, *A handfull of holesome (though homelie) hearbs, gathered*

out of the goodlie garden of Gods most holie word (London, 1584), A2. Hereafter cited in the text.

5. In *A godly Garden*, women are instructed to pray: "I knowledge (O Lord) that justly for our transgression of thy commaundements, thou saydst to the first woman, and in her to all us. I will encrease thy sorowe, when thou art with child, with paine shalt thou bring forth thy children ... a worthy crosse and punishment laid uppon us by they ordinaunce, to the whyche with hart and minde I humbly submit me ..." (pp. 126-26v). In both Becon's *Pomander of prayers* and Bull's *Christian Praiers and Holie Meditations* there are similar prayers.

6. See Marjorie Keniston McIntosh, "Sir Anthony Cooke: Tudor Humanist, Educator, and Religious Reformer," Proceedings of the American Philosophical Society 119 (June 1975), pp. 233-50, particularly pp. 239-41.

7. *Fourtene Sermons of Barnardine Ochyne, concernying the predestinacion and eleccion of god: very expediente to the settynge forth of hys glorye among hys creatures. Translated out of Italian in to oure natyve tounge by A. C.* (London, 1551?), A3.

8. In "The Cooke Sisters: Attitudes toward Learned Women in the Renaissance," in *Silent But for the Word*, pp. 107-25, Mary Ellen Lamb argues that the sisters translated religious works as the one socially acceptable outlet for their education, that translation was a suitably minor activity for women, and that their editors consistently represented strong, intelligent women as demure and shy. Here, the emphasis is on the importance of translation to the development of a women's literary tradition; I would also argue that translation was thoroughly mainstream.

9. The circumstances surrounding Jewel's defense of the English church are explained by J. E. Booty in his introduction to *An Apology of the Church of England by John Jewel* (Folger Shakespeare Library ed., Charlottesville: The University Press of Virginia, 1963). Booty notes the report of the Spanish ambassador, unconfirmed elsewhere, that there was a committee composed of the Archbishops of Canterbury and York, the Bishops of Winchester and Salisbury, Nicholas Bacon and William Cecil, which directed the policy of the English church toward the Pope and which might have initiated its public defense (p. xiii). Perhaps Anne Bacon learned of the need for a translation from her husband.

10. Booty attests to the importance of the *Apology* for the English church. See particularly pp. xliii-xlv. See also William P. Haugaard, *Elizabeth and the English Reformation* (Cambridge: Cambridge University Press, 1968), pp. 242-47.

11. John Jewel, *An Apologie or answere in defence of the Church of Englande with a briefe and plaine declaration of the true Religion professed and used in the same* (London, 1564), The Epistle [p. 1]. Hereafter cited in the text.

12. C. S. Lewis paid tribute to her skills as a translator: "Anne Lady Bacon ... deserves more praise than I have space to give her. Latin prose has a flavour very hard to disguise in translation, but nearly every sentence

in Lady Bacon's work sounds like an original. Again and again she finds the phrase which, once she has found it, we feel to be inevitable. *Sacridiculi* become 'massing priests,' *ineptum* 'a verie toy,' *quidam ex asseclis et parasitis* 'one of his soothing pages and clawebackes,' *lege sodes* 'in goode fellowshipe I pray thee reade,' *operae pretium est videre* 'it is a world to see,' and *magnum silentium* 'all mum, not a worde.' If quality without bulk were enough, Lady Bacon might be put forward as the best of all sixteenth-century translators." *English Literature in the Sixteenth Century* (Oxford: The Clarendon Press, 1954), p. 307.

13. *The Letters and the Life of Francis Bacon*, vol. 1, in *The Works of Francis Bacon*, ed. James Spedding, vol. 8 (London: Longman, Green, Longman, and Roberts, 1861), p. 41.

14. Ibid., pp. 112-13.

15. In Chapter 5 of *Leicester: Patron of Letters* (New York: Columbia University Press, 1955), Eleanor Rosenberg describes the typical translator: "He boasts, in his dedications and prefaces, of serving the commonwealth by providing enlightenment for his unlearned countrymen; he envisions an England made virtuous and powerful by the dissemination of wisdom derived from other tongues. He speaks of his eagerness to undertake further tasks for the public good, and calls attention to his linguistic skill by deprecating it with conventional modesty. In short, his work is usually offered not merely for its own sake but also as a demonstration of his zeal for his country and of his qualifications for employment in public service" (p. 153).

16. See Chapter Eight for further discussion of Tyler in the context of women writing romance.

17. Anne Locke, *Sermons of John Calvin, upon the songe that Ezechias made after he had bene sicke, and afflicted by the hand of God*, Translated out of Frenche into Englishe (London, 1560), The Epistle, A8. Hereafter cited in the text. In "The Role of Women in the English Reformation Illustrated by the Life and Friendships of Anne Locke" (1965), rpt. in *Godly People: Essays on English Protestantism and Puritanism* (London: The Hambledon Press, 1983), pp. 273-87, Patrick Collinson traces Anne Vaughan Locke Dering Prowse through her intense friendship with John Knox with whom "no one was ever closer" (p. 276); her leaving her husband, Henry Locke, to join the English Puritans in Geneva; her second marriage to Edward Dering, the noted preacher; her third marriage and her continued godly activity in Devon. Collinson concludes that her life "spans the whole story of the Reformation in England" (p. 287).

18. *The Monument of Matrones: conteining seven severall Lamps of Virginitie, or distinct treatises ... compiled ... by Thomas Bentley of Graies Inne Student*, London, 1582, title-page. Hereafter cited in the text.

19. In "Elizabeth, Bride and Queen: A Study of Spenser's April Eclogue and the Metaphors of English Protestantism," *Spenser Studies* II (1981), 75-91, Lynn Johnson discusses Bentley's association of Elizabeth with Solomon,

showing how it becomes a metaphor for her political and spiritual leadership, and underlining the "reality" of such thinking for the sixteenth century.

20. Bentley adopts the sixteenth-century tradition of collecting scriptural prayers, a practice Helen White describes as "centrally representative of the scripturalism of the age." The *Tudor Books of Private Devotion* (Madison: University of Wisconsin Press, 1951), p. 134.

21. Marguerite d'Angoulême, Reine de Navarre, *Le Miroir de l'Ame Pécheresse*, ed. Joseph L. Allaire (Munich: Wilhelm Fink Verlag, 1972), Introduction, pp. 15-21. See Chapter Six below for another instance of Marguerite's Reformist role.

22. Bentley used the 1568 edition, edited by James Cancellar. To avoid his changes, I have used the manuscript facsimile. Elizabeth Tudor, *The Mirror of the Sinful Soul*, facs. ed. of 1544, MS Bodleian, intr. Percy Ames (London: Asher and Co., 1897), p. 2. Hereafter cited in the text. See Ruth Hughey, "A Note on Queen Elizabeth's 'Godly Meditation,' " *The Library*, 4th ser., 15 (1935), 238-40.

23. J. E. Neale, *Queen Elizabeth I* (Harmondsworth, England: Penguin, 1971), p. 20.

24. In the Protestant Bible, the passage is I Kings 3:16-28.

25. See Anne Lake Prescott, "The Pearl of the Valois and Elizabeth I: Marguerite de Navarre's *Miroir* and Tudor England," in *Silent But for the Word*, pp. 61-76, for a compelling analysis of Elizabeth's treatment of such passages which have startling relevance to herself as the daughter of Henry VIII and Anne Boleyn. Prescott also discusses Marguerite's importance in England.

26. *English Reformation Literature*, p. 170.

27. *A Godly Medytacyon of the christen sowle concerninge a love towarde God and hys Christe . . . Translated into English by the ryght vertuouse lady Elizabeth*, ed. John Bale (Wesel, 1548), fol. 9v and fol. 42v.

28. William P. Haugaard writes in "Katherine Parr: the Religious Convictions of a Renaissance Queen," *RenQ* 22 (Winter 1969), 359, that "She had not become so enamoured of reformation doctrine that she lost sight of the Erasmian ideal of peace, unity, and understanding in Christian society"; while John King, in "Patronage and Piety: The Influence of Catherine Parr," in *Silent But for the Word*, pp. 43-60, argues convincingly for the importance of Parr and her circle of aristocratic women in "the popularization of Protestant humanism through patronage of devotional manuals and theological translations" as well as by employing Protestant tutors.

29. King, "Patronage and Piety," documents the source of *Prayers or Medytacions* as Thomas à Kempis's *Imitation of Christ*, and comments briefly on *The Lamentation* as a Protestant document (p. 50).

30. The traditional interpretation of events implicates Northumberland, who, having established himself as Lord Protector at the end of Edward

VI's reign, plotted to retain power when the sickly boy king should die by sponsoring Jane Grey's succession to the throne. After convincing Edward to exclude the real heirs, Mary and Elizabeth, on the grounds of their illegitimacy, Northumberland, in collusion with her parents, the Duke and Duchess of Suffolk, put forward Jane Grey, grandaughter of Henry VIII's sister, whom he had married to his own son, Guildford Dudley, on May 21, 1553. Edward died on July 6, and Northumberland proclaimed Jane queen; but the overwhelming support from the people and from the Council for the legitimate heir, Mary, ensured Jane Grey's and Northumberland's downfall. After nine days of rule, the sixteen-year-old queen was deposed and imprisoned, and after Jane's father joined Wyatt's conspiracy, Queen Mary ordered her execution. Although she had grave doubts about assuming the crown, Grey's obedience to her parents and her Reformist piety probably guided her actions. All contemporary accounts praise her as an innocent soul among ambitious and self-seeking advisers. As Catholic Mary's popularity rapidly faded, Jane Grey's courageous death assumed the aura of Protestant martyrdom. In later centuries, Jane Grey became something of a romantic heroine, as in Nicholas Rowe's 1715 play, *The Tragedy of the Lady Jane Gray*. The play's prologue describes her as "A Heroine, a Martyr, and a Queen," "a Beauteous Saint"; it invites the audience's tears to flow "for suff'ring Virtue," and claims that "The only Love that warm'd her blooming Youth,/Was, Husband, *England*, Liberty, and Truth." Ed. Richard J. Sherry, *Salzburg Studies in English Literature* (Salzburg: Institut für Englische Sprache und Literatur, 1980), p. 7. See Hester Chapman, *Lady Jane Grey* (London: Jonathan Cape, 1962), and Alison Plowden, *Lady Jane Grey and the House of Suffolk* (New York: Franklin Watts, 1986).

31. Roger Ascham, *The Scholemaster* (London, 1570), facs. ed. (Menston, England: The Scolar Press Ltd., 1967), pp. 11v-12. In "Lady Jane Grey: Protestant Queen and Martyr," *Silent But for the Word*, pp. 92-106, Carole Levin studies the uncompromising piety of Grey's life and works; about the Ascham passage she notes, "her reply certainly contradicts the traditional picture of a meek and mild Lady Jane" (p. 95).

32. Although Foxe refuses to name the apostate in the *Actes and Monuments*, according to John King, he does identify Harding in a transcript of the letter, as does an earlier copy "among Cecil's papers" (*English Reformation Literature*, p. 420). John Bradford refers to an interview with Dr. Harding the apostate in February 1554. I use Foxe's transcription of the letter in *Actes and Monuments*, pp. 920-22.

33. *The Life, Death and Actions of the Most Chast, learned, and Religious Lady, the Lady Jane Gray, Daughter to the Duke of Suffolke* (London, 1615), C2.

34. In Chapter Ten of *The Tudor Books of Private Devotion*, Helen White documents the new emphasis that the Reformers placed on "the problem of organizing the life of prayer within the framework of ordinary domestic

life lived in the contemporary world" (p. 150) and indicates that the numerous prayer books were essentially pedagogical aids rather than records of personal struggle. Women seem to have found a genre that crossed imperceptibly from the domestic to the public sphere. As in the popular collections of Thomas Becon and Henry Bull, both Tyrwhitt and Aburgavennie compose prayers for time of day and religious occasions.

35. Tyrwhitt heralds the adoption of the ballad measure by other women versifiers. See Chapter Four below.

36. Comprehensiveness was actually a mark of many contemporary prayer books. See White, *Tudor Books*, pp. 164-66.

CHAPTER FOUR

1. See Lewalski, *Protestant Poetics*, pp. 3-27. Also, King, *English Reformation Literature*, pp. 209-21, for a discussion of Protestant Biblical poetry which the Reformers envisioned as "a powerful vehicle that combines aesthetic pleasure with didactic instruction" (p. 210), but in which they "subordinated poetic form and diction to biblical content"(p. 212).

2. My reading of Whitney's poetry as Christian and didactic disagrees with Betty Travitsky's claims that Whitney's "approach to life was secular and pragmatic rather than Christian," and that her poem, "The Copy of a letter" "succeeds in making a personal statement which maintains the dignity of this protesting woman poet." See both Travitsky's article, "The 'Wyll and Testament' of Isabella Whitney," *ELR* 10 (1980), 79 and 80, and her introduction to Whitney's work in *The Paradise of Women*, p. 118.

3. Isabella Whitney, *A sweet Nosegay or pleasant posye. Contayning a hundred and ten Phylosophicall flowers* (London, 1573), Dii. Hereafter cited in the text.

4. *A Choice of Emblemes by Geffrey Whitney*, ed. Henry Green (1866), rpt. (New York: Benjamin Blom, 1967), pp. li-lvi.

5. The author of each of these works is identified as "Is. W.," and the circumstantial evidence of the letters in *A sweet Nosegay* indicates this is Isabella Whitney. In "Isabella Whitney and the Popular Miscellanies of Richard Jones," *Cahiers Elisabethains* 19 (1981), 85-87, Robert J. Fehrenbach argues that three anonymous poems in poetical miscellanies printed by Richard Jones, Whitney's printer, are also by her. He names "The complaint of a woman Lover" in *A Handful of Pleasant Delights* (1566?), and "The Lady beloved exclaymeth of the great untruth of her lover" and "The lamentacion of a Gentilwoman upon the death of her late deceased frend William Gruffith Gent" in *A Gorgeous Gallery of Gallant Inventions* (1578). The evidence for the first two is not compelling, resting on resemblances in subject matter and style to "The Copy of a letter"; however, all the features Fehrenbach names occur constantly in many other poems in the miscellanies and "The complaint" is the rhetorical mate of the succeeding poem, suggesting its feminine persona may be a technique rather than the

voice of a women poet. There are also important differences in approach. The third poem, with its cautious, self-deprecating persona and elaborate secrecy could be Whitney's; William Gruffith may be the "W.G." whose poem, "A Loveletter, or an earnest perswasion of a Lover," was printed with "The Copy of a letter." This does not constitute proof of authorship, however, even if the connection with Richard Jones is suggestive.

6. *The Copy of a letter, lately written in meeter, by a yonge Gentilwoman: to her unconstant Lover* (London, 1567?), A2, stanza 3. Hereafter cited in the text.

7. Sir Hugh Plat (1552–1608) was a scientist, inventor, poet, and moralist. In his introduction to a joint facsimile of Plat's *Floures* and Whitney's *A sweet Nosegay*, Richard J. Panofsky notes that both "typify, but each in different ways, tastes in poetry and in the literature of moral philosophy of the middle years of Elizabeth's reign. Their sententious moralization, social and ethical themes, and a rhetorical elaboration of emotionality place them within the tradition of the short poem initiated by *Tottel's Miscellany* and quickly popularized in a series of anthologies and collections by single authors." *The Floures of Philosophy (1572) by Hugh Plat and A Sweet Nosegay (1573) and The Copy of a Letter (1567) by Isabella Whitney* (New York: Delmar, Scholars' Facsimiles and Reprints, 1982), p. v.

8. Whitney stays close to Plat's matter as she expands his aphorisms into fourteeners. For instance, Number 56 derives from Plat's Number 55, "So account of thy friend nowe, that thou alwayes remember that it is possible for him to be thine enimie" (*The Floures*, rpt. 1982, p. 5). Panofsky suggests that Whitney rarely adds new material "and may miss or blunt the wit of the original," and that she only occasionally elaborates her source (p. ix). Nevertheless, Plat's Number 55 seems a good deal flatter than Whitney's Number 56, so that her choice to versify may have made her considerably shorter, more swiftly moving work more attractive to many readers.

9. Panofsky describes Whitney's complaints as both Heroidean and autobiographical, whereas, I would attribute them to traditional *de contemptu mundi* or to a Calvinist sense of the gap between earthly infection and divine perfection.

10. For example, Whitney places an emphatic *sentence* in the third line of every quatrain:

Peruse these lines, observe these rules
....
To live to dye, to dye, to live.
....
Nor credit every fayned tale
....
Vengeance is his, he wil reveng

As a result, anticlimaxes abound in fourth lines, for which a rhyme with the second line must be found, and the verses often sound clumsy and contrived:

Refer you all to hym,
    that sits above the skyes:
Vengeance is his, he wil reveng,
    you need it not devise.   (Cviii v)

But if her verses lack skill and grace, they possess fervor.

11. In her vision of London and in her contrast between rich and poor, Whitney may be echoing current works. In *The lamentacion of a Christen Agaynst the Cytie of London* (1542), Henry Brinkelow, a well-known gospeler, inveighs against "Idolatrye and other innumerable vices and wickednesses of mans invencyon, dayly committed in the Cytie of London" (Aii). He attacks the rich who make "no honest provysyon for the poore" (Aii v), the Catholic church, and corrupt judges and city officials. Whitney may also have known an old poem to which the Reformers had given new significance: *Piers Plowman*, published and annotated by Robert Crowley in 1550, with its "faire felde ful of folke," its espousal of true Christian poverty and concommitant indictment of a corrupt church and social order appeared to the Reformers to be "a prophecy of the English Reformation" (King, *English Reformation Literature* p. 322), a kind of Wycliffian anticlericalism. While Whitney does not explicitly indict anything, she does envision a world plagued by human sin rather than godliness, and sketches its effects on all orders of society. This reading differs from that of Betty Travitsky who claims Whitney "celebrates the lavish costumes of Renaissance London . . ." and that "despite the references to God in the opening and closing lines . . . the poem's tone is Bohemian rather than pious" ("The 'Wyll,'" p. 82).

12. See (Jean de Serres) *The Three Partes of Commentaries, containing the whole and perfect discourse of the civill warres of Fraunce. . . .* Translated out of Latine into English by Thomas Timme Minister (London, 1574). In his preface to the reader, Timme asserts that "by the reading of these Commentaries, the Faythefull shall finde many things which they maye applye unto themselves, to stay and comfort themselves in the middest of these troubles" (aiv v).

13. *The French Historie* (London, 1589), A2v.

14. See Mario Praz, *Machiavelli and the Elizabethans*, 1928. ([Folcroft, Pa.]: Folcroft Press, 1970), which traces the total misconception the Elizabethans had of the Italian political philosopher, Niccolò Machiavelli, who became "a sort of rallying-point for whatever was most loathsome in statecraft, and indeed in human nature at large" (p. 6). While the rest of the queen's speech reworks material from the *Commentaries* about the relative strength of the Catholics and unpreparedness of the Huguenots (The tenth Booke, p. 12v), Dowriche glosses her verses to press the analogy to Machiavelli: "The queen mother was a good scholer of that divel of Florence, Machivel, of whom she learned manie bad lessons, as this. 1. That a prince must not care to be accompted cruel, so that anie profit come by it. 2. Lesson. A Prince must imitate the natures of a Foxe and a Lion: a Foxe

to allure, and deceive, a Lion to devour without mercie, when occasion is offered. 3. Lesson, That a Prince may not doubt to forsweare, to deceive, and dissemble. This is a wholesome scholemistres for a yong King" (p. 23v).

15. Such opinions by the poet, Alexander Hume, in 1598 and 1599 and by John Livingston in "Eminent Professors in Scotland" (mid-seventeenth century) are quoted in the introduction to a reprint of the 1603 edition, *Ane Godlie Dreame, Compylit in Scottish Meter be M. M. Gentlewoman in Culros, at the requeist of her freindes* (Edinburgh, 1603), in *Early Popular Poetry of Scotland and the Northern Border*, ed. David Laing, LL.D. in 1822 and 1826. Rearranged and Revised with Additions and a Glossary by W. Carew Hazlitt, vol. 2 (London: Reeves and Turner, 1895), pp. 279-301. The Anglicized edition of 1606 has also been consulted and its variants are noted below.

16. Barbara Lewalski calls the pilgrimage "the most pervasive of the metaphors for the Christian life," and indicates that journeying, wayfaring, wandering, seeking a city, and the images of the straight gate and the narrow way are all scriptural variations on the pilgrimage. *Protestant Poetics*, pp. 93-94.

17. Edition of 1606: "wretched world" (A2); "make haste" (A2v); "Lord Jesus come and save thine owne elect" (A2v).

18. 1606: "An Angell bright, with visage shyning cleare" (A3v); "rise up" (A3v).

19. 1606: "thy God for whom thou sighs" (A4);
> I am the way, I 'am the trueth and life,
> I am thy spouse that brings thee store of grace:
> I am thy Lord that soone shall end they strife,
> I am thy love whom thou wouldst faine imbrace.
> I am thy joy, I am thy rest and peace, (A4)

20. 1606: Throgh waters great we were compeld to waid,
> Which was so deepe that I was like to drowne;
> Sometime I sanke, but yet my gratious guide
> Did draw me out halfe dead and in a sowne.
> In woods most wilde, and far from any towne,
> We thirsted thogh, the breares together stack:
> I was so weake their strength did beate me downe,
> That I was forced for feare to flee aback. (A4)

21. 1606: I looked up unto that Castell fair,
> Glistring like gold and shining silver bright:
> The statelie towres did mount above the air,
> They blinded me they cuist so great a light. (B)

22. 1606: "most full of smooke and flamming fire" (B2). Much of Colville's imagery of the journey and the heavenly city recalls Spenser's *Faerie Queene*, Book I.

23. 1606: "the thornie cares of this deceitfull life ... And though ye fall,

yet ly not loitring still:/ Bot call on Christ to helpe you in your neede" (B3v).

24. 1606: "Triumph for joy your enemies are kilde" (B4v).

25. 1606: "his owne" (Cv).

26. *A Mouzell for Melastomus* will be examined in detail in Chapter Nine.

27. Rachel Speght, *Mortalities Memorandum, with a Dreame Prefixed, imaginarie in manner: reall in matter* (London, 1621), A2. Hereafter cited in the text.

28. Speght uses remarkably learned women for her exempla: Cleobulina, celebrated for her learning, judgment, and courage, composed enigmas; Demophila was a sibyl of Cumae; Hypatia, a mathematician, teacher, Platonist, and astronomer of Alexandria; Cornelia, mother of the Gracchi, saved her sons with her eloquence.

Chapter Five

1. Mary Ellen Lamb, "The Myth of the Countess of Pembroke: The Dramatic Circle," *YES* 11 (1981), 194-202, and "The Countess of Pembroke's Patronage," *ELR* 12 (1982), 162-79. Also, Sallye Jeanette Sheppeard, "The Forbidden Muse: Mary Sidney Herbert and Renaissance Poetic Theory and Practice," unpublished Ph.D. Diss. Texas Women's University, Denton, 1980. For a complete bibliography, see Josephine Roberts, "Recent Studies in Women Writers of Tudor England, Part II: Mary Sidney, Countess of Pembroke," *ELR* 14 (1984), 426-39. Margaret Hannay's biography of Mary Sidney is in progress.

2. In "Astrophel. A Pastorall Elegie upon the death of the most Noble and valorous Knight, Sir Philip Sidney," Spenser created the image of Sidney that still exists, of a man so handsome, good, and "gentle," "that all mens hearts with secret ravishment/He stole away, and weetingly beguyld" (ll.15-22). In a letter to Robert Sidney, Sir Henry Sidney instructs Robert to "Imitate hys Vertues, Exercyses, Studyes, and Accyons; he ys a rare Ornament of thys Age, the very Formular, that all well dysposed young Gentylmen of ouer Court, do form allsoe thear Maners and Lyfe by. In Troth I speak yt wythout Flatery of hym, or of myself, he hathe the most rare Vertues that ever I found in any Man," March 25, 1578. *Letters and Memorials of State in the Reigns of Queen Mary, Queen Elizabeth, King James* . . . written and collected by Sir Henry Sydney. . . . The famouse Sir Philip Sidney and his brother Sir Robert Sydney . . . collected by Arthur Collins (London, 1746), I, 246.

3. The letter, dated October 26, 1569, concerns the possible betrothal of Philip to Anne Cecil. See Frances B. Young, *Mary Sidney, Countess of Pembroke* (London: D. Nutt, 1912), pp. 24-25.

4. See Sheppeard, "The Forbidden Muse," pp. 47ff. for similar speculations about the countess's literary activity at this time.

5. William Ringler justly remarks that Sidney's "pose of graceful neg-

ligence" masks the labor of three years and 180,000 words, and that the *Arcadia* "was a composition more carefully structured and more artfully executed than anything in English of its time." *The Poems of Sir Philip Sidney* (Oxford: The Clarendon Press, 1962), p. 383. Like her brother, the countess was entirely reticent about the labor of composition and also devoted to excellence. Frances Young (in *Mary Sidney*, p. 56) quotes her letter to Edward Wotton in which she refers to one of her works as "a certaine Idle passion."

6. "The Countess of Pembroke's Patronage," p. 178.

7. Emphasizing her physical resemblance to Philip, Spenser included the countess among the dedicatees of the *Faerie Queene* specifically as her brother's literary heir. In the preface to his unsanctioned version of Sidney's *Astrophel and Stella*, Thomas Nashe addressed the countess as "fayre sister of *Phoebus* ... whom Artes doe adore as a second *Minerva* and our Poets extoll as the Patronesse of their invention; for in thee, the *Lesbian Sappho* with her lirick Harpe is disgraced, and the Laurel Garlande which thy Brother so bravely advaunst on his Launce, is still kept greene in the Temple of *Pallas.*" *Syr P. S. His Astrophel and Stella*, London 1591, facs. ed. (Menston: Scolar Press, 1970), A4.

8. Samuel Daniel, *Delia and Rosamond Augmented. Cleopatra.* (London, 1594), A4. Hereafter cited in the text.

9. *HERΩOLOGIA Anglica ...* H. H. (London, 1620), p. 116; Thomas Churchyard, *A Pleasant conceite penned in verse* (London, 1593), Bv; Abraham Fraunce, *The Lamentations of Amyntas for the death of Phillis* (London, 1587), dedicatory title; Abraham Fraunce, *The Arcadian Rhetorike* (London, 1588), dedicatory verse; *Caroli Fitzgeofridi Affaniae sive Epigrammatum* (Oxford, 1601), G7.

10. See Andrew Weiner, "The Sidney Milieu," in *Sir Philip Sidney and the Poetics of Protestantism* (Minneapolis: University of Minnesota Press, 1978), pp. 3-18. In "'Doo What Men May Sing': Mary Sidney and the Tradition of Admonitory Dedication" in *Silent But for the Word*, pp. 149-65, Margaret Hannay argues that two of Mary Sidney's poems constitute a political admonition to Queen Elizabeth to support the militant Protestants exemplified by the Sidney family and Philip Sidney in particular.

11. "The Countesse of Penbrook's Passion," in Nicholas Breton, *The Works in Prose and Verse*, ed. Alexander B. Grosart (1879), rpt. Georg Olms Verlagsbuchhandlung (Hildesheim, 1969), p. 3, st. 12.

12. Weiner suggests Philip Sidney's "close relationship with de Mornay, who was in England for eighteen months during 1577 and 1578, during which time de Mornay worked on his book, fathered a child for which Sidney stood as godfather, and [like Sidney] argued heartily against Elizabeth's marriage to Monsieur" ("The Sidney Milieu," p. 192, n. 25). Perhaps Sidney recommended the man and his work to his sister.

13. *A Discourse of Life and Death. Written in French by Ph. Mornay. Antonius. A Tragoedie written also in French by Ro. Garnier. Both done in*

English by the Countesse of Pembroke. (London, 1592), E3. Hereafter cited in the text. See Diane Bornstein, ed., *The Countess of Pembroke's Translation of Philippe de Mornay's Discourse of Life and Death* (Detroit, 1983).

14. In "The Style of the Countess of Pembroke's Translation of Philippe de Mornay's *Discours de la vie et de la mort*," *Silent But for the Word*, pp. 126-34, Diane Bornstein compares Mary Sidney's translation to the French and to Edward Aggas' earlier translation and finds that "she followed the meaning and the graceful, balanced prose style of the original" (p. 128) and on occasion improved it.

15. Both Bornstein (above) and Mary Ellen Lamb, "The Countess of Pembroke and the Art of Dying," in *Women in the Middle Ages and the Renaissance*, find Stoicism at the heart of de Mornay's work. Lamb speculates that Stoicism would appeal greatly to a sixteenth-century woman because it exalted "the ability to suffer without complaint, to endure any affliction with fortitude" (p. 209); she also analyzes the countess's part in the *ars moriendi* tradition. My reading of de Mornay emphasizes his Christian attitudes and Mary Sidney's Protestantism as the basis of her ideology and creativity.

16. Raymond Lebègue notes how important moral teaching is in Garnier's plays, and in *Marc-Antoine* "il choisit dans les guerres civiles de Rome non plus des modèles d'amour conjugal, mais l'histoire d'un couple qui paie de sa vie son abandon à une passion non moins funeste." Robert Garnier, *Marc-Antoine, Hippolyte*, ed. Raymond Lebègue (Paris: Société les Belles Lettres, 1974), p. 208. Christine M. Hill and Mary G. Morrison describe Garnier as a stern moralist who presents a universe guided by moral laws, in which characters ascribe their downfall "to their own sins and faults," demonstrate the "disastrous effects of the passion of love," and often speak in *sentences*. Both Antony and Cleopatra are exempla of "the disastrous effects of excessive passion." Robert Garnier, *Two Tragedies: Hippolyte and Marc-Antoine* (London: The Athlone Press, 1975), pp. 8-10, 18. See Lamb, "The Art of Dying," pp. 213-20, for a reading of Cleopatra as heroic, the embodiment of the Stoic ideal. The 1599 text is reprinted in Geoffrey Bullough, *Narrative and Dramatic Sources of Shakespeare*, vol. 5 (New York: Columbia University Press, 1964).

17. It may be that Garnier and Mary Sidney saw in the story of Antony and Cleopatra an example of passion bringing about a new fall; particularly in Calvinist doctrine, lust was synonymous with original sin. See Arthur Golding's "Epistle Dedicatory" to his 1571 translation of Calvin's *Commentary on the Book of Psalms*: "For doubtlesse, although *Antichrist* were abolished, although *Sathan* were a sleepe, although the world were at one with us, although wicked counsel were utterly put too silence, although no evil example were given us, although no outwarde stumbling-blocke were cast in our waye; yit have wee one thing in our selves and of our selves, (even originall sinne, concupiscence, or lust,) which never ceaseth too egge us from God, and too staine us with all kinde of unclennes,

according as Sainct James sayth: Every man is tempted of his owne lust."
John Calvin, *Commentary on the Book of Psalms*, tr. from Latin and collated
with the author's French version by Rev. James Anderson (Grand Rapids,
Mich.: William B. Eardman Publishing Co., 1949), pp. xxx-xxxi.

18. *"The Triumphe of Death" Translated out of Italian by the Countesse of
Pembrooke*, ed. Frances B. Young, *PMLA* 27 (1912), 1, 5-9. Hereafter cited
in the text. Young prints the Countess's manuscript beside Petrarch's
Trionfo della Morte (Firenze, 1903), an edition based on the version the
countess used. For convenience, the text here is from Young's edition but
with emendations from Gary F. Waller's edition in *The "Triumph of Death"
and other Unpublished and Uncollected Poems by Mary Sidney, Countess of
Pembroke (1561-1621)*, Salzburg Studies in English Literature (Salzburg:
Institut für Englische Sprache und Literatur, 1977). See Robert Coogan,
"Petrarch's *Trionfi* and the English Renaissance," *SP* 67 (1970), 306-27:
"The accuracy of the translation and the excellence of the verse make Mary
Sidney's 'Triumph of Death' the finest translation of this triumph in the
English language" (p. 324). See also Lamb, "The Art of Dying," pp. 220-
22.

19. In the Commentary on "The Dolefull Lay" in Spenser's *Works*, several
scholars attribute this elegy to Spenser on the grounds of "Spenserian"
style, punctuation, and rhetorical ability, with an accompanying denial of
the countess's poetic skills. Such opinions are not convincing in the light
of her education, environment, and other works; any similarities to Spenser
probably derive from their common tradition and the countess's ability to
harmonize with the style of other poets. In *Colin Clout's Come Home Again*
(1595), where the elegies on Sidney first appeared, the printer clearly sets
"Clorinda" apart from Spenser's "Astrophel." Waller summarizes the arguments in *Uncollected Poems*, pp. 53-59, and reprints the Lay as Mary
Sidney's, pp. 176-79.

20. The scriptural metaphor of Christ the shepherd was an exegetical
commonplace that generated many related images in Renaissance pastoral
elegies. See, for instance, Spenser's *Shepheardes Calender* in which he contrasts earth's pastoral landscape, the "trustlesse state of earthly things," and
the promise of eternal life after death: "No daunger there the shepheard
can astert:/Fayre fields and pleasaunt layes there bene,/The fieldes ay fresh,
the grasse ay greene. ..." Edmund Spenser, *The Shepheardes Calender*,
"November" l.153, ll.188-90. *Poetical Works*, ed. J. C. Smith and E. De
Selincourt (London: Oxford University Press, 1965), p. 462. In another vein,
Drayton tells the "Reader of his Pastorals," that "in the *Angels* Song to
Shepheards at our Saviours Nativitie Pastorall Poesie seemes consecrated."
Pastorals. Contayning Eglogues, in *Works*, ed. J. W. Hebel (Oxford: Blackwell,
1961), p. 517.

21. Foxe's *Actes and Monuments*, possessed by every church in England,
is but one example of the propaganda that encouraged the English to believe
in their country as God's elect nation, the archfoe of the Roman Antichrist.

See William Haller, *The Elect Nation: The Meaning and Relevance of Foxe's Book of Martyrs* (New York: Harper & Row, 1963), in which he records the common belief that "England was called to lead mankind and Elizabeth to lead England to ultimate redemption" (p. 109). The recent victory over Spain in 1588, attributed by some contemporary sources to God's wind blowing against the Spanish fleet, confirmed the sense of a godly mission.

22. See Frances A. Yates, "Queen Elizabeth as Astraea," *JWCI* 10 (1947), 27-82. After Elizabeth's death, a line from an Oxford memorial volume claimed, "Rettulit imperio Deboram, pietate Davidem." E. C. Wilson, *England's Eliza*, rpt. (New York: Octagon Books, 1966), p. 378, also pp. 64-65. See Hannay, "Admonitory Dedication," for a discussion of Mary Sidney's political and spiritual purposes in so addressing Elizabeth.

23. First published in [Francis Davison] *A Poetical Rapsody Containing Diverse Sonnets, Odes, Elegies, Madrigalls, and other Poesies* ... (London, 1602), B5-B6. Reprinted in Waller, *Uncollected Poems*, pp. 181-83.

24. In "Mary Sidney's 'Two Shepherds,' " *AN&Q* 9 (1971), 100-102, Gary F. Waller suggests that Thenot represents "courtly and neo-Platonic" praise and Piers the "Protestant, who stresses the Calvinist-derived doctrine of the absolute transcendence of the divine and the inability of man's unaided mind to attain to genuine truth." Thenot's roots seem to be in sonnet language. I hesitate to divide the two voices into opposing "doctrines" when they seem to be working together on the central poetic problem of language.

25. In 1962 this poem and "To the Angell spirit of the most excellent Sir Phillip Sidney" were printed from a manuscript of the Psalms dated 1599: Bent Juel-Jensen, *Two Poems by the Countess of Pembroke* (Oxford: Oxford University Press, 1962); "Even now that Care" is reprinted in *The Female Spectator*, pp. 66-69; and in Waller, *Uncollected Poems*, pp. 88-91.

26. *The Monument of Matrones*, p. 306.

27. See Arthur Golding's "Epistle Dedicatory" to his translation of Calvin's *Commentary on the Book of Psalms*: "It was written by Prophets, Preestes, and Kinges, inspired with the Holye Ghost, the fountaine of all understanding, wysedom, and truth, and avouched unto us by Christ, the Sonne of the everlasting God ... it conteineth a treatise of the Doctrine of lyfe and everlasting Salvation ..." (pp. xxxi-xxxii). Also *Davids Harpe ful of moost delectable armony* ... by Theodore Basille [Thomas Becon] (1541): "Certes the Psalmody of David maye well be called the Treasure house of the holye Scripture. For it contaynethe what so ever is necessary for a christen man to knowe" (a7v). In "Milton's Psalm Translations: Petition and Praise," *ELR* 2 (1972), 243-59, Carolyn P. Collette explains that the Psalms were vital to the reformers of the sixteenth and seventeenth centuries because of "the importance they were found to have had for the earliest Christians" (p. 244) and because "they were well suited to a religion which stressed inward meditation, the study of the Bible, and personal salvation—rather than good works and priestly mediation—as the way to salvation" (p. 245).

28. *The Psalmes of David, Truly Opened and explained by Paraphrasis* ... Set foorth in Latin by that excellent learned man THEODORE BEZA. And faithfully translated into English by ANTHONIE GILBIE (London, 1590), a3v. Hereafter cited in the text.

29. Rathmell's 1963 edition, *The Psalms of Sir Philip Sidney and the Countess of Pembroke* (New York: New York University Press, 1963) is based on fourteen manuscript versions; hereafter cited in the text. In "The Text and Manuscript Variants of The Countess of Pembroke's Psalms," *RES* 26 (1975), 1-18, Gary F. Waller suggests that "the manuscripts reveal a process of constant alteration and experimentation which adds up to nothing less than a poet's self-education" (p. 6). If the Psalms were finished in 1599, the year the countess wrote the dedication to Queen Elizabeth, that process of becoming a poet may have extended over twenty years.

30. John Donne, the first critic of the Sidneian Psalms, refers to "their sweet learned labours" and claims, "They tell us *why*, and teach us *how* to sing" ("Upon the translation of the Psalmes by Sir Philip Sydney, and the Countesse of Pembroke his Sister," Rathmell, *The Psalms*, ix-x). Modern scholarship on the Psalms includes J.C.A. Rathmell's introduction, in which he claims that "one of the most significant features of the collection lies in the way the two poets, especially the Countess of Pembroke, attempt to reveal by an accurate and intelligent use of the scholarly commentaries the latent meaning of the Hebrew originals, and to convey within the conventions of Elizabethan verse the sense of intimate, personal urgency that gives the Psalms, even in prose form, their poetic force" (p. xix); Coburn Freer, *Music for a King: George Herbert's Style and the Metrical Psalms* (Baltimore and London: The Johns Hopkins University Press, 1972), 89-108, who argues that the countess is "not a particularly good poet," but that she is "historically important" (p. 90); Sallye Jeanette Sheppeard who does a good job of countering some of Freer's specific readings ("The Forbidden Muse," pp. 164ff.); Barbara Lewalski, *Protestant Poetics*, pp. 241-44, who describes the Psalmist "transfigured as an Elizabethan poet, expressing a contemporary religious sensibility with rare and delicate artistry" (p. 241); Gary F. Waller, *Mary Sidney, Countess of Pembroke: A Critical Study of her Writings and Literary Milieu, Salzburg Studies in English Literature* (Salzburg: Institut für Englische Sprache und Literatur, 1979), pp. 152-256, who comments on many of the Psalms which "constitute a major claim for the Countess of Pembroke's literary stature"; and Beth Wynne Fisken, "Mary Sidney's Psalms: Education and Wisdom," in *Silent But for the Word*, pp. 166-83, who stresses Sidney's growth as a poet, and considers how her public and private roles engendered her poetic voice.

31. This was one of the three "truly devine" Psalms by the countess that Sir John Harington sent to Lucy, Countess of Bedford (Rathmell, *The Psalms*, xxvii). See Waller, *Mary Sidney*, pp. 231-41; Sheppeard, "The Forbidden Muse," pp. 177-96.

32. *The Geneva Bible* (1560), facs. ed. (Madison: University of Wisconsin Press, 1969), p. 245.

33. Beza, who calls this Psalm "one of the principle Psalmes of David," emphasizes its meaning, "what exceeding mercie the most gratious and most mightie God doth shew to everie one that doth repent." *The Psalmes of David*, pp. 112-13.

CHAPTER SIX

1. Typical of the treatment of good women is Robert Greene's *Penelope's Web* (1587) in which the three qualities "requisite in every woman," obedience, silence, and chastity, are explained in three tales told by Penelope, herself the paragon of womanly virtue. Spenser's ambivalence about heroic women is evident in the battle between Britomart and Radigund, and in his separation of Britomart (and Elizabeth) from other women, for "vertuous women wisely understand,/That they were borne to base humilitie,/ Unlesse the heavens them lift to lawfull soveraintie" (*The Faerie Queene*, v.v.25). See Simon Shepherd, *Amazons and Warrior Women: Varieties of Feminism in Seventeenth-Century Drama* (New York: St. Martin's Press, 1981) for a study of these two opposing dramatic types.

2. Lisa Jardine discusses the transformation of Elizabeth into a symbol and an exception beyond other women, real or fictional, in Chapter 6 of *Still Harping on Daughters*, pp. 169-79.

3. See Jardine, ibid., pp. 182-93, for a discussion of Griselda and Lucretia.

4. Influenced by "English Seneca" and French Garnier, English closet drama usually concerned issues of public morality, treated philosophically, didactically, or politically. In his analysis of Daniel's *Cleopatra*, for instance, Russell Leavenworth studies "the penetrating political and moral discussion which becomes the organizing purpose of *Cleopatra* and may be seen informing character, choruses, and description throughout the poem." *Daniel's "Cleopatra": A Critical Study*, Salzburg Studies in English Literature (Salzburg: Institut für Englische Sprache und Literatur, 1974), p. 13.

5. *Iphigenia at Aulis Translated by Lady Lumley*, ed. Harold H. Child (Malone Society, 1909), p. v.

6. J. G. Nichols quotes the letter in *The Gentlemen's Magazine* 154 (1833), pt. 2, p. 495. But see "Lady Lumley and Greek Tragedy," *CJ* 36 (1941), 537-47, in which David H. Greene shows that Lumley used Erasmus' Latin translation of the play, probably in the 1524 edition which contained the Greek text.

7. Sears Jayne, *Library Catalogues of the English Renaissance* (Berkeley: University of California Press, 1956), p. 45.

8. "John Lumley," *DNB*, 12:272-74.

9. *Sir Nicholas Bacon's Great House Sententiae*, tr., intr. Elizabeth McCutcheon, *ELR* Supplements 3 (1977), p. 66.

10. Greene suggests Lumley read the play in Greek and briefly praises

her efforts before condemning her "total lack of taste and critical ability" (p. 542). Frank D. Crane, in "Euripides, Erasmus, and Lady Lumley," *CJ* 39 (1944), 223-28, judges that Lumley "shows no knowledge of Greek, and none of poetry in any language" (p. 228). Such harshness probably derives from Lumley's failure to produce an accurate, complete, poetic account of the play; however, if her interest was mainly in Iphigenia's character, she may not have cared to do so.

11. The Greek claims that a noble man is better than 10,000 women, while Erasmus' Latin says one man is worthier than many thousands of women, indicating either that Lumley confused her numbers, or thought the comparison excessive. Desiderius Erasmus, *Opera Omnia*, 1703, rpt. Georg Olms Verlagsbuchhandlung (Hildesheim, 1961), vol. 1, 1181.

12. *The Education of a Christian Prince by Desiderius Erasmus*, tr. Lester K. Born (New York: Columbia University Press, 1936), p. 149.

13. So consistent are the Christian echoes that they are surely intentional. For instance, the line that echoes Revelation translates from Greek as "For this day saw your child dead and beholding (the light of the sun)," but from Erasmus as "this one day has seen your daughter both dead and alive": "hic unus filiam mulier tuam/Et mortuam conspexit et vivam dies" (1186); compare to the Vulgate: "ego sum primus et novissimus, et vivus, et fui mortuus, et ecce sum vivens in saecula saeculorum." Earlier, Lumley's "remedie all thes thinges withe my deathe," with its Christian diction, derives from Erasmus, "Haec profecto cuncta redimam morte (si cadam) mea" (1181), "If I die, I shall truly redeem this whole state of affairs with my death." The Greek says, "By dying I shall protect all these things. . . ." Professor Nancy Zumwalt of the Classics Department, University of Massachusetts, Boston, kindly translated and annotated these Greek passages.

14. *The History of the Rebellion and Civil Wars in England, begun in the year 1641 by Edward, Earl of Clarendon*, ed. W. Dunn Macray (Oxford, 1888), 3:180; Douglas Bush, *English Literature in the Earlier Seventeenth Century* (Oxford: The Clarendon Press, 1966), p. 343.

15. *The Lady Falkland: Her Life*, ed. R. S. from a manuscript in the Imperial Archives at Lille (London: Catholic Publishing and Bookselling Co., Ltd., 1861). In his biography of Lucius Cary, Kurt Weber suggests that a "proper discount" should be made on the biography because it was written under "pious influences" as a religious duty. Still, Weber himself makes substantial use of the *Life*. *Lucius Cary*, Columbia Studies in English 147 (New York, 1940), pp. 11-12. Donald Stauffer praises the biography, calling it "a notable piece of individualization." He continues, "its subtle appraisals and almost brazen analyses of motives are written with a certain dry intelligence that puts to shame the effusive contemporary masculine biographers." After criticizing the style, Stauffer concludes, "as a whole the life is distinctive and original, and succeeds in the highest aim of biography: the reconstruction of a personality in thought and actions."

English Biography before 1700 (Cambridge: Harvard University Press, 1930), pp. 148-50.

16. The play was written between 1602 and 1612, probably in the earlier part of that period. See Beilin, "Elizabeth Cary and *The Tragedie of Mariam*," *PLL* 16 (1980), n. 6.

17. In *The True Tragedy of Herod and Antipater: With the Death of faire Marriam* (1622), Gervase Markham and William Sampson focus on the father and son; in Massinger's *The Duke of Milan* (1623), the central character is the Herod figure.

18. The Homilie reads, "Now as concerning the wives duety, what shall become her? Shall she abuse the gentlenesse and humanity of her husband and, at her pleasure, turne all things upside downe? No surely. For that is far repugnant against Gods commandement, For thus doeth *Saint Peter* preach to them, Yee wives, be ye in subjection to obey your owne husbands. ..." *Certaine Sermones or Homilies, appointed to be read in Churches, in the time of Queene Elizabeth I*, Scholars Facsimile (Gainesville, Fla., 1968), p. 242. In *Basilikon Doron*, James writes, "Ye are the heade, she is your body: It is your office to command, and hers to obey, but yet with suche a sweete harmonie, as she should be as readie to obey as ye to command; as willing to follow, as ye to go before: your love beeing whollie knit unto her, and all her affections lovingly bent to followe your will." *The Basilikon Doron of King James VI*, ed. James Craigie (Edinburgh and London: Blackwood & Sons, Ltd., 1944), pp. 133-35.

19. In *A Bride-Bush: or, A Direction for Married Persons* (London, 1619), William Whately does enjoin mutual aid and benevolence, but instructs the husband to keep and use his authority, because it is ultimately God's (chs. 8, 9). In William Gouge's *Of Domesticall Duties. Eight Treatises* (London, 1622), subjection is the main topic of the third treatise on the "particular Duties of Wives": "And good reason it is that she who first drew man into sin should be now subject to him, lest by like womanish weaknesse she fall againe" (p. 269).

20. Cary dedicated "The mirror of the Worlde translated out of French" to her great-uncle, Sir Henry Lee. The manuscript is in the church at Burford, Oxfordshire. See Kenneth Murdock, "Passion and Infirmities: The Pilgrimage of Elizabeth Cary, Viscountess Falkland, 1585?-1639," *The Sun at Noon: Three Biographical Sketches* (New York: Macmillan, 1939), pp. 10-11. A play set in Sicily, mentioned by John Davies in his dedication to Cary of *The Muses Sacrifice*, seems to be lost. So does the "Life of Tamberlaine" in verse, mentioned in the *Life* as "that which was said to be the best" of all that she had by then written (p. 9). In the late 1620s, the *Life* also records that "she began her translation of Cardinal Perron's works, of which she translated the reply to the king's answer in thirty days ... some time after she procured it to be printed, dedicating it to her Majesty; but Dr. Abbots, then lord of Canterbury, seized on it coming into England, and burnt it; but some few copies came to her hands. ... She

likewise here began the rest of his works, which she finished long after, but was never able to print it" (pp. 38-39).

In *The Reply of the Cardinall of Perron, to the Answeare of the Most Excellent King of Great Britaine*, Translated into English (Douay, 1630), the author tells the reader, "I will not make use of that worne-out forme of saying, I printed it against my will, mooved by the importunitie of Friends: I was mooved to it by my beleefe, that it might make those English that understand not French ... reade *Perron*." Calling the author "a most noble heroine," a prefatory poem makes much of her speed and skill in translation: "One woman, in one Month, so large a Booke,/ In such a full emphatik stile to turne. ...."

The *Life* also attributes to this period the composition of the versified saints' lives "and both before and after, many verses to our Blessed Lady ... and of many other saints" (p. 39), all now apparently lost.

A work entitled *The History of the Life, Reign, and Death of Edward II*, signed "E.F." and dated 1627 was found among Henry Falkland's papers and "Printed verbatim from the Original" in 1680. In his study of the influence of drama on historical biography, Donald A. Stauffer speculated that the author was not Henry Falkland, as was long supposed, but Elizabeth Falkland. His evidence included the initials, Elizabeth's interest in drama, and the aptness to her life of the "deep and sad passion" professed by "E.F." in the preface. If the last point signifies at all, it must be because of Elizabeth Falkland's own experiences, not, as Stauffer suggests, because she was the mother of the passionate and sensitive Lucius Cary. Stauffer detects similarities between *Edward II* and *Mariam*: "fatal uniformity of technique, thoughts circumscribed in two verses, almost invariably end-stopped lines, and lengthy philosophical disquisitions." "A Deep and Sad Passion," *Essays in Dramatic Literature: The Parrott Presentation Volume*, ed. Hardin Craig (New York: Russell and Russell, 1935), p. 314. This description could, however, apply to many other plays, and there are numerous differences between the two works. In a note, Stauffer indicates that "E.F." is identified as Edward Fannant in the British Museum copy, and he does conclude conditionally by saying, "If this work be hers. ...." In *The Paradise of Women*, Betty Travitsky appears to refer to Stauffer when she asserts that *Edward II* "has been shown to have been written by Lady Falkland," but she introduces no new evidence (p. 210). In her review of Travitsky, Muriel Bradbrook accepts the attribution, adding that the work "was surely meant as mirror for the subjection of the reigning king to his favorite Buckingham. It is more courageous, and more seditious, than is recognized." *TSWL* 1 (Spring 1982), 93. The best evidence is the initials. Perhaps significant is E.F.'s admission, "nor fear I Censure, since at the worst, 'twas but one Month mis-spent," the same claim that Elizabeth Falkland made for the Perron translation.

21. "Sir Laurence Tanfield," *DNB*, 19:357.

22. The biographer also tells a story of how her mother as a child of

ten cleverly brought justice to her father's court by seeing through the intimidation of the defendant. If the story is apocryphal, Elizabeth Cary may still have had the wit and fearlessness to prompt such an anecdote.

23. In Act 4 of *Mariam*, Herod, believing Mariam to be false, goes off "To try if I can sleepe away my woe."

24. The biographer's credibility increases when other sources corroborate the main drift of her characterizations, particularly that of her father. *DNB* relays the character of Lord Falkland as Lord Deputy of Ireland after 1622: "In office he showed himself both bigoted in his opinions and timid in carrying out a policy which continually dallied with extremes; though conscientious, he was easily offended, and he lamentably failed to conduct himself with credit when confronted with any unusual difficulties." "Henry Cary," 3:1150.

25. A. C. Dunstan, *Examination of two English Dramas: "The Tragedy of Mariam" by Elizabeth Carew; and "The True Tragedy of Herod and Antipater: with the Death of Faire Mariam," by Gervase Markham, and William Sampson* (Königsberg, 1908), p. 49; A. M. Witherspoon, *The Influence of Robert Garnier on Elizabethan Drama*, Yale Studies in English 65 (New Haven, 1924), 154; Bush, *English Literature in the Earlier Seventeenth Century*, p. 23; Brodwin, *Elizabethan Love Tragedy 1587–1625* (New York: New York University Press, 1971, and London: University of London, 1972), p. 389, n. 2; Pearse, "Elizabeth Cary, Renaissance Playwright," *TSLL* 18 (Winter 1977), 605, and also Nancy Cotton, *Women Playwrights in England c. 1363–1750* (Lewisburg: Bucknell University Press, 1980), pp. 31-37; Fischer, "Elizabeth Cary and Tyranny, Domestic and Religious," in *Silent But for the Word*, p. 227.

26. *The Tragedie of Mariam, The Faire Queene of Jewry* (London, 1613), The Argument. Hereafter cited in the text.

27. *The Famous and Memorable Workes of Josephus, A Man of Much Honour and Learning Among the Jewes, Faithfully translated out of the Latine, and French, by Tho. Lodge, Doctor in Physicke* (London, 1602). Hereafter cited in the text.

28. In the Wakefield cycle *Herod the Great*, Herod is so characterized. Many Renaissance works of art depict the Slaughter of the Innocents, usually showing Herod giving the command for the massacre to begin.

29. Josephus's description of Salome's actions is Cary's source, although she gives Salome all her dramatic life. Josephus says, "Not long after it happened, that *Salome* fell at debate with *Constabarus* for which cause she sent a libell of divorse to her husband, notwithstanding it were against the lawes and ordinary customes of the Jewes. For according to our ordinances, it is onely lawfull for the husband to do the same. . . . But *Salome* without respect of the lawes of the countrey, grounding her selfe too much upon her owne authoritie, forsooke her husband . . ." (p. 400).

30. In Chapter 7 of *Women and the English Renaissance*, Linda Wood-bridge argues that in the late sixteenth and early seventeenth centuries, the

appearance on London streets of women dressed as men influenced a series of literary counterparts: "All through these years, literature maintained a steady interest in female mannishness, male effeminacy, and the whole question of the 'nature' of men and women, often suggesting that traditional sex roles were undergoing pronounced mutation in the modern world" (p. 153). While Salome could easily have evolved from the long literary tradition of women attempting to dominate men (Eve, Deianira, Cleopatra), perhaps Cary was influenced by contemporary concern, particularly through her great interest in the drama. See Lisa Jardine's discussion of strong women and the "female bogey" on stage in Chapter 3 of *Still Harping on Daughters*.

31. The battle for sovereignty between husband and wife is a common dramatic theme, although most treatments are comic, intended to satirize the uxorious husband and the folly of female rule. See *Johan Johan the Husbande* (1533) and Jonson's *Epicoene* (1609). Also comically handled is the popular theme of the rebellious woman returned to her proper place; see Marston's *The Courtesan* (1604), Fletcher's *The Sea Voyage* (1622) and *Rule a Wife and Have a Wife* (1624), and Massinger's *The City Madam* (1632). In tragedy, the fatal dangers of wife ruling husband are suggested in Lady Macbeth and Goneril, and in Beaumont and Fletcher's *The Maid's Tragedy* (1610). *Mariam* resembles *Othello* in opposing two married couples, as well as in the parallel characters of Othello and Herod, Desdemona and Mariam. Both plays raise the issue of female sexuality: Desdemona's passion for Othello and Emilia's lusty commentary suggest women are men's equals in "affections, /Desires for sport, and frailty." Unlike the inevitable tragedy of passion in *Othello*, however, the outcome of *Mariam* depends partly on history and partly on Cary's profound interest in redeeming Mariam. Once Salome has fulfilled her functions of propounding feminine power and endangering Mariam, she fades from the play, and Mariam becomes increasingly spiritual.

32. *The Araignment of Lewde, idle, froward and unconstant women* (1615) is Joseph Swetnam's virulent attack on women. See Chapter 9 below.

33. Cary clearly alters the explicitly sexual rebellion she found in her source: "When as about midday the king had withdrawne himself into his chamber to take his rest, he called *Mariamme* unto him to sport with her, being incited thereunto by the great affection that he bare unto her. Upon this his commaund she came in unto him; yet would she not lie with him, nor entertaine his courtings with friendly acceptance, but upbraided him bitterly with her fathers and brothers death" (*Josephus*, p. 398).

34. Florence McCulloch notes that "all versions of Physiologus agree that the phoenix symbolizes Christ, who had the power to come back to life." *Medieval Latin and French Bestiaries* (Chapel Hill: University of North Carolina Press, 1960), p. 158.

35. See Matthew 27:5. There is no such reference to the butler's end in Josephus.

CHAPTER SEVEN

1. Barbara Lewalski writes that "Most of the praises of great ladies are characterized by the speaker's quasi-Petrarchan stance, the topos of the celestial lady, and many of the familiar Petrarchan conceits." *Donne's "Anniversaries" and the Poetry of Praise: The Creation of a Symbolic Mode* (Princeton: Princeton University Press, 1973), p. 31. Praise of Queen Elizabeth often followed this pattern, as did panegyrics on the Countess of Pembroke (see Chapter 5) and other ladies cast as traditional types of virtue.

2. Ibid., p. 302. It is difficult to do justice here to the brilliant scholarship and insight behind this reading of Donne's poems.

3. Ben Jonson, *Epigrammes*, 76, "On Lucy Countesse of Bedford," *Ben Jonson*, ed. C. H. Herford, Percy Simpson, and Evelyn Simpson (Oxford: The Clarendon Press, 1952), vol. 8, p. 52.

4. John Donne, "An Anatomie of the World. Wherein, By occasion of the untimely death of Mistris ELIZABETH DRURY, the frailty and the decay of this whole World is represented. The first Anniversary." *Donne: Poetical Works*, ed. Herbert Grierson (London: Oxford University Press, 1933), rpt. 1968, ll.175-83.

5. *Salve Deus Rex Judaeorum* appears in the Stationer's Register for October 2, 1610. Lewalski and others think that Donne began to write on Elizabeth Drury shortly after her death in December 1610 (*Donne's "Anniversaries,"* p. 221).

6. *Le tombeau de Marguerite de Valois Royne de Navarre* (Paris, 1551). Anne Lake Prescott suggests a political setting for the volume in "The Pearl of the Valois and Elizabeth I," pp. 73-76.

7. *Le tombeau*, Av-Avii. Ronsard says that Orpheus could only sing of the natural world, but "ces Vierges chantent mieus/Le vray Manouvrier des cieux,/Nostre demeure eternelle,/Et ceulx qui vivent en elle" (ll.53-56). The tradition that the Sirens play an earthly version of inaudible heavenly music for human beings to hear elevates the Seymours' verses to divine poetry.

8. A. L. Rowse generated considerable heat, but less light, when he claimed that Aemilia Lanyer was Shakespeare's mistress and indeed, his Dark Lady of the Sonnets. His evidence is at best weak and has been generally discredited. See Rowse's tendentious introduction to an unexceptionable text of *Salve Deus Rex Judaeorum* in *The Poems of Shakespeare's Dark Lady* (New York: Clarkson N. Potter, 1979). Rowse's theory has been ably countered in *ShN* 23 (May 1973) and (September 1973); *SQ* 25 (1974) 131-33; Paul Ramsey, *The Fickle Glass: A Study of Shakespeare's Sonnets* (New York: AMS Press, 1979), p. 20. Perhaps the last word should belong to J. P. Kenyon who wrote that "this seems a conundrum of slight practical importance." *Times*, Feb. 23, 1973, p. 17.

9. Aemilia Lanyer, *Salve Deus Rex Judaeorum* (London, 1611), Dedications. While the first edition, second issue (STC 15227.5) has been consulted

NOTES TO CHAPTER SEVEN

in every case, page numbers in Rowse's edition are cited for convenience; here, p. 53, p. 137, p. 60.

10. See *CSPD* James I, v. 8, Aug. 23, 1604, p. 146; v. 9, Nov. 23, 1613, p. 210; and Nov. 22, 1616, p. 407. Also *CSPD* Charles I, v. 7, Feb. 19, 1634–1635, pp. 516-17.

11. In "Of God and Good Women: The Poems of Aemilia Lanyer," in *Silent But for the Word*, pp. 203-24, Barbara Lewalski illuminates the poem by reading it as "a comprehensive 'Book of Good Women,' fusing religious devotion and feminism so as to assert the essential harmony of those two impulses." Lewalski gives bibliographical and biographical information; shows how the dedications compose a "contemporary community of good women," most of whom were connected to the militantly Protestant Earl of Leicester; examines the Passion poem "as the focus for all the forms of female goodness—and masculine evil—her poems treat" (p. 207); and reads "Cookham" as giving "mythic dimension to Lanyer's dominant concerns: the Eden now lost is portrayed as a female paradise inhabited solely by women" (p. 220). Although my study uses different terms and concentrates on different aspects of Lanyer's work (the idea of praise, the concept of feminine virtue, the scriptural imagery, and her relation to a feminine literary tradition), my reading is compatible with Professor Lewalski's. I would not agree, however, that Lanyer was a feminist, because her advocacy for women begins with spiritual power and ends with poetry; and in fact, she assumes that men control society, art, and the worldly destiny of women, including herself.

12. In *The Enduring Monument: A Study in the Idea of Praise in Renaissance Literary Theory and Practice* (Chapel Hill: University of North Carolina Press, 1962), O. B. Hardison argues that "Renaissance poems on the Passion ... provide a kind of archetype, and ... Christian elegies are in some measure adaptations of this archetype" (p. 155). He notes that both his examples, Sannazaro and Chapman, compare Christ to the epic hero (p. 159). In another Passion poem, "The Countesse of Penbrook's Passion," cited in Chapter Five, Nicholas Breton adopts the persona of the Countess of Pembroke to convey the traditional topics of lamentation, praise, and consolation, but the poem is not specific to her womanhood, only to her Christian piety.

13. While she does attribute Lanyer's dedicatory praises to pride in her sex, "a major theme" of the poem, Betty Travitsky also believes that her "obsequiousness is obvious" and that she had "to flatter for favor." *The Paradise of Women*, p. 92. Muriel Bradbrook ascribes the dedications to "practical politics," and assumes that Lanyer's main interest was "the usual expectation" of £2 per dedication. Review, *TSWL* 1 (1982), 92. Barbara Lewalski, in "Good Women," says that "these dedications are obviously intended to call Aemilia Lanyer to the attention of past patronesses, and perhaps to attract new ones" (p. 206), but she also emphasizes that Lanyer

creates "a contemporary community of learned and virtuous women with the poet Aemilia their associate and celebrant" (p. 212).

14. Edmund Spenser, *The Faerie Queene* II. vii. 15:7.

15. The cast here resembles that of a masque, perhaps in deference to Anne's favorite court entertainment. Alfonso Lanyer's position as court musician may have allowed his wife to see such spectacles, or at least to hear a firsthand report.

16. These ladies were not uniformly learned and virtuous. Arabella Stuart was known for her learning. In a report of the Venetian Ambassador in 1607, she is described as "not very beautiful, but highly accomplished, for besides being of most refined manners she speaks fluently Latin, Italian, French, Spanish, reads Greek and Hebrew, and is always studying." *James I By His Contemporaries*, ed. Robert Ashton (London: Hutchinson & Co., 1969), p. 96. Her royal blood made her a continuous threat to James's security, and although she was briefly in favor in 1609, her secret marriage to William Seymour and her attempted flight ensured that her last four years would be spent in the Tower.

Lucy Harington Russell, Countess of Bedford, also bore a reputation for learning and piety. In discussing her as Donne's patron, P. Thomson writes, "she was a learned lady, with a knowledge of classical antiquities and of painting. Florio praised her skill in French and Italian." "John Donne and the Countess of Bedford," *MLR* 44 (1949), 329. Thomson also makes a point relevant here that in the early seventeenth century the countess's financial situation was perilous, and may even have precipitated her withdrawal of support from Donne (pp. 335-39). Besides Florio and Donne, the countess's other literary connections included Samuel Daniel, Michael Drayton, and Ben Jonson.

Mary Sidney, Countess of Pembroke, has already been discussed in Chapter Five. Margaret Russell, Countess Dowager of Cumberland is discussed below. Her daughter, Anne Clifford (1590–1676), was an extraordinary woman, known for her strong character, learning, virtue, piety, and good works, although her life was not without its financial and marital woes. Samuel Daniel was her tutor, and Bishop Rainbow's funeral elegy describes how nature "had endowed her Soul with such excellent abilities as made her ready to build up herself in the knowledge of all things decent and praiseworthy in her Sex. She had great sharpness of Wit, a faithful Memory, and deep Judgement, so that by the help of these, much Reading, and conversation with Persons eminent for Learning, she had early gain'd a knowledge, as of the best things, so an ability to discourse in all Commendable Arts and Sciences, as well as in those things which belonged to Persons of her Birth and Sex to know." George C. Williamson, *Lady Anne Clifford, Countess of Dorset, Pembroke, and Montgomery 1590–1676. Her Life, Letters and Work*. Second edition (Yorkshire: S. R. Publishers Ltd., 1967), p. 325.

The Lady Elizabeth, daughter of King James and Queen Anne, who afterward became the "winter Queen" of Bohemia, was tutored by the Countess of Bedford's father, Lord John Harington of Exton, and was said to be very close to her serious and accomplished brother, Prince Henry.

The learning and virtue of Susan Bertie, Countess Dowager of Kent, seems to have gone unrecorded. She was the daughter of the famous Reformer, Catherine Willoughby, Duchess of Suffolk, and was married first to Reginald Grey, Earl of Kent, and after his death to Sir John Wingfield.

Katherine Knyvet, Countess of Suffolk, seems to be the most dubious member of Lanyer's gallery. Married to the naval hero, and after 1614, the Lord Treasurer, Lord Thomas Howard, she had, says *DNB* "a great ascendancy over her husband, and undoubtedly used his high office to enrich herself." The embezzlement scandal did not break until 1618, however; but earlier, the countess had accepted a £1,000 annual Spanish pension for which "she supplied information from time to time in return" (*DNB*).

Although it is clear why Lanyer would begin her dedications with the queen, Anne of Denmark is perhaps the most puzzling figure. Described by the Venetian Ambassador as "very gracious, moderately good looking. She is a Lutheran. The King tried to make her a Protestant; others a Catholic; to this she was and is much inclined, hence the rumour that she is one. She likes enjoyment and is very fond of dancing and of fetes. She is intelligent and prudent; and knows the disorders of government, in which she has no part, though many hold that as the King is most devoted to her she might play as large a role as she wished. . . . She is full of kindness for those who support her, but on the other hand she is terrible, proud, unendurable to those she dislikes" (*James I*, p. 95). She is still remembered as an extravagant spender; Antonia Fraser remarks that art historians have at least vindicated the results. *King James VI of Scotland, I of England* (New York: Knopf, 1975), p. 54.

17. Robert Chester, *Love's Martyr or Rosalins Complaint* (1601), ed. Alexander B. Grosart (London: New Shakespeare Society, 1878), pp. 29-32.

18. Rosemond Tuve, *Allegorical Imagery: Some Medieval Books and Their Posterity* (Princeton: Princeton University Press, 1966), p. 92.

19. See ibid. pp. 85-89, and Appendix.

20. Authorial sycophancy does not really explain Lanyer's purpose in so comprehensively detailing the virtues of these women. She could have offered sufficient flattery to the queen in less than these 27 stanzas which broach important themes and images for her poem and establish her persona. That she chose a series of strong, independently minded women may signify, as may their aristocratic titles which would qualify them to lead other women.

21. *Historical Memoirs of the House of Russell from the Time of the Norman Conquest* (London: J. H. Wiffen, 1833), 1, 508-509. The passage is an excerpt from Anne Clifford's diary. Following a childhood arrangement, Margaret Russell married George Clifford, 3rd Earl of Cumberland in 1577, but the

marriage was not a happy one. After 1586, the earl began his naval wanderings. He impoverished his estates, and eventually, as his daughter wrote, "fell to love a lady of quality." At his death in 1605, he was reunited with the countess, but his estate passed to another branch of the family. The countess spent the remaining eleven years of her life attempting to restore the inheritance to her daughter, Anne Clifford. Although she did not succeed, Anne Clifford took up the suits, and by outliving all her relations, finally inherited in 1643.

22. *Lady Anne Clifford*, Appendix, pp. 490, 495.

23. Pilate's wife appears in earlier defenses of women as a virtuous example. In the English translation of Agrippa, *The Nobilitie and Excellencie of Womankynde* (1542), appears the claim that "the very wyfe of Pylate, an hethen woman went aboute, and laboured more to save Jesus than any man, yea any of these men, that beleved in hym" (Cviii). And in *The prayse of all women called Mulierum Pean* (1542), Edward Gosynhyll writes that "The wyfe of Pylate dyd pytie more/ The turnement of our Savyoure/ Than all the men that than there were" (Div).

24. According to John W. Brooks in *Holy Trinity Church Cookham: An illustrated Guide to Church & Village*, Henry III, Edward I, and Richard II assigned the income from the Royal Manor of Cookham to their queens, and Henry VIII made two of his queens Ladies of the Manor. In addition, Anne of Cleves had a house on Winter Hill overlooking the Thames Valley (p. 11).

25. In "Good Women," Barbara Lewalski calls "The Description of Cooke-ham" "the gem of the volume," and shows that in it, "a female Eden suffers a new fall" (pp. 220-24). My reading concentrates on Lanyer's depiction of Margaret Russell as a redeemed Eve whose presence inspires both piety and poetry.

26. "To Penshurst" cannot be dated precisely, although it was certainly written between 1603 and 1612. If Jonson wrote the poem after a visit there, some evidence suggests the latter end of this period. In "Jonson, Lord Lisle, and Penshurst," *ELR* 1(1971), J.C.A. Rathmell deduces that Jonson was at Penshurst for William Sidney's twenty-first birthday on November 10, 1611 (p. 251). In addition, Rathmell notes that "If Jonson's allusion to the rearing of walls 'of the countrey stone' is intended as a reference to a contemporary event it constitutes an important clue as to the date of the poem, since the wall was erected in May 1612" (pp. 252-53). Lewalski notes that Lanyer's poem "can certainly claim priority in publication" (p. 204).

27. "Palma, typus esse solet triumphi, & victoriae Christi, ... Palma etiam crucem Christi, in qua diabolus est victus, & mundus redemptus, designare potest. ... Palma quandoque significat sanctam Ecclesiam. ... Palma saepe pro fortitudine sumitur, quia resistit ponderi. ... Et peculiariter designat victoriam Sanctorum post hanc vitam ..." [The palm signifies the triumphs of Christ; also the cross on which the devil was beaten and the world

redeemed; also the holy Church; it is often cited for its strength, because it withstands weight, and it especially signifies the victory of the Saints after this life]. "Potest etiam cedrus designare Apostolos & Prophetas, propter vitae eorum excellentiam, & doctrinae sublimitatem, qua aedificant ecclesiam Dei.... Cedrus magna, quam plantavit Deus, Christum designare potest: & etiam Ecclesiam ..." [The cedar signifies the Apostles and Prophets, because of the excellence of their life and the loftiness of their teaching, by which they build the church of God; the great cedar, which God planted, may signify Christ and also the Church]. Hieronymus Lauretus, *Silva Allegoriarum Totius Sacrae Scripturae* (Barcelona, 1570), rpt. 10th ed. 1681 (Munich: Wilhelm Fink Verlag, 1971), pp. 763, 223.

28. The female figure in nature has a classical history, although Lanyer's version differs quite notably. In discussing Marvell's "Upon Appleton House," Rosalie Colie mentions Waller's poem to Penshurst as a "feminine type" of house-poem, and notes that "the feminine house-poem takes its major conceit from the pastoral compliment to a lady who is said to improve nature by her presence in it, a thematic commonplace (cf. Virgil, *Ecl.* VII, 45-48) Leishman has called simply 'pastoral hyperbole.'" *My Echoing Song: Andrew Marvell's Poetry of Criticism* (Princeton: Princeton University Press, 1970), p. 284. Lanyer anticipates something of Marvell's concept of Mary Fairfax in "Upon Appleton House." See also Ruth Wallerstein, "Marvell's 'Upon Appleton House' and 'The Garden,'" *Seventeenth Century Poetic* (Madison: University of Wisconsin Press, 1950), p. 299; and Marien-Sofie Rostvig, "Upon Appleton House," *Marvell: Modern Judgements*, ed. Michael Wilding (London: Macmillan, 1969), pp. 219, 229.

Chapter Eight

1. Josephine Roberts writes the most complete biography to date in her edition of *The Poems of Lady Mary Wroth* (Baton Rouge: Louisiana State University Press, 1983), pp. 3-40. See also Roberts, "The Biographical Problem of *Pamphilia to Amphilanthus*," *TSWL* 1 (1982), 43-51.

2. Robert Sidney wrote to Lady Sidney from Flushing in 1597, urging her not to bring the three oldest children over with her: "I know yowr Delight in them, makes yow not Care, what is best for them; and rather than you will part with them, yow wil not heare of any Place, where to leave them behind yow." He wishes her to send Mary and Kate to the Countess of Huntington and the Countess of Warwick for their education, for "though I cannot find Fault hether unto, with their Bringing up, yet I know now every Day more and more, it wil bee fit for them to bee owt of their Fathers Hows. For heer they cannot learne, what they may do in other Places. ..." He concludes by reassuring his wife that "I know also, that a better, and more carefull Mother there is not, then you are; and indeed, I doe not feare any Thing so much as your to much Fondnes." *Letters and Memorials of State ... of the Sidney Family*, ed. Arthur Collins

(London, 1746), II, 43. The letter is mistitled "Sir Thomas Sydney to his Lady." Peter J. Croft discusses Barbara Sidney's illiteracy and her close relationship with her husband in *The Poems of Robert Sidney* (Oxford: Clarendon Press, 1984), pp. 69-81.

3. *Letters and Memorials*, II, 153.

4. On December 28, 1602, Rowland Whyte wrote to Robert Sidney that "Mrs. *Mary* upon *St. Stevens* Day, in the Afternoone, dawnced before the Queen two Galliards, with one Mr. *Palmer*, the admirable Dawncer of this Tyme; both were much commended by her Majestie, then she dawnced with hym a Corante. . . ." Ibid., p. 262.

5. See Roberts, *Poems*, pp. 11-12. Jonson's remark appears in *Conversations with William Drummond of Hawthornden* in *Works*, I, 142, line 355.

6. *The Letters of John Chamberlain*, ed. Norman E. McClure (Philadelphia: American Philosophical Society, 1939), pp. 512, 519.

7. *CSPD*, James I, 1623-1625, pp. 155, 344, 473. *CSPD*, Charles I, 1627-1628, p. 136. *CSPD*, Charles I, 1628-1629, p. 44. Most entries refer to her receiving royal protection from her creditors.

8. Roberts, *Poems*, pp. 24-26 and pp. 43-44; "Biographical Problem," pp. 48-51.

9. Nathaniel Baxter, *Sir Philip Sydneys Ourania* (London, 1606), A4. Robert Jones, *The Muses Garden for Delight Or the fift Booke of Ayres* (London, 1610).

10. In dedicating his elegy on her brother, William Sidney, to the Sidney family, Joshua Sylvester writes of Mary Wroth that she is a Sidney "In whom, her *Uncle*'s noble Veine renewes. . . ." "An Elegiac Epistle Consolatorie . . . ," in *Lachrymae Lachrymarum* (London, 1613), H2.

11. Ben Jonson, *Epigrammes* CIII and CV in *Works*, VIII, 66-68; "A Sonnet, To the noble Lady, the Lady MARY WROTH," *The Underwood*, XXVIII, in *Works*, VIII, 182.

12. See Thomas M. Greene, "Ben Jonson and the Centered Self," *SEL* 10 (1970), 325-48, and below.

13. See Josephine Roberts, "An Unpublished Literary Quarrel Concerning the Suppression of Mary Wroth's *Urania* (1621)," *N&Q* 222 (1977), 532-35, and *Poems*, pp. 31-35; Paul Salzman, "Contemporary References in Mary Wroth's *Urania*," *RES* 29 (1978), 178-81. John Chamberlain sent Denny's "bitter verses" to Dudley Carleton on March 9, 1622, "for that in her book of Urania she doth palpablie and grossely play upon him and his late daughter the Lady Hayes, besides many others she makes bold with, and they say takes great libertie or rather licence to traduce whom she please, and thincks she daunces in a net: I have seen an aunswer of hers to these rimes, but I thought yt not worth the writing out." *Letters*, vol. 2, p. 427.

14. The basis for discussion here is the 1621 volume containing *Urania* and *Pamphilia to Amphilanthus*. The manuscript continuation of *Urania*, now in the Newberry Library, reflects some change in Wroth's original

plans for her main characters, but the relation between the two parts must be discussed elsewhere. According to Josephine Roberts, a critical edition of the manuscript play, *Love's Victorie*, is being prepared from the complete copy in private hands in England. A copy lacking part of Act One and all of Act Five is in the Huntington Library; Roberts publishes the songs from the play in *Poems*, pp. 210-15.

15. Margaret Tyler, *The Mirrour of Princely Deeds and Knighthood* (London, 1578), A3.

16. Tyler joins a perennial debate. Following Vives, many sixteenth- and seventeenth-century writers banned romances for women readers, but at the end of the sixteenth century, many romances were being dedicated to women in general or to specific figures. See Hull, *Chaste, Silent & Obedient*, pp. 71-82. Nevertheless, given the usual content of romance, Tyler probably overstates the easy transition between reading and writing.

17. Philip Sidney, *The Defence of Poesie* in *Works*, ed. Albert Feuillerat (Cambridge: Cambridge University Press, 1965), vol. 3, p. 22.

18. In another interesting case of "lateness," L. A. Beaurline argues that Ben Jonson attempted to revive the comic romance in his late play, *The New Inne* (1629), giving the Caroline audience what he thought they wanted, while still adapting the form to teach what he wanted about "love and virtuous action." *Jonson and Elizabethan Comedy: Essays in Dramatic Rhetoric* (San Marino: The Huntington Library, 1978), pp. 257-74.

19. Romantic heroines tend to be like Lodge's Rosalynde, "the paragon of all earthly perfection," meaning that they are beautiful, chaste, and wise, and spend all their time involved in the love plot. In Lodge's *Margarite of America*, the quietly chaste Margarite is finally murdered by her false lover. Interesting figures like Lady Porcia in Barnabe Riche's *The Straunge and Wonderful Adventures of Don Simonides* also die early because they have no living love interest, and so they evolve into symbols. In "Feminine Identity in Lady Mary Wroth's *Urania*," *ELR* 14 (1984), 328-46, Carolyn Ruth Swift argues that Wroth modifies romance convention by giving women new roles and by blaming their unhappiness on male inconstancy, although not without contradictions.

20. See William Percy, *Sonnets to the Fairest Coelia*, particularly Sonnet 19, "It shall be said I died for COELIA," which ends, "One solace I shall find, when I am over;/ It will be known I died a constant lover." See also Richard Linche's *Diella*, Sonnet 35, "End this enchantment, Love! of my desires!" in which the lover says, "Constant have I been, still in Fancy fast,/ ordained by heavens to doat upon my Fair."

21. In "Lady Mary Wroth's *Urania*," *Proceedings of the Leeds Philosophical and Literary Society*, 16 (1975), pp. 51-60, Graham Parry calls the *Urania* "an imitation of the *Arcadia*" (p. 52) and claims "it is written in a style that is almost indistinguishable from Sidney's: the passage of thirty years between the two books is not apparent in the prose" (p. 54). Later, however, he judges that "it is fairly evident that Urania has lost the phil-

osophic garb of the *Arcadia* and has become the central figure in an infinitely convoluted history that lacks the intellectual strength of Sidney's work. Lady Mary tells a good story, but one that lacks resonance, or suggestion of veiled meaning or spiritual allegory" (p. 55). Naomi Miller's Harvard dissertation, "The Strange Labyrinth: Pattern as Process in Sir Philip Sidney's *Arcadia* and Lady Mary Wroth's *Urania*" (1987) studies the relationship between *Arcadia* and *Urania*.

22. Philip Sidney, *The Countess of Pembrokes Arcadia 1590* in *Works*, ed. Feuillerat, vol. 1, Book 1, p. 20. Hereafter cited in the text by book and page number.

23. In "The Heroic Ideal in Sidney's Revised *Arcadia*," *SEL* 10 (1970), 63-82, Myron Turner argues convincingly that Pamela is Sidney's "ideal woman," who unites and balances "pride and humility, magnanimous self-sufficiency and Christian dependence on God ..." (p. 73).

24. Kohler, *The Elizabethan Woman of Letters*, p. 209.

25. *The Countesse of Montgomeries Urania*, written by the right honorable the Lady Mary Wroth, Daughter to the right Noble Robert Earle of Leicester, And Neece to the ever famous, and renowned S͏ʳ Phillip Sidney knight. And to the most exelent Lady Mary Countesse of Pembroke late deceased. (London, 1621), p. 452. Hereafter cited in the text.

26. See Swift, "Feminine Identity," pp. 336-37, for a discussion of constancy in love. I emphasize the importance of Pamphilia's public aspect.

27. Henry Peacham, *Minerva Britanna 1612*, English Emblem Books 5 (Menston, Yorkshire: Scolar Press, 1969), p. 167. In another emblem, "Manlie Constancie" is pictured as a "mightie Rock" amid waves, weathering a great storm (p. 158). In a work well known to Jonson, Cesare Ripa defines Constancy as "una dispositione ferma di non cedere a dolori corporali, ne lasciarsi vincere a tristezza, o fatica; ne a travaglio alcuno per la via della virtu, in tutte l'attione." *Iconologia* (Padua, 1611; rpt New York: Garland Publishing, 1976), p. 98. Shakespeare develops the idea of "persistive constancy" in Agamemnon's speech in *Troilus and Cressida* I.iii.17-30.

28. Ben Jonson, *Epigrammes* XCVIII, *Works*, VIII, 63. See Richard Peterson, *Imitation and Praise in the Poems of Ben Jonson* (New Haven and London: Yale University Press, 1981), Chapter Two, "The Stand: Noble Natures Raised." In "Ben Jonson and the Centered Self," Thomas Greene writes that "Virtually all the heroes and heroines (the terms are not missapplied) of the verse seem to possess this quality of fixed stability" (p. 330). For discussion of Jonson and references, I am indebted to John Lemly.

29. Wroth's description particularly recalls the "Pelican" portrait of Elizabeth in which her gown is reddish-brown, sewn with pearls, embroidered with leaves and flowers, and decorated with bows; she holds a glove in her left hand. However, each of these features appears separately in almost every portrait. In *The English Icon* (New York: Pantheon Books, 1969), Roy Strong gives murrey as a color emblematic of steadfastness in love and tawney of melancholy and mourning (p. 34), so that Pamphilia's dress

reflects her destiny. The pearl has a long association with purity and divinity; Lynn Staley Johnson notes that "in exegetical literature, the pearl of great price is a symbol for purity, grace, Christ, healing, penance, and Christian doctrine. . . ." *The Voice of the "Gawain"-Poet* (Madison: University of Wisconsin Press, 1984), p. 262. Spenser made Arthur's shield out of "Diamond perfect pure and cleene" (*FQ* I.vii.33). The possibility of a religious interpretation of Pamphilia's appearance is strengthened by her subsequent actions. See René Graziani, " 'The Rainbow Portrait' of Queen Elizabeth and Its Religious Symbolism," *JWCI* 35(1972), 247-59. In "Masques Performed before the Queen, 1592," Elizabeth frees ladies from "Unconstancie." John Nichols, ed., *The Progresses and Public Processions of Queen Elizabeth* (London: John Nichols and Son, 1823), III, 199. In "The Princely Pleasures at the Courte at Kenelwoorth" in 1575, the lady in the lake is freed from Sir Bruce sans pitie "by the presence of a better maide than herself." *Progresses*, I, 492.

30. Roy Strong notes that the crowned pillars referred to Elizabeth's constancy in two of Sir Henry Lee's entertainments for 1590 and 1592. *The Cult of Elizabeth* (New York: Thames and Hudson, 1977), pp. 75, 154.

31. As in the *Arcadia*, this Urania probably evolves from Venus Urania or the celestial Venus, the original divine archetype of human love. Plato's description of two Venuses or two loves had a strong Renaissance tradition. See Edgar Wind, *Pagan Mysteries in the Renaissance* (Harmondsworth, England: Penguin, 1967), pp. 138-39.

32. Paul Johnson gives specific details of Elizabeth's solicitude for her subjects in *Elizabeth I: A Study in Power and Intellect* (London: Omega, 1976), pp. 234-36. For the Tilbury speech, see *Progresses*, II, 536. See also Frances Yates, "Queen Elizabeth as Astraea," *JWCI* 10 (1947), 27-82.

33. William Camden, *The History of the Most Renowned and Victorious Princess Elizabeth*, selected chapters, ed. Wallace T. MacCaffrey (Chicago: University of Chicago Press, 1970), p. 29. See also William Birch's "A Songe betwene the Quene's Majestie and England," stanza 4, in E. C. Wilson, *England's Eliza* (New York: Octagon Books, 1966), pp. 4-5:

> Bessy. Here is my hand,
>> My dere lover Englande,
> I am thine both with mind and hart,
>> For ever to endure,
>> Thou maiest be sure,
> Untill death us two do part.

34. Less than twenty years after her death, Elizabeth had almost achieved the aura of sainthood. An engraving by Frances Delaram c. 1617–1619 shows the queen in heavenly glory. An earlier posthumous tribute declared, "She was and is, what can there more be said,/ In earth the first, in heaven the second maid." *Progresses*, III, 652.

35. These two scenes may echo *The Faerie Queene* (III. xi. 30-31), in which the enchanter, Busyrane, lays bare Amoret's heart and uses her

lifeblood to figure "straunge characters of his art," trying to force her to love him.

36. This may be a Garden of Deduit, a false paradise, reflecting Amphilanthus's continual breach of faith.

37. Parry says of *Pamphilia to Amphilanthus* that "this sequence contains much competent writing in the Petrarchan fashion; the feeling throughout is late Elizabethan" ("Wroth's *Urania*," p. 57). The sonnet sequence is appended to the *Urania*, but separately paginated. Quotations here are from Josephine Roberts's excellent edition of the sonnets in *The Poems of Lady Mary Wroth*, although reference is also made to the 1621 text. Sonnets are cited by their number in the sequence and by page number.

38. A number of parallels between the poems of father and daughter are suggested by W. H. Kelleher and Katherine Duncan-Jones in "A Manuscript of Poems by Sir Robert Sidney: Some Early Impressions," *British Library Journal* 1 (1975), 114-15. In another article, Duncan-Jones writes that Wroth "models a substantial number of poems on her father's." " 'Rosis and Lysa': Selections from the Poems of Sir Robert Sidney," *ELR* 9 (1979), 243. Now that all the texts are available, a full study of the relationships among the three sequences of father, uncle, and daughter is needed. See Croft, *The Poems of Robert Sidney*, Appendix C, Echoes of Robert's Sequence in his Daughter Mary Wroth's Verse; and Roberts, *Poems*, in which resemblances are given in the notes to individual sonnets.

39. The *Princeton Encyclopedia of Poetry and Poetics* (p. 174) defines a crown of sonnets as "Traditionally a sequence of 7 It[alian] sonnets so interwoven as to form a 'crown' of panegyric for the one to whom they are addressed. The interweaving is accomplished by using the last line of each of the first six sonnets as the first line of the succeeding sonnet, with the last line of the seventh being a repetition of the opening line of the first. A further restriction prohibits the repetition of any given rhyme sound once it is used in the crown." Philip Sidney uses the form memorably in the fourth singing dialogue of the second eclogues of the *Arcadia* in which Strephon and Klaius mourn the absent Urania; Robert Sidney has an unfinished crown of four sonnets and a fragment, *Poems*, pp. 174-81. In other sequences, poets use the technique for up to four sonnets, but the extended repetition to as many as fourteen sonnets seem to be unique to Wroth's sequence.

40. The crown of sonnets is also a crown of praise for love, reminiscent of the iconography of a crowned virtuous love. See Ripa's "Amor di virtu," a naked, winged youth crowned with a wreath of laurel and holding three more laurel wreaths, "per mostrare che l'amor d'essa non e corruttibile, anzi come l'alloro sempre verdeggia, e come corona, o ghirlande che di figura sferica non ha giamai alcun termine" (*Iconologia*, p. 20). Alciati's "Amor virtutis" is identically equipped and claims to have woven the wreaths out of virtue itself, including the wreath of wisdom on his brow. Andrea Alciati, *Emblemata*, p. 459.

41. Ibid., pp. 457, 461.

42. See R. V. Merrill, "Eros and Anteros," *Speculum* 19 (1944), 265-84, for a history of the rival interpretations. Merrill describes Marguerite de Navarre's "La Distinction du vray amour par dixains" as similar to Alciati's emblems, but with Marguerite's own intent of showing how divine love is purified "of the cruelty of blindness . . . which characterizes earthly passion" (p. 28). In *The Masque of Beautie* in which Wroth had appeared, Ben Jonson introduces multiple Cupids and notes, "I make these different from him, which they fayne, *caecum cupidine*, or *petulantem* as I expresse beneath in the third song, these being chaste *Loves* that attend a more divine beautie, then that of *Loves* commune *parent*." *Works*, VII, 192.

43. In "The Biographical Problem," Josephine Roberts also recognizes two Cupids; however, Roberts's conclusion is that the two Cupids are an "Anacreontic Cupid," the playful trifler, and "a mature, esteemed king, in the tradition of the medieval courts of love," who "stands as the symbol of noble, generous love" (p. 50); see also *Poems*, p. 45. Of all the sequences Sidney Lee publishes in *Elizabethan Sonnets* (New York: Cooper Square Publishers, 1964), none approaches the number of references to Cupid in *Pamphilia to Amphilanthus*—except *Astrophil and Stella* with 27.

44. In "Shakespeare and the Sonnet Sequence," *English Poetry and Prose 1540–1674*, ed. Christopher Ricks (London: Barrie and Jenkins, 1970), 101-17, Thomas P. Roche writes of the sonnet ladies that "the vitality of the sonnet sequence comes not from real life but from the multiple significances inherent in these female figures who symbolize all that is desirable and unobtainable in human life. We need not refer to outmoded theories of courtly love to explain the intensity and endurance of the tradition; we need only consider the later sequences, derived from Dante and Petrarch, to see that most of them emphasize only one half of the story these poets tell, and that half-story stresses again and again the unhappiness attendant on the poet's not obtaining his lady's love. In both Dante and Petrarch this unhappiness leads to the greater happiness of suffering—through to wisdom and virtue, but in all of the sonnet sequences I have read, with the exception of Spenser's *Amoretti*, the poet is enslaved by despair at the end, trapped by his unobtainable passion" (p. 104). Roche concludes that a Renaissance reader would not greatly sympathize with the sonneteer's ultimate despair over love, and indeed that the sequence would have been a warning to lovers.

45. In the 1621 text, the spelling is "Prophet." The transformation of Cupid here to prophet and teacher is perhaps akin to the seventeenth-century emblems which metamorphosed boy-Cupid into infant Jesus. In *Studies in Seventeenth-Century Imagery*, 2nd ed. (Rome: Edizioni di Storia e Letteratura, 1964), Mario Praz writes that "the Infant Jesus, the heart, the cross—these are the new devotions which flourish in the seventeenth century. Alexandrian love has become spiritual; Cupid has yielded up his wings and arrows to the little Redeemer" (p. 155).

CHAPTER NINE

1. Those who study the Renaissance debate on the woman question will benefit greatly from reading Linda Woodbridge's *Women and the English Renaissance*. The instances in which I differ from Woodbridge's analysis of the female defenders will become clear during the course of my argument.

In her discussion of Edward Gosynhyll who published both a defense of and an attack on women, Woodbridge remarks that "The debater who rebuts himself can be suspected of holding the Ramist view that to dispute well is logic's chiefest end. The facility with which one writer can argue opposing propositions must caution the reader against too blithely accepting any Renaissance pronouncement on women as reflecting the attitudes of his contemporaries" (p. 37). About other defenders of women, Woodbridge observes that they "accomplish little more for women's cause than to create a stereotype of the 'good' woman to counter the misogynist's stereotype of the 'bad.'" (p. 38). Even the extraordinary Agrippa mounts a defense of Eve that Woodbridge cannot believe "was meant to be taken seriously" (p. 40).

2. Woodbridge remarks that "Anger's essay injects new life into a stagnating genre" (p. 64), and that it includes "sardonic reversals of familiar conventions" (p. 65).

3. Of Swetnam's work, Woodbridge writes, "Everything in it was dismally stale, a good deal of it plagiarized from works like *The Golden Book of Marcus Aurelius* and *Euphues*. It is longer than most misogynistic attacks, but one cannot call it sustained—rambling or long-winded, perhaps" (p. 81).

4. *Jane Anger her Protection for Women* (London, 1589), title page. Hereafter cited in the text. The identity of the "Surfeiting Lover" is not known, although Anger refers in her text to *Boke his surfeit in love*, entered 1588, now lost. Jane Anger is reprinted in *First Feminists: British Women Writers 1578-1799*, pp. 58-73. See Betty Travitsky, "The Lady Doth Protest: Protest in the Popular Writings of Renaissance Englishwomen," *ELR* 14 (1984), 255-83, for a consideration of the works of Jane Anger, Rachel Speght, Ester Sowernam, and Constantia Munda as essentially feminine texts.

5. *A Mouzell for Melastomus, The Cynical Bayter of and foule mouthed Barker against Evahs Sex . . .* By Rachel Speght (London, 1617), A3. Hereafter cited in the text.

6. Woodbridge rightly judges that "Speght's historical relativism is impressive; it was a rare quality" (*Women and the English Renaissance*, p. 90).

7. Like Puritan writers on marriage, Speght assumes that to make the husband a beneficent ruler of a willingly obedient wife raises the status of marriage and women. For a discussion of the contradictions in the Puritan position, see David M. Harralson, "The Puritan Art of Love: Henry Smith's 'A Preparative to Marriage,'" *BSUF* 16 (1975), 46-55, esp. p. 52.

8. *Ester hath hang'd Haman: or an Answere to a lewd Pamphlet, entituled,*

The Araignment of Women.... Written by Ester Sowernam (London, 1617), A2. Hereafter cited in the text.

9. A play, *Swetnam the Woman-hater, Arraigned by Women* was published in 1620. Its treatment of the woman question is examined at length by Linda Woodbridge, pp. 300-22. See also Coryl Crandall, *Swetnam the Woman-hater: The Controversy and the Play, A Critical Edition With Introduction and Notes* (Purdue University Studies, 1969).

10. "Redargution" carries the added meaning of confutation, reprehension, or reproof.

11. *The Worming of a mad Dogge. Or, A Soppe for Cerberus the Jaylor of Hell....* By Constantia Munda (London, 1617). Hereafter cited in the text. Perhaps "Lady Prudentia" indicates Constantia Munda's own station as a gentlewoman.

12. Archilochus, a Greek poet of the seventh century B.C., was forbidden to marry the woman he loved by her father and avenged himself by writing biting satires. Father and daughter are said to have hanged themselves. Phalaris, a Sicilian tyrant (c. 6 B.C.), roasted his victims in a brazen bull invented by Perillus who was the first to die in it.

13. In "The New Mother of the English Renaissance: Her Writings on Motherhood," in *The Lost Tradition: Mothers and Daughters in Literature*, ed. Cathy N. Davidson and E. M. Broner (New York: Frederick Ungar, 1980), pp. 33-43, Betty Travitsky suggests that the writing mother "in the context of Renaissance reality, would one day hope to find in her experience as a mother the outlet for her creative, spiritual, and intellectual needs" (p. 33). See also Christine W. Sizemore, "Early Seventeenth-Century Advice Books: The Female Viewpoint," *SAB* 41 (1976), 41-48, for the suggestion that the piety in each book reflected a "tradition of middle-class womanhood."

14. Elizabeth Grymeston, *Miscelanea, Meditations, Memoratives* (London, 1604), A3. Hereafter cited in the text. Three subsequent, expanded editions were dated by Ruth Hughey and Philip Hereford as 1605 or 1606; before 1609; about 1618. "Elizabeth Grymeston and her *Miscellanea*," *The Library* 15 (1934–1935), 61-91, esp. p. 71.

15. Ibid., pp. 76-81.

16. So wrote Simon Grahame in his sonnet "to the Authour" (Bv).

17. *Englands Parnassus* quotes *FQ* III.iv.17 accurately except it gives "Theaters" for "th'altars" in l.4. Grymeston changes the last line, "So fell proud *Marinell* upon the precious shore" to "So downe I fell on wordlesse precious shore" (B4). Other changes are orthographic. See *Englands Parnassus or The choysest Flowers of our Modern Poets, with their Poeticall comparisons* [ed. Robert Allott] (London, 1600), pp. 453-54.

18. In *Englands Parnassus* (p. 133) the lines appear:

> A deadly gulfe, where nought but rubbish growes,
> With foule blacke swelth in thickned lumps that lies:
> Which vp in th'aire such stinking vapour throwes.

That over, there may fly no fowle but dies,
Choakt with th'pestilent savours that arise.

Grymeston omits the second line, perhaps because she wanted two couplets for pithy effect. She changes "fowle" to "bird" (B4v).

19. In *Englands Parnassus* (p. 230), the lines from Drayton are:

Our fond preferments are but childrens toyes,
And as a shadow all our pleasures passe:
As yeares increase, so waining are our joyes,
And beautie crazed like a broken glasse,
A prettie tale of that which never was.

Grymeston writes (C):

Your fond preferments are but childrens toyes.
And as a shadow all your pleasures passe.
As yeeres increase, so waning are your joyes.
Your blesse is brittle, like a broken glasse,
Or as a tale of that which never was.

Grymeston appears to prefer the standard image to Drayton's variation. Another example of her conflating originals in order to write concise couplets occurs in her stanza (C):

What in this life we have or can desire,
Hath time of growth, and moment of retire.
So feeble is mans state as sure it will not stand,
Till it disordered be from earthly band.

The first two lines are from Lodge and are accurately quoted from *Englands Parnassus*, p. 168. The next two lines (p. 169) are from Spenser, coming from the end of the stanza:

So feeble is mans state, and life unsound,
That in assurance it may never stand,
Till it disordered be from earthly band.

For the Harington quotation, see *Englands Parnassus*, pp. 120-21; for Daniel, p. 265. Hughey and Hereford suggest that Grymeston might have used a book like Hugh Platt's *Flores Patrum* (i.e., Hugonis Platti armig. *manuale, sententias aliquot Divinas & Morales complectens: partim e Sacris Patribus. Partim e Petrarcha philosopho & Poeta celeberrimo decerptas*, London, 1594) for her prose quotations, but they add that "it is certain that she treated her quotations as she did those from English writers" ("Elizabeth Grymeston," p. 90). Hughey and Hereford trace a number of Grymeston's allusions and borrowings, showing briefly how she "made the borrowings very much her own."

20. Elizabeth Jocelin, *The Mothers Legacie to her unborn Childe* (London, 1624), A3-A3v. Hereafter cited in the text.

21. Dorothy Leigh, *The Mothers Blessing: Or, The godly Counsaile of a*

Gentle-woman.... The seventh Edition (London, 1621), title page. Hereafter cited in the text.

22. *The Countess of Lincolnes Nurserie* (Oxford, 1622), p. 13. Hereafter cited in the text.

23. M.R., *The Mothers Counsell, or, Live within Compasse* (London, 163[0?]), p. 1. Hereafter cited in the text.

24. M.R. writes, "Chastitie is a veile which Innocents adorne,/ th'ungathered rose defended with the thorne" (p. 5), basing the lines on Daniel, "The unstained vaile which innocents adorne,/Th'ungather'd rose defended with the thorne" (*Englands Parnassus*, p. 26). The quotations from Drayton and from Harington appear in *Englands Parnassus*, p. 27.

25. The first two lines are Drayton's (*Englands Parnassus*, p. 311), and the last are Harington's (*Englands Parnassus*, p. 311), altered to make two couplets.

26. STC notes that *The Mothers Counsell* (STC 20583) was probably issued with the tenth impression of *Keepe within Compasse* (14900). The latter was entered in the Stationer's Register first in 1619, then assigned to John Wright on January 24, 1623, when *The Mothers Counsell* is also entered to him.

27. That M.R. wrote her advice in response to *Keepe within Compasse* is likely, not only from the similarity in titles, but from consistent echoes of language: the father writes, "He is happily religious, whom no feare troubleth, no sorrow consumeth, no fleshly lust tormenteth, no desire of worldly wealth afflicteth, nor any foolishnesse moveth unto mirth" (A3); M.R. writes, "That chaste woman hath got to the height of felicitie, whom no feare troubleth, no pensiveness consumeth, no carnall concupiscence tormenteth, no desire of worldly wealth afflicteth, nor any foolishnesse moveth unto mirth" (p. 4).

LIST OF WORKS BY WOMEN, 1521-1624

THIS LIST indicates the availability of texts: citation of first editions is followed by selected later editions and microfilm reel numbers. Place of publication is London unless otherwise noted.

Aburgavennie, Frances. "The Praiers made by the right Honourable Ladie Frances Aburgavennie." In *The Monument of Matrones*, 139-213.

Anger, Jane. *Jane Anger her Protection for Women*. 1589. Selection in *First Feminists: British Women Writers 1578-1799*. Ed. Moira Ferguson. Bloomington and Old Westbury, 1985, 58-73. Reel 165.

Askew, Anne. *The first examinacyon of Anne Askewe, lately martyred in Smythfelde, by the Romysh popes upholders, with the Elucydacyon of Johan Bale*. Wesel, 1546. Reel 21.

————. *The lattre examinacyon of the worthye servaunt of God mastres Anne Askewe*. Wesel, 1547. Reel 21. See John Foxe, *Actes and Monuments of these Latter and Perillous Dayes*. 1563. (Ed. Cattley, 1838; rpt. 1965; vol. 5, pp. 537-50.) Also, *Select Works of John Bale*, ed. Henry Christmas. Parker Society, 1849, rpt. 1968; and *Writings of Edward the Sixth, William Hugh, Queen Catherine Parr, Anne Askew, Lady Jane Grey, Hamilton, and Balnaves*. Philadelphia, n.d. Selection in *The Paradise of Women: Writings by Englishwomen of the Renaissance*. Ed. Betty Travitsky. Westport, Ct., 1981. 173-86.

Bacon, Anne Cooke, tr. *An Apologie or answere in defence of the Church of Englande with a briefe and plaine declaration of the true Religion professed and used in the same*. 1564. Rpt. *An apology of the Church of England by John Jewel*. Folger Library, ed. John Booty. Charlottesville: The University Press of Virginia, 1963. Reel 963.

————. *Fourtene Sermons of Barnardine Ochyne, concernying the predestinacion and eleccion of god: very expediente to the settynge forth of hys glorye among hys creatures. Translated out of Italian in to oure natyve tounge by A.C.* 1551? Reel 121.

Cary, Elizabeth, Lady Falkland, tr. *The Reply of the Cardinall of Perron, to the Answeare of the Most Excellent King of Great Britaine*. Douay, 1630. Reel 985.

————. *The Tragedie of Mariam, The Faire Queene of Jewry*. 1613. Rpt. Malone Society, 1914. Reel 830.

Clifford, Anne. *The Diary of the Lady Anne Clifford*. Ed. V. Sackville-West. 1923.

Clinton, Elizabeth, Countess of Lincoln. *The Countess of Lincolnes Nurserie*. Oxford, 1622. Selection in *The Paradise of Women*, 57-60. Reel 984.

Colville, Elizabeth Melville. *A Godlie Dreame, Compyled by Elizabeth Melvill, Ladie Culros yonger at the request of a friend.* 1606 (English version). Reel 1247. Scottish version rpt., *Ane Godlie Dreame, Compylit in Scottish Meter be M. M. Gentlewoman in Culros, at the requeist of her freindes,* Edinburgh, 1603, in *Early Popular Poetry of Scotland and the Northern Border,* ed. David Laing, LL.D. in 1822 and 1826. Rearranged and Revised with Additions and a Glossary by W. Carew Hazlitt. Vol. 2. 1895. 279-301.

Constantia Munda, pseud. *The Worming of a mad Dogge: Or, A Soppe for Cerberus the Jaylor of Hell.* 1617. Selection in *Half Humankind: Contexts and Texts of the Controversy about Women in England, 1540–1640.* Ed. Katherine Usher Henderson and Barbara F. McManus. 244-63. Reel 967.

Dowriche, Anne. *The French Historie: A Lamentable Discourse of three of the chiefe, and most famous bloodie broiles that have happened in France for the Gospell of Jesus Christ.* 1589. Reel 289.

Elizabeth Tudor. *The Mirror of the Sinful Soul.* facs. ed. of 1544 MS Bodleian. Intr. Percy Ames. 1897. Also *A Godly Medytacyon of the christen sowle concerninge a love towarde God and hys Christe....Translated into English by the ryght vertuouse lady Elizabeth.* Ed. John Bale. Wesel, 1548. See *The Monument of Matrones,* Second Lampe, 1-34. Reel 56.

Ester Sowernam, pseud. *Ester hath hang'd Haman: or an Answere to a lewd Pamphlet, entituled, The Araignment of Women.* 1617. Selections in *Half Humankind,* 217-43, and *First Feminists,* 74-79. Reel 1188.

Grey, Jane. "A certaine effectuall praier" and "An exhortation" in *The Monument of Matrones,* Second Lampe, 98-102. See Foxe, *Actes and Monuments,* 918-20.

————. "An Epistle to a learned man," in Foxe, *Actes and Monuments,* 920-22.

————. *The Life, Death and Actions of the Most Chast, learned, and Religious Lady, the Lady Jane Grey, Daughter to the Duke of Suffolke.* 1615. Reel 955.

Grymeston, Elizabeth. *Miscelanea, Meditations, Memoratives.* 1604. Selection in *The Paradise of Women,* 52-55. Reel 1068.

Hoby, Margaret. *The Diary of Lady Hoby.* Ed. Dorothy M. Meads. 1930.

Jocelin, Elizabeth. *The Mothers Legacie to her unborn Childe.* 1624. Selection in *The Paradise of Women,* 60-63. Reel 745.

Lanyer, Aemilia. *Salve Deus Rex Judaeorum.* 1611. Rpt. *The Poems of Shakespeare's Dark Lady.* Ed. A. L. Rowse. New York, 1979. Reel 803.

Leigh, Dorothy. *The Mothers Blessing: Or, The godly Counsaile of a Gentlewoman.* Seventh edition. 1621. Reel 1278.

Locke, Anne Vaughan [Dering; Prowse], tr. *Of the markes of the children of God, and of their afflictions. To the faithfull of the Low Countrie. By John Taffin.* 1590. Reel 358.

————. *Sermons of John Calvin, upon the songe that Ezechias made after he had bene sicke, and afflicted by the hand of God.* 1560.

Lumley, Joanna [Jane], tr. *Iphigenia at Aulis Translated by Lady Lumley.* Ed. Harold H. Child. Malone Society, 1909.

M. R. *The Mothers Counsell, or, Live within Compasse.* Ent. 1623. Published 163[o]. Reel 1033.

Martin, Dorcas, tr. "An instruction for Christians ... translated out of French into English," in *The Monument of Matrones,* Second Lampe, 221-46.

Mildmay, Grace. "Journal." In Rachel Wiegall, "An Elizabethan Gentlewoman," *Quarterly Review* 215 (1911), 119-38.

The Monument of Matrones: conteining seven severall Lamps of Virginitie, or distinct treatises ... compiled ... by Thomas Bentley of Graies Inne Student. 1582. Reel 174.

Parr, Katherine. *The Lamentacion of a Sinner.* 1547. Reel 29.

————. *Prayers stirryng the mynd unto heavenlye medytacions.* 1545. Reel 61. Both works rpt. in *The Monument of Matrones,* Second Lampe, 37-98.

Roper, Margaret More, tr. *A devout treatise upon the Pater noster.* 1524. Rpt. *Moreana* 7 (1965), 9-64; 9 (1966), 65-92; 10 (1966), 91-110; 11 (1966), 109-118. Reel 37.

Russell, Elizabeth Cooke, tr. *A Way of Reconciliation of a good and learned man.* 1605. Reel 974.

Seymour, Anne, Margaret, and Jane. *Le tombeau de Marguerite de Valois Royne de Navarre.* Paris, 1551.

Sidney, Mary, Countess of Pembroke. "A Dialogue betweene two shepheards, Thenot and Piers, in praise of Astraea." In [Francis Davison], *A Poetical Rapsody.* 1602. Rpt. in *The "Triumph of Death" and other Unpublished and Uncollected Poems by Mary Sidney, Countess of Pembroke (1561–1621).* Ed. Gary F. Waller. Salzburg, 1977. 181-83.

————, tr. *A Discourse of Life and Death. Written in French by Ph. Mornay. Antonius. A Tragoedie written also in French by Ro. Garnier.* Both done in English by the Countesse of Pembroke. 1592. Reel 440. Rpt. *The Countess of Pembroke's Translation of Philippe de Mornay's Discourse of Life and Death.* Ed. Diane Bornstein. Detroit: Michigan Consortium for Medieval and Early Modern Studies, 1983. *Antonius* rpt. in Geoffrey Bullough, *Narrative and Dramatic Sources of Shakespeare,* Vol. 5. New York, 1964.

————. "The Dolefull Lay of Clorinda." In Edmund Spenser, *Colin Clout's Come Home Again.* 1595. Rpt. in *Uncollected Poems,* 176-79.

————. "Even now that Care which on thy Crown attends." See Bent Juel-Jensen, *Two Poems by the Countess of Pembroke.* Oxford, 1962. Rpt. in *Uncollected Poems,* 88-91; and in *The Female Spectator: English Women Writers Before 1800.* Ed. Mary R. Mahl and Helene Koon. Bloomington and Old Westbury, 1977, 66-69.

Sidney, Mary, Countess of Pembroke. *The Psalms of Sir Philip Sidney and the Countess of Pembroke.* Ed. J.C.A. Rathmell. New York, 1963.

———. *"The Triumphe of Death" Translated out of Italian by the Countess of Pembroke.* Ed. Frances B. Young. *PMLA* 27 (1912), 47-75. Also *Uncollected Poems,* 66-79.

Speght, Rachel. *Mortalities Memorandum, with a Dreame Prefixed, imaginarie in manner: reall in matter.* 1621. Reel 1220.

———. *A Mouzell for Melastomus, The Cynical Bayter of and foule mouthed Barker against Evahs Sex.* 1617. Reel 939.

Tyler, Margaret. tr. *The Mirrour of Princely Deeds and Knighthood.* 1578. Dedication and Epistle rpt. in *First Feminists,* 50-57. Reel 1029.

Tyrwhitt, Elizabeth. "Morning and Evening praiers, with diverse Psalmes, Hymnes, and Meditations." In *The Monument of Matrones,* Second Lampe, 103-138.

Wheathill, Anne. *A handfull of holesome (though homelie) hearbs, gathered out of the goodlie garden of Gods most holie word.* 1584. Reel 719.

Whitney, Isabella. *The Copy of a letter, lately written in meeter, by a yonge Gentilwoman: to her unconstant Lover.* 1567. Selection in *The Paradise of Women,* 118-20. Reel 1016.

———. *A sweet Nosegay or pleasant posye. Contayning a hundred and ten Phylosophicall flowers.* 1573. Rpt. in *The Floures of Philosophy (1572) by Hugh Plat and A Sweet Nosegay (1573) and The Copy of a Letter (1567) by Isabella Whitney.* Facs. Ed. Richard J. Panofsky. New York, 1982. See Betty Travitsky, "The 'Wyll and Testament' of Isabella Whitney," *ELR* 10 (1980), 83-94. Reel 1048.

Wroth, Mary. *The Countesse of Montgomeries Urania.* 1621. Reel 980.

———. *Pamphilia to Amphilanthus.* 1621. Printed with *Urania.* Rpt. in *The Poems of Lady Mary Wroth.* Ed. Josephine Roberts. Baton Rouge, 1983. See also *Pamphilia to Amphilanthus.* Ed. Gary F. Waller. Salzburg, 1977.

For a list of secondary sources, the reader is referred to "Recent Studies in Women Writers of Tudor England," *ELR* 14 (1984); Elizabeth Hageman, Part I: "Women Writers, 1485–1603," 409-25; Josephine Roberts, Part II: "Mary Sidney, Countess of Pembroke," 426-39.

INDEX

Aburgavennie, Frances Manners, 83-84, 303
Agrippa, Heinrich Cornelius, xviii, 323
Alciati, Andrea, 329
Ane Godlie Dreame. See Colville, Elizabeth Melville
Anger, Jane, 248, 249, 250-53, 285, 331
Anne of Denmark, 185, 321, 322
Apology of the Church of England. See Bacon, Anne Cooke
Araignment of Lewde, idle, froward, and unconstant Women. See Swetnam, Joseph
Ascham, Roger, 294, 302. *See also* Grey, Jane
Askew, Anne, 29-47, 73, 79, 295, 296; ballad of, 44; compared to Blandina, 33; compared to Margaret Roper, 46; *First examinacyon*, 37-42, 296; iconography, 33, 297; *Lattre examinacyon*, 42-44, 297; in Lincoln minster, 35; marriage and divorce, 34, 297; as public figure, 36; and Scripture, 40, 44, 47; spiritual autobiography, 30-32, 37, 296

Bacon, Anne Cooke, 50, 55-61, 154, 299; letters, 60-61; translation of Jewel's *Apology*, 55, 57-59; translation of Ochino's sermons, 56
Bacon, Anthony, 60
Bacon, Francis, 60
Bacon, Nicholas, 57, 154
Bale, John, 67; "Elucydacyon" of

Askew's *Examinations*, 30, 33, 34, 38, 42, 44, 295, 296, 297
Ballard, George, 289, 293, 295
Baxter, Nathaniel, 210
Beaufort, Margaret, 61
Beaumont, Francis, 318
Beaurline, L. A., 326
Becon, Thomas, 290, 299, 311
Bentley, Thomas. See *Monument of Matrones*
Bertie, Susan (Countess of Kent), 188, 189, 322
Beza, Theodore, 144, 145, 312, 313
Bonner, Edmund (Bishop), 32, 35, 40, 41
Booty, J. E., 299
Bornstein, Diane, 288, 309
Bradbrook, Muriel, 316, 320
Bradford, John, 302
Brathwaite, Richard, 8, 292
Breton, Nicholas, 125, 127, 308, 320
bride of Christ, 179, 182, 193, 199, 207, 241
Brinkelow, Henry, 305
Brodwin, Leonora, 317
Brooks, John W., 323
Bruto, Giovanni Michele, 4, 14-15, 292
Bush, Douglas, 314, 317
Bynum, Caroline Walker, 296

Calvin, John, 62, 144, 160, 309, 310, 311
Cary, Elizabeth (Viscountess Falkland), xvi, 152, 157-76, 177, 247, 292; biography of, 157, 158-64, 174, 314; Catholicism of, 160,

Library of Congress Cataloging-in-Publication Data

Beilin, Elaine V., 1948-

Redeeming Eve.
Includes index.
1. English literature—Early modern, 1500-1700—
History and criticism. 2. English literature—
Women authors—History and criticism. I. Title.
II. Title: Women writers of the English Renaissance.
PR113.B45 1987   820'.9'9287   87-6926
ISBN 0-691-06715-5

*Elaine V. Beilin is Assistant Professor of English at
Framingham State College, Framingham, Massachusetts.*